CUSTOMS VALUATION
in the UNITED STATES

CUSTOMS VALUATION
in the UNITED STATES

A Study in Tariff Administration

By

R. ELBERTON SMITH

THE UNIVERSITY OF CHICAGO PRESS
CHICAGO · ILLINOIS

THE UNIVERSITY OF CHICAGO PRESS, CHICAGO 37
Cambridge University Press, London, N.W. 1, England
W. J. Gage & Co., Limited, Toronto 2B, Canada

TO VERNA

THE APPRAISER

"... There is no office in this government, from the President of the United States down, that requires such varied acquirements as that of an appraiser. He must know the language of every country sufficiently to construe the invoices; he must know the currency of every country—francs, florins, piastres, rupees.... He must know the weights and measures of every country. He must know the value of every article of merchandise known to commerce, its quality and value in every country of the world, on every day of the week; and he must know human nature perfectly—the motives and springs of action which govern men in their transactions with the customs, that he may protect the honest importer against the fraudulent one, and keep in legitimate channels the trade of the country.... He must present [sic] no man for malice, hatred, or revenge; nor must he spare him for love, friendship, or regard. There is no office where skill, tact, good judgment, untiring industry and firmness, and decision of character are more demanded; while integrity, fidelity, and discretion are only a few of the requisites to make him an accomplished public officer."

SAMUEL J. BRIDGES

Testimony before Senate Committee on Finance in 1887 (*Senate Report No. 1990* [49th Cong., 2d sess.], pp. 242–43).

PREFACE

THE primary purpose of this book is to make available a body of information on a much-neglected subject—the problem of valuing imports for tariff purposes. With some changes in form and content it represents essentially the author's doctoral dissertation written at the University of Chicago. As such its original purpose was the description and interpretation of the law of dutiable value in the United States from the economic standpoint, i.e., from the standpoint of the various alternatives in the determination of dutiable value, and the economic implications of the valuation methods actually employed.

Like most economic institutions, customs valuation presents many different aspects and its subject matter penetrates a number of separate but interrelated fields of inquiry. Partly because of the impossibility of divorcing the economic from the other aspects and partly because of the desirability of bridging a major gap in the extant literature of tariff administration, this work has taken the form of a general study in economics, history, public administration, and law. Although the economic theme predominates, its significance as well as its very existence is functionally interrelated with the other important aspects indicated.

The work is divided into four parts—an introduction, a historical section, a section on contemporary valuation law and problems, and a summary and conclusion. The introduction attempts to indicate the nature and significance of the problem at hand. The historical section serves a number of purposes. It begins with a review of the origins of dutiable value and valuation procedures in the United States and traces the significant developments up to the present. In the process of establishing the study firmly on the foundation of the positive experience of the past, many analytical problems are resolved which would otherwise require separate treatment. Indeed, the historical approach is indispensable to an adequate understanding of perhaps the fundamental problem of the entire study—an examination and evaluation of the alternative forms or bases of dutiable value. The other major aspect of the study—the problem, or complex of problems, surrounding the administration of dutiable value upon a given valuation base—likewise requires for its understanding the factual background and insights made available by history. The historical section is unconcerned with a systematic tracing of the origin and evolution of the minor value components and minutiae of administrative procedure. It seeks, however, in addition to the objectives already stated, to make available to the student of customs history a knowledge of conditions and events associated with the valuation problem and leading to important changes in customs organization and administration.

Part III attempts to present a representative description of customs valuation as it exists today. Its primary objective is to provide an analysis of each of the several forms of dutiable value currently in effect in the United States. Much of this is accomplished in the chapter on foreign and export value, since many of the problems pertaining to valuation are common to several of the different value bases and are most completely represented in the definition and interpretation of foreign value. In addition to the analysis of the forms of dutiable value, Part III is also concerned with the more important special problems associated with customs valuation. Although these problems appear recurrently in the historical section, their systematic treatment is reserved until this time. It is believed that this arrangement, apart from advantages in exposition, will be of convenience to students whose principal concern is with the contemporary situation. A final chapter in Part III presents a brief discussion of valuation methods in foreign countries and of international efforts to prevent the use of valuation procedures as tools of administrative protection. Part IV is a condensation of the findings of the entire study and suggests certain changes in valuation methods in the United States.

A word or two should perhaps be said with respect to the audience for which this book is intended. It is hoped that economists generally will find in this study an illuminating case history of the kinds of problems encountered in an attempt to administer economic activity over even a relatively simple and restricted area. Since many of the problems of economic policy at the present time as well as in the foreseeable future imply the possibility of extensive public administration, an additional institutional study of "administered economics" is not without relevance. The work will be of more direct concern, however, to students of international trade and commercial policy, to economic historians (Part II), and to specialists in the fields of tariff administration and customs jurisprudence. Although not definitive of the law of dutiable value, a substantial portion of the book should be useful for historical and reference purposes to customs brokers, customs administrators, and the customs bar.

In closing these prefatory remarks, the author wishes to state that he is well aware that this study constitutes at best but an introduction to a highly complex and technical subject. For the omission or cursory treatment of many important issues in the economics as well as in the jurisprudence of customs valuation the author can plead only limitations of time and space. If the book succeeds in stimulating interest in a surprisingly neglected but important field, its inadequacies may eventually be rectified by the contributions of others. It would take many volumes of many pages to exploit fully this field, which is still virtually pioneer territory.

R. E. S.

Evanston, Illinois
January 30, 1948

ACKNOWLEDGMENTS

THE author has been fortunate in the interest which has been displayed by various persons in the completion of this study. A number of government officers have furnished valuable advice, criticism, and sources of information. Special mention should be made of Mr. Robert L. Sammons, chief, International Economics Division, Office of Business Economics, Department of Commerce, Washington, D.C.; Mr. Robert W. Chambers, chief counsel, Bureau of Customs, Washington, D.C.; Mr. George R. Gulick, appraiser of merchandise at Los Angeles, California; Mr. Charles Kruszewski, formerly U.S. Treasury representative at Berlin, more recently special customs investigator in the Chicago district; and Mr. William Hannan, appraiser at Chicago. Mr. Hannan's wealth of experience in the appraisement of merchandise for a period of over forty years, combined with his scholarly interest in the present study and his willingness at all times to be of assistance, has been one of the bright spots in an endeavor not altogether devoid of frustration.

Several members of the business and legal community have also added to the author's sources of information. Mr. E. R. Dreves, general traffic manager, Marshall Field and Company, and Mr. Charles Hoy, formerly head of the foreign office, Carson, Pirie, Scott and Company, at Chicago, gave willingly of their time. Mr. Harry Radcliffe, executive secretary of the National Council of American Importers, furnished valuable materials through the mail. Mr. Philip Stein, of Los Angeles, and Mr. Allerton deC. Thompkins, of Washington, D.C., customs attorneys, contributed special information and data on the legal aspects of valuation. Likewise, Mr. W. C. Sullivan and Mr. F. L. Conrad, of the firm of W. C. Sullivan and Company, custom-house brokers, Chicago, provided an especially illuminating discussion of the problems of clearing merchandise through the customs. Mr. S. W. Findley and Mr. W. T. Couch, of the University of Chicago Press, contributed special insight into the problems surrounding the importation of books.

Constructive advice and criticism were given by the members of the author's doctoral dissertation committee at the University of Chicago—Professors Jacob Viner (chairman), Chester Wright, Theodore Yntema, and Leonard W. White. In particular, the author is permanently indebted to Professor Viner—in addition to a larger obligation to him—for his rigorous and detailed criticism, his prolific sources of information, and his remarkable patience in reading and re-reading the manuscript at various stages of completion.

It is perhaps desirable to state formally that which is implicit in any work of this kind, namely, that any errors or other shortcomings in the present study are the responsibility of the author alone and cannot be charged to any whose names appear above or whose contributions have not been mentioned for lack of space. Finally, two additional acknowledgments are in order: one to a generous government, which made possible this undertaking through the medium of Public Law 346, otherwise known as the "G.I. Bill of Rights"; the other to a courageous wife, without whose inspiration and insight this study could not have been completed.

R. E. S.

TABLE OF CONTENTS

PART I. INTRODUCTION

PART II. THE HISTORY OF CUSTOMS VALUATION IN THE UNITED STATES

xiii

PART III. CONTEMPORARY VALUATION LAW AND PROCEDURE

Table of Contents

PART IV. SUMMARY AND CONCLUSION

BIBLIOGRAPHY

TABLE OF CASES CITED

INDEXES

PART I

Introduction

CHAPTER I

The Problem and Its Setting

FEW subjects in the domain of economics have been more widely discussed than the tariff. It was largely in the discussion of the influence of tariffs and similar restraints upon the free flow of trade that the doctrine of laissez faire and the classical school of economics originated and received initial impetus. Some of the earliest explicit statements of the effects and implications of elasticity of demand are to be found in writings dealing with the relationship between the height of customs duties and the receipts of customs revenue.[1] The implications of tariff levies for price levels, wage rates, standards of living, the balance of payments, the location of industry, and so on ad infinitum have been studied, discussed, and written into the history of economic thought.

However widely discussed in principle, the tariff has received relatively little scholarly attention from the standpoint of the substance and effects of administrative practice. By its very nature, a knowledge of the intricacies of tariff administration is confined to a few—principally customs brokers and lawyers and customs officials. Moreover, there seems to have existed in academic circles and elsewhere the tacit assumption that administrative practice has negligible or no economic implications. Only since the growth of quotas, exchange controls, clearing agreements, and other restrictive measures arising out of exaggerated national policy has the term "administrative protection"

1. E.g., Roger Coke, *A Treatise Wherein It Is Demonstrated, that the Church and State of England, Are in Equal Danger with the Trade of It*, Treatise II: "Reasons of the Increase of the Dutch Trade, etc." (London, 1671), p. 122: "Nor is this all the benefit the Dutch receive by the smallness of their Customs, which Sir *Walter Raleigh* affirms not to be the 19 part so much as the *English;* (though in truth they are much less) yet by this means they draw all Nations to Traffick with them; and though the Duties they receive be but small, yet the multitudes of all sorts of Commodities brought in by themselves and others, and carried out by themselves and others, is so great, that they receive more Customs and duties to their State in one year by the greatness of their Commerce, than *England* does in two by the greatness of their Customs."

received currency and its underlying phenomena serious consideration. Even as yet there has been little attention devoted to the kind of administrative protection which is necessarily or potentially connected with the operation of the tariff as contrasted with other administrative restrictions.[2] The latter, though more spectacular, have been intermittent and fortuitous—the former continuous and persistent. The cumulative effects of tariff administrative policy have had substantial long-run economic and political significance little realized by students of the tariff history of the United States.

There has been another reason for the divorce of tariff theory from tariff practice in general discussion, particularly in the United States. From the passage of the first tariff act in 1789 for upward of a hundred years there was a separation of the tariff acts proper from the customs administrative laws in the statutes.[3] While the tariff acts received the concentrated attention and talents of such congressional orators as Calhoun, Clay, and Webster, the customs administrative laws, with a few outstanding exceptions, elicited relatively little interest as they passed through the legislative mill.[4] Nevertheless, as rates of duty became higher and higher and administrative practice therefore—as well as for independent reasons—more significant, greater consideration was given in tariff hearings to the effects of the administrative sections

2. Two notable exceptions have been John Day Larkin, *The President's Control of the Tariff* (Cambridge, Mass., 1936), and Percy Wells Bidwell, *The Invisible Tariff* (New York, 1939). Prior to the 1930's the Economic Council of the League of Nations had recognized the restrictive effects of customs formalities but was able to do relatively little toward their removal. The term "administrative protection" as used in the recent literature with respect to the imposition of exchange controls, quotas, and similar measures is really a misnomer. Like the tariff, these are substantive policy measures requiring administration for their implementation; but the nature of the measures themselves should not be confused with the administrative methods used to execute them. Administrative protection in the strict sense is that protection which results from the methods by which a policy is administered as distinct from the effects of the substantive policy itself.

3. Although the Payne-Aldrich Tariff of 1909 made substantial progress in the matter, it was not until the passage of the Fordney-McCumber Tariff of 1922 that the two branches of tariff law were effectively consolidated.

4. "From the early days of the republic, Congress has always been very loath to undertake the work of perfecting customs procedure, partly because its members were unfamiliar with the practical problems facing government officers in charge of the administration of the tariff laws, and partly because its time and energies had invariably been exhausted in framing the schedules, so that the administrative features, vitally important as they are, were suffered to be let alone" (I. Newton Hoffman, "Customs Administration under the 1913 Tariff Act," *Journal of Political Economy*, XXII [November, 1914], 845).

of the law. By 1923 it was possible with considerable justification for an importers' representative to say, "Let me write the Administrative Act and I care not who writes the rates of duty."[5] Repeatedly the statement has been made in congressional hearings by widely divergent interests that whether or not a given tariff law is "good" or "bad" depends upon the manner in which it is administered.

Once it is recognized that the mode of administration of the tariff has significant economic consequences, the importance of adequate attention to the administrative features becomes obvious. Other considerations lead to the same conclusion. A knowledge of the practical operation of the tariff lends realism to theoretical discussion. It tends to reduce "crackpot" legislation and provides an insight into the important intangibles of the tariff. It reveals the importer as a representative citizen and businessman and helps dispel many naïve and distorted notions which inhibit rational thinking in matters of international trade.[6] Finally, it affords some indication of the nature and costs of the mechanism which has been charged with the somewhat dubious task of collecting revenue under legislative acts which are designed primarily to reduce or eliminate revenue by excluding imports.[7]

The Nature and Significance of Customs Valuation

The need for appraisement or valuation of merchandise in customs administration arises primarily from the existence of tariff duties which depend for their amount upon the value of the article taxed. Although there are in principle only two classes of tariff rate[8]—ad valorem and specific—there are in fact a number of subtypes belonging to either or both classes.[9] Specific rates are expressed in terms of a

5. Benjamin Arthur Levett, *Through the Customs Maze* (New York, 1923), p. 11.

6. Among these is the semijudicial notion existing in some circles that importing is a "privilege" as opposed to the "right" to conduct domestic manufacture.

7. No matter how restrictive of imports and therefore of customs revenue, virtually all tariff and customs laws are couched in terms of "protecting the revenue."

8. A distinction should here be made between *duties* and *rates* of duty. Rates are the unit levies, whether ad valorem or specific, expressed in the tariff schedules. The term "duty" is more comprehensive and may signify either a rate or (especially in the plural form) the total assessment for a given quantum (value or physical quantity) of merchandise. It is convenient, among other uses, to apply the term "duty" when the implications of either the rate or the total assessment may be involved.

9. A third class—duties collectible in kind (such as the 1-in-10 provisions for tobacco exports in certain of the American colonies)—may be considered as a type

fixed monetary amount per physical unit, however defined, of a given article. Ad valorem rates, in the narrow and technically correct sense, are expressed in terms of a percentage of the value of the merchandise taxed. There are, however, a number of distinct types of duty whose rate and/or amount depends in one way or another upon the value of the merchandise. Such duties as a class are sometimes loosely referred to as ad valorem duties.[10] Included in this general class and requiring valuation procedures for their assessment and collection are the following types of duty, with actual illustrations taken from the Tariff Act of 1930 (unless otherwise specified):

1. *Simple ad valorem duties*
   Dolls and dolls' clothing, 90 per centum ad valorem (par. 1513)
2. *Compound and complex duties*
   a) *Compound rates.* Print rollers . . . $5 each and 72 per centum ad valorem (par. 395)
   b) *Complex rates.* Hat bodies, etc., . . . 40 cents per pound and 75 per centum ad valorem; and in addition thereto, . . . 25 cents per article (par. 1115[b])
3. *Duties subject to classification by value brackets*
   a) *Specific rates.* Clay pipes, valued at not more than 40 cents per gross, 15 cents per gross (par. 1552)
   b) *Ad valorem rates.* Iridescent, imitation, solid pearl beads, valued at not more than 10 cents per inch, 90 per centum ad valorum; valued at more than 10 cents per inch, 60 per centum ad valorem[11] (par. 1503)
   c) *Compound rates.*—Razors and parts thereof . . . valued at
   Less than 75 cents per dozen . . . . 18 cents *each*[12]
   75 cents and less than $1.50 per dozen . . . . 25 cents *each*
   $1.50 and less than $3.00 per dozen . . . . 30 cents *each*
   $3.00 and less than $4.00 per dozen . . . . 35 cents *each*
   $4.00 or more per dozen . . . . 45 cents *each*
   and in addition thereto, on all the foregoing, 30 per centum ad valorem (par. 358)

---

of ad valorem duty for which the value measure is the commodity taxed. In so far as the commodity taxed was itself circulated as money (e.g., tobacco), the ad valorem nature of such duties is readily apparent.

10. In order to preserve the distinction between simple ad valorem duties and the general class, the tariff law refers to the latter as duties "based upon or regulated in any manner by . . . value" (Tariff Act of 1930, sec. 489).

11. Note the highly regressive nature of this tax and the incentive for overvaluation as the breaking point is approached.

12. Italics added. The determination of the ad valorem equivalents of the compound rates is left to the reader.

4. *Duties subject to an ad valorem minimum*

   Gloves ... $6 per dozen pairs ... and in addition $5 per dozen pairs ... provided further, that all the foregoing shall be dutiable at not less than 50 per centum ad valorem (par. 1532[a])

5. *Duties subject to an ad valorem maximum*

   Bicycles and parts thereof ... but in no case shall such duty exceed 50 per centum ad valorem (par. 371)

6. *Minimum valuation duties*

   a) *Simple minimum valuation.*—All cotton cloths whatsoever ... the original cost of which, at the place whence imported ... shall be less than 35 cents the square yard, shall be taken and deemed to have cost 35 cents the square yard, and charged with duty accordingly (Sec. 7, Act of May 19, 1828, "Tariff of Abominations")

   b) *Valuation by value brackets.*—Woolen manufactures ... (values per square yard):

Actual Value	Dutiable Value
Not exceeding $0.50	$0.50
In excess of $0.50 but not $1.00	1.00
In excess of $1.00 but not $2.50	2.50
In excess of $2.50 but not $4.00	4.00
In excess of $4.00	Actual value

   (Condensation of sec. 2, pars. 2–6, Act of May 19, 1828, "Tariff of Abominations")

7. *Duties subject to "chief value" provisions*

   a) *Specific rates.*—Cordage, including cable ... wholly or in chief value of hemp, 3¼ cents per pound (par. 1005[a][3])

   b) *Ad valorem rates.*—Hats, bonnets, hoods, wholly or in chief value of any braid not provided for in paragraph 1504 ... 90 per centum ad valorem (par. 1505)

The foregoing examples are sufficient to indicate the basic purposes of customs valuation so far as the levy of duties is concerned. It should be observed at this point that the assessment of all duties, whether ad valorem or specific, requires an act of *classification,* that is, the determination of the applicable rate of duty under the tariff schedules for the particular merchandise in question. This not only is an exceedingly difficult problem for many importations but is always highly important inasmuch as a simple act of classification may determine whether a given article is duty free or subject to a prohibitively high rate. Notwithstanding the importance of classification and its applicability to all importations, valuation is considered to be of even greater complexity and of greater importance in the total machinery of tariff administration.[13] Moreover, in many cases it is impossible to make a definitive classification until a valuation or appraisement has first been made. This is true of all merchandise subject to value brackets and frequently of merchandise subject to "chief value" provisions, although valuation for the latter is technically not called an appraisement.

Customs valuation is not confined in purpose to the levy of duties. During its history in the United States it has been employed to accomplish at least six distinct purposes:

1. To determine dutiable value
2. To permit classification
3. To establish rates of duty, as for dumping duties and other special cases[14]
4. To provide statistics of foreign trade
5. To establish amounts of penalties, fines, and forfeitures
6. To facilitate the sale of forfeited and abandoned merchandise

The manner in which valuation procedures have been employed to fulfil these functions will become apparent as this study progresses. For the present it is sufficient to state that, from the standpoint of substantive importance, administrative complexity, and legislative history, customs valuation is undoubtedly the most significant as well as the most representative problem in the field of tariff administration. Its ramifications run through every department of tariff practice, and a study of it affords an excellent opportunity to observe the actual working of tariff-enforcement machinery.

In order to indicate the broad significance of customs valuation in terms of its consequences, the following subsections briefly describe the implications of valuation with respect to (1) the effects of valuation upon the level of duties; (2) administrative effects of valuation; (3) other effects.

13. "By far the greater difficulty is as to the value. The question as to what is the proper rate is very often complex; but it is always a question of law and is solved through the application of more or less settled rules of construction" (Levett, *op. cit.*, p. 16). In addition to having been the subject of far greater controversy than classification in the history of tariff legislation, valuation involves a much wider range of problems of interest to the economist.

14. Valuation was necessary for the proration downward of specific rates of duty under the blanket tariff reduction provided in the Compromise Act of 1833. It has also been a factor in establishing revised duties under the flexible provisions of the current tariff law.

EFFECTS OF VALUATION UPON THE LEVEL OF DUTIES

In a consideration of the relationship of valuation to the level of duties, it is necessary to distinguish between the *rate* component and the *value* component of ad valorem duties. Total duties, per importation or per unit of import, when levied on an ad valorem basis, depend for their amount upon *two* factors or variables: the *rate* of duty and the *valuation* to which the rate is applied. The actual duty and tariff burden upon a given article of import will be the same whether the rate be 50 per cent upon a dutiable base of $1.00 or 25 per cent upon a base of $2.00. If the "true" value of imported articles existed in some simple, single, and easily ascertainable form and if duties were always levied upon the basis of such "true" values, the foregoing mathematical truism could be dismissed as obvious and unimportant. From the standpoint of actual practice, however, with rates of duty fixed by statute, valuation becomes the practically significant variable upon which actual duties "depend."

The foregoing is not intended to imply that value for duty purposes is determined fortuitously or is in general subject to capricious fluctuation. It is meant, rather, to indicate the substantive importance of the valuation base itself and to pave the way for an examination into the possible range or spread in values under alternative methods of valuation. That the potential variation in the value base is many times greater than any probable variation in rates of duty from one tariff act to another is revealed by studies of the United States Tariff Commission showing the spread between purchase prices in foreign markets and selling prices in the United States of various imported articles. Many such markups have exceeded 400 per cent, some have exceeded 500 per cent, and a spread of over 600 per cent is not unknown.[15] In view of these possibilities of variation in actual duties resulting from the selection of different bases of valuation, it is pertinent to examine some of the implications of such variation.

15. U.S. Tariff Commission, *Domestic Value—Conversion of Rates: Report No. 45* (2d ser.; Washington, 1932) (for purposes of simplification, reference to Washington as the place of publication of government documents is hereinafter omitted). Specific examples of such markups, partly reflecting the existence of high tariff duties, may be found on pp. 672, 716, 792, 803, and 804. Extreme examples of divergence in value of a given article, depending upon the base, may be found in U.S. Congress, Senate Committee on Finance, *Imported Merchandise and Retail Price* (1922). This study, partly reflecting the effects of depreciated currencies, shows domestic values of imported goods as high as 4,000 per cent of foreign value and over 2,500 per cent of landed cost.

Implications for government revenue.—Customs duties are one form of taxation, hence of direct fiscal significance to the government. For many decades after the establishment of the federal government, customs revenue constituted almost the entire source of federal income.[16] With the increasing use of the tariff for protective purposes and the development of other forms of taxation for revenue, the fiscal importance of the tariff has markedly declined until it recently supplied less than 7 per cent of ordinary federal receipts.[17] Nevertheless, until 1929 absolute receipts from tariff duties showed a secular trend upward to a peak of over $600,000,000 in that year. In the five-year period from July 1, 1935, to June 30, 1940, they amounted to an annual average of approximately $380,000,000.[18]

Historically the proportion of total customs revenue proceeding from the levy of ad valorem duties has varied considerably, depending upon the policy expressed in various customs and tariff acts. The Act of 1789 carried predominantly specific rates; but even under it ad valorem rates accounted for approximately a third of the revenue.[19] Under the Walker Tariff of 1846 all rates were made ad valorem, reflecting the desire to maintain constant and readily recognizable ratios of duty to value. Subsequently, with a change in political parties and the ascendancy of protectionism, this policy was reversed. Specific rates, which tend to conceal the degree of protection afforded, were substituted wherever feasible, and an increasing number of compound rates were employed to insure, so far as possible, the desired degree of protection under varying price conditions. During the first year of the operation of the Tariff Act of 1930, revenue from simple ad valorem rates constituted roughly a fourth of total customs receipts, a ratio notably less than the ratio of the value of the merchandise involved to the value of total dutiable imports.[20]

A factor tending to make the determination of value for duty purposes of greater dollar importance to the government in recent decades has been the historical increase in ad valorem rates from the

16. From 1800 to 1820 average annual customs receipts were $12,046,000, or 92.3 per cent of average annual federal revenue of $13,056,000 (*Statistical Abstract of the United States, 1940* [1941], p. 167).
17. Five-year average ending June 30, 1940: 6.8 per cent (*ibid.*).
18. *Ibid.*
19. "Not much short of one-third of the whole amount of the duties is received from articles rated as ad valorem" (Letter of Alexander Hamilton to Congress, January 31, 1795, *American State Papers: Finance*, I, 438).

5 to 15 per cent levels in the days of Alexander Hamilton to levels ranging as high as 90 per cent in the Hawley-Smoot Tariff of 1930.[21] A difference in dutiable value is therefore likely to produce a much greater difference in customs revenue in terms of absolute amounts than it would under the original low rates of duty. This has been further augmented by the secular increase in price levels. From the standpoint of total government revenue, however, the relative decline in importance of revenue from customs duties of all kinds has been such as to reduce the significance of valuation methods to a minor role in the total fiscal policy of the government.

Significance for competing interests.—It is a truism where the tariff is concerned that any factor tending to raise or to lower effective duties is inevitably the subject of spirited controversy between the opposing interests involved. Because of the great difficulty experienced in developing a satisfactory definition of dutiable value and the no less serious difficulties in the application of a given definition, valuation procedures have afforded scope for wide differences of opinion among the interests concerned. The kinds of controversy and the issues involved will become apparent hereinafter; at present it is necessary merely to state the basic group alignments and conflicting interests at stake.

The sharpest cleavage over valuation matters has been between domestic producers and importers. Throughout the nineteenth century and into the twentieth, domestic manufacturing interests have supplemented their demands for high statutory tariff rates with demands for the use of valuation methods which increase and con-

20. U.S. Tariff Commission, *Methods of Valuation*, pp. 10–11. For the year ended September 30, 1931, import and collection ratios by type of duty were as follows:

Type of Duty	Percentage of Dutiable Imports	Percentage of Total Duties
Ad valorem	35.0	24.1
Specific	53.7	63.1
Compound	7.6	9.6
Unsegregated	3.7	3.2
	100.0	100.0

21. Despite the high level of ad valorem rates in the current tariff, the most highly protective duties are specific and compound rates. Tariff framers believe, not without justification, that percentage rates much above 90 per cent do not "look good" in the statute.

ceal effective rates of duty and which subject the importer to a maximum of administrative barriers and penalties. Importers, on the other
hand, have attempted to prevent the adoption of all such methods
and to minimize their effects by turning the letter of the law to their
own advantage whenever possible. Among the more dramatic features of the general controversy over valuation, and serving to illustrate the conflicting interests between manufacturers and importers,
have been the circumstances surrounding the nullification movement
and the Compromise Act of 1833; the charges and countercharges
concerning fraudulent undervaluation and the notorious custom-
house scandals, chiefly at New York, in the nineteenth century; and
the "American valuation" battle, which reached its climax in 1921–22.

A less significant area of conflict has been the dissension between
importers or groups of importers over valuation practices in particular lines of merchandise or over legislation having discriminatory effects in actual operation. In both cases a considerable portion of the
antagonism was directed at foreigners. So far as particular lines of
merchandise were concerned, questionable practices were frequently
indulged in by less reputable firms regardless of the citizenship of the
owners; but the greater vulnerability of well-established American
firms to the civil and criminal penalties of the law and to unfavorable
publicity attending revelations of fraud had the effect of making
them less likely than foreigners to take the risks of undervaluation.
In the matter of discriminatory operation of the law, certain technicalities of the early statutes permitted importation by foreign manufacturers on their own account or through agents at lower valuations
than required for goods purchased abroad and imported by American merchants. Much of the criticism directed at "foreigners" was,
however, originated by domestic manufacturers who sought to identify as foreign and therefore undesirable all importing in whatever
form and by whomever conducted.[22]

A third area of conflict over customs valuation has been geographical in nature. On the one hand, this has taken the form of local rivalry
between different ports of entry, finding expression in allegations by

22. The issues in this general controversy are discussed *infra*, chap. iii; cf. also
W. H. Osborn, *The Administration and Undervaluation Frauds on the Customs
Revenue* (New York, 1887), as indicating the mixed motives and complex align-
ments typical of valuation controversy in the nineteenth century.

the commercial interests of one port against those of another that laxity and fraud were being deliberately or otherwise used to draw legitimate trade away from its natural channels.[23] On a larger scale, valuation methods during the first half of the nineteenth century were a sectional issue, aligning southern interests against the North in the minimum-value and home-valuation controversies of that period. The sectional issue was partly a question of interport competition between the North and the South and partly the result of divergent interests with respect to the larger issue of tariff protection.

Organization and commercial practice of importing.—The difference in duties under alternative methods of valuation permitted or suggested by law have been in many cases a deciding factor in the organization and commercial practice of foreign manufacturers and importers. As indicated in some detail in Part II of this study, the basis for valuation in certain tariff acts made it decidedly profitable, apart from other considerations, for a foreign manufacturer to establish a branch or an agency in this country and to handle all his business on a consignment basis instead of through the traditional wholesale channels in his own country.

Valuation policy with respect to the so-called "charges" has had substantial effects upon packing and shipping methods and terms, the kind and quality of containers furnished, and the extent to which goods are finished abroad or imported in an unfinished condition. In the case of the application of the "similar merchandise" and "chief-value" provisions, as well as in other areas of valuation procedure, the manufactured products themselves have been altered or differentiated in order to minimize valuation and resultant duties. Even the domestic price policy of a foreign manufacturer is sometimes determined by considerations of customs valuation in the United States. It is difficult to determine the extent to which such modifications of commercial practice have actually taken place, for the reason that the question of their legality for duty purposes often turns upon the issue of whether the tariff provisions were the sole or merely a concomitant

23. Valuation matters have not been a matter of substantial interport rivalry in recent years. More important issues, such as the St. Lawrence waterway project and the establishment of free zones, particularly on the West Coast, have been the major items of such dissension. The question of uniform appraisement at the several ports is, however, of importance to the government from the standpoint of sound administration and the prevention of fraud.

motivation for the change. The subject matter is therefore frequently and understandably classified under the heading of trade secrets.

Effects in general.—In general, the significance of valuation methods, so far as the question of duty levels is concerned, is the same as the significance of higher or of lower tariff rates in the statutes. The implications therefore extend to domestic price levels, effects upon consumption, the establishment and location of industry, and all other issues comprehended by the protectionist–free-trade controversy—issues which lie outside the scope of this investigation.[24]

CUSTOMS VALUATION AND ADMINISTRATIVE PROTECTION

The line of demarcation between policy and administration is at best a thin one. Legislation in the United States not only expresses policy measures but frequently specifies in considerable detail the procedures which shall be taken to administer the policy. Likewise, the interpretation of the statutes by administrators and courts often allows wide scope for what amounts to policy-making. This is true regardless of the detailed nature of the statutes; and statutory detail is itself more often than not the result of previous experience and decisions of administrators and courts. Thus what begins as the opinion of an administrator often ends as "the will of Congress."

In view of these interrelationships, as well as for independent reasons, the most appropriate definition of "administrative protection" as applied to the tariff in general and customs valuation in particular is that additional burden upon importation, over and above the normal pecuniary burden of tariff duties, which results from all administrative

24. It might be stated at this juncture that valuation methods frequently have served to provide conclusive protection or otherwise to determine the course of trade. The American cotton manufacturing industry was established behind the protection of the minimum-valuation proviso in the Tariff Act of 1816, which was alleged to have cost consumers in the United States some $26,000,000 between 1816 and 1828. The American chemical and dye industry since World War I has grown up under the protection provided by "American valuation." Conversely, English manufacturers of woolens, French winegrowers, and other foreign producers were said at various times to have completely dominated the American importing business, eliminating the competition of domestic importers under provisions enabling them to pay duty on a low cost-of-production rather than on a foreign-market-value basis. Canadian producers of ferro-silicon were able to compete on favorable terms for the American market as long as they were able to take advantage of a low valuation basis for their exports to this country. Numerous instances can be found in which the valuation features of the tariff have played a decisive role in the profitability of either the importing or the domestic interests concerned.

measures employed in the collection of duties. This includes both "necessary" and "unnecessary" administrative burdens regardless of whether their origin lies in the statutory will of Congress, in the regulations of administrators, in the decisions of courts, or in the particular exigencies of day-to-day practice.

Customs valuation in the United States is a branch of tariff administration unique in the multiplicity of ways in which it may actually or potentially contribute to tariff protection. As already indicated, it may operate directly to increase tariff levies. In addition, it has exhibited at one time or another virtually all types of procedural barrier associated with administrative protection. These have included burdensome requirements for the procurement of sworn consular invoices from abroad; complicated entrance formalities under pressure of inadequate time; expensive bonding requirements; delays in appraisement for months or even years, creating an uncertain and contingent liability for increased duties which may well threaten an importer's solvency long after the merchandise has been sold; drastic penalties for undervaluation in the form of additional duties, fines, forfeitures, and seizures of merchandise; expensive and protracted litigation; and a complex of minor legal and equitable anomalies which in some instances have provoked more irritation and antipathy than the major exactions.[25]

After the measure of administrative protection associated with customs valuation is understood, it then becomes pertinent to distinguish between those practices essential to sound valuation procedure and those which are relatively unnecessary. It also becomes pertinent, in order to seek the appropriate remedy, to determine whether and to what extent undesirable practices are the result of administrative action, judicial interpretation, or legislative enactment. Both the history of customs valuation and the discussion of contemporary valuation law appearing hereinafter indicate the difficulty of determining the essentiality and appropriateness of particular solutions to given administrative problems, the trial-and-error nature of the administrative process, the frequent difficulty of determining from the wording of the statutes the "true" or even the apparent will of Congress, the possibility of widely differing results all consistent with the letter

25. For examples of vexatious valuation provisions which are sometimes the despair of importers cf. Levett, *op. cit.*, pp. 32–67, 91–118.

of the law, and the occasional departure from the expressed will of Congress because of either the unworkability or the misinterpretation of particular statutory provisions. In short, a study of customs valuation reveals the essentially interrelated and overlapping nature of administrative protection and public administration.

CUSTOMS VALUATION AND FOREIGN-TRADE STATISTICS

The Bureau of Customs is the basic fact-gathering agency for supplying statistics of imports and exports of goods moving in the foreign trade of the United States.[26] The methods and formulas employed in the valuation of such goods are therefore highly significant for the determination of the resultant aggregates and for the uses to which foreign-trade statistics are put. Although a statement of the detailed implications of valuation procedure for statistical purposes is beyond the scope of this study, a few general observations are pertinent at this time.[27]

The most important test of the validity and usefulness of foreign-trade statistics is the equivalence of reported values and actual settlement prices. To the extent that these diverge, balance-of-payments studies and aggregate-value estimates of foreign trade are erroneous. Two factors in customs valuation in the United States operate to create a divergence between reported and transaction values: (1) the widespread use of valuation methods which necessarily result in such divergence; (2) inaccuracies in reporting.

Import statistics comprehend three classes of merchandise: (1) goods subject to duties based upon value; (2) specific-duty goods; (3) goods on the free list. Goods in class 1 are subjected to the most exacting appraisement procedures, resulting in maximum accuracy

26. Cf. U.S. Department of Commerce, Bureau of the Census, *Regulations for the Collection of Statistics of Foreign Commerce and Navigation of the United States* (rev. to May, 1946), sec. 30.1, 6, 9.

27. Further remarks on a special aspect of the subject are made *infra*, pp. 246–48, but it is considered desirable to dispose of the statistical implications of custom valuation for the purposes of this study at this point. Two articles useful as background material for this subject are Frank R. Rutter, "Statistics of Imports and Exports," *Journal of the American Statistical Association*, XV (March, 1916), 16–34; and Eliot Mears, "The Foreign Trade Statistics of the United States," *Journal of the American Statistical Association*, XXX (September, 1935), 501–16. The best concise introduction to the problem is to be found in U.S. Department of Commerce, Bureau of the Census, *Foreign Commerce and Navigation of the United States for the Calendar Year 1944*, "Explanation of Statistics," pp. ix, xiv–xvi.

from the standpoint of reporting. Goods in classes 2 and 3, although technically required to be entered and appraised under the regular dutiable-value provisions, are actually valued perfunctorily at the figures shown in importers' entries—generally on an invoice basis. In anticipation of the analysis in Part III, hereinafter, it may be said that dutiable value exceeds actual transaction prices in perhaps a majority of appraisements, often by very substantial amounts. The resulting anomaly for all import statistics is that the figures most likely to be accurate are least likely to represent transaction prices, while those most likely to represent transaction prices are least likely to be accurate.[28]

The procedure for gathering export statistics is even less formal than that for imported goods on the free list. Export values are recorded from exporters' sworn declarations which are required before clearance of the carrying vessel. The valuation formula for exports is relatively simple, but the absence of any check for other than manifest error leaves substantial latitude for departure from accuracy and consistency.[29]

28. Although progress has been made, the implications of the statement "commercial statistics have been described as a customs by-product" still hold (cf. Rutter, *op. cit.*, p. 16). An excellent study of deviations of reported values from transaction prices for balance-of-payments purposes was made by the W.P.A. under the sponsorship of the Bureau of Foreign and Domestic Commerce. This study indicated that from 70 to 80 per cent of all entries under observation stated values inaccurately for balance-of-payments purposes. Unfortunately, only specific-duty goods and goods on the free list were studied. The reason underlying much, if not most, of the deviation was "overvaluation" resulting from additions by importers of inland freight in foreign countries, the normal safe procedure in meeting import valuation requirements for duty purposes (cf. U.S. Department of Commerce, Bureau of Foreign and Domestic Commerce, *Merchandise Import Statistics in the Balance of International Payments: Report on Official W.P.A. Project No. 365-97-3-20* [1939]).

29. Exports are to be declared at their selling price, if sold, or at actual cost, if not sold, unless consigned, in which case their market value in the United States applies. Eventual sales of consigned merchandise at dumping prices thus result in overvaluation of exports relative to transaction prices. Since most dumping prices are probably established prior to exportation, their use in foreign-trade statistics results in an understatement of the value of exports relative to the domestic trade in the United States. Actual or estimated transportation charges to the border or port of exportation are to be included in the value of all exports. For reasons underlying the inaccuracy of export valuations cf. *Foreign Commerce and Navigation of the United States, 1944*, p. xiv; also Mears, *op. cit.*, pp. 511–12. In 1850 the Secretary of the Treasury, in discussing heavy fluctuations in the prices and quantities of cotton exports, reported the following: "It must be borne in mind, however, that these values as reported are not always the prices realized on sales abroad.

These issues raise important questions as to the validity of the figures for merchandise account in the balance-of-payments studies of the Department of Commerce. Since this account is by far the largest and most important in the total balance, it is rather surprising that such studies have devoted relatively little attention to the merchandise adjustment account and rarely allude to the lack of relationship between dutiable values and transaction prices.[30]

There is no way, short of an extensive empirical study, of determining the average excess of dutiable values over transaction prices; but in view of the many factors tending in this direction—the existence of foreign consumption-taxes frequently included in dutiable value but not in purchase price, the effect of court interpretations of "usual wholesale quantity," the use of the "American selling price" basis of dutiable value, the excess of dutiable values over remittances in the case of consignments and branch-plant importations, etc.—it would appear that this excess may be substantial.

There are of course many other considerations to be dealt with in obtaining maximum accuracy in the statistical valuation of merchandise imports and exports.[31] The Bureau of the Census, in its explanation of the statistics of foreign commerce and navigation, recognizes

---

They are the declared values of the exporters from our country, against which bills of exchange are usually drawn, and not the prices received on actual sales; and it is notorious that the immense losses on shipments of cotton during the last year have reduced the amount actually realized by the sales in Europe very far below the official value in the custom-house returns" (U.S. Treasury, *Annual Report, 1851,* p. 11).

30. The author has been unable to find in this series any explicit recognition of the inevitable excess of dutiable values over transaction values for a large proportion of all importations. In one instance reference is made to "additions to invoice values . . . to place dutiable value on basis required by special provisions of existing tariff legislation" (*Balance of International Payments of the United States, 1937,* p. 11). More frequent reference is made to upward adjustments to compensate for "undervaluation" of imports (*ibid., 1935,* p. 16; *1938,* p. 30). These references pertain to the statistical undervaluation of reported values relative to transaction prices resulting from the existence of noncommercial trade, smuggling, foreign inland freight not included in dutiable value, etc. For reasons appearing later in this study, substantial *over*valuation relative to transaction prices is necessary in order to enter a large portion of total importations at correct dutiable values. Since such entries are the basis of import statistics, a corresponding adjustment *downward* would be necessary to reflect actual transaction prices.

31. Cf. Nicholas M. Petruzzelli, *Some Technical Aspects of Foreign Trade Statistics with Special Reference to Valuation* (Washington, 1946), for an extended treatment of the general problem, including discussion of foreign systems and much useful bibliographical material.

the possibility of divergence of dutiable values and transaction prices but makes no statement as to the probable direction or degree of such divergence. It is to be hoped, as intimated in the W.P.A. study cited above, that the Bureau of Foreign and Domestic Commerce will soon find the staff and facilities for a detailed investigation of the empirical relationship between dutiable values and transaction prices. The findings of such a study might well result in material refinement and improvement in the balance-of-payments estimates for the United States.[32]

CUSTOMS VALUATION AND FOREIGN RELATIONS

The institution of customs valuation has had a continuous, and at times notorious, influence upon the foreign relations of the United States. This influence has resulted from several distinct aspects of the problem. The first of these has been the requirement of sworn consular invoices, originally only for goods shipped on consignment by foreign manufacturers and later for all importations. Foreign exporters were required to appear before the United States consul in the district of manufacture and take oath as to the correctness of the values appearing in the invoice. This exaction, apart from the element of compulsion and the consular fees involved, was especially irritating and onerous to those manufacturers who were required to travel long distances to appear before the appropriate consul.[33] The requirement also ran counter to laws in certain countries which provided that aliens were not legally competent to administer oaths. It is not certain to what extent the enactment of such laws was the result of the consular oath requirement, but the Treasury Department was obliged to recognize oaths before foreign notaries and officials, on both legal and practical grounds, since an oath not considered legally

32. The Office of Business Economics of the International Economics Division of the Department of Commerce is now endeavoring to devote more detailed attention to the problems under consideration. The success of this endeavor will depend largely upon the adequacy of staff and related facilities. A brief but penetrating study raising substantially similar issues for Canadian balance-of-payments estimates and indicating steps taken toward their improvement is Herbert Marshall, "Recent Developments in Balance of International Payments Statistics," in *Essays in Transportation in Honour of W. T. Jackman*, ed. H. A. Innis (Toronto, 1941), pp. 145–57.

33. Cf. *infra*, p. 63, n. 16, for illustrations of the kind of hardship frequently resulting from this requirement and the penalty for sending an agent in the place of an owner or manufacturer.

binding upon the foreigner would be of little value.[34] Throughout the nineteenth century the handling of invoices was the principal function of the majority of foreign consulates of the United States, and the collection of consular fees for this service more than supported the entire organization.[35] The importance of this function even at the present time is indicated by the elaborate instructions in force governing the discharge of the duties in question.[36]

Another aspect of customs valuation of much more spectacular effect upon the foreign relations of the United States has been the role of United States Treasury agents abroad and the general problem of value investigations in foreign countries. Shortly after the Civil War the Treasury sent its first revenue agents to Europe to ascertain foreign market values in an effort to detect undervaluations and to augment the informational facilities of appraisers in this country.[37] Even when conducted with the greatest of decorum, these investigations have been odious to foreign manufacturers and governments. As valuation law in the United States became more complex, the simple gathering of price lists, quotations, and routine information abroad did not suffice. It became necessary for a foreign manufacturer to throw open his books to American agents and to divulge prices, discounts, terms, and conditions of sale for all his customers whether in his own country or in third countries remote from the United States. This requirement and its numerous by-products have been a constant source of foreign irritation and the subject of numerous diplomatic exchanges over the years.

On several occasions the irritation from this source, combined with

34. Cf. Treasury Circular, September 20, 1853, in U.S. Treasury, *Annual Report, 1852–53*, pp. 350–52. The old expression "not worth a custom-house oath" suggests the probable value of an oath taken by an exporter 3,000 miles away from the custom house before an alien not competent to administer a binding oath.

35. Cf. *infra*, p. 119, n. 26. Many of the foreign officers in the U.S. diplomatic service had little or no duties other than the consulation of invoices. The story is told of an ex-saloonkeeper in charge of one such office who gave expression to the uniform character of his duties by the stock greeting: "Well, gentlemen, what'll it be, an invoice or a cocktail?" (Graham H. Stuart, *American Diplomatic and Consular Practice* [New York, 1936], p. 362, quoted from George Horton, *Recollections Grave and Gay* [Indianapolis, 1927], p. 87).

36. Cf. U.S. State Department, *Foreign Service Regulations of the United States of America* ("Looseleaf Series"), chap. xv: "Documentation of Merchandise."

37. Cf. *infra*, chap. iv, for account of the activities of the first United States revenue agents abroad.

punitive administrative practices in the United States, has threatened a serious rupture in friendly relations with foreign governments. One such occasion was the near tariff war with Germany in 1906–7, in which valuation methods and investigations abroad played a leading role. As a result of German representations President Theodore Roosevelt dispatched an investigating commission to Germany. The consequences were a minor revolution in customs administration, a new commercial agreement with Germany, and a lengthy passage in the annual message of the President to Congress for 1907.[38]

Even more serious was the rift with France in the 1920's. By this time the "cost-of-production" formula in the dutiable-value provisions

38. "In this inquiry I became satisfied that certain vicious and unjustifiable practices had grown up in our customs administration, notably the practice of determining values of imports upon detective reports never disclosed to the persons whose interests were affected. The use of detectives, though often necessary, tends towards abuse, and should be carefully guarded. Under our practice as I found it to exist in this case, the abuse had become gross and discreditable. Under it, instead of seeking information as to the market value of merchandise from the well-known and respected members of the commercial community in the country of its production, secret statements were obtained from informers and discharged employees and business rivals, and upon this kind of secret evidence the values of imported goods were frequently raised and heavy penalties were frequently imposed upon importers who were never permitted to know what the evidence was and who never had an opportunity to meet it. It is quite probable that this system tended toward an increase of the duties colleced upon imported goods, but I conceive it to be a violation of the law to exact more duties than the law provides, just as it is a violation to admit goods upon the payment of less than the legal rates of duty. This practice was repugnant to the spirit of American law and to American sense of justice. In the judgment of the most competent experts of the Treasury Department and the Department of Commerce and Labor it was wholly unnecessary for the due collection of customs revenues and the attempt to defend it merely illustrates the demoralization which naturally follows from a long continued course of reliance upon such methods.

"I accordingly caused the regulations governing this branch of the customs service to be modified so that values are determined upon a hearing in which all the parties interested have an opportunity to be heard and to know the evidence against them. Moreover our Treasury Agents are accredited to the Government of the country in which they seek information, and in Germany receive the assistance of the quasi-official chambers of commerce in determining the actual market value of goods, in accordance with what I am advised to be the true construction of the law" (U.S. State Department, *Papers Relating to the Foreign Relations of the United States, 1907*, Vol. I: "Message of the President," at pp. lxvi ff.) (hereinafter cited as *"Foreign Relations of the United States"*). The new commercial treaty with Germany, concluded April 22, 1907, carried several appendixes containing provisions for the interpretation of dutiable value and the revision of value-investigation procedures. The same arrangements were offered to a number of other nations and formed the subject of considerable negotiation (*ibid.,* pp. 487–510).

had become well established and was applied with increasing frequency. This feature was the subject of even more bitter foreign denunciation than were price investigations, since it required inspection of a manufacturer's cost accounts. Many manufacturers considered this as a direct demand upon them to divulge their trade secrets and refused to open their books to United States agents. In order to force compliance upon foreign firms, Congress included in the Tariff Act of 1922 a provision prohibiting the importation into the United States of merchandise from persons or firms refusing to submit books and accounts to Treasury agents. All such merchandise reaching the United States was to be forfeited and sold at auction if the failure to exhibit such records persisted for the space of one year.[39]

This harsh and arrogant provision was understandably resented by foreign nations, and in the case of France it became a major issue. The refusal of an influential French firm to open its books, followed by an embargo on its products in the United States, led to protracted representations and even threatened to scuttle the pending debt agreement with France.[40] France maintained that the activities of American customs representatives were a violation of French sovereignty, that they amounted to a form of espionage, that price- and cost-information gleaned from manufacturers' books would be used not only to make unjustifiable increases in dutiable values but also to raise tariff rates under the "flexible provisions" of the tariff, and that even French government officials under the law were not accorded the privilege demanded by American agents. As a result, all United States customs attachés were withdrawn from France, effective February 1, 1928.

39. Tariff Act of 1922, sec. 510.

40. Cf. telegram of Ambassador Herrick to Secretary of State, June 4, 1926: "Berenger stated task of obtaining ratification of French debt agreement would be facilitated if the U.S. Treasury would raise embargo against Boue Sœurs as a mark of good will. This might furthermore deter the French press from outbursts against our customs representatives abroad for their alleged inquisitorial methods" (*Foreign Relations of the United States, 1926*, II, 94–96). Although the United States insisted on treating the debt agreement as a separate question, it is interesting to note that the embargo was lifted June 8 (*ibid.*). Boue Sœurs was a manufacturer of ladies' silk underwear, a fact which led to the calling of the entire incident by the descriptive title "la guerre des chemises" (Stuart, *op. cit.*, p. 361). Much contemporary material on the attitude of France during this period may be found in the *New York Times* in the latter part of 1928; cf. especially issues of October 31, p. 5, col. 1; November 8, p. 28, col. 8.

Similar resentment was expressed by Switzerland[41] and by Sweden,[42] and even Great Britain declined, as a matter of principle, to accord United States Treasury representatives diplomatic status.[43]

With a few important exceptions, such as the Reciprocal Trade Agreements program under the leadership of Secretary Hull, the tariff policy of the United States has been a source of irritation to foreign governments. The annoyances incidental to customs valuation represent a typical and, over the long run, a substantial consequence of this policy.[44]

41. *Foreign Relations of the United States, 1925,* II, 731 ff.

42. *Ibid.,* pp. 725–27.

43. In order to facilitate value investigations abroad, Congress passed an act (43 U.S. Statutes 748, effective January 13, 1925) providing that customs attachés be regularly and officially attached to diplomatic missions. This act failed to produce the desired results, as foreign nations refused to accredit customs agents. The diplomatic correspondence and instructions of the U.S. State Department to foreign offices in connection with this problem furnish perhaps the best material available on the whole subject of foreign value investigations (cf. *Foreign Relations of the United States, 1925,* I, 211–54).

44. Many other illustrations might be given of the relationship between customs valuation and foreign relations. As far back as 1842 a group of British importers and agents resident in New York appealed to their government for official intervention to restrain the collector at New York from further oppressive seizures for alleged undervaluations (cf. *House Executive Document No. 212* [27th Cong., 2d sess.], p. 272). In 1913 Assistant Secretary of the Treasury Curtis testified that diplomatic representations had led to nonenforcement of the requirement that cost-of-production statements accompany all entries of consigned goods (cf. *House Document No. 1447: Tariff Hearings before the Committee on Ways and Means* [62d Cong., 3d sess.], VI, 6327); also reference of Representative Harrison to protests of delegation from the Parliament of Bermuda and the Bahamas against appraisements of vegetables from the islands (*ibid.,* p. 6329). Hoffman cites the case of an American customs investigator who was given twenty-four hours' notice to leave town, under pain of physical expulsion thereafter, by German municipal authorities (Hoffman, *op. cit.,* pp. 854–55). European resentment toward American investigators even penetrated academic and professional circles: "Besonders die brutalen Methoden des amerikanischen Zollbehörden haben in Europa immer wieder zu lasten Beschwerden geführt" (Gottfried Haberler, *Der Internationale Handel* [Berlin, 1933], p. 253, n. 1). A Swiss lawyer and student of tariff administration, writing in 1905, punctuated his opinion of the institution in question: "Le gouvernement des États-Unis à un certain nombre d'agents spéciaux— d'espisses!—chargés de faire des enquêtes et de signaler les fraudes ou erreurs d'évaluation qu'ils ont découvertes dans le pays d'origine" (James Valloton, *De la juridiction administrative fédérale des États-Unis et de la Suisse en matière de douanes* [Lausanne, 1905], p. 18, n. 1).

The Concept of Dutiable Value

The foregoing analysis has indicated in a general way the nature and significance of customs valuation. It is now proper to give a more precise definition of terms and of the principal problem with which this study is concerned.

The necessity of ascertaining the value of an article of import for duty purposes has given rise to the concept of "dutiable value."[45] Dutiable value is the legally applicable valuation of an article for the assessment of duties which are based upon, or regulated by, value. Such duties have included not only the types listed above (pp. 6–7) but, on occasion, even specific duties.[46] Customs valuation comprehends more than the determination of dutiable value; it includes the valuation of all imports, whether subject to specific or ad valorem duties and whether dutiable or free;[47] it also includes the valuation of exports, both for statistical purposes and (as in Colonial times) for the levy of duties. Customs valuation is likewise a broader concept than is appraisement, since it comprehends the theory underlying legislation and embraces alternative valuation practices and systems not utilizing appraisement procedure.

Dutiable value is fundamentally a *legal* concept. It has economic origins and economic consequences, but its essence is statutory definition, amplified by administrative regulation and judicial interpretation. An understanding of the concept is complicated by the fact that there are many possible alternative economic concepts or bases from which to choose in formulating the law of dutiable value. Moreover, in addition to economic valuation concepts or bases, there are a number of purely administrative definitions of value for customs purposes which frequently have a determining influence on the actual amount of

45. The earliest use of the term "dutiable value" encountered in the course of this study is found in a "Treasury Circular" dated October 12, 1830. It is interesting to note that it was about this time that the concept itself first became differentiated from "cost," "actual value," "price current," and similarly vague conceptions.

46. The administration of the reduced duties of the Compromise Act of 1833 involved the valuation of imports subject to specific duties. This act required an administrative reduction of all duties then in effect to a 20 per cent ad valorem equivalent in successive stages over a period of nine years.

47. With only minor exceptions all articles imported into the United States must by law be appraised (cf. Tariff Act of 1930, secs. 484, 488, 490, and 500).

duties collected.[48] Not only do the economic and administrative concepts overlap categorically, i.e., any administrative value category might represent any economic valuation, depending upon the circumstances, but the value components included within or added to the applicable valuation base may be extremely numerous and complex. Such value components, in addition to the basic value of the goods involved, may include various transportation, insurance, packing, and other "cost" items, as well as foreign drawbacks, tax abatements, bounties, or private subsidies, and special elements peculiar to particular importations.

In view of this complexity it may help to examine the concept of dutiable value in the light of several broad and rather loose categories, arranged to indicate different aspects and various possible alternatives in the determination of value for customs purposes, which have faced legislators and others in defining and refining the concept:

A. *Structural aspects.*—Elements or ingredients potentially entering into dutiable value
  1. The basis or starting point,[49] namely, putative value of the "naked goods"
  2. Cost components over and above 1, such as charges for finishing, packing, containers, drayage, transportation, insurance, etc.
  3. Commissions, brokerage fees, discounts, profits, etc., prior to exportation
  4. Additions by statute or court interpretation to offset real or fancied advantages of the foreign producer: drawbacks, tax refunds or abatements, bounties, subsidies by cartels, etc.

B. *Geographical aspects.*—Alternative places or markets to be considered in determining value
  1. Place of production
  2. Principal market in country of export
  3. Port of exportation

48. Economic, as distinguished from administrative, valuation concepts are those substantive bases of valuation defined by statute and used to determine the amount of dutiable value. "Cost of production," "foreign-market value," "American selling price," and other statutory valuation bases are economic notions, each having definite and distinct economic significance. Purely administrative valuation concepts are those procedural categories representing actual or potential dutiable value at various stages in customs procedure, e.g., invoice, entered, appraised value, and modifications of these.

49. The value of goods per se is the "starting point" in pure theory, to which value may be made various additions as indicated. In practice, however, this value or the dutiable value sought is often reached by making appropriate *deductions* from invoice or other prices.

    4. Port of importation
    5. Principal market in United States

C. *Temporal aspects.*—Date for basing valuation
    1. Date of sale or contract
    2. Date of exportation
    3. Date of importation
    4. Date of entry for consumption
    5. Average over a fixed period prior to any of these

D. *Monetary aspects.*—Selection and basis of currency conversion
    1. Selection of currency
       a) Currency of purchase
       b) Currency of country of exportation
       c) Currency normally used in country of exportation
    2. Basis for currency conversion
       a) Mint parity
       b) Foreign exchange rate; if so, what exchange market, which among dual or multiple rates, etc.
       c) Arbitrary or proclaimed conversion rate
    3. Time basis of conversion: any of C, above

E. *Normative aspects.*—Problem of selecting representative criteria to permit determination of "the" market price among an array, the "principal" market among many, "the" standard or representative rate of commission, discount, profit, etc.

F. *Evidentiary aspects.*—Documentary proof or acceptable evidence of valuation data
    1. Invoice: commercial, consular, or *pro forma*
    2. Sworn entry and declaration
    3. Correspondence, contracts, affidavits, etc., admissible by courts or recognized by customs
    4. Price information and cost studies of appraisers, consuls, Treasury attachés, or others

The foregoing classification is illustrative of the complexity of the problem of defining dutiable value specifically and completely enough to cover the majority of actual importations or of interpreting the definition once it has been made with reasonable clarity. It also implies the existence of many questions concerning the administrative workability of any definition, to say nothing of the relative economic or equitable desirability of the possible alternatives. In actual practice it has been found impossible to choose any single definition of dutiable value which will fit the facts of the market place sufficiently well to render it applicable to all commodities or types of importation. Accordingly, there have been developed a number of alternate definitions which have been incorporated into the statute and which are applied in a prescribed order under rigorously defined conditions to determine the dutiable value of any particular importation. A brief description of each of these alternatives appears in the following subdivision on the forms of dutiable value.

The Bases of Dutiable Value

The following list and preliminary definitions are offered only as an abbreviated and tentative introduction to the specific forms or bases of dutiable value actually in use or under consideration in the United States, either now or in the past, for purposes of customs valuation. The several forms indicated are distinctive concepts and with appropriate changes in nomenclature and minor modifications in form also exhaust the list of valuation concepts in foreign countries. A preview of these facilitates an appreciation of the nature of the valuation problem and of the historical section which precedes the detailed exposition in Part III.

I. Economic or substantive valuation concepts
 1. Specific purchase price
 2. Foreign value and foreign market value
 3. Export value
 4. United States value
 5. Cost of production
 6. Domestic value
 7. American selling price
 8. Landed cost or c.i.f. value
 9. Official values
II. Administrative valuation concepts
 1. Invoice value (consular or *pro forma* invoice)
 2. Entered value (includes amended entry value)
 3. Appraised value (includes reappraised or subsequently appraised value)

1. *Specific purchase price* of the imported goods (referred to in early statutes as "prime cost," "true cost," or "actual cost") is one possible basis for dutiable value. To the layman, particularly one who is entering his goods for the first time, this would appear to be the only logical or "true" value upon which to assess duties. With some modification this was the basis used in the early tariff acts of the United States. For reasons appearing hereafter, the United States discontinued the use of purchase price in favor of various "ideal" types based on some concept of market price.

2. *Foreign value* is the primary legally applicable value for duty purposes in the United States today. In brief, it is a specially defined type of market price—originally intended to be the general market price (as contrasted with specific purchase price)—of the imported goods in the princi-

pal markets of the country of export. As will be seen later, there are numerous qualifications surrounding the definition of foreign value (as of all other forms) which substantially affect its amount or may even result in its exclusion as the applicable basis for the assessment of duties. *Foreign market value,* the primary legal basis of valuation for dumping duties, is a modification of foreign value.

3. *Export value* is applicable in the absence of, or when higher than, foreign value. It is in general the market price of such or similar goods sold for export to the United States. This basis finds wide application in lieu of foreign value and approximates actual transaction prices much more closely than foreign value.

4. *United States value* is a hypothetical or constructive foreign value arrived at by working backward from the selling price of the imported article in the United States. Allowable deductions from the selling price in this country include duty, ocean freight, insurance, general expenses, profit, and commission. The term "United States value" is something of a misnomer since it approximates more nearly foreign value and takes value in the United States only as a starting point for calculation.

5. *Cost of production,* as specially defined in the statute, is the applicable dutiable value in the absence of any of the foregoing, such as in the case of goods in process imported for assembly or completion by a branch plant and involving no commercial transaction or normal selling price in their imported condition. The difficulties of interpretation and application of the cost-of-production formula are numerous.

6. *Domestic value* is the selling price in the United States of the imported article. It has no legal status as dutiable value in the United States (although in modified form it is used in forfeiture cases) but was the subject of much controversy along with American selling price during the hearings preceding the 1922 and 1930 acts. As a result, the Tariff Act of 1930 (sec. 340) carefully defined domestic value and required the Tariff Commission to investigate and report to Congress the conversion of rates necessary to place the entire tariff on a domestic value basis. The results of this study are discussed in a subsequent chapter.

7. *American selling price,* popularly referred to as "American valuation," is the selling price in the United States not of the imported article but of comparable merchandise produced in the United States. This basis for dutiable value is applied to coal-tar intermediates and products and to particular commodities after presidential proclamation resulting from findings of the Tariff Commission under the so-called "flexible" provisions of the 1922 and 1930 acts.

8. *Landed cost,* or c.i.f. value, is the total cost of importation prior to duty. It is ordinarily the sum of the purchase price and of all other components, such as insurance, packing, freight, etc., necessary to land the goods at the port of importation. Though not in use in the United States at the present time, landed cost is applied by many countries in one form or another and in modified form was used in early tariff acts of this country.

9. *Official values* (alternatively referred to as "proclaimed," "arbitrary," or "fixed" valuations) consist of a schedule of specially established values for duty purposes. Official values are used by a number of countries, including Canada, as the principal, or a subordinate, feature of total valuation procedure. Proclaimed valuations may have as their object the simplification of customs procedure, or they may, as in the case of the minimum-value provisions in early tariffs of the United States, represent a device to impose prohibitive or highly protective duties under nominal or apparently representative rates of duty.

The Tariff Commission, in its study of methods of valuation,[50] divides all forms of dutiable value into four general classes: foreign value, landed cost, domestic value, and American valuation. Under this classification items 1 through 5, above, would fall under the heading of foreign value; items 6, 7, and 8 would each fall in the class taking its name. Item 9 is not provided for in this classification inasmuch as it has no necessary relation to any of the other forms. Another broad classification would place all forms of dutiable value into three classes: "foreign," "home," and "arbitrary" valuation. All such broad classifications, whether based on apparent geographical or other considerations, must be used with care since the individual members of a class may exhibit much greater divergence than the classes themselves. Moreover, the significance of none of the individual bases can properly be appreciated until the important implications of the statute and of judicial interpretation are adequately explored.

The administrative valuation concepts listed above are relevant primarily to the United States and will be made clear in subsequent treatment of administrative aspects of customs valuation.

50. U.S. Tariff Commission, *Methods of Valuation: Report No. 70* (2d ser., 1933), pp. 1–2, 21–43.

PART II

The History of Customs Valuation
in the United States

CHAPTER II

The Initial Period—Colonial Times to 1816

The Colonial Period[1]

CUSTOMS valuation in what is now the United States had its origins more than three centuries ago in the administration of early Colonial duties. Under the barter or near-barter conditions which at first existed in the several colonies, percentage rates of duty presented no valuation problem because duties were collectible in kind by simple appropriation.[2] As barter gave way to the more extensive use of money, these duties became payable in money as well as in kind, and the problem of valuation for customs purposes became significant.

As early as 1629, in the Charter of Liberties to Patroons and Colonists granted by the States-General preliminary to the settlement of New Netherland, we find reference to the valuation of imports for the assessment of transportation charges. Article X of the charter, in specifying the terms for carriage of colonists and their goods to America,

---

1. An account of Colonial customs administration is to be found in John Dean Goss, *A History of Tariff Administration in the United States* ("Columbia University Studies in History, Economics, and Public Law," Vol. I [New York, 1892]); see also William H. Futrell, *The History of American Customs Jurisprudence* (New York, 1941), pp. 13–19.

2. Cf. the New York 5 per cent export duty on tobacco, payable in kind, levied by ordinance of August 19, 1638, cited in Goss, *op. cit.*, p. 18. One year later Maryland is said to have levied a similar 5 per cent export duty on tobacco (*Bacon's Laws of Maryland, 1639*, Act XXXVI, as cited in Futrell, *op. cit.*, p. 15). The collection of tobacco duties in kind throughout the colonies reflected a transitional, rather than pure, barter phenomenon inasmuch as tobacco itself was the prevailing currency in wide areas. In Virginia one of the items of business before the first legislative assembly at Jamestown, ending July, 1619, was the fixing of the value of tobacco as currency: "The value of tobacco to be taken either for commodities, or for bills, at 3 shillings a pound for the best, and 18 pence a pound for the second quality" (Henry Wirt, "The First Legislative Assembly in America," in *Annual Report of the American Historical Association for the Year 1893* [Washington, 1894], pp. 311–12). Collection in kind is not limited to barter economies; among other uses, it appears in the form of "pre-emption" and "abandonment" in the tariff systems of some foreign countries (cf. discussion *infra*, p. 313, n. 45, and references cited therein).

provides payment to the West India Company "for freight of the goods five per cent ready money, to be reckoned on the prime cost of the goods here."[3] This proviso may well have influenced the later adoption of "prime cost" in the country of exportation as the basis for the levy of ad valorem customs duties.

In 1642 an ordinance of the director and council of New Netherland levied general import duties of 10 per cent and required formal entry of all goods with the receiver of revenue or his representative.[4] With the increase in trade and the more widespread application of duties, custom-house formalities became more elaborate and detailed. Some of them reflect practices of the mother countries; most were developed experimentally as particular needs became manifest. Export duties typically preceded duties on imports and set the pattern for administrative procedure. For example, one of the earliest Colonial statutes designed to prevent undervaluation was the New Netherland ordinance of June 23, 1661.[5] This required formal inspection and appraisement of all exports at the company store. In Virginia customs duties became payable "in money or good bills of exchange."[6]

The New York Colonial laws subsequent to English assumption of sovereignty reveal several valuation practices of interest, some of which later became important in the customs system of the United States. The revenue act of 1683 provided for ad valorem duties based on "prime cost" and required that importers be placed under oath in doubtful cases.

... If any difference should arise about the value of such goods, Then the Collector or any appointed for the Collector of Said dutyes Customes or Excise may administer to all or any such person or persons making such Entry their Corporall Oath, that said Entry is according to the Invoyce or Invoyces sent to them from the place or places from whence such goods did come.[7]

3. *Collections of the New York Historical Society* (2d ser.; New York, 1841), I, 372.

4. *Laws and Ordinances of New Netherland, 1638–74* (Ordinance of April 3, 1642) (Albany, N.Y., 1868).

5. *Ibid.*

6. Goss, *op. cit.*, p. 12.

7. *The Colonial Laws of New York from the Year 1664 to the Revolution* (Albany, N.Y., 1894), I, 119: "A Continued Bill for Defraying the Requisite Charges of the Government: Passed October 30, 1683."

The same act also established the so-called "moieties system"—or distribution of forfeitures, which became prominent in the nineteenth-century customs administration in the United States—by providing forfeiture of goods landed without entry and division of the forfeiture "one third to his Royal Highnesse One third to the Governour and one third to the Informer that shall sue as above."[8]

The provisions for entry and oath in the 1683 law were not sufficient for practical disposition of the valuation problem, and the following year two new features were added to the law. One of these established arbitrary or official values for "Indian goods".

> Whereas there may Arise Differences between His Royall Highness Collector and the merchants trafficquing to this province by the uncertainty of the first Cost mentioned. . . . Be it enacted that the Certain Duty of ten per Cent established by the said Act upon merchandises Commonly Called Indian goods that shall be valued after the manner hereafter specified, and not otherwise That is to say for all Indian goods Called Indian Duffells . . . two shillings and foure pence [etc.].[9]

The influence of English customs procedure is evident in the foregoing provision inasmuch as arbitrary valuations, or "Books of Rates," had been in use in England as early as 1507.[10] The same section of the 1684 law also contained the forerunner of provisions for a system of merchant appraisement, which later appeared in both Colonial and United States laws.

> . . . If any misunderstanding should arise between his Royall Highness Collector and Merchants or others Trafficquing and Importing any merchandise into this Province, about the value of prime Cost as Established in said Act It shall and may be Lawfull for the Descission of such misunderstanding or Difference to appoint two indifferent persons, who shall value said merchandise Imported According to the manner expressed in said Act att prime Cost att which value so estimated, The said merchant or Importer shall pay his duty, without further delay or molestation.

8. *Ibid.* This did not, as did the moieties provisions of the United States laws, apply to undervaluation cases. Strictly speaking, the term "moieties" does not apply to the Colonial system inasmuch as it did not divide the forfeiture one-half to the government and one-half to individuals.

9. *Ibid.*, p. 170: "An Explanation of the Continued Bill for Defraying the Requisite Charges of the Government: Passed October 29, 1684."

10. Cf. "A rate made of the prisys of allmaner of warys by the kyngs cownsell' . . . the xv daye of July in the xvii yere of the rayne of ower' Soverayne Lorde Kynge Hary the VII . . ." (reproduced in N. S. B. Gras, *The Early English Customs System* [Cambridge, Mass., 1918], p. 694).

With the multiplication and specialization of trade during the following half-century the qualification of "indifference" no longer sufficed for arbitration in appraisement disputes. In 1740 the basis of selection was changed as indicated:

> ... And if no such Invoice is produced, or that any Disputes shall arise concerning such Value, the Treasurer is to nominate and appoint one credible Merchant, and the Importer another, who are to appraise such Goods to the best of their Judgments; and according to such Appraisement, which is to be at the sole Charge of the Importer, the real Value of such Goods is to be ascertained.[11]

These provisions, as well as the "prime-cost" basis of dutiable value, were successively re-enacted and with minor changes remained in effect until the adoption of the federal Constitution.

The statutes of Massachusetts also furnish an insight into the inherent difficulties of arriving at an administratively workable definition of dutiable value. In 1669 the Colonial legislature enacted a law[12] containing one of the earliest specific definitions of value for customs purposes in this country. This act levied an import duty of 1 penny for each 20 shillings value—this to be ascertained by adding 20 per cent to the value at the place whence imported. The act required the owner or importer, before landing the goods, to "signify the true value thereof by showing the just invoice to the collector."

If the invoice were "falsified, concealed, or not produced," the treasurer or collector with the selectmen of each town concerned were to rate the goods "according to their best discretion at not less than £4 per tun." Thus, at this early date, are evident three of the fundamental ingredients of customs valuation which were incorporated into the first United States customs administrative law one hundred and twenty years later: (1) foreign valuation as the base, with the addition of an arbitrary percentage in order to approximate landed cost; (2) the use of the invoice as primary evidence of dutiable value; (3) the application of appraisement procedure in special or doubtful cases.

In the law of June 24, 1692,[13] there was a discrimination between English goods and all others, the latter to be assessed on "value here."

---

11. *Laws of New York, from the Year 1691 to 1751, Inclusive: Published According to an Act of the General Assembly* (New York, 1752), p. 287.

12. *Records of Massachusetts Bay Colony*, IV, Part II, 418, cited by Goss, *op. cit.*, p. 15.

13. *Massachusetts Province Laws* (1st sess., 1692–93), c. 5, sec. 4.

This application of the lower foreign value for English goods and "home value" for all others is one manifestation of English colonial and mercantile policy. In England discriminatory valuations had long existed but appeared in the form of differences in official values favoring certain products of English colonies. Thus in the 1660 tonnage and poundage subsidy granted to Charles II the tobacco of English colonies was valued at 1s. 8d. per pound, as contrasted with 10s. for tobacco from foreign plantations.[14]

In the 1695 law[15] oaths were required as to "the truth of the writing in the invoice." In 1717 the oath required swearing that the importer's entry of the goods was equal to the "true value, as per invoice, and not less than the real cost thereof."[16] This is apparently an attempt to prevent the use of false invoices rather than to define dutiable value as foreign-market or purchase price, whichever was higher. But this was found to be unsatisfactory, and in 1735 reference to cost was dropped and the word "value" used throughout, without any definite statement or even implication of what was meant by the word. Further confusion is evident in the change in wording adopted by the 1742 enactment. In this act the reading of the oath upon entry was as follows: "I, A B, do swear that the entry now made, exhibits the present price of said goods at this market, and that, *bona fide,* according to my best skill and judgment, it is not less than the real value thereof."[17]

Just how this provision was interpreted in actual practice is uncertain. It is probable that, instead of effecting a change from foreign to domestic valuation, the words "this market" represent an attempt to recognize that the imposition of the 20 per cent addition to foreign purchase price really resulted in a constructive landed cost at the place of importation.[18] Subsequent enactments indicate that not only the foregoing but virtually every other phrasing of the statute was inadequate for administrative purposes. For example (italics added):

14. The 1660 act persisted as the basic "branch" of the English customs system for over one hundred years. The valuations cited were still in effect as late as 1718 (cf. William Edgar, *Vestigalium systema, or, a New Book of Rates* [2d ed.; London, 1718], pp. 182–83).

15. *Massachusetts Province Laws* (4th sess., 1694–95), c. 27.

16. *Ibid.* (1st sess., 1717–18), c. 6.

17. *Ibid.* (5th sess., 1741–42), c. 24.

18. For a similar confusion of landed cost and domestic value cf. *infra,* p. 40, n. 23.

1758 law You, A B, do swear that the entry . . . exhibits the *sterling value* of such goods, and that . . . it is not less than *that value.*

1764 law . . . the entry exhibits the *present value* of said goods, and is not less than the *real value* thereof.

1765 law . . . the entry made, and the value thereof annexed, . . . is agreeable to the price current or the *market price* of said goods.[19]

It is small wonder, in view of the infantile status of value theory in the seventeenth and eighteenth centuries, that the notions of cost, price, and value were hopelessly confused in the minds of Colonial legislators and that their attempts to frame a satisfactory law for the administration of ad valorem duties met with such stubborn resistance by the facts of the market place. But it is likewise not difficult to discern, by reading the successive statutes quoted above, the gradual development of the concept of value as market price and its significance in terms of a workable basis for the levy of duties. Indeed, in view of the pre-eminence of the custom house in the eighteenth century as a laboratory for the study of trade and markets, it is not surprising that the "father of economic theory" should have been intimately associated with customs administration;[20] certainly few other influences were as well qualified to inspire an unremitting search for a formal and correct definition of value.

Apart from the difficulty of defining value, the foregoing account reveals in broad outline the two major problems of customs valuation: (1) the selection of a *basis* for dutiable value; (2) the *administration* of the basis actually selected. Experience demonstrates the mutual interdependence of the two. In the case of Massachusetts, statutory definition began with specific purchase price and ended with market price. This change was essential primarily because of the impossibility of relying upon the invoice as a true representation of the price actually paid. Likewise, the apparent shift from foreign to home valuation and back again was the result of administrative difficulties. The more

19. The phraseology of the 1765 law was maintained in subsequent acts until the Revolutionary War.

20. Adam Smith was the son of a Scottish comptroller of customs and was himself made commissioner of customs in Scotland shortly after the appearance of the first edition of *The Wealth of Nations*. While he held this position, he was able to bring out successive new editions of his great work until his death in 1790 (cf. Erich Roll, *A History of Economic Thought* [New York, 1939], p. 144; also, Introd. by E. R. A. Seligman to Adam Smith, *The Wealth of Nations* [Everyman ed.; New York, 1933], p. viii).

exact nature of these difficulties is observed in the later and more comprehensive experience of the United States.

The First Tariff System of the United States

The first tariff act of the United States, the law of July 4, 1789, contained both specific and ad valorem duties. The ad valorem rates fell into four classes: 7½, 10, and 15 per cent, respectively, for three groups of enumerated commodities, and a general 5 per cent duty on all imports not specifically named in the act. The only hint as to the basis for dutiable value is found in the 5 per cent general clause: "On all other goods, wares, and merchandise, five per centum on the value thereof at the time and place of importation."

On the surface this appears to be a species of "home valuation" and on occasion has been cited by defenders of the home-valuation principle as a precedent.[21] But in order to construe this clause properly and to learn precisely the original basis for dutiable value in the United States, it is necessary to consult the first customs administrative act, designed to implement the new tariff system.[22]

Under section 13 of the collection act all persons who imported goods were required to enter them at the custom house, specifying the "nett prime cost thereof," and to produce the original invoice and bill of lading, taking oath that "said invoice contains, to the best of his knowledge and belief, the nett prime cost thereof." If goods were damaged during the voyage or were not "accompanied with the original invoice of their cost," the collector and consignee were each to appoint a merchant, "who being sworn or affirmed by the collector well and truly to appraise such goods, shall value them accordingly, and the duties upon such goods shall be estimated according to such valuation."

In section 17 of the collection act we come to the actual definition of dutiable value:

The ad valorem rates of duty upon all goods, wares, and merchandise, at the place of importation, shall be estimated by adding twenty per cent to the actual cost thereof, if imported from the Cape of Good Hope, or

21. Cf. U.S. Tariff Commission, *American Valuation as the Basis for Assessing Duties Ad Valorem: Report No. 70* (2d ser., 1921), Appen. V, p. 114.
22. The first "collection act," 1 U.S. Statutes 29 (Act of July 31, 1789).

from any place beyond the same; and ten per cent on the actual cost thereof, if imported from any other place or country, exclusive of charges.

Thus we learn that the original basis for dutiable value was none of the forms found in existence in the United States today. It was rather a variant of landed cost, similar to that already observed in Massachusetts, determined by adding to the specific purchase price of the goods arbitrarily differentials as a rough approximation of transportation and other charges.[23] But, by basing dutiable value upon specific purchase price, the statute failed to reap the fruits of over a century of experience in Massachusetts, where purchase price had been tried and found inadequate.

Whatever the circumstances shaping the legislation,[24] the statute as actually written poses a number of obvious questions. Two general questions occur immediately: (1) Precisely what is meant by "actual cost ... exclusive of charges"? (2) What adequate check would customs officials have upon the validity of the invoice?

The answer to the first was left entirely to the administration and the courts. Many of the issues connected with this question were ultimately clarified by statute on the basis of experience; others were left permanently to codification in the form of comprehensive customs regulations. This is essentially the problem of the substantive law of dutiable value and is treated in detail in Part III of this study.

The statutory attempt to answer the second question is found in the penalty clause of the collection act, section 22:

And ... when it shall appear that any goods, wares, or merchandise of which entry shall have been made, in the office of a collector, are not invoiced, according to the actual cost thereof at the place of exportation, and that the difference was made with design to defraud the revenue, all such goods ... or the value thereof to be recovered of the person making

23. Secretary of the Treasury Ingham, in his annual report to Congress for 1830, confuses landed cost with "value" or "sale price" in his interpretation of the purpose of the 10 and 20 per cent differentials: "The aggregate of these items on which the duties are laid is presumed to be the value of the goods when offered for sale in the United States market, but such is rarely the case." It would indeed be a rare transaction in which an importer would accept a 10 or 20 per cent mark-up over purchase price in foreign markets when, in addition to payment of transportation, insurance, and other costs, he had to pay a 20 or 30 per cent duty on the total (for an abridged version of the Ingham report cf. U.S. Tariff Commission, *American Valuation*, p. 26).

24. Goss, *op. cit.*, p. 24, says of the 1789 collection law: "It is plainly a hasty compilation from the laws of the various states—following very closely the late laws of New York, and even copying whole sections almost verbatim."

the entry, shall be forfeited; and in any such case, or where the collector is suspicious of fraud, and that any such goods . . . are not invoiced at a sum equal to that for which they have usually been sold, in the place or country from which they were imported, it shall be the duty of such collector to take the said goods . . . into his possession, and retain the same at the risk and expense of the owner or consignee thereof, until their value, at the time and place of importation, according to the principles for estimating the same, established by this act, shall be ascertained by two reputable merchants, mutually chosen by the said collector, and owner or consignee, and the duties arising upon such valuation shall first be paid, or secured to be paid, as required by this act in other cases or importation.

It is difficult to place any single, consistent interpretation upon this ambiguously worded section. The most reasonable construction of it, taken together with the rest of the law, appears to be as follows:

1. Dutiable value is the actual purchase price of the goods, f.o.b. the port of exportation, plus the 10 or 20 per cent differential.

2. Appraisement is to be made whenever the collector believes the invoice to be fraudulent.

3. An invoice price below the foreign-market prices of the goods furnishes a presumption of undervaluation, upon which the collector may, if he sees fit, order an appraisement.

4. The resulting appraised value is the dutiable value. If the excess of appraised value over invoice value is great enough, the collector may institute forfeiture proceedings.

The difficulties confronting the merchant appraisers, to say nothing of the collector, once appraisement proceedings were undertaken, are evident from the record, as well as fairly obvious on a priori grounds. The appraisers' instructions in the statute were to ascertain the value of the goods "according to the principles for estimating the same, established by this act." These "principles" are to add 10 or 20 per cent to the "actual cost" of the goods. Since the invoice, by assumption, is ruled out as evidence of "actual cost," what possible evidence could the appraisers have upon which to sustain a different valuation? Later acts gave customs officers the power to impound all the correspondence and books of account of importers, and these could conceivably yield incriminating evidence that would hold up in forfeiture proceedings before the courts. But under the early collection laws, the whole compulsory appraisement operation was based upon suspicion—sometimes well grounded in fact but not in evidence. The result was that merchant appraisers were often loath to participate in such proceedings and, even after the statute was clarified by subsequent acts, had to be drafted.[25]

It is not surprising, in view of the looseness of the statute, that interpretation and administration by both collectors and appraisers often ran to extremes. On the one hand, the majority of appraisers were inclined to favor the importer.[26] On the other, as will be seen later, the collector, in addition to his normal solicitude for law enforcement, stood to gain personally by a rigorous or even harsh policy of appraisement. It is reasonable to assume that the appraiser chosen by the collector would be one inclined toward a strict interpretation of the revenue laws, particularly where his "foreign" competitors were concerned. Later laws even provided that where the two merchant appraisers disagreed, the collector would have the power to resolve the question by adopting one of the two reports. But even before the first collection act had been in operation a year, the penalty clause began to weigh heavily upon importers.[27] That private businessmen should thus be placed in the position of making intimate and important decisions in the business of their associates and competitors is testimony to the rudimentary and informal status of public administration in the early days of the nation.

The anomaly of the wording of section 22 was soon recognized and was substantially improved in the second collection law, that of

25. Cf. Act of April 20, 1818, 3 U.S. Statutes 433, sec. 10, and subsequent acts, imposing a $50 fine for refusal or neglect of merchant appraisers, chosen by either the collector or the importer, to assist. The system of merchant appraisement was taken from New York Colonial practice and was not finally abandoned until late in the nineteenth century.

26. Secretary Crawford, in a letter to the House, January 20, 1818, cites a number of reasons for this preference. In substance they were as follows: (1) "morbid sensibility" on the part of appraisers, resulting in sacrifice of the interests of the nation to those of the individual; (2) individual bias in favor of the importer, since his reputation, in the event of an adverse decision, "must be seriously affected" thereby; (3) fear of retaliation; (4) collusion, community feeling among merchants (cf. *Annals of Congress*, XXXII, 2323–30).

27. Cf. letter, Alexander Hamilton to the House, January 19, 1790, in *American State Papers: Finance*, I, 37: ". . . considerable forfeitures have been incurred manifestly through inadvertence and want of information—circumstances which cannot fail to attend the recent promulgation of laws of such a nature, and seem to indicate the necessity of vesting . . . a discretionary power of relief."

August 4, 1790.[28] Among other changes, this law eliminated the contradictory phrase "according to the principles for estimating the same, established by this act," thus giving the appraisers a clear-cut directive to find market value. This applied only to goods undergoing appraisement; specific purchase price was still the general basis for dutiable value. Nevertheless, although it clarified the matter considerably, the 1790 act, as did its immediate successors, failed to get at the root of the problem—the inadequacy of specific purchase price as a satisfactory administrative basis for dutiable value.

Another interesting feature of the collection act of 1789, as well as of subsequent administrative acts, was the statutory establishment of

TABLE 1

Coin	Country	Rate	Coin	Country	Rate
£ sterling.........	Great Britain	4.44	Ruble............	Russia	1.00
			Real plate........	Spain	0.10
Livre tournois.....	France	0.18½	Milree............	Portugal	1.24
Florin or guilder...	Un. Netherlands	0.39	£ sterling.........	Ireland	4.10
Mark banco.......	Hamburgh	0.33⅓	Tale [tael]........	China	1.48
Rix dollar.........	Denmark	1.00	Pagoda...........	India	1.94
Rix dollar.........	Sweden	1.00	Rupee............	Bengal	0.55½

foreign-currency conversion ratios for valuation purposes. The following mint ratios, listed in section 18 of the 1789 act, and the coins involved, are of interest in revealing not only the parities then existing but the coins most generally used in international trade in the respective currency systems (see Table 1). Section 18 further provides that all other denominations were to be converted "in value as near as may be to the said rates; and the invoices shall be made out in the currency of the place or country from which the importation shall be made, and not otherwise."

It is of interest to note that no reference is made to the use of foreign-exchange rates prevailing in the international money markets and no anticipation of the problem of currency depreciation. The act very properly removed from importers and foreign exporters the privilege

28. Goss, *op. cit.*, is overly critical of the 1790 act. This act, though it left much to be desired, clarified many ambiguities and made specific provision for numerous administrative details omitted by the first collection act.

of expressing invoices in terms of currencies of their own choosing.[29] However, by restricting collectors to statutorily defined conversion ratios, the act made it necessary for them to resort to central authority for advice in special circumstances.[30] Numerous circulars and memo-

29. Current provisions are at once more liberal and more exacting. For many years the law has required the invoice to be made in the currency of actual purchase, regardless of the country of export. The collection act of 1790, whether inadvertently or not, omitted the currency restriction on invoices. This omission was continued by the act of 1799. Hence, in 1816 we find a recommendation from Secretary Dallas to Congress "that provision be made more effectively to secure the revenue from fraud and imposition, in making out invoices in the money of foreign countries, particularly of such countries as employ a depreciated currency" (*American State Papers: Finance*, I, 85–99).

30. The following letter from Alexander Hamilton to the collectors of customs, dated June 4, 1792, is illustrative of the close attention paid by him to customs matters during his first three years in office. Shortly thereafter, in October, 1792, Hamilton relinquished the immediate superintendence of the collection of duties to the newly appointed comptroller of the Treasury. The letter is one of the New Orleans Custom House Collection in the Library of Congress:

"The 17th Section of the Act entitled 'an Act for raising a further sum of Money ... etc.' having abolished the rate heretofore annexed to the livre tournois of France, it becomes proper to give some general direction concerning the mode of estimating the value of goods imported from France.

"It will be understood that the cause of this alteration in the law is the depreciated state of the assignats, which now essentially constitute the current money of that country.

"To distinguish therefore the natural and *real* from the artificial and *nominal* value of the goods imported is the point to be aimed at. To assist in doing that, it is easier to indicate some general criterions, than to establish a precise rule.

"The criterions which have occurred are either

"1. The actual difference between specie and assignats at the time and place of exportation.

"2. The actual state of foreign exchange at the time and place of exportation.

"3. The prices of similar articles prior to the present revolution in France.

"4. An appraisement as in the case of goods not invoiced according to the 36th Section of the Collection Law.

"The first of these is the least to be relied upon. It was found in numerous instances in the course of the late war with Great Britain, that the comparative prices of goods in specie or paper did not correspond with the actual difference between them, and that they were otherwise artificially affected by the depreciation, so as to vary from the natural Standards of intrinsic value. The same thing is said to be remarked in France.

"The second affords a better rule though one not free from objections. Commercial circumstances operate upon the rate of exchange so as to render it an inaccurate test of the intrinsic value of any circulating medium. As far as this rule is allowed to guide, the exchange with Amsterdam or London, must regulate the calculating.

"The third is the best of the criterions mentioned, as often as it can be ascertained, and ought to be preferred. It is however not free from objection, as prices

randa, as well as legislative enactments during the next twenty-five years, testify to the troubled state of world currency systems in this period of history and the extent to which currency problems plagued collectors of customs. In the United States, which was then in the process of establishing its own currency system, many foreign coins circulated as legal tender and were acceptable in payment of customs duties, a privilege denied as late as 1933 to certain currency of the United States.[31]

Section 38 of the first collection law established what was to become one of the major scandals in the history of customs administration, namely, the so-called "moieties" system for distributing the proceeds of fines and forfeitures collected for various frauds against the revenue. As previously stated, undervaluation was included in the category of frauds punishable by forfeiture, although the grosser types of fraud, such as smuggling and relanding goods for benefit of drawback, were particularly indicated. The section provided that "one moiety" (half) of the forfeitures, after deducting costs of prosecution and collection, was payable into the United States Treasury. The other half was evenly divided among the three principal officers—the collector, naval officer (comptroller), and surveyor—of the port or district concerned. In smaller ports or districts the collector might have to share with only one alternate or with none where none was assigned. If an informer was involved, other than one of the aforesaid officers,

---

vary from causes, which ought to render the actual prices at the time of computation, the ground of it. But when they cannot be ascertained intrinsically, as in the present instance, no better substitute occurs.

"The last rule is liable to some objection of weight. The appraisers it is obvious would want some certain guide as much as the officers. There are cases nevertheless in which a defect of competent lights otherwise may render it advisable to employ this expedient.

"With these indications, it must be left to the respective Collectors to exercise a prudent discretion in the several cases which will arise; combining a due regard to the public interest with a spirit of justice to individuals."

The foregoing letter is significant not only for its substantive content but as indicative of the wide latitude allowed collectors in resolving the problem. Papers in the New Orleans Custom House Collection, except for Treasury circulars of known general circulation, will hereafter be cited as "*N.O.C.H.P.,*" the appropriate box- or bundle-number being indicated by a Roman numeral.

31. The 1789 act, sec. 30, specified acceptable coins for payment of customs duties. United States notes were not legally acceptable for this purpose until May 12, 1933, when they were made full legal tender.

he was entitled to half the officers' moiety, the remainder being distributed as indicated.[32]

The object of the provision, which is understandable in view of the then existing conditions and standards of public administration, was of course to overcome any laxity on the part of the officers in enforcing the law. Customs officers were always faced with the opportunity for personal enrichment through bribery and similar considerations.[33] Together with the contingent nature of the compensation of the principal officers—consisting of established fees and, in the case of the collector, of a specified percentage of net customs receipts—the moieties provision was designed to inspire adequate zeal in the collection of duties. Subsequent events, in many instances, proved the incentive to be more than adequate.

Nevertheless, these inducements—however gratifying and effective for the more favorably situated officers—were inadequate to insure complete protection to the revenue. A few years later, Hamilton, in a communication to the House urging the wider adoption of specific duties as a means of preventing undervaluation, clearly indicated the relationship between the compensation of all customs personnel and the safety of the revenue:

> The security of the revenue, in every branch, turns (it will not be too strong to say) principally upon the officers of the lowest grade. Hence, it is a policy no less mistaken than common, to leave those officers without such compensations as will admit of a proper selection of character, and prevent the temptation, from indigence, to abuse the trust. It is certain that, in many places, the present allowance to inspectors, on the most liberal application of it, is inadequate to those important ends.
>
> A similar reasoning will apply to those officers of the principal grades, who, being in districts which produce little, are ill compensated by the emoluments to which they are at present entitled. It cannot escape, that the safety of the revenue must depend on equal fidelity and due vigilance in all the districts; else it may become in many cases, worth the while to resort to particular districts, because there is a deficiency of the one or the other. Besides, that it is in itself just and proper, that all who are in the

32. Goss, *op. cit.*, p. 27, is in error in stating that an informer would receive the moiety normally apportioned to the United States.

33. The minimum penalty for conviction of bribery was a fine of $200 for each offense and permanent disability from holding any office of trust or profit under the United States. Customs officers were also forbidden to have any financial interest in any importation anywhere in the United States.

public service should receive adequate rewards for their time, attention, and trouble.[34]

This passage is particularly pertinent to the subject of customs valuation not only because of its direct relationship to the problem of undervaluation but also because it foreshadowed an important consideration which later contributed to the defeat of "home valuation" in 1842. This consideration is the necessity, always of concern to customs and treasury officials, of insuring equal treatment at the various ports of entry throughout the country. Important as are considerations of equity and justice, the practical compulsion behind uniformity at the different ports is the relative fluidity of large classes of imports and their tendency to gravitate to the port of preferred treatment. Even if the preference be assumed to result from the differential exercise of latitude allowed by statute, the consequences would be more far-reaching than merely loss of revenue. They would involve the subjection of the entire customs system to charges of regional and sectional favoritism, of stimulating national disunity, and of effecting substantial changes in importing organization and practice.

Such, in general, were the valuation provisions established at the beginning of the first tariff system of the United States. During the remainder of the period under discussion (1789–1816) various refinements were made administratively as well as through the medium of various tariff and collection acts, but no major changes were made in dutiable value. The special act of January 29, 1795, which was passed to clarify certain doubts as to the dutiability of "charges," defines the value base as "the actual cost at the place of exportation, including all charges (commission, outside packages, and insurance only excepted)." This attempted to make certain that appropriate deduction of the charges indicated would be made from invoice price in ascertaining the "nett prime cost" specified in the collection act. The 10 and

---

34. Letter of Alexander Hamilton, Secretary of the Treasury, to the House, February 2, 1795, *American State Papers: Finance*, I, 348–50. A single year of tariff administration was sufficient to show that the compensation of customs personnel was badly proportioned. The collection act of 1790 made a number of changes, reducing the collectors' percentage at the major ports (e.g., New York and Philadelphia from 1 per cent to ¾ per cent) and placing collectors in many outlying districts upon a fixed annual salary. The influence of Hamilton's message is seen in the act of March 3, 1797, and in subsequent acts within the period of a few years.

20 per cent additions were presumed to be an adequate equivalent for all charges between the place of exportation and the place of importation.[35]

The most important piece of legislation during this period was the comprehensive collection act of 1799.[36] This law canceled in whole or in part the provisions of twenty-six previous acts and remained in effect as the basic customs administrative act for almost a century. It was drafted by the Treasury Department in response to congressional resolution,[37] prompted by the development of new territory and the consequent need for reorganization of old districts, establishment of new ones, and the codification of many scattered enactments. The act was by far the lengthiest on the statute books for some time to come and reveals, in one document, the culmination of the first ten years of experience in our national tariff administration.

Among the changes of interest for this study, other than those already mentioned, are the provisions for executive establishment of regulations for dealing with depreciated currency; changes in the moieties clause to permit officers of the newly established revenue-cutter service to share; the requirement of United States consular verification of landing certificates for drawback on goods re-exported to foreign countries;[38] and more detailed specification of oaths and entry formalities. Importers of goods unaccompanied by invoice had the choice of storing the goods in customs custody until they could produce the invoice or entering the goods on appraisement by the merchant appraisers. The latter were to take oath, in all appraisement proceedings, "that the several prices by us affixed to each article are, to the best of our skill and judgment, the true and actual value or cost

35. The 1795 act did not, as sometimes stated by twentieth-century protectionists, "substitute foreign valuation for dutiable purposes" (cf. Tariff Commission, *Methods of Valuation*, Appen. V, p. 114). It did not disturb the *basis* of dutiable value, but merely clarified, in conjunction with the collection law, the definition of the *elements* of value. In this connection, cf. statement of the Secretary of the Treasury in his *Annual Report, 1841*, quoted *infra*, pp. 88–89.

36. 1 U.S. Statutes 627 (Act of March 2, 1799).

37. Goss attributed the drafting of the act to Congress (*op. cit.*, p. 29). Actually the Treasury Department worked for almost a year on the project (cf. letter of Oliver Wolcott, Secretary of the Treasury, to House, January 24, 1798, in *American State Papers: Finance*, I, 506–7).

38. This marks the beginning of the participation of U.S. consuls abroad in tariff administration, paving the way for the consular verification of all invoices of imports.

thereof, at the place of exportation." The ambiguity of this phrase-ology is patent. In the light of import practice and subsequent legis-lative history it is probably correct to infer that appraisers were to determine, if possible, actual "cost" (price) to the importer in the case of purchased goods, and a reasonable "value" for goods shipped directly or on consignment by the manufacturer and therefore involv-ing no actual purchase price. But, as will be seen later, the wording gave the foreign manufacturer-and-exporter the option of claiming his cost of production as the correct valuation, a basis more favorable than the purchase-price basis applying to American importers.

Conclusion of the Initial Period

The initial period of customs valuation in the United States proper-ly ends with the end of the War of 1812 and the definite consolidation of the movement for protection immediately thereafter. Professor Taussig has indicated the effects of over seven years of nonintercourse, beginning with the Embargo in 1807, extended by the Nonintercourse Act of 1809, and completed by the War of 1812.[39] The virtually com-plete exclusion of imports during this period was equivalent to a protective tariff of prohibitive levels. Domestic industry received unprecedented stimulus. Two of the young industries most vocal in later tariff history—the cotton and woolen manufactures—are out-standing for their rate of growth during this period. The end of the war brought the return of heavy competition from well-established foreign industries, particularly those of England, and the demand for tariff protection was rapidly converted into a philosophical creed em-braced with religious zeal by many adherents. The rapid growth of this movement and its consequences during the succeeding twenty years accounts for a substantial portion of the legislative and political history of the times. With all these developments the institution of customs valuation is intimately connected.

The first twenty-five years of national tariff administration were, in principle, largely a continuation of Colonial practice and experi-ence.[40] As we have seen, so far as customs valuation is concerned,

39. F. W. Taussig, *The Tariff History of the United States* (7th ed.; New York, 1923), p. 16.
40. "The year 1789 marks no such epoch in economic as it does in political history" (*ibid.*, p. 10).

there was no significant gain over the principles developed previously in Massachusetts and New York. This is quite different from stating that little was accomplished. The consolidation and integration of the former separate and scattered Colonial systems into the customs system of the United States, and its extension into new territory, was no small undertaking.[41]

Perhaps of greatest significance for our study is the fact that there did not exist during the period under discussion any great need for the refinements of later decades. With the low ad valorem rates of duty which prevailed during the first twenty-five years of federal history there was relatively little inducement to undervaluation. In such circumstances the specific purchase price was, in general, a simple, satisfactory, and logical basis upon which to apply the rates of duty. Such evasions as there were, rather than typifying the basic administrative problem of the time, foreshadowed the problems of the future under continually rising levels of duty. For these reasons it may be concluded that the legislative and administrative provisions which appear so crude today were not unduly inadequate for their own time.

41. A review of the documents in the New Orleans Custom House Collection (cf. *supra*, p. 44, n. 30), indicates the many problems of centralized control under primitive conditions of transportation and communication. This custom house was also faced with peculiar problems of its own, including the absconding of a collector with $90,000 of government funds; an unusually difficult smuggling problem, marked by armed conflict and undeclared warfare with the pirates of the bayous; and the complications arising from the inheritance of the French civil law.

CHAPTER III

Valuation under Rising Protection
1816–61

The Early Protective Movement

THE TARIFF ACT OF 1816

THE ending of the War of 1812 ushered in a new period of American economic history. The seven-year absence of foreign competition, combined with contemporary developments in manufacturing technology and the rapid industrial growth appropriate to a new country, had set the stage for the economic activity and conflict which were to follow. One of the best indications of the prevailing atmosphere at the end of the war, with particular relevance to the present study, is found in the following extracts from Secretary Dallas' circular letter of February 25, 1815, to all collectors of customs:

The peace, which has been concluded between the United States and Great Britain, will immediately revive our commerce and navigation; and arrangements should be speedily made at the custom-houses, to facilitate the business of the merchants, and to guard against every species of fraud upon the revenue. For the accomplishment of both objects, you may rely upon the cooperation of the department; and, as it is designed to exact from every public officer the strictest official responsibility, I do not hesitate to promise, with the approbation of the President, that the officers of the customs shall be supplied with all the means, which are requisite, for an efficient performance of their important duties. . . . The duties and powers of the officers of the customs are sufficiently described and defined in those laws. And it is only necessary, at this period, to recommend to your attention, some of the leading objects of the trust.

. . . .

5. The entries of merchandise should be admitted with every possible circumspection in the examination of the invoice and other documents; and every detection of an entry, upon a fictitious invoice, should be prosecuted with the utmost rigor of the law. If there be a doubt of the good faith of the transaction, the power of inspection and appraisement of the goods, with a view to form an estimate of the duties, should be freely executed.[1]

1. Circular letter, A. J. Dallas, Secretary of the Treasury, to collectors and naval officers, February 25, 1815, *N.O.C.H.P.*, II.

Concurrently with these preparations for tariff administration, the shapers of tariff policy were preparing for the economic contest which loomed on the horizon. There were two factors influencing the direction of tariff legislation: the need for revenue and the rising demand for protection of infant industries. In his annual report to Congress, in December, 1815, Secretary Dallas, anticipating a deficit of three and one-half million dollars for the following year, recommended the extension of the wartime emergency duties[2] until a suitable tariff, with a "competent addition" to the permanent rates previously in effect, would be prepared and enacted. Congress responded with an extension until June 30, at which time the rates of duty established by the Tariff Act of 1816, passed on April 27 of that year, became effective.

In the meantime, the events of the market place were rapidly converging to bring into focus the prevailing scattered and somewhat vague demands for protection. The Secretary's earlier prediction of increased commerce was fulfilled before the year was up. The supplies of goods which had been accumulating abroad, particularly in England, during the period of nonimportation, were shipped to the Western Hemisphere in unprecedented quantities, financed by a speculative bubble not unlike that which accompanied the earlier Dutch-tulip fiasco. Total imports into the United States, which had fallen from a peak of $138 million in 1807 to less than $13 million in 1814, rose to $113 million in 1815, and $147 million in 1816. By the middle of 1816, imported goods were glutting the markets and prices declined rapidly. The infant industries of the country, particularly cotton and woolen manufactures, suffered a severe setback, and the resulting bitterness against imports lent stimulus to the movement for protection which was already manifest in the framing of the tariff earlier the same year.

There has been some difference of opinion and interpretation as to whether the act of 1816 marked the beginning of protective policy in the United States. Professor Taussig dissents from what is apparently a majority view[3] by claiming that a coherent protectionist movement,

2. These were the additional duties enacted July 1, 1812, to expire one year after the end of the war. In addition to doubling all existing tariff duties this act imposed additional discriminating duties upon foreign shipping. They would have expired on February 17, 1816.

3. The following are samples of the representative point of view: "The Tariff Act of 1816 was the first distinctly protectionist tariff of the United States" (Jacob Viner, *Dumping: A Problem in International Trade* [Chicago, 1923], p. 43); "The

and, by extension, protectionist policy, did not come into existence until after 1819:

> The protective movement in this country has been said to date from the year 1789, even from before 1789; and more frequently it has been said to begin with the tariff act of 1816. But whatever may have been, in earlier years, the utterances of individual public men, or the occasional drift of an uncertain public opinion, no strong popular movement for protection can be traced before the crisis of 1818–19. The act of 1816, which is generally said to mark the beginning of a distinctly protective policy in this country, belongs rather to the earlier series of acts, beginning with that of 1789, than to the group of acts of 1824, 1828, and 1832. Its highest permanent rate of duty was twenty per cent, an increase over previous rates which is chiefly accounted for by the heavy interest charge on the debt incurred during the war. But after the crash of 1819, a movement in favor of protection set in, which was backed by a strong popular feeling such as had been absent in the earlier years.[4]

Both views have merit, and the correctness of each is largely a matter of definition of terms and issues. A study of the valuation provisions of the 1816 act, however, tends decidedly to place it in the same class as the later protective acts of 1824 and 1828 rather than in the Colonial and early United States acts. The act of 1816 introduced the celebrated minimum valuation principle which was later to become the focal point of attack upon the rising protectionist movement. For the next thirty years the literature of antiprotectionism abounds with scathing denunciations of the minimum. It is not incorrect to state that this provision was, more than any other single tariff feature, the *cause célèbre* of the nullification movement in South Carolina which nearly led to civil war in 1833.

The minimum-value provision, which in the 1816 act applied only to cotton goods and yarn, was a device to guarantee the domestic manufacturer a minimum protective duty while seemingly levying an ad valorem duty of only 25 per cent. The highest ad valorem rate in the tariff was 25 per cent, and this applied to a number of articles.

---

four protective tariffs were enacted in 1816, 1824, 1828, and 1842" (Secretary Walker in U.S. Treasury, *Annual Report for 1846*, pp. 142–43); "A cry for more protection arose. The result was the Tariff Act of 1816. . .; this tariff reflects the beginning of the shift toward a policy of protection" (Chester W. Wright, *Economic History of the United States* [New York, 1941], p. 394).

4. Taussig, *The Tariff History of the United States* (7th ed.; New York, 1923), pp. 68–69. The reference to a "highest permanent rate of duty" of only 20 per cent is misleading in view of specific duties and other provisions presently to be considered.

But in a lengthy paragraph, devoted exclusively to cotton manufactures, the following proviso appeared:

That on all cotton cloths, or cloths of which cotten is the material of chief value, (excepting nankeens imported direct from China) the original cost of which at the place whence imported, with the addition of twenty per cent, if imported from the Cape of Good Hope or from places beyond it, and of ten per cent if imported from any other place, shall be less than 25 cents per square yard, shall, with such addition, be taken and deemed to have cost 25 cents per square yard, and shall be charged with duty accordingly.

Uncolored cotton yarn or thread was given a minimum value of 60 cents per pound, and colored yarn 75 cents. The effect of the 25-cent

TABLE 2

(1) Foreign-Market Value (Cents)	(2) Additional 20 Per Cent (Cents)	(3) Normal Dutiable Value (Cents)	(4) Minimum Duty (Cents)	(5) Duty/Dutiable Value (Per Cent)	(6) Duty/Foreign-Market Value (Per Cent)	(7) Actual Rate (5)/ 25 Per Cent Rate (Per Cent)	(8) Domestic Value (Cents)
20.0	4.0	24.0	6.25	26.0	31.2	104.0	30.2
17.5	3.5	21.0	6.25	29.8	35.7	119.2	27.2
15.0	3.0	18.0	6.25	35.0	41.7	140.0	24.2
10.0	2.0	12.0	6.25	52.1	62.5	208.4	18.2
8.0	1.6	9.6	6.25	65.1	81.4	260.4	15.8
6.0	1.2	7.2	6.25	86.8	104.2	347.2	13.4
4.0	0.8	4.8	6.25	130.2	156.2	520.8	11.0

minimum, depending upon the price of cloth, can be seen from Table 2 for various foreign-market values of from 20 cents down to 4 cents per yard. Column 8—"Domestic Value"—indicates the minimum sale price in this country of the imported article, on the stringent assumption that the 20 per cent differential[5] would adequately cover transportation, insurance, and other landed costs, as well as the importer's margin. It can readily be seen not only that the minimum granted practically exclusive protection as the selling price of the competing domestically produced article declined substantially below the minimum valuation but that the actual rate of duty became more than five times the ostensible rate of 25 per cent on imports priced to

5. Coarse cottons from India furnished the chief competition against which the minimum provision was initially directed. In its actual operation over a period of years England was the chief foreign country affected. Goods imported from England were subject to only a 10 per cent addition.

compete with the domestic product selling at 11 cents per yard or less. Later events proved that these high rates were to become actually effective and not merely hypothetical.

An examination of the circumstances surrounding the establishment of the minimum—and the subsequent price history of cotton goods—sheds additional light on the subject. The man who was perhaps most responsible for the minimum-valuation proviso, as well as for the subsequent decline in the price of cotton cloth, was Mr. Francis Lowell, one of the pioneers in the perfection of the power loom and the development of the cotton manufacture in this country. Mr. Nathan Appleton, one of his business associates and later a member of Congress, recounts the circumstances in his memoirs:

> In 1816 a new tariff was to be made. The Rhode Island manufacturers were clamoring for a very high specific duty. Mr. Lowell was at Washington, for a considerable time, during the session of Congress. His views on the tariff were much more moderate, and he finally brought Mr. Lowndes and Mr. Calhoun, to support the minimum of 6¼ cents the square yard, which was carried.
>
> . . . .
>
> Mr. Lowell adopted an entirely new arrangement to save labor, in passing from one process to another; and he is unquestionably entitled to the credit of being the first person who arranged all the processes for the conversion of cotton into cloth, within the walls of the same building. It is remarkable how few changes have been made from the arrangements established by him, in the first mill built at Waltham. It is also remarkable, how accurate were his calculations, as to the expense at which goods could be made. He used to say, that the only circumstance which made him distrust his own calculations, was, that he could bring them to no other result but one which was too favorable to be credible.[6]

Appleton goes on to state that it is unlikely that Lowell foresaw that "the same goods which were then selling at thirty cents a yard, would ever be sold at six cents, and without a loss to the manufacturer, as has since been done in 1843." It is, however, highly probable that Lowell did realize what effect the power loom would have upon the general trend of prices in the next decade and that the provision which he was successful in securing from Congress would be more than adequate protection in the future. The price of cotton goods fell from around 30 cents a yard in 1816 to 21 cents in 1819. In another

6. Nathan Appleton, *Introduction of the Power Loom and Origin of Lowell* (Lowell, Mass., 1858), pp. 13 ff.

ten years—in 1829—the price was down to 8½ cents. It is unnecessary to state that long before 1829 the minimum-value provision had become prohibitive to all importations of lower-grade cotton goods.[7]

The foregoing account has portrayed the first notable instance in which customs valuation was used in the United States to secure and disguise[8] a substantial increase in tariff protection. The minimum-valuation device was employed because of its apparent innocuousness at a time when existing prices rendered it of relatively little significance. An equivalent specific duty would have afforded the same protection but would have had difficulty passing Congress because of its more obvious implications. At that time all specific duties were assessed upon articles by weight, dimension, or other physical unit. To have obtained the same protective effect, it would have been necessary to introduce a new principle in the application of specific duties—the levy of a specific duty with classification based on *value*, thus requiring valuation procedure for its implementation. This would probably have drawn much more attention than the simple

7. Cf. Taussig, *op. cit.*, p. 30, where he concedes the prohibitive effect of the minimum under the act of 1816. Prices of foreign goods fell even lower than those of the domestic product, which were frequently held by American manufacturers just below the landed cost plus duty of the foreign article. In 1831–32, when the minimum under the Tariff of Abominations was 35 cents, yielding a duty of 8¾ cents per yard, British shirtings were selling at 7½ cents. The comparable American product was priced at this time at 15 to 15½ cents. Cf. speech of Mr. Cambreleng, of New York, in the House of Representatives early in 1832: "Thus were British shirtings excluded by the wise, just, and patriotic laws which enable us to supply Mexico with those very cottons while we prohibit our own countrymen from consuming them" (*Congressional Debates*, VIII, Part II, 1610). The conclusive protection of the minimum was frankly admitted by the protectionists: "The original idea extended only to the manufacture of coarse cottons, to take the place of those imported from India. Not only were these excluded almost immediately, but under the influence of a small extension of the minimum in 1824, and again in 1828, by each of which an additional duty of 1¼ cents the square yard was added to that imposed in 1816, the manufacture has been carried up into the finer and higher branches, to an extent and with a rapidity which I will venture to say has no parallel in the history of commerce" (speech of Mr. Nathan Appleton in the House, *ibid.*, p. 1599). Much valuable material on the history and practical operation of the minimum may be found in this series of debates (*ibid.*, pp. 1599–1615).

8. The following is typical of the resentment in informed circles against the minimum duties because of their concealed nature: "These enormous duties, however, are not exhibited on our statute books, but are imposed by a legislative contrivance, as if intentionally resorted to, to protect the public from seeing the extent of the tax which they are called upon to pay for the support of cotton manufactures" (*Free Trade Advocate and Journal of Political Economy*, I [1829], 119–20).

minimum-value proviso in the appropriate ad valorem section of the tariff. The employment of this device is an indication of the feeling on the part of the legislators that the public at large was not sufficiently protectionist-minded to countenance, consciously and openly, the duty levels actually obtained. To this extent, Taussig's position, as given above, was well taken. On the other hand, the whole history of tariff legislation in the United States is the demonstration par excellence of the simple but generally unappreciated fact that effective national policy is by no means synonymous with the conscious will of the public at large. The tariff of 1816 may not have reflected the desires of the majority; but it definitely established protection and provided the pattern upon which the succeeding more highly protective tariffs were based.

<h2 style="text-align:center">THE ACT OF MARCH 3, 1817</h2>

The question of what charges were to be included in the "actual cost of the goods at the place of exportation" was always a source of dispute between importers and collectors. These difficulties were enhanced by the fact that the cost elements in question were seldom specifically mentioned in the statutes or were indiscriminately added or omitted from one statute to another without apparent reason. Apart from the addition of the 10 and 20 per cent differentials, the 1799 act—as well as that of 1795, already mentioned—based dutiable value upon "the actual cost at the place of exportation, including all charges (commission, outside packages and insurance only excepted)." The valuation clause in the 1816 act changed the basis to "the net cost of the article at the place whence imported (exclusive of packages, commissions and all charges)." A year later, the special act of March 3, 1817,[9] consisting of only a single paragraph, clarifying the treatment of charges, added further exemptions by making "charges of transportation and export duty" permissible deductions in the determination of dutiable value.

These exclusions in the calculation of "net cost" were unusually liberal and undoubtedly gave rise to abuse. The vagueness of the term "all other charges" presented an especially large loophole for the evasion of duties. Foreign manufacturers seized upon this to include in the category of "charges" payment for numerous "services"

9. 3 U.S. Statutes 369.

such as bleaching, dyeing, and finishing, which were really part of the cost of the goods in their completed condition prior to sale. The word "packages" (as opposed to "outside packages") could be construed in a variety of ways to include not only the expenses of packaging incidental to the voyage, but cartons, boxes, containers, and the like, which either possessed considerable value of their own or substantially enhanced the value of the contents for the ultimate consumer. By excluding them from the dutiable value of the basic merchandise they were thus importable duty free.

Discounts and commissions also gave trouble in administration. Since a bona fide discount was a necessary consideration in the determination of the actual purchase price, it could not be denied as a legitimate deduction. To complicate matters, there was no uniformity either in the rate of discount allowed in a particular trade or in the matter of indicating it on the invoice. It was the general policy of the Treasury Department to deny the deduction of discount not shown on the invoice. But even when it was shown, there was always the suspicion that it was overstated or non–bona fide.[10] The same was true of commissions, which were later made part of dutiable value at a minimum of 2½ per cent of the invoice.

Transportation to the port of final exportation was normally considered as a cost ingredient to be included in dutiable value. A strict interpretation of this often resulted in anomalies, especially where goods for one reason or another were rerouted or reshipped; what was normally a duty-free component of landed cost at the port of importation then became dutiable as a cost ingredient prior to exportation. It was probably on the basis of complaints in specific instances of this kind that the exclusion of transportation charges was made in the 1817 act.

The specific exemption of export taxes in the 1817 act suggests certain logical problems in the administration of dutiable value based on specific purchase price. The purchase price depended upon the terms of sale, and, if goods were purchased on the basis of delivered prices at the port of importation, the amount of the export tax would be reflected in the invoice price. In the absence of statutory exemp-

10. Cf. Treasury Circular, August 15, 1826: "Informant advises that the potters of England have agreed to allow only 15% discount hereafter on everything. Be on the lookout, as this is considerably different from the usual 35% to 37½%."

tion, the Treasury with some degree of plausibility in such cases apparently took the position that since the export taxes accrued within the country "whence imported" they were properly a part of the price at the "place whence imported," as called for in the statutory rule of dutiable value. On the other hand, merchandise purchased f.o.b. the foreign factory or market would in all probability not include the amount of the export tax. Thus, in the absence of clearly defined rules providing for various contingencies, the use of specific purchase price led to differences in dutiable value for identical merchandise purchased under different terms. Export bounties posed a somewhat similar problem but were administratively allowed, when shown on the invoice, as adequate explanation of a price paid by the importer lower than that prevailing in foreign markets for home consumption.[11] All this was essentially the problem of fraudulent undervaluation based on fictitious invoices[12] and further

11. Letter, comptroller of Treasury to collector, New Orleans, July 12, 1819, in *N.O.C.H.P.*, III: "Deduction for bounty allowed only when clearly specified on original invoice." The necessity for showing the amount of the export bounty on the invoice indicates that foreign-market value was used at this time as a check upon the truthfulness of the purchase price stated in the invoice.

12. The following example, taken from the Treasury Circular of August 15, 1826, is a good illustration of the techniques used and provides an insight into the number and nature of the various charges in vogue during the general period under discussion: "Also a new and unprecedented course pursued by agents residing in Paris, who purchase goods for merchants residing in this country, by omitting with the avowed purpose of saving the duties thereon, to include the commissions and other incidental charges in the invoice sent to the importer, transmitting them in separate letters, containing a particular specification. Informant selected the following specimens:

According to invoice:

Net cost of 60 cases of goods, without charges		f. 70,833 20
Add for charges:	275	
Cases, packing, etc.	275	
Custom House duty, drayage, etc.	65	340
		f. 71,173 20

According to separate letter:

60 cases of goods	f. 70,833 20
Add:	
For 21 mahogany scales for clocks	73 50
" cases, packing, paper, etc.	694 40
" custom house expenses and drayage	240
" emballage of silk goods	26
" commission at Lyon on sundry cases	415 40
" carriage on cases from country	230
" dying [sic] rose crepe lisse	24
" cartons in sundry cases	106 15
" commissions on the above	2,179 25
	f. 74,821 90

Besides these, it is alleged, that the usual shipping charges at Havre, amount to f. 753 15."

indicated the administrative difficulty of preventing fraud as long as dutiable value was based on specific purchase price. The statutory exemption of specified charges aggravated the problem, but the principal difficulty was the basing of dutiable value upon "actual cost"— a quantity which rarely if ever could be proved satisfactorily by any party to the controversy. This promoted the omission of dutiable charges from the invoice, or even the use of double invoices—the fraudulent one for customs, the correct one for settlement of the actual terms of sale.

THE APPRAISEMENT ACT OF 1818

By 1818 the tremendous volume of importations, the decline in prices, and the depression in home industry were sufficiently felt for Congress to respond to the demands for increased protection. On April 20 of that year several acts were passed, all designed for protective purposes. While there were increases in both specific and ad valorem duties, the most drastic changes were made by the Appraisement Act of this date. Underlying the passage of this act was the feeling that foreign importations were largely to blame for the country's distress and that foreign manufacturers—particularly the English—were determined to prevent American industry, still in its infancy, from maintaining its precarious foothold.[13]

There was also the widespread complaint that the importing business was rapidly gravitating into the hands of foreigners because of the mechanism of customs valuation. This was a grievance to be heard for many years to come, and one which played an important part in the various controversies in the history of tariff administration.

The details of the act were proposed by the Treasury Department on January 20, 1818, in response to an earlier House resolution.[14] Unfortunately, the suggested details, instead of being submitted in the form of a completely drafted, internally consistent bill, were merely listed in general fashion. As a result, the act as passed was hopelessly confused and self-contradictory.

13. Cf. Viner, *op. cit.*, pp. 39–45, for an illuminating discussion of the period, particularly the circumstances surrounding the speech of Lord Brougham, April 9, 1816, in the House of Commons, and its effects upon American sentiment.

14. Cf. "Revision of the Revenue Laws," *American State Papers: Finance*, III, 234–41.

The first four sections were reasonably clear. Section 1 provided that goods unaccompanied by the original invoice would be stored at the owner's expense in the public warehouse until the invoice was produced. If this was not accomplished within six months (nine months for goods originating beyond the Cape of Good Hope), the goods would be removed and appraised and the duties levied accordingly. Section 2 permitted the Secretary of the Treasury, when he deemed it expedient, to allow the admission of the goods on appraisement before the expiration of the stated periods, provided bond was given for the later production of the invoice. Unredeemed bonds were forfeit at the end of eight and fifteen months, respectively, for the two categories stated above. Section 3 required an oath as to the correct ownership of the goods.

The fourth section provided a more restrictive definition of dutiable value, so far as charges were concerned, than the 1816 and 1817 acts: "ad valorem rates of duty . . . shall be estimated by adding . . . [the 10- and 20-per-cent differentials] . . . to the actual cost thereof . . . including all charges, except commission, outside packages, and insurance." It will be noted that specific purchase price was still the basis of dutiable value; the treatment of charges was returned to its status under the 1795 and 1799 acts.

Despite the very specific language of section 4, section 5 required an oath on entry of any ad valorem goods that "the invoice produced by him exhibits the *true value* [italics added] of such goods . . . in their actual state of manufacture at the place from which the same were imported." This provision was originally intended to cover the foreign manufacturer who shipped his goods to this country on consignment. Previously he could show his "actual cost," which was very much lower than that of the importer whose actual cost abroad was the foreign-market or specific purchase price rather than the cost of production. The result was not only a legal rate of duty less than the American importer paid but substantial fraudulent undervaluation, in addition, because of the impossibility of any check upon the foreign manufacturer's costs. There appears to be adequate evidence, apart from the numerous memorials and testimonials of businessmen, that by 1818 American merchants and importers had lost a substantial portion of their business to direct foreign importations on consignment, which were sold at auction or by representatives of foreign concerns.[15] From these circumstances, as well as from the wording in the Treasury Department recommendation and the statute itself, it seems clear that section 5 was intended to require the showing of market value only on the foreign producer's *pro forma* invoice and entry. But the wording of section 5 made it apply to *all* importations, thereby compelling all importers to swear to something that might or might not be true and in many cases was manifestly impossible of being true—namely, that the invoice price and market price were identical.

On top of this hopelessly inconsistent requirement, the act provided for the usual appraisement upon suspicion of undervaluation, with the further stipulation that, if the appraised value exceeded the invoice value by 25 per cent, the goods would be assessed a heavy penalty, in the form of a 50 per cent increase in valuation, on the *appraised* value. As if this were not sufficient to discourage all "foreigners," the act made the unfortunate importer pay for the expenses of appraisement, unless he were lucky enough to emerge with an invoice value in excess of the appraised value, in which case he was assessed duty on the invoice value. To cap the climax, the penalized importer had the satisfaction of knowing that the very individual who initiated appraise-

---

15. Letters from collectors of customs, reports of the Secretary of the Treasury, and speeches in Congress all confirm the view that the tendency of the importing business to be concentrated in the hands of foreigners was a reality (cf. "Protection to the Manufacturing and Mercantile Interests," *American State Papers: Finance*, III, 168). Much literature on this issue can be found in the discussions of the effects of the auction system and customs credits, e.g., Philadelphia Chamber of Commerce, *Essay on the Warehousing System and Government Credits of the United States* (Philadelphia, 1828), esp. pp. 17–19; *Report of a Special Committee of the American Institute on the Subject of Cash Duties, the Auction System, etc., January 12, 1829* (New York, 1829); "Auction System in New York," *Hunt's Merchant Magazine and Commercial Review*, X (1844), 154. An authoritative study and appraisal of the auction system in the United States in the early nineteenth century is Ray Bert Westerfield, "Early History of American Auctions: A Chapter in Commercial History," *Transactions of the Connecticut Academy of Arts and Sciences*, XXIII (May, 1920), 159–210, esp. pp. 191–93, confirming the relationship of undervaluation to concentration of importing into the hands of foreigners. The auction system facilitated undervaluation by furnishing the foreign manufacturer or agent with a simple, inexpensive, and rapid means of disposing of his goods. Once goods had been sold at auction, fraud was difficult to detect and substantiate with documentary proof; moreover, penalties were difficult of enforcement, since the goods had escaped forfeiture; the foreign agent, if found, had little or no assets; and criminal convictions were almost impossible to obtain. A brief discussion of the auction system is also found in Norman Sydney Buck, *The Development of the Organization of Anglo-American Trade, 1800–1850* (New Haven, 1925), esp. pp. 135–44.

ment proceedings and who had a large voice in custom-house operations generally, namely, the collector, would, by section 14 of the act,
share one-half of the 50 per cent penalty duty with the other principal
officers of the port.

These were not the only harsh requirements of the Appraisement
Act of 1818. The act stipulated that any importer who resided abroad
must verify, under oath, the invoice of the goods in question before
the United States consul in the port of exportation or before a consul
in the country of such port if none resided in the port. This was interpreted to mean that the owner himself—or a partner, in the case of a
firm—was personally required to travel halfway across his country, if
necessary, to take the prescribed oath. Only if he were incapacitated
or absent from his residence for a prolonged period could substitution
be made, and then only by his known agent or factor.

If this onerous requirement was neglected for some reason (possibly because the owner of a large manufacturing plant might be expected to have other things to do), then section 13 came into operation. This aptly numbered section provided that goods "for want of the
verification required by the eighth section of this act, not admitted to
entry, shall be subject to the same appraisement, and to the same addition to the appraised value, as are prescribed by the eleventh section
of this act, in the case of fraudulent invoices." On the surface of it, and
under any reasonable interpretation, this section was eminently fair.
It provided, in plain language, for the same treatment as goods
appraised because of doubts as to their value, which would result in a
50 per cent penalty *if* the appraised value exceeded the invoice value
by 25 per cent. This was not, however, the interpretation placed upon
the matter by the Treasury Department, which took the position that
the phrase, "shall be subject . . . to the same addition to the appraised
value," meant that regardless of the relationship between invoice and
appraised value, the 50 per cent penalty accrued automatically for all
omissions of the sworn consular invoice.[16]

16. Par. 3 of Treasury Circular (apparently addressed to consuls as well as to
collectors) of March 26, 1819, reads as follows: "All cases embodied by the 13th
section of the act are subject to the addition of fifty per cent; the failure to produce
invoices duly verified being, in contemplation of the act, equivalent to merchan-
dize fraudulently invoiced at twenty-five per cent below its appraised value." An
actual illustration of the severity of the Treasury Department's interpretation is
found in a letter of Joseph Anderson, comptroller of the Treasury, to Beverly
Chew, collector at New Orleans, March 29, 1820, in *N.O.C.H.P.*, IV: "Sir, I have

Another notable provision of the act of 1818 was the appointment of two full-time appraisers at each of the six principal ports—Boston, New York, Philadelphia, Baltimore, Charleston, and New Orleans. These two appraisers were to collaborate with one merchant appraiser chosen by the party in interest. In other ports the collector was to choose two merchant appraisers, and the importer one, and "the appraisement so made by them, or a majority of them, shall be valid and effectual in law." This was the first step in the supplanting of merchant appraisers by specially appointed government officials. Nevertheless, as previously indicated, the presence of those merchants actually selected for appraisement proceedings was implemented by section 10, which provided for a fine of fifty dollars and costs of prosecution for failure to attend.

Like the minimum provision of the 1816 act, the entire act of 1818 was initially given a limited life, in this case "two years from and after the passing thereof." Also, like the minimum provision, it was kept alive by subsequent legislation until it was superseded by more drastic and severe protective legislation. At the time of its passage, however, even the Secretary of the Treasury had a "tongue-in-cheek" attitude toward it:

> The act supplementary to the collection laws, passed on April 20, last, being entirely experimental, it is an object of the highest importance to ascertain, with precision, the effects produced by it upon the commerce and revenue of the nation.

. . . .

---

received a communication . . . [in which case] the invoice and appraised value are the same, but 50% assessed for verification by *agent* at Liverpool, instead of the owners and manufacturers of the goods residing at Sutten Park, Birmingham." In this case there was no question of fraud; the appraisers' returns were the same as the invoice value. Nor were the consular invoice and certification of the oath lacking. The sole reason for assessing the penalty was the execution of the consular oath by an agent instead of the owner. The comptroller concluded by stating that only sickness or prolonged absence relieved the owner of the personal responsibility required.

Similar hardship obtained in the case of the American buyer abroad. Regardless of the inconvenience involved, he was obliged to appear before the consul at the point of shipment. A buyer might "order shipment to the United States, on account of his house in Boston, from Leghorn when he is himself in Dublin, and from Bordeaux when he is in London, as the exigencies of the times and opportunity of markets" might require (Memorial of T. H. Perkins and two hundred others on "Revision of Revenue Laws," December 23, 1822, in *American State Papers: Finance,* IV, 3). This lengthy but clearly written testimonial is an excellent discussion of the actual operation of the Appraisement Act.

Should the ordinary trade of the ports, where official appraisers are provided by law, take, from that or any other cause, a different direction, and concentrate in any one or more of the ports where such officers had not been provided, you will not fail to notify the department of such change, and of the causes and circumstances which are supposed to have produced it.[17]

In two short months after the passage of the act the various ports were so crowded with goods awaiting arrival of invoices that Secretary Crawford advised all collectors to admit goods on appraisement until the following November.[18]

The weaknesses of the Appraisement Act of 1818, as indicated above, were numerous and glaring. The framers missed an excellent opportunity, while making so extensive a revision of valuation procedure and law, of putting an end to the anomalous use of specific purchase price as the basis for dutiable value. Instead, they compounded the error by retaining the old basis[19] and penalizing the importer for

17. Treasury Department Circular, May 29, 1818.
18. *Ibid.*, June 22, 1818.
19. The Treasury Department apparently took the position that the act did change the general basis of dutiable value to the market value: "I will merely add that, it is not the *cost* of the goods, but their *true value* in their actual state of manufacture, that is now to govern in estimating the duties; which value is ascertained from the *general prices given,* and the state of the market at the time of purchase. This distinction will be obvious from a comparison of the provisions of the Collection Law of 1799, with those of the supplementary law of April, 1818" (Joseph Anderson, comptroller of the Treasury to collectors, March 13, 1819). Cf. also letter of the comptroller to the collector, New Orleans, April 14, 1819, in *N.O.C.H.P.*, III: "According to the Collection Law of 1799, invoices were to exhibit the *actual and real cost of the goods;* but by the supplementary act of 20th April, 1818, they are to exhibit the *true value* of the goods, in their actual state of manufacture, at the place from which the same were imported. . . . Under the Old collection law, many impositions, it is apprehended, were practiced on the revenue, by false invoices, predicated on fictitious sales, etc., which impositions were the more readily carried into execution, from the circumstance that the invoices were to exhibit the *costs,* and not the *value,* of the goods." This interpretation cannot be sustained by a reading of Section 4, quoted in part above, which defines dutiable value. Moreover, seemingly conclusive evidence on the subject is found in Treasury Department Circular to collectors, written on October 12, 1830, more than twelve years later: "I take occasion to add, that the decision of the appraisers that goods have been charged too low, is not of itself conclusive evidence of fraudulent intent. The act of 1828 directs the appraisers to ascertain the 'true value,' which it is believed was not intended to be synonymous with 'actual cost'— the words used in the former acts to indicate the dutiable value of goods. This idea is corroborated by the 3rd section of the act of 1830, where it is provided, that, before the importer can appeal from the appraisement made under that act, he must take oath 'that the appraisement is higher than the actual cost and proper charges on which duty is to be charged, and that he verily believes it is higher than the "current value" of the said goods, including said charges at the place of exportation.'"

their own lack of insight. In fact, the more skilful the importer—or his agent or partner abroad—in buying goods at favorable prices, the more he exposed himself to the inequitable operation of the law. If he refused to take the consular oath, knowing that his buying price and therefore invoice price was lower than the market in a particular instance, he subjected himself to a 50 per cent penalty. On the other hand, if he did take the oath, he subjected himself to the same penalty and possibly even to forfeiture of the goods. Although the legislation was reputedly directed against foreign manufacturers, American importers and buyers abroad often suffered greater hardships under it than did the former. In any event, the act of 1818 is the first clear case of the use, in the United States, of what had later come to be known as "administrative protection." At the same time, it should in all fairness be stated that the act represented a marked advance in appraisement organization and hastened the day when a practicable concept of dutiable value would be recognized and adopted.

Abomination, Nullification, and Compromise

The fifteen-year period following the Appraisement Act of 1818 was probably the most important era in the tariff history of the United States. During this period the issue of protectionism became the dominant economic and political issue in the nation. The cotton manufacturing industry, under the stimulus of technological advance, of increasing tariff protection, and of independently rising demand, became firmly established as the nation's leading manufacture. The woolen industry, borrowing from the technical and political experience of the cotton trades, likewise secured an established place in the American economy. The iron industry, although lagging behind that of England technologically, was able, with the aid of highly protective specific duties, to achieve substantial control over the domestic market and a powerful voice in the business and legislative councils of the country. The transition of the United States from an agricultural and commercial community to that of a diversified economy proceeded rapidly.[20]

The extent to which the tariff accelerated this diversification will always remain a moot question in economic controversy. It is certain,

20. Cf. Taussig, *op. cit.*, p. 106.

however, that during the period under discussion the tariff was felt by the unprotected groups as well as by the protected interests to be of primary influence in shaping the economic development of the nation. The debates in Congress, the memorials and testimonials preserved in state papers and government documents, the numerous privately printed pamphlets which have survived to tell their story, the newspapers and the more substantial periodicals of the time—all combine to reveal the felt importance of the tariff issue to all classes. As the decade of the 1820's advanced, the alignment of the contending political groups became more and more a division upon the stand of protection. While it is true that partisan politics, particularly before and during the enactment of the tariff of 1828, used the tariff issue in the furtherance of other political ends, the consequences were that shortly thereafter this issue became basic to the question as to whether or not the Union would survive.

The nullification movement and its train of consequences had far-reaching effects upon the institution of customs valuation. But, before we trace the intimate relationships therein involved, two developments earlier in the period are deserving of brief attention.

The first is the enactment in 1820 of a fairly comprehensive law[21] for the systematic gathering of foreign-trade statistics. This task was assigned to the customs service and required the valuation of both imports and exports. It was required that "the kinds, quantities, and values" of all imports and exports be reported annually to Congress and quarterly by collectors to the Treasury. Such reports were to classify foreign trade by country of origin or destination and by foreign or domestic production (to enable segregation of the re-export and re-import trade). Imports free of duty or subject to specific duties were to have their values ascertained "in the same manner in which the values of imports subject to duties ad valorem are ascertained." Originally this required merely the use of the values exhibited on the importers' sworn invoice and entry. Subsequently, in 1828 and thereafter, appraisement of all ad valorem imports became mandatory, and by the wording of the 1820 statistical law, appraisement was automatically extended to free goods and those subject to specific duties.[22]

---

21. 3 U.S. Statutes 541 (Act of February 10, 1820).

22. "The value of free goods must, for statistical purposes and returns, be ascertained by appraisement, as in the case of goods liable by law to the payment

Export valuation, however, was accomplished without appraisement, the sworn export manifest of owners and shippers of cargo, which was required before clearance was granted to vessels, being deemed sufficiently accurate. Manifests were required to show the value of goods "according to their actual cost, or the values which they truly bear at the port and time of exportation." The 1820 act made available for the first time reasonably accurate export figures and, by expanding the scope of customs valuation and administration, gave the customs authorities more intimate knowledge and wider control of all goods moving in the foreign trade of the United States.

The other development was the elimination of the major incongruities of the Appraisement Act of 1818, by the passage of a much more complete and more intelligently drafted statute in 1823.[23] This law very clearly distinguished between the two classes of import—purchased goods and goods obtained otherwise than by purchase. The former were made dutiable upon their cost to the importer and the latter upon their actual market value, both with the usual additions. In the case of purchased goods, the invoice was required to show what an invoice is normally intended to show, namely, the purchase price, including all charges. Invoices for goods obtained otherwise than by purchase were to show the market value in the actual state of manufacture. The forms of oaths were made to correspond with these changes and were separately drawn for the three classes of deponent: (1) importer, consignee, or agent; (2) owner by purchase; (3) manufacturer. One or more of these oaths was required for each importation, depending upon its nature, the purpose being in every case to bind the owner of the goods as well as the person making entry. The authority to admit goods without invoice to entry on appraisement

---

of import duties" (U.S. Treasury Department, *General Regulations under the Revenue and Collection Laws of the United States* [1857], p. 437; at the time this was published there were no specific duties, all duties having been made ad valorem in the Walker Tariff of 1846).

23. 3 U.S. Statutes 729 (Act of March 1, 1823). This act was the result of numerous requests for revision of the 1818 act, the most important of which was the petition signed by two hundred merchants referred to *supra*, p. 00, n. 16. Contemporary debates in Congress also refer to a similar memorial by the Philadelphia Chamber of Commerce (cf. U.S. Congress, *Annals*, XL, 630–32, and references in indexes to *Annals* under "Duties"). Mr. Ingham, Secretary of the Treasury, was one of the sponsors of the new act (cf. also "Letter from the Secretary of the Treasury in relation to the Collection of Duties on Imports and Tonnage, January 29, 1823," *House Document No. 50* [17th Cong. 2d sess.]).

was given to collectors, instead of residing in the Secretary of the Treasury. The Secretary was specifically authorized to admit, in his discretion, goods of nonresidents unaccompanied by consular invoice. Section 13, prescribing the 50 per cent penalty when appraised value exceeded invoiced value by more than 25 per cent, carried a proviso that nothing in the act could be construed to impose the penalty "for a variance between the bona fide invoice of goods . . . and the current value of said merchandise." This removed one of the chief defects of the 1818 act and made clear the distinction, theretofore nebulous in all previous statutes, between market and specific purchase price. Although the act still based dutiable value upon the specific purchase price, it relieved the importer of the imputation of fraud merely because of an apparently excessive deviation from market price. To this extent the administrative difficulties resulting from the basing of dutiable value upon specific price were reduced in comparison even with the acts previous to 1818. Finally, the importer was given the right of appeal after appraisement, first to two reputable merchants hired by himself—that is, the importer selected the appraisers, presumably from a qualified panel approved by the collector,[24] and paid the standard appraisement fees fixed by law. If still dissatisfied, the importer could appeal to the Secretary of the Treasury. It is plain that the 1823 act, which resulted from numerous appeals by importers and merchants to Congress, was a step forward in the direction of sound customs administration.

The Tariff Act of 1824, although of definite significance in the general tariff history of the United States because of its further aggravation and consolidation of the antiprotectionists, has otherwise little relevance for the present study. It contained virtually no administrative features and failed, by three votes, in extending the minimum valuation principle to woolen goods. It did, however, increase the cotton minimum valuation to 30 cents, which was further increased four years later to 35 cents.

24. This is a reasonable assumption. Certainly the collector would have a voice, directly or indirectly, in the interpretation of the word "respectable" as applied to merchant appraisers in the statute, and he administered the oaths which stated that they had no interest whatsoever in the merchandise. But Mr. Mallary read a letter before Congress a number of years later citing the case of one merchant appraiser who was a British factor and the other an auctioneer, both of whom were presumed therefore to be untrustworthy (cf. *infra*, p. 74, n. 31).

The Tariff Act of 1828[25]—the Tariff of Abominations—made far-reaching changes in valuation procedure. It was the first act to place dutiable value completely and unequivocally upon the basis of market value—"actual value, any invoice or affidavit thereto to the contrary notwithstanding, at the time purchased, and place from whence same shall have been imported"—instead of "actual cost" or specific-purchase price paid by the importer. Moreover, also by section 8—the lengthiest section on valuation procedure in any act up to that time—it closed the door to any further clearance of ad valorem goods through the custom house without appraisement. It required an appraisement "in all cases where the duty . . . shall by law be regulated by, or be directed to be estimated or levied upon the value of . . . any quantity or parcel thereof, and in all cases where there is or shall be imposed any ad valorem rate of duty." By former acts appraisement was unnecessary except in cases of suspicion of undervaluation. The 1828 act made appraisement mandatory not only on all ad valorem goods but on all goods coming under the minimum-value provision, on all goods subject to specific duties under value brackets or gradations, and on all goods, whether ad valorem or specific, subject to the "chief-value" clause.[26] It also narrowed the permissible excess of appraised value over invoice value, in connection with the assessment of the 50 per cent penalty valuation, to 10 per cent.

One of the principal "abominations" of the 1828 act was the inclusion of minimum valuations on woolen goods, similar in underlying

25. 4 U.S. Statutes 270 (Act of May 19, 1828); cf. Taussig, *op. cit.*, pp. 80–103, for a detailed discussion of the steps leading to the final form of this act.

26. The first such clause appeared in the act of August 10, 1790, in connection with the 7½ per cent duty on leather and "all manufactures of which leather is the article of chief value, except such as are herein otherwise rated." This provision was also applied to lead in the act of March 2, 1791, and to the principal metals in that of May 2, 1792. At first the chief-value clause created little or no administrative difficulty, inasmuch as the classification problems of the time were relatively simple, requiring only casual inspection for their determination. With advances in technology and the multiplication of products and product components, the problem of classification on the basis of value has in many instances become a highly technical problem. For example, in 1889 the chief-value clause gave considerable trouble in the classification of imported lead-, silver-, and gold-bearing ores. If lead was found to be the material of chief value, an entire importation paid the lead duty of 1½ cents per pound. If the gold or silver content of the same ores was found to have greater value, the entire importation was duty free (cf. U.S. Treasury, *Annual Report, 1889*, p. xxxiii). For important court decisions on the chief-value provision cf. *Seeburger* v. *Hardy*, 150 U.S. 420 (1893); *Turner & Co. et al.* v. *United States*, 12 C.C.A. 48 (1924).

principle to those of the 1816 act on cottons,[27] and to those which had been unsuccessfully sought for woolens in the Tariff of 1824. The woolens minimums, with one major exception, were those requested by the Harrisburg Convention the year before. This convention, made up of the leading protectionists in the country, had a definite influence in the passage of the 1828 act. The Harrisburg plan had contemplated a 50 per cent duty with minimum-value brackets of $0.40, $2.50, and $4.00. As is obvious, this would result in enormous duties at the lower limits of the several ranges and would bear with prohibitive weight on the large quantities of goods actually being imported at the $1.00 – $1.50 level. But the House Committee on Manufactures,[28] which framed the bill, drove a wedge into the valuation scale by inserting a

27. The effectiveness of the 1816 cotton minimums and the feeling of the anti-protectionists toward them are indicated by remarks of Mr. Cambreleng, of New York, in a speech before the House during the debates on the 1828 bill: "The American system can never benefit an agricultural population; they will never be indemnified for their proportion of the six and twenty millions of dollars which had been levied on the consumption of the country since 1816, under the minimum on cotton" (cf. *Congressional Debates*, IV, Part II, 2357). The South, and especially South Carolina, was intensely bitter over the prospect of extending the minimum principle to woolens and fought its adoption both in and out of Congress (cf. *Speech of Mr. M'Cord at a Meeting of Inhabitants in the Town Hall of Columbia, S.C., Opposed to the Proposed Woolens Bill, 2 July 1827* [Columbia, S.C., 1827]). The attitude of the South Carolinians was not mollified by the attempt on the part of a leading protectionist and cotton manufacturer to attribute the original adoption of the minimum principle to South Carolina because it was passed at a time when Mr. Lowndes of South Carolina was chairman of the House Committee on Manufactures: "The minimum, therefore, whatever its character, is a child of South Carolina; and if it require defence, South Carolina should defend it. Will she do so? No, Mr. Speaker; even here, on the spot of its birth, South Carolina brands, with every opprobrious epithet, her own offspring. And yet, sir, is not the act entitled to defence? I think it is. And, however much I may regret that it should have fallen to so feeble hands, I will defend this act of South Carolina, even against herself" (speech of Nathan Appleton, House of Representatives, January 21, 1832, in *Congressional Debates*, VIII, Part II, 1599 ff.). This charge was effectively refuted by Mr. McDuffie of South Carolina (*ibid.*). There was also strong sentiment in New England against the adoption of the woolens minimums, as well as of the other increases contemplated by the Tariff of Abominations. Perhaps the best available discussion and analysis in this connection is to be found in the two hundred-page document, *Report of a Committee of the Citizens of Boston and Vicinity Opposed to a Further Increase of Duties on Importations* (Boston, 1827); cf. esp. pp. 13–15 for discussion of rates of duty in relation to under-valuation.

28. The committee had as its chairman Representative Mallary of Vermont, a thoroughgoing protectionist and woolens man and member of the Harrisburg Convention. The majority of the committee, however, were Jacksonian adherents who were determined, with their colleagues in both houses, to make the tariff bill so odious to all concerned that it would be defeated.

$1.00 breaking point; also, of less importance, it reduced the rate to 40 per cent for the first year and 45 per cent thereafter. The inclusion of the $1.00 minimum was fought bitterly but carried in the final adoption.

The act as passed thus carried the scale of duties on woolens shown in Table 3. It will be observed that the woolens minimums introduced a new principle not associated with the cotton minimums, namely, the establishment of value brackets. The cotton provisions represented a simple, distinct minimum for each of three different kinds of cotton manufacture—cotton cloths, uncolored yarn, and colored yarn. All cot-

TABLE 3

RATE (PER CENT)		VALUE (PER SQUARE YARD)	
Initial	After June 30 1829	Actual	Dutiable
40	45	$0.50 or less	$0.50
40	45	Over $0.50 but not over $1.00	1.00
40	45	Over $1.00 but not over $2.50	2.50
40	45	Over $2.50 but not over $4.00	4.00
45	50	$4.00	Actual value

ton articles whose actual value was above the minimum paid duty upon actual value. But, in the case of woolens, no article below the luxury level of $4.00 per yard was dutiable upon actual value except in the rare and unlikely event of actual valuation at the top of a given class. Thus an article valued at $1.25 paid duty on $2.50, or the equivalent of 90 per cent under the permanent rate. One wonders what the Tariff of Abominations might have been labeled had the members of the Harrisburg Convention succeeded in obtaining the omission of the $1.00 breaking point; in such case an article worth $0.51 would have paid duty on $2.50, or an actual ad valorem equivalent of nearly 225 per cent.[29] Yet one woolens spokesman in Congress bitterly termed

29. It is apparent that the woolens minimums, although obviously the precursor to the modern value-bracket system, were of a different species. The modern device is a system of *classification* by value brackets; the woolens minimums represented a system of *valuation* by value brackets (although in the case of the highest bracket it also changed the classification). By adopting this series of fictitious values for woolens the Tariff of Abominations achieved not only the concealment and additional protection conferred by the simple minimums for cottons but ex-

the inclusion of the $1.00 breaking point as a blow which "falls into the center of the great body of American business."[30]

Perhaps equally disappointing to the woolens group, however demonstrative of retributive justice, were the heavy increases, under new compound duties, of the taxes on imports of raw wool used by the manufacturers, which were supported as a last resort by the antiprotectionists (with the ostensible purpose of protecting domestic woolgrowers) for taking the profit out of the newly obtained minimums on woolen products. A still further disappointment to the woolens men was the later ruling by the Secretary of the Treasury that the customary 10 and 20 per cent differentials were not to be added to the minimum valuations. This was a proper ruling in view of the fictitious nature of the valuations, but the protectionists thought that by making the duties ad valorem in form the differentials would automatically be added. The woolen interests were able, nevertheless, to have incorporated into the general valuation section an arbitrary provision that all manufactures of which wool was a component part, imported in an unfinished condition, "shall be taken, deemed, and estimated. . . as of as great value as if the same had been entirely finished."

One early result of the Tariff of Abominations was a revival of the charges and countercharges concerning alleged "frauds upon the revenue." It cannot be denied that the exorbitant rates of duty under the minimum provisions furnished a powerful incentive for undervaluation. In addition to the pecuniary incentives to fraud, because of the serious sectional and ideological division on the score of the tariff—particularly after 1828—an indignation was felt by many which was transformed into a disrespect for the tariff, with its prohibitive features, not unlike the sentiment against the National Prohibition Act of a century later. It was stated on the floor of Congress and elsewhere that the indifference to the enforcement of the revenue laws was aided and abetted by newspapers that made light of the whole subject of evasion. It was said to be well-nigh impossible to get a jury to convict for revenue frauds, even upon abundant evidence. Admissions were

tended their effectiveness throughout the entire range of woolen manufactures. The term "minimum" throughout the period under discussion was applied to the duties on both cottons and woolens, in the later case denoting any breaking point between brackets. The use of the term hereinafter should be clear from the foregoing and from the appropriate context.

30. Cf. Taussig, *op. cit.*, p. 95, n. 1.

regretfully made that the dishonesty and corruption which were to be expected of foreigners had spread to American merchants and importers as well. Even the Treasury Department was cited for indifference to law enforcement by overruling collectors who were desirous of doing their duty.[31]

A not uninteresting feature of the acrimonious discussions upon the "revenue frauds" is the patent fact that neither side to the controversy —least of all, those who laid claim to the greatest concern on the score —was seriously perturbed about this aspect of the question. But the terms "fraud" and "revenue" were convenient shibboleths to which lip service could be paid with appropriate piety and righteousness.[32] The complete insincerity of the majority of protectionists in the matter was evident from the threefold set of circumstances well known to them that (1) government revenue during this period was redundant more often than not, sometimes becoming a positive embarrassment and requiring pork-barrel methods of distribution; (2) the way to increase revenue, if needed, was not to extinguish it by prohibitive duties, but to gear the tariff to "the revenue standard"; (3) the revenue argument was used largely in desperation to defend the constitutionality of tariff protection.

There is no doubt that many devices, both legal and illegal, were resorted to in order to bring valuations below the appropriate minimum. One of the commonest types of fraudulent undervaluation was the familiar double invoice, already referred to. The practice was allegedly so common that importers had difficulty keeping track of their invoices and frequently made the mistake of selling their merchandise on the basis of the fictitious invoice, discovering later, to their dismay, that they had actually lost money on the transaction![33] Another ingenious and technically legal device was one currently used in the evasion of price ceilings, namely, a verbal tying agreement with the foreign manufacturer or seller. A buyer abroad would be quoted a given price per yard for a large stock of goods. He would thereupon

31. Cf. speech of Mr. Mallary, April 15, 1830, in *Congressional Debates*, VI, Part II, 795.

32. A typical statement is the following, made by Mr. Ellsworth of New York at the New York Convention of Manufacturers in 1831: "This difference caused the government to lose no less than $400 on every one of those bales. It was thus that our manufacturers were deceived and betrayed" (*Niles' Weekly Register*, XLI [November 12, 1831], 202).

33. Speech by Mr. Mallary, *op. cit.*, p. 797.

offer to purchase the entire stock in two parts, the one invoiced substantially below the asking price, the other at a corresponding price above. The seller would of course receive his aggregate asking price and the buyer could import one half of the goods "honestly" invoiced below the normally applicable minimum and supported by sworn testimony and consular authentication as to the price actually paid. The other half of the goods could then be resold abroad, possibly to another importer, at the usual price or else shipped in another vessel to another port of entry. Frequently the undervalued invoice would pass as market value and escape the higher minimum. In any event, by virtue of the sworn and authenticated invoice the importer would escape the 50 per cent penalty for suspected undervaluation.

Akin to this was the practice of averaging the prices of goods of several grades imported in the same package. The packages were made up in such a way that the average value of the goods per yard was just below the minimum, and all were invoiced at the average price. The invoice was duly sworn and the goods all entered on that basis. Only one in fifty[34] packages covered by a given invoice was required by law to be opened and inspected by the appraisers. The designated packages would often await appraisement for weeks or even months. The remainder of the shipment, after the posting of bond for duties, was released from customs custody and promptly auctioned off or disposed of through other commercial channels. If the average price failed to hold as the appraised value for all the goods and the dutiable value of the better grades was raised above the minimum, the importer was no worse off than he would have been had the different grades been invoiced and entered at their several real prices. If forfeiture for fraudulent undervaluation was decreed, only the designated package was forfeit. With duties often well over 100 per cent, the importer could still come out ahead on a partial forfeiture.[35]

---

34. At first made one in fifty by sec. 22 of the Appraisement Act of 1818, the inspection requirements were increased to one in twenty by sec. 4 of the act of May 28, 1830. Current requirements are one in ten, subject to specific exemptions for classes of merchandise as allowed by the Secretary of the Treasury.

35. Importers felt that they were morally, if not legally, entitled to the use of "averaging" procedure in order not to "waste" any allowable value remaining for goods whose values were below a given breaking point. For example, a buyer abroad might purchase one thousand yards each of two different designs of woolen goods, one normally priced by the foreign manufacturer at 90 cents per square yard, the other at $1.05. The manufacturer would logically be willing to sell and

In order to stem these abuses, Chairman Mallary of the Committee on Manufactures introduced a bill calling for the addition of four assistant appraisers at New York (the port subject to the greatest criticism) and two each at Boston and Philadelphia. The collector was to have power, when he deemed the appraisement too low, to order reappraisement either by the principal appraiser or by two merchants, one chosen by him and one by the importer. Reappraisement was also obtainable by the importer, upon appeal in writing to the collector, stating reasons why he considered the appraisement too high. In case of disagreement, the two merchants were to agree on an umpire to decide. All cotton and woolen products were to be held in customs custody until appraisement was made. If the designated packages contained any undervalued articles, the remainder of the shipment was to be inspected. Also, packages containing goods of different quality were to be appraised at the value of the best article in the package. The 50 per cent penalty valuation for fraudulent undervaluation was abolished and forfeiture of the goods substituted. Distribution of forfeitures under the moieties system was continued with the specific proviso that appraisers were not to share therein. The bill was passed on May 28, 1830.[36]

Probably the greatest hardship imposed by this law was the provision that the value of the best article in the package was to be taken as the average of the whole package. Commercial practice, as well as economy in packing and shipping of many goods, such as laces, required the packing of several grades together. Many importers were unable to notify their suppliers abroad in time to change their packing procedure before the effective date of the law (October 1, 1830), thus subjecting many importations, properly and honestly invoiced, to excessive duties. Congress provided at least partial relief in the act of March 2, 1831,[37] which retroactively exempted all importations prior to January 1, of that year, from the operation of the provision, provided due diligence was proved to the satisfaction of the collector.

But the state of the Union was not a happy one in the year 1831, and

---

invoice both grades at 97½ cents, especially if a long-term contract might result. The importer would then, if successful in passing his goods on this basis, pay duties of 45 per cent on $2,000, or $900, instead of 45 per cent on $3,500, or $1,575, thus saving $675 in duties which he felt represented "tribute" to domestic manufacturers.

36. 4 U.S. Statutes 409.   37. *Ibid.*, p. 451.

no administrative change could have sufficed to avert the inevitable showdown on tariff policy. Meetings and conventions were held in all parts of the country, pleading the respective cases for and against protection. The southern states, the rural portions of the northern and western states, and the shipping and mercantile interests of the New England states, were all predominantly antiprotectionist but had a minority in Congress. South Carolina, under the leadership of McDuffie and Calhoun, was adamant in her stand that the use of the taxing power to confer special benefits upon manufacturers at the expense of the consumers, under the guise of collecting revenue, was unconstitutional. Her demand was a return of tariff legislation to the revenue standard, namely, a level of duties no higher than necessary to yield sufficient revenue to defray the reasonable and legitimate expenses of government.

The Tariff Act of 1832 was a partial concession to the ominous rumblings of secession. It abolished the minimum system on woolens,[38] which was regarded by the woolens men themselves as being unsatisfactory, substituting ad valorem rates of 50 per cent, and in some cases specific or compound rates, depending upon the material. It made a number of reductions in other areas, mitigating the more notable "abominations," and in general reflecting the results of antiprotectionist pressure.[39] A permanent improvement in the basis for dutiable value was made by section 4, which eliminated the long-standing 10 and 20 per cent differentials by repealing them specifically from "any act of Congress." They were never restored as such, although later tariffs contained similar geographical differentials as discrimination on goods carried in foreign bottoms, subject to removal by treaties of reciprocity.[40]

38. Professor Taussig was in error in stating that "the entire minimum system was abolished" (*op. cit.*, p. 103). The cotton minimums were retained.

39. "In fact, the protective system was put back, in the main, to where it had been in 1824. The result was to clear the tariff of the excrescences which had grown on it in 1828 and to put it in a form in which the protectionists could advocate its permanent retention" (*ibid.*, p. 105).

40. E.g., sec. 11 of the Tariff Act of 1842 provided, subject to treaty obligations, for an additional duty of 10 per cent on all importations in foreign vessels and a further addition of 10 per cent on such importations from any port or place east of Good Hope. The opening of the Suez Canal rendered the Good Hope rule obsolete, and it was repealed, effective May 4, 1882, by 22 U.S. Statutes 58, c. 120. Since the later discriminations applied to goods subject to specific duties and those on the free list, they were not a revival of those which were discontinued in 1832, as indicated in Tariff Commission, *American Valuation*, p. 21.

A curious reversion to the "actual-cost" basis of dutiable value appeared in section 15:

> . . . The ad valorem rates of duty on goods . . . shall be estimated in the manner following: to the actual cost, if the same shall have been actually purchased, or the actual value, if the same shall have been procured otherwise than by purchase, at the time when and where purchased, or otherwise procured, or to the appraised value, if appraised, shall be added all charges, except insurance.

In view of the fact that, by section 7, appraisement on the basis of "actual value" was mandatory for all ad valorem goods and that section 15 provided for the addition of charges "to the appraised value, if appraised," it is difficult to see wherein the "actual cost" would be applied. Its inclusion was possibly the result of the unconsidered incorporation of wording used in the provision in effect prior to 1828.

Of greater significance for this study than the act itself is the fact that the first important discussion of the "home valuation" principle on the floor of Congress occurred during the debates on the 1832 tariff bill. The possibilities of home valuation had been called to the attention of Congress at some length by Secretary Ingham in his annual report for 1830 recommending its adoption. He based his recommendations largely upon the alleged defects of foreign valuation and the supposition that some kind of home valuation would overcome its difficulties. His objections to foreign-market value were for the most part specious, the same criticisms, in many instances, applying a fortiori to any kind of home valuation. The following is a condensation of Ingham's citation of the consequences of foreign valuation:

1. Lack of uniformity of duties at different ports because of differences in available information and abilities of appraisers at the nearly one hundred separate custom houses.
2. Inequity to importers, consumers, and the government, in connection with price fluctuations of the imported goods in this country. Depressed prices compelled the importer to absorb part or all of the duty, often resulting in failure, with loss to the government; advanced prices under brisk demand compelled consumers to pay "not only the duty but nearly as great a price . . . as if the duty were laid on true value at the place of importation," thus conferring on the importer "a portion of what ought to accrue to the government."
3. Bestowing advantage upon those with special opportunities for purchasing goods abroad, namely, foreigners, who were able, particularly under the minimum system, successfully to purchase and/or invoice goods at figures giving conclusive advantage.

4. Loss and inequity resulting from currency conversion problems, because of either depreciated currencies or differences in "the relative values of gold and silver, as established by the different nations."[41]

The idea of home valuation was well received by domestic interests. Even before the discussions on the 1832 bill, it was considered as a potentially fruitful device to be resorted to when circumstances became propitious.[42] Accordingly, no time was lost when the 1832 bill reached the floor of the House. Valuation "in the principal markets of the United States" was proposed by Mr. Jewett,[43] apparently only for application to woolen manufactures and as a substitute for the minimums which were removed by this act. The proposal was voted down, later to be introduced with reference to the woolen section by Mr. Davis of Massachusetts, who proposed "the current wholesale market value thereof in the principal markets of the United States."[44] It was at this time that John Quincy Adams, who sponsored the 1832 tariff bill, gave the home-valuation principle his indorsement, stating that the abandonment of the minimums was conditioned upon the change to home valuation, that its purpose was to overcome fraud, and that it presented no difficulties which could not be overcome. It is apparent from the record, however, that Mr. Adams was unfamiliar with the ramifications of the principle involved. Mr. Cambreleng of New York, an ardent advocate of low duties, if not of free trade, pointed out that home valuation of necessity contemplated the payment of a duty upon a duty, stating that it would raise duties to 95 per cent, would operate as a prohibitory clause, and was altogether "too monstrous a proposition to be debated by reasonable men."[45]

The most detailed criticism of home valuation in this series of debates was presented by Mr. Dayan of New York. He stated that the

41. Discussion of the several issues involved is omitted at this juncture in view of later developments in the history of customs valuation, as well as the explicit treatment *infra*, Part III. The complete remarks of Secretary Ingham may be found in U.S. Tariff Commission, *American Valuation*, p. 26.
42. Cf. minutes of the New York Convention of Manufacturers in 1831, in *Niles' Weekly Register*, XL (November 12, 1831), 203: "Mr. Brown: Valuation here would effectually remedy the evil [undervaluation]. . . . Present rate of duties would be found too high if applied to the value of goods here. They would amount to a prohibition. For his own part he would not oppose a prohibitory duty; . . . it would involve the whole question of the tariff, which he had considered would not be expedient at this time."
43. *Congressional Debates*, VIII, Part II, 3654.
44. *Ibid.*, p. 3656.   45. *Ibid.*, p. 3657.

adoption of home valuation would place the importer at the mercy of domestic interests, that the latter would manipulate supply in the home market to raise values and duties during periods of heavy importation, and that there would be hopeless confusion in the determination of the principal markets of the United States. He inquired how the proponents of home valuation proposed to reconcile widely divergent prices in Charleston, New York, Philadelphia, and Baltimore and what kind of average would be used to obtain a satisfactory valuation. He posed an interesting problem in monopsony as well as in monopoly by stating that the woolen manufacturers, by restricting the supply of cloth in the market, not only would increase the valuation of wolen products but would simultaneously depress the prices of wool and control the woolgrowers as well as the importers.[46] Mr. Burges of Rhode Island replied to the effect that he was against the home-valuation amendment for substantially opposite reasons, that no real control over market prices in this country would be exercised by domestic interests, but that in "the eternal war waged against them by the English manufacturers" the latter would prevail by their predatory dumping techniques:

> ... An English manufacturer, by throwing suddenly upon the market a large quantity of goods, could at once reduce the market value below even the cost of the goods. Having thus accomplished a fall in price, there was nothing to prevent him from making still further larger shipments, upon which, as the duty was to be paid at the market value, he would pay the lowest duty, and afterward could, by holding over, realize his own prices. He rather thought that the foreign valuation, when prices were more equally made, in places not subject to the danger of such a fluctuation, would be more safe for the home manufacturer.[47]

By this time Mr. Adams was apparently convinced that the home-valuation principle was unsound, and he abandoned it.[48] But in view

46. *Ibid.*, p. 3777.

47. *Ibid.*, p. 3779.

48. "Mr. Adams said ... he had not understood that it was his colleague's intention ... to include in the market valuation the duty upon the article. The effect of that part of the amendment had been demonstrated most forcibly by the gentleman from South Carolina to be most unjust in principle—a duty upon a duty being a thing unknown in any country in the world. He must therefore vote against it" (*ibid.*, p. 3777). This reaction of Mr. Adams is not quoted in citations to his support of the home-valuation measure in 1832 (cf. U.S. Tariff Commission, *American Valuation*, p. 19; cf. also Taussig, *op. cit.*, p. 105, n. 1; also Larkin, *op. cit.*, pp. 79–80).

of the many complaints "that frauds were committed in consequence of the foreign valuations, and by which the drab-gaitered gentry, as they were called, monopolized the trade to the exclusion of the American merchant," he prepared a measure which "would obviate the objection of the manufacturers, and secure the Government in the duties ... by making it the interest of the importer of the foreign goods to make fair and honest returns of the value of his woolens, or take the consequences." This was a proposal, based upon English practice, to have the government arbitrarily take goods deemed to be undervalued, pay the importer 10 per cent above the appraised value, and sell them at auction. This proposal, though possessing all the attributes of "poetic" justice, could not be said to satisfy either the canons of practical justice or sound administration, to say nothing of the due-process clause, and was voted down.[49]

This first congressional discussion of home valuation is of interest as exhibiting considerable confusion over both the nature and the consequences of "home valuation." The difference of opinion as to whether the importing or domestic interests would control valuations, although partly based on prejudice, was the result of a failure to distinguish between the selling price of the imported article ("domestic value" in present-day terminology) and that of the domestically produced article ("American selling price"). The substantial difference between these two, as to both the price levels and the element of control, were perhaps implicit in the sentiments of the debaters; but because of the novelty of the proposal and the fact that the discussion ran largely in terms of woolen goods, where the elements of similarity were perhaps greater than for imports as a whole, the distinction was never explicitly made. The discussion also served to indicate the ideological alignment of protectionists on the side of home valuation,

49. This proposal as a suggested means of combatting undervaluation cropped up repeatedly during the nineteenth century. It was later, in more severe form, incorporated as section 9 of the tariff bill of 1846 but was struck out at the last minute before the bill's passage; cf. Edward Stanwood, *Tariff Controversies in the Nineteenth Century* (Boston, 1903), II, 79: "The ninth section provided a new remedy against undervaluation." At this time the proposal was to pay the "declared value" plus 5 per cent. Mr. Benton strongly opposed the clause, declaring it unconstitutional, and, upon Mr. Webster's motion, the whole section was struck out. Far from being a "new" remedy, this was first proposed, as an optional penalty, by Secretary Dallas in his special report to Congress of February 12, 1816 (cf. *American State Papers: Finance*, III, 85–99). For discussion of the defects of the pre-emption system cf. *infra*, p. 313, n. 45, and references cited.

however defined, and the opponents of protection as definitely opposed to it.

The changes wrought by the act of 1832 were mere palliatives in the eyes of the opponents of protection, and, on November 24 of that year, South Carolina issued the famous Nullification Ordinance, declaring the Tariff Acts of 1828 and 1832, from and after February 1, 1833, null and void and no law in the state of South Carolina. The Nullification Ordinance was not an act of the state legislature but the product of a special convention of the people of South Carolina. The convention was called by special act of the legislature and was presided over by the governor for the purpose of determining and effectuating the "sovereign will of the people," an important feature in the constitutional issue. Accompanying the publication of the Nullification Ordinance, was the "Address to the People of the United States by the Convention of South Carolina," presenting a "clear and distinct exposition of the principles" upon which the ordinance was based. There is no doubt that, despite its weaknesses in both economic[50] and political theory, this frank appeal to sentiments of justice, coupled with the evident determination to execute the purposes of the convention, must have modified the attitudes of many who had previously found themselves aligned on the side of protection. Certainly it was clear to thoughtful men that the continuation of the Union was at stake and that, if civil war with South Carolina should ensue, it might easily spread to adjacent states.

The convention left the way open to conciliation:

Having now presented, for the consideration of the Federal Government and our confederate States, the fixed and final determination of this State in relation to the protecting system, it remains for us to submit a plan of taxation in which we would be willing to acquiesce. . . .

. . . .

With a distinct declaration that it is a concession on our part, we will consent that the same rate of duty may be imposed upon the protected articles that shall be upon the unprotected, provided that no more revenue be raised

---

50. The economic argument in the nullification papers was in the main correct, namely, that the tariff reduced the export of cotton and other agricultural staples of South Carolina and that it turned the terms of trade against her with respect to her purchase of both domestic and foreign goods. The error lay chiefly in the quantitative estimate of the damage done. The "Address to the People," as well as Jackson's proclamation, and related papers on nullification can be found in *Congressional Debates*, IX, Part II, Appen., 145–202.

than is necessary to meet the demands of the Government for Constitutional purposes, and provided also, that a duty, substantially uniform, be imposed upon all foreign imports.

The Nullification Ordinance was in effect an ultimatum to Congress either to reduce duties to the revenue standard or to prepare for secession at the first sign of forcible federal intervention. The third alternative, federal acquiescence in nullification, was unthinkable. Even before the convention had met, the Secretary of the Treasury had anticipated the result and, in a confidential letter of instructions to the collector at the port of Charleston on November 6, had given him wide latitude for the handling of any eventuality which might arise.[51] The collector was instructed to continue the full execution of the revenue laws and, if expedient, to remove the seat of customs administration for the district to Castle Pinckney or such other place as would permit the effective discharge of his duties. He was advised to utilize the full assistance of the federal courts and of the revenue cutters already assigned and en route to his district. All incoming vessels were to be boarded by a sufficient number of officers and inspectors as soon as possible after entering the district and required to comply with all requirements of entry, including the securing of duties, before receiving landing permits.

These instructions reflected President Jackson's determination to preserve the integrity of the Union and were followed by similar instructions by the War and Navy departments to officers in the field to prepare for possible action. On December 10, President Jackson issued his celebrated proclamation[52] refuting the constitutional, and

51. *Ibid.* This letter, which was dispatched shortly after the convention had been called by the state legislature, may also be found in *Niles' Weekly Register,* XLIV (March 2, 1833), 15–16.

52. The proclamation—which should be required reading for all students of constitutional, as well as tariff, history—was apparently written by Livingstone, Jackson's Secretary of State. "It was written by Livingstone, who as we have seen, had taken up a position against nullification more than two years before. . . . Jackson did not like the constitutional doctrines of the proclamation, which are Madisonian federalist, and not such as he held, but he let it go on account of lack of time to modify it" (William Graham Sumner, *Andrew Jackson* ["American Statesmen"] [Boston, 1900], p. 328). But Parton, Jackson's biographer, indicates with a dramatic flourish that Jackson himself was largely responsible: "Though he regarded those proceedings as the fruit of John C. Calhoun's treasonable ambition . . . he rose, on this occasion, above personal considerations. . . . He went to his office alone, and began to dash off page after page of the remarkable Proclamation which was soon to electrify the country. . . . The warmth, the glow, the passion and

to some extent the economic, arguments advanced in the nullification papers and pleading with the people of South Carolina to abstain from rash action inspired by false leaders. He indicated that even then Congress had gathered to consider action which might well remove much of the basis for conflict but that in any case he was determined, as chief magistrate, faithfully to execute the laws of the United States.

Under the circumstances, the protectionist majority in Congress showed a willingness to concede the wisdom, if not the justice, of conciliation. Two measures were proposed: one, a drastic increase of federal powers for enforcing the collection laws, known as the Force Bill; the other, a bill to reduce duties. Henry Clay, anxious to perfect his role as "the Great Compromiser," begun in 1820, was working on a bill which was substituted for the House bill and eventually passed. On the surface of it, the bill seemed to meet the demands of South Carolina. It reduced all duties by successive reductions to 20 per cent by July 1, 1842. After four biennial reductions of 10 per cent of the excess over 20 per cent, beginning on January 1, 1834, the remaining excess was to be dropped within a six-month period—half on January 1, and half on July 1, 1842. It is thus apparent that no substantial reduction was to occur until more than nine years later. The bill also provided that from and after July 1, 1842, all duties would be payable in cash and that such duties "shall be laid for the purpose of raising revenue for the economical administration of the government." All conflicting portions of former acts were repealed, and interim adjustments of rates to meet revenue needs, prior to 1842, were subject to the proviso that no such rates should exceed 20 per cent.

When Clay introduced his bill, everyone seemed to be agreeable to its passage in order to put an end to the dispute. But he had committed himself to the introduction of an amendment which provided for home valuation after June 30, 1842, and it was this amendment which came nearest to scuttling the whole bill.[53] The amendment provided

---

eloquence of that proclamation, were produced then and there by the President's own hand." Parton continues, saying that Jackson gave the manuscript to Livingstone to put in proper "form," that Livingstone returned the draft three days later, but that Jackson was not in agreement with certain passages and requested alterations. "This was done, and the second draft being satisfactory, he ordered it to be published" (James Parton, *Life of Andrew Jackson* [New York, 1860], III, 466).

53. For the discussions upon the home-valuation amendment to the Compromise Act cf. *Congressional Debates*, IX, Part I, 694–709.

that duties on all goods after June 30, 1842, "shall be assessed upon the value thereof at the port where the same shall be entered, under such regulations as may be prescribed by law." Calhoun, who had apparently agreed with Clay in advance to accept the amendment if necessary, rose to state that he hoped that neither the friends nor the opponents of the proposal, which he termed "merely a speculative point open for future legislation," would allow their differences to stand in the way of the major objective. Nevertheless, violent opposition to the amendment was voiced by the southern members, who claimed that it was a further discrimination against the South, calculated to draw the entire import trade to New York, since goods "were known to be at all times cheaper in New York than the commercial cities south of it."[54] It was denounced as unequal, unjust, impracticable, productive of confusion, and a thinly disguised attempt by "the great pacificator" to raise duties with one hand while "offering the olive branch" with the other. Clay defended the amendment on the grounds that

we do not adopt it now; only the principle, leaving it to future legislation. . . . Besides it would be the restoration of an ancient principle, known since the foundation of the government. It was but at the last session that the discriminating duties of 10 and 20 per cent, from this side, and beyond the Cape of Good Hope, were repealed. On what principle was it, said he, that these discriminations ever prevailed? On the principle of home valuation. Frauds make the amendment necessary.[55]

Clay thus placed the modified "landed-cost" basis, for dutiable value originally in effect, in the category of home valuation, justifying the shift to domestic value, proposed by the amendment, on the grounds of administrative necessity for prevention of undervaluation.

Mr. Calhoun then declared that home valuation in any form would be unsatisfactory; that a true landed-cost basis of value violated the constitution because it resulted in different duties at different ports, giving some a preference over others; that the market price in this country was even worse because it included many additional variables over and above transportation costs; and, finally, that it required the payment of a duty upon a duty. In spite of this, however, he would vote for the amendment in order to put an end to the discussion.[56]

54. *Ibid.*, p. 695.   55. *Ibid.*
56. Calhoun, as well as the majority, appeared to be anxious to settle the whole issue as quickly as possible by any legislative act, however unsatisfactory for the

Daniel Webster stated that, as far as he was concerned, home valuation, to any extent, was "impracticable, unprecedented, and unknown in any legislation." He went on to state that the "great vice" of the compromise bill was the fact that it converted all specific duties to ad valorem rates, opening the way for gross frauds under either home or foreign valuation.

But the amendment was insisted upon by the more rabid protectionists, chiefly Mr. Clayton of Delaware, and the amended bill passed the Senate by 29 to 16 votes and the House by 119 to 85. Both the Compromise Act and the Force Bill were passed March 3, 1833, the date when the 1832 Tariff Act would have become effective. The leading nullifiers, in a special meeting, had extended the February 1 deadline of their ultimatum to the date of the adjournment of Congress, in view of the pending legislation. Calhoun hurried home immediately after March 3 and persuaded the nullifiers into acceptance of the Compromise Act as a reasonable redress of their wrongs. The nullifiers then withdrew the Nullification Ordinance but, as a parting shot, declared the Force Bill null and void.

Declining Duties—1833–61

The administration of the Compromise Act placed a special burden upon the machinery of customs valuation. As indicated above, all specific duties were, in effect, converted to an ad valorem basis by virtue of the terms of the requirement of periodic percentage reductions. The Treasury Department, by its circular of April 20, 1833, instructed collectors to apply immediately the same methods of valuation to goods subject to specific duties as to those under ad valorem rates.[57] This resulted in the accumulation of valuation data upon which to estimate the ad valorem equivalents of specific duties during the base year, 1833, a prerequisite to the reduction procedure. The lower the initial computed ad valorem equivalent, the lower would be the rate of duty at any stage in the reduction process until the 20 per cent level

---

long run, which would save face for all concerned. Clay himself believed that the act would be superseded before 1842 (cf. Taussig, *op. cit.*, p. 112, n. 1).

57. Although free goods and those subject to specific duties were supposedly appraised in order to comply with the Statistical Act of 1820, such appraisement was probably perfunctory in view of its irrelevance to the actual collection of duties.

was reached. It was therefore to the long-run advantage of importers of goods subject to other than ad valorem duties to receive a high appraisement upon their imports during the base year. In the case of goods subject to minimum valuations, the problem of the Treasury Department was whether to take the actual or the minimum valuations during the base year as the basis for computation. The department chose the former on the ground that the intent of Congress was to reduce the actual tariff burden from its initial position. This was perhaps the correct interpretation, but it penalized the importer by using the artificial minimum valuation when it was to his disadvantage and rejecting its use when it would have been to his advantage. As a result, the duty on cotton cloth subject to a nominal 25 per cent rate and purchased abroad at 8½ cents per yard in 1833, was still 70 per cent ad valorem on December 31, 1841, more than nine years after the Compromise Act was passed. The use of the minimum valuation of 35 cents for the base year would have resulted in a duty of 23 per cent in 1841.[58]

Whatever the defects of the Compromise Act, both in content and form, it accomplished its fundamental purpose. It restored domestic tranquillity to the national scene and removed the tariff as a major political issue for a space of nearly ten years.[59] During this period both imports and exports reached a new peak,[60] and revenue was more than adequate for federal needs. Despite temporary embarrassments, national economic development and prosperity grew rapidly, and, after twelve years of Jacksonian Democracy, the Secretary of the Treasury was moved to say, in his annual report for 1840: "Regarded as an indication either of the good state of the national credit, or the ample resources of the General Government, or the discreet legislation rela-

58. The rate of duty, R, for any article subject to a specific duty during the base year, may be computed for any stage in the reduction process, as follows:

$$R = 0.20 + Y \left(\frac{D}{V} - 0.20 \right)$$

where $D =$ initial specific or minimum duty; $V =$ initial valuation; and $Y =$ percentage of the excess over 20 per cent remaining at a given stage in the reduction process. Since $D/V =$ the initial rate of duty, it is obvious that subsequent rates would vary inversely with the size of V.

59. There were, of course, other factors working toward the same end (cf. Wright, *op. cit.*, p. 396).

60. In 1836 total imports were valued at $190 million. This figure was not exceeded until 1851.

tive to its fiscal concerns, it will be difficult to discover many eras more prosperous in these respects, whether in the annals of this or any other country." The periodic duty reductions proceeded according to schedule, and the year 1842 arrived with the Compromise Act unchanged.[61]

As the time for the drastic duty reductions approached, to be followed by home valuation under the horizontal 20 per cent duty scale, there was much uncertainty in business and commercial circles. In anticipation of the reductions scheduled in 1842, importations dropped substantially below their previous trend. The resultant contraction in federal income, in addition to the heavy disbursements in the distribution of the proceeds of the public lands to the states, left the Treasury virtually destitute of funds. Moreover, the accession of the Whigs to power in 1841 indicated a change in tariff policy and an almost certain increase in duties. Added to these circumstances was the Treasury Department's concern over the impending change to home valuation, involving a complete departure from the principles and rules adopted during a half-century of tariff administration. In the absence of specific legislation to implement home valuation the Treasury would be obliged not only to adopt a wholly new body of administrative techniques and procedures but, by executive action, to assume the role theretofore jealously guarded by Congress in creating what were believed to be substantive provisions of law.[62]

The concern of the Treasury is well expressed in the annual report for 1841:

Hitherto, throughout the whole history of the Government, the cost or value in the foreign market has been assumed as the basis for the calculation of ad valorem duties, and to this cost or value certain additions have been made, supposed to be equivalent to the charges of importation ... if Congress shall not at this session prescribe regulations for assessing duties upon a valuation to be made at the port of entry, or pass some law modifying the

61. The act of September 11, 1841, was largely a revenue measure, raising all duties, with specified exceptions, to 20 per cent and establishing the similitude clause for non-enumerated articles.

62. It will be recalled that the administration of home valuation was to be accomplished "under such regulations as may be prescribed by law." An attempt had been made during the debates on the compromise bill to delete the word "law" and insert the words "the Secretary of the Treasury, with the approbation of the President of the United States." This was rejected, Mr. Clay stating that the object of his proposal was "to leave it to a future Congress to act in detail, on the principle of the home valuation amendment." Other objections were that it would give "the President and his Secretary too much power over the principle" (*Congressional Debates*, IX, Part I, 711–13).

act of 1833, it may well be questioned whether any ad valorem duties can be collected after the 30th of June. . . . In support of this opinion he would first mention the great, if not insurmountable difficulties of establishing a home valuation at our various ports, without incurring the risk of producing such diversity in the estimates of value as should not only lead to practical inconvenience, but interfere, also, in effect, with the constitutional provision that the duties on imports shall be equal in all the States.[63]

Congress, however, was unready to come to any conclusions respecting the tariff. Calhoun, still in the Senate, denounced any attempt to change the basic principles of the Compromise Act as an unholy breach of faith. He took the position that the South had waited patiently for nine long years to reap the fruits of the act, and that now, on the very eve of their realization, it was proposed to snatch them away. On the other hand, he was opposed to home valuation, which he declared unconstitutional. This opinion was fairly generally held. Senator Rives, of Virginia, a moderate with respect to the tariff, urged that home valuation be abandoned and that a nominal increase in rates be given, equivalent to the increase contemplated by home valuation.[64]

Meanwhile, the first major valuation scandal of the nineteenth century had broken out in the New York Custom House. A special commission, appointed by the Secretary of the Treasury with the approval of the President, had been at work for almost a year gathering testimony and preparing its report. On April 30, 1842, President Tyler communicated the bulk of the findings, which ultimately consisted of more than two thousand pages of testimony and report, to the House for their disposition by effecting any needed legislation.[65]

63. U.S. Treasury, *Annual Report, 1841,* pp. 464–66.

64. *Congressional Globe,* XI, 216, speech of March 24, 1842: "By agreeing that the duty should be assessed upon the home, instead of the foreign value or invoice price of the article imported, it was certainly intended that the duty should be calculated on a higher value, which should have the same effect in the practical result as increasing the rate of duty. . . . The difference between home and market value is variously computed at from 20 to 30 per cent advance upon the foreign cost."

65. Cf. *House Document No. 212* (27th Cong., 2d sess.). Dissension between the two principal commissioners, former Governor Poindexter of Mississippi and Colonel William M. Steuart, resulted in the writing of separate reports. Both concur in finding widespread corruption, attributable largely to Collector Jesse Hoyt, a Tammany politician appointed during the Van Buren administration. Among the irregularities charged against Mr. Hoyt in one or both reports were: defalcation of large sums of public money; deposit of public funds in a bank known to be unsound while personally speculating in the bank's stock; padding of expense

The principal charge against the New York Custom House was the systematic oppression of importers of woolen goods by harsh and summary condemnation of goods on the ground of fraudulent undervaluation. During 1839 there were numerous seizures of woolens which had been duty paid and cleared through the custom house from one to fourteen months previously. The custom-house "raids" on merchandise cleared through the port of New York extended as far south as Baltimore. A number of the resultant suits were won by the importers, a number by the government, and others were compromised under dubious circumstances. In view of the collector's share in the distribution of the forfeitures, testimony indicating collusion between domestic manufacturers and the collector, and conflicting opinions of appraisers as to the fact and extent of undervaluation, the charges of oppression seem to be substantiated. On the other hand, there is no doubt that some fraudulent, as well as much technical, undervaluation did exist. The chief offenders in this respect were the woolen manufacturers of Saddleworth, Yorkshire, England—known to the trade as the Yorkshiremen—who maintained resident partners or agents in New York for the importation and entry of their goods. All the goods for the English market were sold in the unfinished condition. Goods for the United States were finished and invoiced at low figures to the agents in this country. The question of fraudulent undervaluation appears to have turned largely on the issue of whether the "sales" were bona fide or non–bona fide. It will be recalled that section 15 of the 1832 Tariff Act based dutiable value on "actual cost" in the case of goods actually purchased but that for goods acquired other-

---

accounts and falsifying public vouchers; personal enrichment by control of the public warehouse and cartage business; and the levy of political tribute in behalf of Tammany Hall upon subordinate officers and personnel in the custom house as a condition of retention in office. The Poindexter report is the longer of the two reports and, despite its tendency to exaggeration, seems to have been preferred by the House Committee on Public Expenditures. The committee reported the Poindexter version to the House with the statement: "It is believed that the wickedness of public officers herein exposed is unparalleled in the history of any civilized Government; and public interest, the interest of the injured and unjustly oppressed citizens, and, above all, public honor, imperiously demand a remedy at the hands of Representatives of the people." Colonel Steuart concluded that domestic manufacturers had not used illegal influence upon appraisement proceedings at the custom house. For additional material on the investigation see *House Document No. 77, No. 213, and No. 230,* (27th Cong., 3d sess.); *House Report No. 669* (27th Cong., 2d sess.); *Senate Report No. 83* (27th Cong., 3d sess.); and *Senate Document No. 196* (27th Cong., 3d sess.).

wise than by purchase the actual "value" was to obtain. Upon examination in court it appeared that virtually all the transactions from Saddleworth, purporting to be sales at low prices, were non–bona fide. On the other hand the record is not clear that the appraised value was determined other than by the opinions of appraisers said to have been under the influence of the collector and domestic interests.[66]

The great amount of publicity attending this investigation gave added significance to the reports. Both reports adverted to the projected change to home valuation on June 30 and contained strong recommendations that foreign valuation be maintained.[67] The reasons cited included the familiar constitutional argument, the administrative difficulties, and the relative lack of stability involved in the use of importers' selling prices in this country instead of the more stable wholesale price abroad. The Steuart report recommended the establishment of a national board of appraisers who would make frequent inspections at the various ports and standardize valuations throughout the country, thus preventing the progressive deterioration of valuation levels through the competition of ports in different sections of the Union.

The recommendations of these reports lent added weight to the general pressure to revoke the home-valuation provisions before July 1. On April 9 the Secretary of the Treasury transmitted to Congress the draft of a new tariff bill which would provide increased duties as well as the retention of foreign valuation. The bill passed Congress but was vetoed by President Tyler because of a rider concerning the distribution of the proceeds of public lands. This placed the Treasury in an embarrassing position in view of the Secretary's previous statements that in the absence of enabling legislation to implement home valuation it was doubtful that any duties could be collected after July 1. The Secretary accordingly laid the matter before the Attorney-General, who rendered an opinion[68] that, although the situation was not without difficulty, duties were nonetheless collectible and that the

66. An interesting account of the experiences and fortunes of the Yorkshiremen and their difficulties with American customs administration may be found in Herbert Heaton, "Yorkshire Cloth Traders in the United States, 1770–1840," *Publications of the Thoresby Society: Miscellany*, XXXVIII, Part III (1941 vol. issued in April, 1944), 225–87, esp. 275–86.

67. *House Document No. 212* (27th Cong., 2d sess.), pp. 52–53, 360–61.

68. 4 Op. Atty. Gen. 56, 63; opinions of June 23 and 24, 1842.

Secretary had the power, under the appraisement and valuation provisions of the Tariff Act of 1832, to prescribe the necessary regulations.
On June 23 the Treasury Department issued a circular instructing
collectors to ascertain the value of the imported article at the place of
importation with due regard to "the prices obtained at cash sales in
the fair and regular course of trade." This would, in effect, involve the
payment of a duty upon a duty. On July 1, the day that home valuation went into effect, another circular was issued changing these instructions and prescribing the deduction of the duty from market
value to make dutiable value, namely, to deduct one-sixth of the market value to determine dutiable value. This would result in a valuation
which, with the addition of the flat 20 per cent rate of duty, would
equal market value. This last-minute move was no doubt made in the
knowledge that the whole proceedings were certain to come before
the Supreme Court and that the government might be in a more favorable position to sustain its right to collect duties if the Treasury regulations avoided the connotation of assessing a "duty upon a duty."

Payment of duties after July 1, 1842, was apparently protested generally[69] by importers, and the issue was ultimately carried to the
Supreme Court. On July 23, during the first month of home valuation,
the House Committee on the Judiciary issued a belabored report[70]
purporting to prove that no duties were collectible under existing
legislation, that the President's wilful rejection of the tariff bill was
exceeded only by his presumption in undertaking the role of legislator
by attempting to collect duties on the basis of home valuation, and
that, even though a new tariff bill was virtually ready for the consideration of Congress, it would be well to pass a special act retroactively
establishing the validity of the tariff laws subsequent to June 30. This
recommendation was not followed, but on August 30 the Tariff Act of
1842 was passed, effective immediately, restoring foreign valuation as
the permanent basis for dutiable value, raising duties to a high protective level, and imposing new penalties on undervaluation. Thus, home
valuation was in actual operation for less than two months.

The Supreme Court in 1845 finally decided the legality of tariff

69. Cf. *Niles' National Register*, LXII (July 16, 1842), 307. The total amount
of duties involved in the litigation before the Supreme Court approximated one
million five hundred thousand dollars.
70. *House Report No. 943* (27th Cong., 2d sess.).

duties collected during the two-month period of home valuation. Although counsel for the importers and Justice McLean, who dissented, presented interesting arguments, the majority opinion of the court, written by Chief Justice Taney, is the more convincing. The substance of the decision was that the Compromise Act was merely a modification of pre-existing laws, that nowhere did it specifically repeal any duties after June 30, 1842, and that existing legislation, especially sections 7–9 of the Tariff Act of 1832, supplied the legal basis for the collection of duties on the basis of home valuation.[71]

The act of 1842, which was partly the product of a quarrel between the Whig Congress and a Democratic president, in some respects exceeded the exactions of the Tariff of Abominations. It re-established minimum valuations on cotton goods; restored the 50 per cent penalty addition to appraised value, this time when the latter exceeded invoice value by only 10 per cent; required that one in every ten packages be examined; and provided a fine up to $5,000 or a maximum of two years' imprisonment for smuggling or the use of false invoices. Dutiable value was defined as the "market value or wholesale price" of the goods "at the time when purchased in the principal markets of the country from which the same shall have been imported," to which were to be added all costs and charges except insurance. It will be seen that the lapse to the "actual-cost" basis in the 1832 act was corrected and the application of the wholesale price, which had already been used administratively, was made specific by statute. Section 17 of the 1842 act provided that, in cases of disagreement between appraisers in reappraisement proceedings, the collector was to "decide between them."

The most significant administrative change occurring in 1842, and one which had indirect bearing on customs valuation, was the requirement, effective July 1, of cash payment for all duties. Hitherto, credit had been allowed, varying with the commodity and the country of origin, subject to the posting of bonds with acceptable sureties. Originally, cash payment was required only for duties less than $50 and a discount of 10 per cent was allowed for prompt payment of amounts over that sum. Bonds were to run up to twelve months, depending upon the class of goods. By the act of March 1, 1823, the discount was

71. *Aldridge* v. *Williams,* 3 Howard 9 (1845).

reduced to 4 per cent per annum during the remainder of the bond, and in 1832 the minimum amount of duties eligible for credit was raised to $200. At this time half the duties were payable in three months and the remaining half in six. Woolen goods, because of frauds previously alluded to, could not be withdrawn from customs custody until full payment of duties and were subject to a 6 per cent interest charge on the deferred duties. If the duty instalments on woolens were not paid when due, a sufficient portion of the goods was to be sold to cover the duties. Under the 1842 act goods not duty paid but remaining in the public stores after sixty days (ninety days when from beyond the Cape of Good Hope) were to be appraised and after due notice sold at public sale. The act provided that "at such public sale, distinct printed catalogues, descriptive of said goods, with the appraised value affixed thereto, shall be distributed among the persons present at said sale," thus indicating a function of customs valuation distinct from the assessment of duties.

An interesting feature of the credit system was the fact that the importer was often placed in a more favorable financial position in the face of high duties than he would have been in the absence of any duties at all. Assuming the duties not to be prohibitive, he could import under bond a consignment of goods, say at a 33⅓ per cent duty, sell them at auction, and retain the duties as working capital for a whole year. It was not unusual for an importer to turn over his working capital three times a year. He could thus, by the use of government credit, create a working capital at the rate of 100 per cent per year upon the appraised value of the imported goods. This condition promoted a substantial amount of speculation in imports and resulted in numerous failures during the downward swing of the speculative cycle.

The curtailment of credit in 1842 led to numerous demands for the establishment of the warehousing system in the United States similar to that which had existed in England since 1803. This proposal had been made many times previously but lacked the element of compulsion which arose from the cash duty requirement. Finally, on August 6, 1846, under the strong representations of Secretary Walker, the warehousing system was formally established. At this time, duty-free storage of all except perishable goods was permissible for one year, the duties being secured by bond. Goods withdrawn during that period could be re-exported duty free or entered for consumption. In 1854 the warehousing period was extended to three years. The important bearing of the warehousing system upon customs valuation was that the privilege of withdrawal for consumption at any time during the warehousing period enabled importers to choose, within the limitations of judgment, the most favorable time after importation for entry and appraisement of goods. Goods entered for consumption immediately upon importation were subject to valuation as of the date of purchase.

On July 30, 1846, the well-known Walker Tariff was enacted. This tariff not only embodied to some extent the low-duty philosophy of its sponsor, Secretary Walker, but also introduced a new standard of clear and orderly draftsmanship. The act classified all commodities into a limited number of schedules—the form maintained in major tariff acts to the present time—each subject to a given percentage rate of duty. All minimum valuations were abolished and all duties placed on an ad valorem basis. Several administrative changes were made to overcome the harshness of those in the 1842 act already mentioned. The penalty addition to appraised value when the latter exceeded entered value by 10 per cent was reduced from 50 to 20 per cent, and importers were permitted to add such sum to the invoice upon entry to make the entered value equal to market value.[72] Under no circumstances, however, was the dutiable value to be less than the invoice value. This provision to allow additions to invoice upon entry enabled the importer to remove any imputation of fraud because of the deviation of the invoice, from whatever causes, from the market value of the goods and was especially necessary in view of the heavy criminal as well as civil penalties—established in 1842—attending fraudulent invoices.

At this time the controversy surrounding the relative merits of ad valorem and specific duties was at its height. The protectionists were almost uniformly in favor of specific or minimum duties and violently opposed to ad valorem duties. Their position was that specific duties were certain in amount, simpler to administer, less easy of evasion; that they provided dependable protection in times of depression

72. This applied only to goods obtained by purchase. The privilege was extended to goods obtained otherwise in the special act of March 3, 1857, 11 U.S. Statutes 199.

when protection was most needed; and that they prevented the importation of the cheaper and less desirable grades of merchandise. Advocates of low duties or free trade opposed specific and minimum duties because of their regressive nature—constituting a greater tax upon the consumption of the poor than of the rich—and on the ground that they were used to disguise their true protective height and burden upon consumption and that they bore unequally during changes in price levels. The opponents of ad valorem duties claimed that such duties opened wide the door to fraud; that, although the rate of duty was fixed by law, the determination of the value base was left completely to interested foreigners, to the detriment of the honest importer, the domestic producer, and the revenue. Those who favored ad valorem duties countered that the extent of fraudulent undervaluation was grossly exaggerated, that specific duties were subject to even greater evasion by reclassification devices, and that a true revenue standard with relatively low duties and uniform levels for large classes of imports would eliminate the incentives to under-valuation. In his annual reports for 1845 and 1846 Secretary Walker devoted many pages to this controversy and was outspoken in his denunciation of minimum and specific duties. His views prevailed, and ad valorem duties became the standard until the outbreak of the Civil War.[73]

73. Walker's celebrated report of 1845 is reproduced in its entirety in F. W. Taussig, *State Papers and Speeches on the Tariff* (Cambridge, Mass., 1893). For representative material on the ad valorem–specific-duty controversy of that period cf. "Bundelcund," *The Protective System Considered in Connection with the Present Tariff* (Palmyra, N.Y.: Wayne Sentinel, 1846); Abbott Lawrence, *Letters from the Hon. Abbott Lawrence to the Hon. William C. Rives of Virginia* (Boston, 1846); and speeches in Congress during the debates on the Walker bill. By this time Henry Clay had come to favor ad valorem duties, as is shown in a speech by Mr. Chase of Tennessee, June 26, 1846 (in *Congressional Globe* [29th Cong., 1st sess.], Appen., p. 754), quoting in part Clay's speech of March 1, 1842: " 'We have had the ad valorem principle in force ever since the Compromise Act was passed; and there has been no difficulty in administering the duties of the Treasury on that principle. Compare the system of specific and the ad valorem system of duties, and I maintain that the latter is justly entitled to the preference. The one principle declares that the duty shall be paid on the real value of the article taxed; the specific principle imposes an equal duty on articles greatly unequal in value. . . . I believe that if we adopt a fixed rate ad valorem, wherever it can be done, the revenue will be subjected to fewer frauds than the injustice and frauds incident to specific duties. One of the most prolific sources of the violation of our revenue laws has been, as everybody knows, the effort to get goods of a higher quality and higher value admitted under the lower rate of duty required for those of lower value.' "

The next legislative enactment of significance for customs valuation was the act of March 3, 1851,[74] authorizing the President to appoint, subject to Senate confirmation, four appraisers to "be employed in visiting such ports of entry in the United States," under the direction of the Secretary of the Treasury, "as may be deemed useful by him ... to protect and insure uniformity in the collection of the revenue from customs." This was a precursor to the later Board of General Appraisers which was eventually independent of the Treasury Department and ultimately established as the United States Customs Court, an integral part of the judiciary system of the United States. The United States appraisers appointed under the 1851 act were to participate, wherever practicable, in reappraisement cases. The collector, upon appeal, was to select one "discreet and experienced merchant" to be associated with the United States appraiser. In case of disagreement between these two, the collector was to decide between them. Such appraisement was final and deemed to be the true value of the goods, "any act of Congress to the contrary notwithstanding."

The same act made an important change concerning the time period of valuation. Formerly, dutiable value had been defined as that existing on the date of purchase, except in the case of articles imported from countries other than where grown or manufactured, in which case "the period [date] of exportation" applied. By a strained interpretation of the law, Secretary Walker had issued a circular, on July 6, 1847, instructing the use of the period of exportation with respect to all importations. This manifestly erroneous interpretation of the clear wording of the law was overruled by the Supreme Court.[75] This state of the law, however, resulted in certain apparent

---

74. 9 U.S. Statutes 629.

75. *Greely v. Thompson et al.*, 10 Howard 225 (1850). This case involved the shipment of a cargo of railroad iron from Newport, Wales, to Boston. The invoice price was £5 per ton. The initial appraisement by the U.S. appraisers was £6 per ton, representing the market value as of February 24, 1849, the date of shipment (also the date on the invoice, which was made up as of the date of shipment). Appeal to merchant appraisers resulted in appraisement at £5 15s., which still required the imposition of the 20 per cent penalty duty. The importer introduced evidence that the iron was actually contracted for on January 24, at which time the market value was only £5. The court held for the importer, stating, in effect, that the written statute was so clear that "the custom house and courts and juries would not comply with their oaths to follow the law, unless all were governed by the value at the time of purchase or procurement."

anomalies, such as different valuations for identical goods imported on the same ship but having different dates of purchase. It also permitted the substitution of fictitious dates on invoices to take advantage of favorable market trends, a type of evasion administratively difficult, if not impossible, to circumvent. Moreover, by the court's determination that the time of purchase *or procurement* was to govern, manufacturers were given the opportunity to use the time of manufacture or sale, whichever suited their interest. The 1851 act, upon the recommendation of the Treasury Department,[76] defined dutiable value to be "the actual market value or wholesale price thereof at the period of exportation to the United States." This was construed to mean the date of clearance of the ship from the port of exportation.

There were several recurrences of the home-valuation proposal during the 1850's. In December, 1849, Secretary Meredith recommended that ad valorem duties "be levied on the market value in the principal markets of our own country at the time of arrival." In 1850, 1851, and 1852, President Fillmore, who had been chairman of the Ways and Means Committee during the home-valuation experiment of 1842, recommended in his annual messages the adoption of home valuation where specific duties were not practicable. On June 7, 1856, Secretary Guthrie, in anticipation of possible congressional action, addressed a lengthy communication to the chairman of the Ways and Means Committee setting forth in greater detail and with greater cogency than had been done previously the arguments against the adoption of home valuation in any form. He pointed out that the elements of freight, insurance, duty, and profits constituted the essential difference between value in foreign and domestic markets and that some of these were not the proper subject of taxation. The duty and profits constituted no part of the price paid by the importer and, so far as they depended upon the ultimate selling price, were merely contingent and conjectural. The elements of freight and insurance, because of their variability, would, if taxed, result in unequal levies upon importers residing in different parts of the Union. Neither valuation at the port of importation or in the principal markets of the United States would be satisfactory: the former would necessarily be unconstitutional and the latter so fraught with delays in ascertain-

76. Cf. "Treasury Department Report to Senate, September 26, 1850," contained as inclosure "T" in *Annual Report, 1850.*

ment and communication that entries would have to be suspended and merchandise withheld from the importer for unworkably long periods. In both cases prices would be subject to manipulation by combinations of importers. Secretary Guthrie's lengthy exposition of the problems involved apparently forestalled whatever legislation had been contemplated.[77]

An indication of the extent to which the components of dutiable value had grown in number by the end of the period under discussion is to be found in the Treasury Circular of August 25, 1853.[78] Dutiable costs and charges at this time included the following:

1. Purchasing, carriage, bleaching, dyeing, dressing, finishing, putting up and packing, together with the value of the sack, package, box, crate, hogshead, barrel, bale, cask, can, and covering of all kinds, bottles, jars, vessels, and demijohns.

2. Commissions at the usual rate but in no case less than 2½ per cent, and where there is a distinct brokerage, or where brokerage is a usual charge at the place of shipment or purchase, that to be added likewise.

3. Export duties, cost of placing cargoes on board ship, including drayage, labor, bill of lading, lighterage, town dues, and shipping charges, dock, or wharf dues; and all charges to place the article on ship board, and fire insurance, if effected for a period prior to the shipment of goods to the United States.

. . . When goods are transported from an interior country for shipment to the United States, the cost of transportation to the foreign port of shipment must also be included among the dutiable charges.

The same circular pointed out that the dutiable charges were to be excluded from all calculations to determine whether or not penalty duties for undervaluation were applicable. The reasonableness of this ruling is obvious when it is considered that the inclusion of charges was frequently a matter of interpretation[79] and that the amounts

77. The complete letter may be found in U.S. Tariff Commission, *American Valuation*, pp. 28–32; cf. also Albert Sidney Bolles, *Financial History of the United States, 1789 to 1860* (New York, 1883), pp. 488–89: "During President Pierce's administration it was proposed to apply the idea, but Guthrie, the secretary of the treasury, was opposed to it and furnished cogent reasons why the experiment should not be tried. Guthrie's views prevailed; and since his day no one has had the hardihood to champion the idea."

78. This circular is reproduced in U.S. Treasury, *Annual Report, 1853,* pp. 342 ff.

79. Although the amounts of the charges were known to the importers who bore them, the question of their dutiability was often debatable, requiring court decision to resolve the issue; cf. *infra,* pp. 191–95, for illustrations of the difficul-

involved might easily in themselves account for the entire 10 per cent margin allowable without penalty between entered and appraised value.

It should be noted at this point that while the question of the inclusion of charges in dutiable value was, in one sense, a matter of valuation, it was also a question of law similar to classification matters. The original remedy for disagreements between the collector and importer on "questions of law"—which usually involved decision as to whether a given importation was free or dutiable or subject to a lower or a higher rate—was a suit against the collector to be tried by jury. The unsatisfactoriness of this method led to the adoption, in the Appropriation Act of March 3, 1839,[80] of an administrative remedy by the Secretary of the Treasury, who was authorized to draw a warrant upon the Treasurer in favor of persons entitled to refund where more money had been paid than the law required. Shortly thereafter the Supreme Court ruled that this proviso eliminated the judicial remedy and that thereafter no suits could lie against the collector. This was also unsatisfactory, as it appeared, among other defects, to violate due process. Congress, accordingly, by the act of February 26, 1845,[81] restored the judicial remedy and prohibited the Secretary of the Treasury from making refunds upon his own decision. In section 5, Tariff Act of 1857, both remedies were made available. The importer was allowed, in the first instance, to file a protest with the collector. If the protest was not granted, appeal to the Secretary of the Treasury within thirty days was permitted. If the Secretary's decision was unfavorable, suit could be instituted within thirty days thereafter.

An interesting comment on the multiplicity of tariff and customs laws existing in whole or in part after more than half a century of legislation, appears in a House report in 1855:

> There are now standing on our statute books, unrepealed in terms, more than four hundred [revenue] laws, running through more than five hundred large octavo pages. . . . This uncertainty and complexity of the laws obliges the importer to resort to others supposed to be well versed in the revenue system and forms to transact his business at the custom house. Hence, to

---

ties sometimes encountered in determining whether or not a given charge is dutiable.

80. 5 U.S. Statutes 348.   81. *Ibid.*, p. 727.

meet the necessity of the case, a large class of agents or brokers has grown up at our principal ports, who attend, at liberal compensation, to the importer's business at the custom house. This operates as a tax on the consumer, because it is an expense which in the end must be paid by the goods.[82]

Although it was many years before appreciable results in the codification of the revenue laws were obtained, Congress, in 1857, took a more direct means to reduce the tax on the consumer. A Democratic Congress, in keeping with party tradition and in view of the abundance of revenue, made substantial reductions by the Tariff Act of 1857, resulting in the lowest schedule of duties since 1816. The Secretary of the Treasury, in his annual report for 1857, commenting unfavorably upon proposals to raise the newly reduced rates, made the pronouncement that "the day has passed in this country for increasing restrictions upon commerce, and it is hoped that the same remark will soon be applicable to all other countries." What might have been the subsequent tariff history of the United States, had not the Civil War interrupted a fifteen-year trend of low duties, will never be known.

82. *Navigation, Revenue, and Collection Laws: House Report No. 145* (33d Cong., 2d sess.; March 3, 1855).

CHAPTER IV

Valuation under High Protection
1861–1940

The Civil War and Its Aftermath—1861–90

THE CIVIL WAR furnishes no exception to the proposition that prior to World War II every major war fought by the United States has been accompanied or followed by a substantial increase in protective tariff legislation. Indeed, the Civil War is perhaps the outstanding example of the general tendency under observation, since it not only reversed a preceding trend of declining rates of duty but had more far-reaching consequences than any other war for the long-run tariff policy of the United States.[1]

The Morrill Tariff Act of March 3, 1861, was conceived in peacetime under Republican sponsorship in the House over a year before the war, but passed the Senate only a few weeks before the firing on Fort Sumter. Though in this respect not a war tariff, it may be classified, in terms of its consequences, with the whole series of wartime tariffs which rapidly and steeply increased duties on all commodities. It sharply reversed the fifteen-year policy of levying ad valorem duties exclusively by a return to specific duties at higher ad valorem equivalents for a large number of commodities. In general, it returned the tariff to the high rates of 1842.

Section 28 of this act modified the time period required for valuation by providing that dutiable value was to be "the foreign-market

---

1. It is an interesting fact that rates of duty were, on an average, declining before each important war of the United States. Prior to World War I, this was the result of the Democratic Underwood Tariff of 1913; prior to World War II, of the Democratic Reciprocal Trade Agreements Act of 1934. The pre–Civil War reductions were general reductions of *all* duties rather than piecemeal reductions, as in the later instances. Professor Taussig says of the Civil War duties: "The high duties which the war thus caused to be imposed, at first regarded as temporary, were retained, increased, systematized, so developing gradually into a system of extreme protection" (*Tariff History*, p. 155).

value on the day of actual shipment whenever a bill of lading shall be presented showing the date of shipment, and which shall be certified by a certificate of the United States consul, commercial agent, or other legally authorized deputy." As distinguished from "the period of exportation" generally applicable, this meant the date the goods left their point of origin, whether in the interior or at the actual port of exportation. This was consistent with the policy of requiring consular certification by the United States consul nearest the place of manufacture rather than by the consul at the port of exportation.

After the outbreak of war, tariff and internal-revenue taxes were extended and increased rapidly. On July 13, 1861, an act "further to provide for the collection of duties," somewhat similar to the Force Bill of the nullification period, was enacted, permitting collectors, under presidential authority, to move ports of entry and to perform other acts necessary to the collection of duties. On August 5 Congress passed an elaborate act increasing import duties, requiring payment of duties on warehoused goods within three months of importation, levying direct taxes on each of the states, and providing extensive additional internal-revenue administrative machinery. On December 24 of the same year duties on all teas were increased to twenty cents per pound and on coffee and sugar to five cents per pound, and further duties were laid on products containing sugar. By the middle of 1862 it was evident that the financial burden of the war would not easily be carried. Accordingly, a comprehensive internal-revenue act was passed on July 1, followed by a compensatory, equally comprehensive tariff act on July 14. Section 17 of this act contained an important administrative provision pertaining to customs valuation. It provided that after March 1, 1862, no imports would be admitted without consular certification of invoices. Previously, it will be recalled, only goods imported by nonresidents were subject to this requirement. At the same time, the owner was required to take oath before the consul, subscribing to the same on the consular invoice, that the invoice exhibited the *actual cost*, including all charges, in the case of purchased goods, and the *actual market value* for all goods consigned or obtained otherwise than by purchase. This was similar to earlier requirements but forcibly called the exporter's attention to the requirements of the law and gave consuls the opportunity to arrest violations at the source. A fee of $1.00 was charged for consular authentication, and consuls were instructed, by section 17, to report any fraudulent practices to the appropriate collector of customs or to the Secretary of the Treasury. This was the first of a series of provisions established during the Civil War period which had far-reaching effects upon customs administration.

On June 30, 1864, the second comprehensive tariff act was enacted under circumstances very similar to its predecessor of 1862. As before, a new internal-revenue act had been passed, and the same considerations which had been operative in 1862 were at work two years later. As Professor Taussig has pointed out, these not only included the ostensible purposes of providing additional revenue and compensating domestic producers for the increased internal taxes but also afforded a substantial measure of protection. Mr. Morrill, chairman of the Committee on Ways and Means, introduced the bill in the House, as he had in 1862. Debate in the House was restricted after one day, and the act was passed with a total of five days—three in the House, two in the Senate—devoted by Congress to its discussion.[2]

THE CLIMAX AND ABOLITION OF THE MOIETIES SYSTEM

The high taxes and duties imposed by the legislation just mentioned put a premium on evasion and required additional administrative and enforcement machinery. The first step, the requirement of consular invoices for all importations, has already been mentioned. Subsequent developments culminated in what was probably the most spectacular, as well as the most sordid, chapter in the history of

2. The following words of Professor Taussig, in discussing the Tariff Act of 1864, are quoted in detail because of their pertinence to customs administration during the period under discussion. Taussig had in mind tariff schedules and other substantive legislation: "The habit of putting on as high rates as any one asked had become so strong that it could hardly be shaken off; and even after the war, almost any increase in duties demanded by domestic producers was readily made. The war had in many ways a bracing and ennobling influence on our national life; but its immediate effect on business affairs, and on all legislation affecting moneyed interests, was demoralizing. The line between public duty and private interests was often lost sight of by legislators. Great fortunes were made by changes in legislation urged and brought about by those who were benefitted by them; and the country has seen with sorrow that the honor and honesty of public men did not remain undefiled. The tariff, like other legislation on matters of finance, was affected by these causes. Schemes for money-making were incorporated in it, and were hardly questioned by Congress. When more enlightened and unselfish views began to make their way, and protests were made against the abuses and excessive duties of the war period, these had obtained, as we shall see, too strong a hold to be easily shaken off" (*ibid.*, pp. 166–67).

customs administration in this country. It is impossible adequately to present the events leading to the abolition of the moieties system without reference to certain of the leading individuals involved. These individuals undeniably exercised a predominant influence on both legislation and administration for the enforcement of customs valuation during the period in question and have left a permanent record of their activity in various government documents of the times.

The first of these, and seemingly the "prime mover" in the chain of events under consideration, was one Montgomery Gibbs, a New York lawyer who had engaged in various forms of legal and business practice during the 1850's. Mr. Gibbs was from all indications an energetic and talented individual whose propensities ran largely in the direction of personal ambition and professional charlatanry. In 1854 he published a legal handbook known as *Gibbs' Practical Forms and Precedents,* quoting the various laws on "the collection of debts in all the states," "the exemption laws of each state," "the statute of limitations of each state," "legal rates of interest and penalties for usury in each state", "provisions for securing bounty lands," etc. His legal practice, such as it was, appears to have been largely at the periphery of professional ethics, including the operation of a bill-collection agency of dubious reputation, the performance of various services as an intermediary on a contingent basis, and eventually the adoption of the role of informer in customs undervaluation cases. It was in this capacity, in 1859, that he first came prominently to the attention of customs officials. A portion of his testimony before the House Committee on Public Expenditures a number of years later best describes the sequence of events:

I discovered a very important and extensive fraud upon the revenue committed by a merchant in New York. I indicated the result of my investigation to the collector of the port, and it was communicated to the then Secretary of the Treasury. This led to my employment as counsel for the United States in that case, and to a visit by me to various parts of Europe. The case was the United States *vs.* Herrick. Herrick was an American merchant in New York City. In my investigations in connection with that case, I discovered that the commission of frauds upon the revenue, by exporters, was very grave; that the government had, in fact, no checks, except in its custom-houses at home, upon the commission of frauds by undervaluation; no record of the transactions of importers was left in Europe. Only one invoice of merchandise was necessary, and that invoice might as well have been made by the importer himself as by the consular agents abroad. No arrangement had been made for the prevention of frauds at the place where they were all or nearly all conceived and carried on. My connection with that case, and my investigations abroad, led me to make a report on the subject to Secretary Chase, on the 15th of January, 1862, which report was printed.[3]

Mr. Gibbs proposed to the Secretary of the Treasury that a system of triplicate consular invoices for all importations be adopted by law. The original, after consular certification, was to be given to the exporter for transmittal to the importer as the basis for his custom-house entry. The verified duplicate was to be mailed by the consul to the collector at the port of importation as corroboration of the legitimacy of the original. The triplicate was to be retained on file in the office of the consul for subsequent use by special foreign agents of the Treasury to be appointed for the purpose of gathering information on foreign-market prices at the source. Secretary Chase referred the proposal to the solicitor of the Treasury, Mr. Edward Jordan, for his recommendations. The solicitor was much in favor of the plan, and in his annual report to the secretary for 1862, reiterated his recommendation of the adoption of Mr. Gibbs's proposals, including the appointment of foreign agents. He also made the suggestion that "the whole subject of the prevention, detection, and prosecution of violations of the revenue be placed under the general supervision of some officer of the Treasury Department." Mr. Jordan quite logically decided that the most appropriate officer was the solicitor and concluded with the sentiment that "for the very considerable increase in labor and responsibility which would be the result, he might be allowed a very small percentage—probably one-half per cent. would be sufficient—upon the moneys collected under his supervision. While such an allowance would be sufficient for his compensation, it would be too small in any particular case to excite his cupidity, and thereby cloud his judgment, or unduly influence his action."[4] Elsewhere in

---

3. U.S. Congress, House Committee on Public Expenditures, *New York Custom House: House Report No. 30* (39th Cong., 2d sess. [1867]), pp. 177–78. The printed report to Secretary Chase, referred to above, may be found in *Letters to the Secretaries of the Treasury in Relation to the Revenue by Montgomery Gibbs, United States Revenue Agent for Europe* (December, 1867).

4. U.S. Treasury, *Annual Report, 1862*, p. 134. The total "moneys collected under his [the solicitor's] supervision" increased from approximately $461,000 in 1862, when he proposed the ½% commission, to $2,998,000 the following year and $9,559,000 in 1865. Only a portion of these amounts were revenue collections, however, and it is assumed that Mr. Jordan referred only to revenue col-

the report, the solicitor makes another statement anticipatory of coming events:

> With reference to the power of compromising judgments, I will say that, while it is a power which has been held to be vested in the Solicitor of the Treasury, it is one concerning the exercise of which I should feel great hesitation, and which I should certainly not exercise without the advice and approbation of the Secretary of the Treasury. Still I think it is a power which ought to exist as well for the interest of the government as for the sake of judgment debtors, since it is often practicable to obtain a portion of a judgment by compromise when nothing could be obtained by compulsory measures; and I know of no place where such a power could be so appropriately lodged as with the head of the Treasury Department.[5]

The result of these representations was the passage of the act of March 3, 1863, "An act to prevent and punish frauds on the revenue, to provide for the more certain and speedy collection of claims in favor of the United States, and for other purposes."[6] This law has been denominated "the most stringent measure ever applied in our service to the purpose declared by its title."[7] Section 1 of this act is a lengthy exposition of the triplicate-invoice requirement and of the forms of oaths to be taken before consuls and customs officers. Section 2 gave the solicitor of the Treasury cognizance of all frauds and attempted frauds and required the collector to communicate promptly to him notice of all seizures with a statement of facts. Section 7 conferred the power on any district judge to issue a warrant to the collector of customs directing him or his authorized agents to enter any premises for the removal of invoices, books, or papers relating to merchandise imported by persons suspected of fraud, and such invoices and the like were to be retained by the United States subject to the control of the solicitor, as long as necessary.[8] Furthermore, by

---

lections in his proposal for a commission. Even applied to the total given above for 1865, the contingent fees would have been less than the principal officers at the New York Custom House received annually in moieties during this period.

5. *Ibid.*, pp. 132–33.

6. In his testimony before the House committee, Mr. Gibbs stated that he drew up the original bill and that, after consultations with the collector at New York, the solicitor, and the secretary, it was passed substantially as he recommended (Committee on Public Expenditures, *op. cit.*, p. 178).

7. John Dean Goss, *A History of Tariff Administration in the United States from Colonial Times to the McKinley Administration*, p. 59.

8. Goss (*op. cit.*, p. 60), erred in stating that sec. 68 of the collection law of 1799 permitted the seizure of papers. That law permitted the seizure of only the suspected merchandise. Sec. 7 of the 1863 act was without any direct precedent.

section 8, any person concealing or destroying any such papers after demand for them by the collector, or for the purpose of suppressing evidence of fraud, was subject to a fine up to $5,000 and/or imprisonment up to two years. This was a far cry from the provision of section 17 of the 1842 act, which required the forfeiture of $100 for the refusal "to produce such papers."

Section 10 reveals the legalistic bent and foresight of Montgomery Gibbs, in collaboration with Solicitor Jordan, in providing for future contingencies: "that upon a report by a district attorney, or *any special attorney or agent* [italics added] having charge of any claim in favor of the United States, showing, in detail the condition of such claim, and the terms upon which the same may be compromised, and recommending that the same be compromised upon the terms so offered, and upon the recommendation of the solicitor of the Treasury, the Secretary of the Treasury be, and he is hereby, authorized to compromise such claim accordingly." Finally, by section 14, sections of certain previous acts of Congress imposing time limitations upon the commencement of actions for the recovery of fines, penalties, and forfeitures were "hereby repealed."[9] The only notable omission from the act of the recommendations of Mr. Jordan was the failure to include the ½ per cent commission for the solicitor on all collections made under his supervision.

Fifteen days after the enactment of this law Montgomery Gibbs was appointed the first United States revenue agent abroad. After a three months' period of indoctrination and preparation at the New York Custom House, he sailed for Europe and began immediately to collect evidence of foreign-market values. His first endeavors were confined largely to the wine trade from France, and it was not long before he had communicated a mass of information consisting of price lists, invoices and abstracts, correspondence with manufacturers

---

For an interesting and detailed discussion of the history of English and United States law on the seizure of papers, etc., cf. Committee on Public Expenditures, *op. cit.*, pp. 16–18; also *Moieties and Customs Revenue Laws: House Miscellaneous Document No. 264* (43d Cong., 1st sess. [1874]), pp. 66–84.

9. It will be recalled that Gibbs's *Practical Forms and Precedents* contained a section on the statute of limitations for the collection of debts in the various states, and it may be surmised that he had found such limitations inconvenient in the conduct of his debt-collection agency.

and exporters, samples,[10] and general data indicating substantial undervaluation. This information was to be used primarily as a lead to enable customs authorities in the United States to seize the correspondence and books of account of importers, which were expected to yield conclusive evidence of fraud which would stand in court. The results of Mr. Gibbs's appointment appeared highly satisfactory to Mr. Jordan, and the following year a second foreign agent, Mr. W. B. Farwell, was appointed and the system placed on a permanent footing.

The number of seizures, fines, and forfeitures for undervaluation grew rapidly after the passage of the law of 1863 and the appointment of the special foreign agents. The seizure bureau at the New York Custom House, under the direction of a deputy collector, extended its operations and worked closely with the special Treasury agents at home and abroad, and with the solicitor. Under the longstanding provisions of the moieties clause in the customs laws, the proceeds of all fines, forfeitures, and compromises were distributed, 50 per cent to the Treasury, 25 per cent to the informer, and the remaining 25 per cent equally among the collector, naval officer, and surveyor. Although customs officers were not eligible to file claim as informers, it was eventually interpreted that the special Treasury agents were. There thus developed a practically closed system of detection, seizure, forfeiture, and compromise, whereby the same government officers who administered and enforced the law had a vested interest in the initial violation of the law, followed by subsequent harsh, punitive measures.

10. Mr. Gibbs, in checking copies of invoices in consular offices, found that it was virtually impossible, since they were not accompanied by the goods or samples thereof, to determine accurately the quality and therefore the probable market value of goods which had been shipped to the United States under the invoices on file. He therefore advised the consuls to require samples of goods covered by each invoice where the furnishing and retention of samples was supposedly practicable. The Paris consulate accordingly set up what appeared to be a fairly elaborate sample-filing system and issued a circular requiring the submission of samples with each invoice. Upon representations of the onerousness and illegality of this requirement it was temporarily discontinued. Solicitor Jordan was able to have a law passed by Congress the following term giving consuls the power to exact samples. It appears that relatively few consuls exercised their full authority in the matter (cf. Committee on Public Expenditures, *op. cit.,* pp. 115–16, 347–50).

By the end of 1866, complaints of alleged extortion and corruption in the handling of undervaluation cases had reached such proportions that the Committee on Public Expenditures was charged, by a House resolution, with the investigation of both the Boston and New York custom houses. The resolution was precipitated by the much publicized "Williams Case," involving the compromise, for $125,000, of forfeitures for champagne and sherry which had been imported by the Boston firm of J. D. and M. Williams.[11]

The wines in question had been imported for many years without any question of undervaluation. On information gathered abroad by Mr. Farwell, the firm's books were seized and evidence was obtained of the use of fraudulent invoices, undervaluing by one-third all importations dating back to 1846, when the duties had been made ad valorem under the Walker Tariff. It was officially estimated that the champagne undervaluations defrauded the government of $150,000 in duties; that accumulated interest would raise this to $200,000; and that the value of the wines liable to forfeiture since 1846 would, without interest, reach nearly $2,000,000. It was initially agreed by Messrs. Jordan, Farwell, and the collector at Boston to accept $350,000 in settlement of all penalties, but this was refused by counsel for Williams, and the government decided to institute suit. Counsel for Williams then let it be known that they had discovered the nonrepeal of one statute of limitations by the act of 1863. Upon receipt of this information the government accepted $100,000 in complete settlement of the champagne claims, the sherry claims having been previously settled for $25,000. Of the $100,000, paid in greenbacks, $50,000 went to the Treasury, $25,000 to Mr. Farwell as informer, and $25,000 was divided among the collector, naval officer, and surveyor at Boston. Mr. Farwell gave $4,000 to Mr. Jordan, who had made an official determination, while the case was pending, that special agents, as distinct from regular customs officers, were entitled to claim as informers.

The basic issue raised but not resolved by the investigation was whether or not the moieties system should be continued as a part of the legal tariff enforcement machinery. The committee, however, was

11. This was one among many contemporary cases involving European wines. For the complete testimony in the Williams and related cases in Boston cf. U.S. Congress, House Committee on Public Expenditures, *Frauds on the Revenue: House Report No. 15* (39th Cong., 2d sess. [1867]).

divided in its report and failed squarely to face the issue. No positive recommendations were made, the majority glossing over the question of fraud by the importers and condemning the government officers, while the minority took the opposite position. Nevertheless, the testimony obtained in the course of the investigation is valuable as revealing the following abuses which had developed out of the unsatisfactory nature of the law:

1. The moieties system put a premium on the detection of fraud, rather than its prevention, and upon the punishment by financial penalties rather than by the conviction of the guilty persons.

2. Indiscriminate seizures of books permitted "fishing expeditions" into importers' books and correspondence to obtain original evidence of irregularities. Pending the institution of forfeiture proceedings or the issuance of a "clean bill," importers were unable, sometimes for months, to pass any goods through the custom house, and the loss of their books of account forced temporary suspension or serious embarrassment in operations.

3. The compromise procedure had developed into a dangerous tool of extortion, with 50 per cent of the proceeds going into the pockets of government officers, some of whom had nothing whatsoever to do with a majority of the cases involved. As part of the compromise machinery a certain law firm in Boston became practically the sole intermediary between the customs authorities and importers who were "in trouble." Regular counsel for importers were obliged to deal through this firm, which successfully represented that they could "settle any seizure case within twenty-four hours."[12]

4. Under forfeiture proceedings duties were waived, inasmuch as the law did not require both forfeiture and payment of duties. But under compromise procedure, where the goods had passed into consumption, the settlement was often much less than the full value of the goods, and the 50 per cent accruing to the Treasury frequently only a portion of the duties presumably lost. Thus, in effect, what should have been paid into the Treasury as duties went into the pockets of Treasury agents and customs officers. In any case, the amount received by the Treasury had no relation to the duties due the government.

The New York investigation covered a number of custom-house irregularities in addition to seizures for undervaluation. Testimony concerning the latter centered largely upon the behavior of Montgomery Gibbs in Europe[13]—allegations that he obtained retail rather

12. *Ibid.*, p. 259.
13. Objections had been received from a number of sources that Mr. Gibbs was "not a fit person" to represent the United States abroad. His methods of securing price data included the posing as a merchant or buyer under various aliases, the carrying on of extensive correspondence under assumed names, and the hiring of an Austrian former wine-dealer of doubtful reputation as a "front"

than wholesale market prices, that he did not select the principal market abroad, and that his methods of securing price data were such as to obtain smaller price discounts, concessions, etc., than were customarily obtained by the large importers. Again the committee made no vigorous or detailed recommendations other than the recall of foreign Treasury agents and the substitution of specific for ad valorem duties as rapidly as possible.

The weakness of the foregoing reports seemed to confer tacit approval upon the perpetuation of the moieties system, and, although Secretary Boutwell recommended its abolition in his annual report to Congress in 1869 and repeated it from year to year, no positive action was taken by Congress. Between 1870 and 1874 the number of seizures and forfeitures increased further and embraced a wide variety of imports. During this period the foreign agents seem to have subsided from the picture and the chief role in the whole seizure program was assumed by Mr. B. G. Jayne, a special Treasury agent stationed in the United States. An analysis of the record of fines, penalties, and forfeitures distributed during the years 1870–73 reveals that Mr. Jayne received as informer during these four years the enormous sum of $316,700.[14] This represented an average return of nearly $5,400 for each of the fifty-nine cases handled by him during this period, all in addition to his regular salary as special Treasury agent. In the Phelps-Dodge case alone, he is recorded as receiving $65,000. Inasmuch as Mr. Jayne received nearly 65 per cent of all moneys paid to informers at New York from March 1, 1869, to November 30, 1873—a period several months longer than he was actually on duty—it is clear that a definite understanding existed among all the interested customs and Treasury officers and that Mr. Jayne's receipts were sufficiently redistributed to officials and outside informers to protect his claim as informer in all important cases. Indeed, a review of the record shows

---

to procure prices. Correspondence between Gibbs and Leuchtenrath—whom Mr. Bigelow, minister to France, characterized as Gibbs's "stool pigeon"—indicated that Gibbs had proposed that he and Leuchtenrath divide the informer's share in forfeitures to be claimed in the latter's name and even that they withhold evidence of undervaluation from the government upon receipt of a satisfactory consideration from foreign exporters. Gibbs also took it upon himself, while in England, actively to participate in the settlement of U.S. government claims for confederate property abroad, notably in the case of Fraser, Trenholm & Co. and presumably for an undisclosed commission.

14. *House Executive Document No. 124* (43d Cong., 1st sess., 1874).

that practically without exception every important case in the New York district during this period was turned over to him to investigate and lay claim to as informer. In two outstanding cases in Boston he was sent to collaborate with the local customs authorities.[15]

The event which finally led to the abolition of the moieties system was the celebrated Phelps-Dodge case, which was compromised in February, 1873, for the sum of $271,017.23. Phelps, Dodge and Company had been importers of iron and steel and other metals for many years and was considered as one of the leading and most reputable houses in the country. For five years prior to the seizure of their books and correspondence, they had made importations of tin plate through their Liverpool house—Phelps, James and Company—who purchased from various manufacturers, in some cases outright, in others under long-term contracts subject to final adjustment for failure to meet delivery date, shortcomings in quality, and so on. It will be recalled that although dutiable value was defined as the foreign-market price as of the date of exportation, it was in no case to be below the invoice value, and the invoice was required to present the specific purchase price. Inasmuch as the date of exportation of the tin plate, especially in the case of orders for unusual sizes, was frequently several months after the adoption of the basic contract price and since the market price was subject to wide fluctuations (in 1872 tin plate rose from 28 *s.* per box in January to 44 *s.* in July, and was down to 35 *s.* in December) the firm would have been substantially penalized by the necessity of always paying duty on the higher of two widely divergent prices. Apart from the intrinsic inequity of this requirement, identical goods, imported on the same boat, purchased by competitors at the time of exportation, would often have the benefit of decisively lower duties. Since the long-run average purchase price and the long-run average market value tended to coincide, the Liverpool house adopted the practice, in invoicing the goods for exportation to the United States, of adding to, or subtracting from, the contract price to make market

15. One of these was the case of Richard Baker, Jr., *et al.*, involving a settlement for $400,000, one of the largest compromise cases on record (*ibid*). A large part of the story of Jayne's activities is found in his testimony in U.S. Congress, Senate Committee on Investigation and Retrenchment, *New York Custom House Investigation: Senate Report No. 227* (42d Cong., 2d sess. [1871]), II, 481–567. This three-volume report on the New York Custom House contains over twenty-five hundred pages of material and is a serious indictment of conditions under the Grant administration.

price and representing this as the price paid. This was no doubt a violation of the law—subject to the plausible defense that in many cases the prices paid were contingent and might later have been brought into conformity with the law; but it was consistent with the presumed basic intention of the law to levy duties on the fair market value of goods at the time of exportation, and the more so since American consuls were required to certify that the invoice authenticated by them contained the actual market value.[16] Memoranda of such adjustments, in order to keep the record straight, were regularly mailed to the New York house. One of the clerks in the firm, seeing in these memoranda a technical violation of the law and the possibility of a large reward as informer, carefully abstracted the memoranda which showed a marking-down of the invoice price and placed himself in communication with Mr. Jayne.

The result was the seizure of the books and accounts of Phelps, Dodge and Company and a check of all their imports for the previous five years. During that period the company had imported $40,000,000 worth of merchandise, upon which some $8,000,000 in duties had been paid. Of the total number of invoices, the government selected about fifty, held to be fraudulent by virtue of the memorandum slips covering certain items in the invoices. The aggregate value of the goods covered by the invoices was about $1,750,000, the amount technically forfeit, since by law any fraudulent item in an invoice tainted the whole. A *pro forma* suit was instituted against the company for this amount while compromise negotiations took place. The total value of the items actually undervalued was $271,017.23, the amount finally agreed upon in settlement. The undervaluation itself amounted to only $6,658.78 and the actual duties lost to only $1,664.68. Ironically, the firm had paid several times more than this amount in duties in excess of either the purchase-price or the market-price basis, since not all their invoices had been placed on the market basis. But the uncertainty, delay, and other disadvantages consequent upon a protracted suit, the desire to avoid unfavorable publicity, and the alleged intimidation by Mr. Jayne[17] led the firm to make an early settlement.

16. Although the burden of resolving this contradiction fell upon the consul and not upon the exporter, the form of the required consular authentication easily induced the idea that market price was called for in the invoice.

17. The personality of Mr. Jayne and the methods used by him in detecting, investigating, and settling cases of alleged fraud were an important factor in the

The publication of the initial facts in the case followed closely upon the Credit Mobilier scandal which had shaken the country and ruined the reputations of men in high places. The public was hypersensitive to revelations of graft and corruption, and, after the settlement had been effected, Phelps-Dodge issued a statement of their version of the case, which portrayed it as it essentially was—an enormous exaction for a minor violation resulting in an actual loss of duties of less than 1 per cent of the penalty.[18] The public reaction was wholeheartedly behind the firm. Newspapers, magazines, commercial and financial

---

willingness of merchants to compromise at exorbitant figures. In 1871 the minority report of the Senate committee investigating the New York Custom House made the following comments: "Mr. Jayne, it would seem, has a fine eye for dramatic effect in his profession, and he does not fail to cultivate the accessories in his own personal experience and demeanor. Terrorism being one of his favorite, and, as he considers, legitimate arguments, his look and manner are brought into harmony. In his skill as a searcher after moieties, he seems to outstrip his competitors . . . who must needs pale their ineffectual fires before the superior genius of Jayne. That such a man should have been permitted to continue in office after a development of his character and conduct, may well be a cause of astonishment" (*ibid.*, I, cxv). Nevertheless, a year after the Senate investigation Mr. Jayne's activities still continued unabated. By the time of the Phelps-Dodge case, his reputation was so widespread that he symbolized the whole operation of the moieties system. Mr. Dodge, testifying before the Ways and Means Committee in 1874, states his introduction to Mr. Jayne: "The first knowledge or hint, in the forty-odd years of business that I have had with the Government, that I was accused of any dereliction of duty, was when, sitting at the board of one of our large institutions, I received a note from my partner asking me to come to the custom-house. I went there; was taken into the little dark hole, lighted by gas, where this business is done, and there, for the first time, I confronted this man Jayne. . . . We paid the money to get rid of these enormous charges against us, rather than subject ourselves to a forfeiture of $1,750,000. . . . We were fools, but there was terror in all these things; there was terror in that first day when we went into that dark hole in the custom-house; there was terror throughout . . ." (*Moieties and Customs Revenue Laws*, pp. 19, 24). Cf. also, testimony of Mr. James E. Caldwell, Philadelphia merchant: " 'Have you discharged anyone from your employment lately?' I said, 'Yes; a bookkeeper.' He replied, 'That accounts for it; he has stolen all your papers, invoices, etc., and you are now in the hands of B. G. Jayne' " (*ibid.*, p. 259). In Mr. Jayne's behalf it should be said that he was (despite the fact that he was a cripple [*ibid.*, p. 131]), a brilliant, energetic, and thorough investigator and, although ruthless, was virtually always "right" in so far as the law was concerned (cf. his testimony before the same committee [*ibid.*, pp. 1–15, 159–95]). The foregoing protracted observations are made in order to indicate the intangible and unanticipated but nonetheless real and significant forms taken by administrative protection.

18. Cf. *Our Revenue System: History of the Proceedings in the Case of Phelps, Dodge and Co. of New York and Vindication of the Firm* (New York, 1873) (hereinafter cited as "*Our Revenue System*"). This is an eighty-four-page document containing the statement of the firm, a number of government communications in the case, and a large collection of contemporary editorials and articles on the case.

journals, and even the religious press throughout the country took up the cause and demanded a repeal of the moieties system and a reform and simplification of the tariff laws. The following responses are typical:

The acts regulating the tariff upon importations are of many dates within a period of a half a century and more, and they were framed, in many instances, perhaps in almost all, by men innocent of any knowledge of the subject matter about which they undertook to legislate.[19]

Legislation, as we all know, has driven our commerce from the seas; but administration seems now to supplement legislation by driving American merchants out of existence. . . .[20]

The truth is that even bad and imperfect laws, when admininstered by good men with good motives, are very often run on for a long time harmoniously and pleasantly. But when you get technical men, selfish men, who are interested in their enforcement, then you begin to see the hardships of the laws.[21]

Early in 1874 the Committee on Ways and Means held extensive hearings on the subject of moieties.[22] In view of all the testimony, the state of public opinion, and previous recommendations of the Treasury Department,[23] the Anti-Moiety Act was passed, effective June 22, 1874.[24]

The Anti-Moiety Act repealed all laws under which any share of fines, penalties, or forfeitures was paid to informers or customs offi-

19. Editorial, "Obliquities of the Tariff," *New York Evening Post,* April 18, 1873; reprinted in *Our Revenue System,* p. 19.

20. David A. Wells, "The Extraordinary Element in the Case of Phelps, Dodge and Co.," *The Nation,* May 1, 1873; reproduced in *Our Revenue System,* p. 24. Mr. Wells, Special Commissioner of the Revenue in the Treasury Department from 1866 to 1870, was originally a protectionist. During his commission in the Treasury he fell out of sympathy with the cause of protection and became the leading exponent of his day for tariff reduction and general revenue reform. It was apparently he who prepared the Phelps-Dodge brochure already cited. In addition to this he wrote a much longer case history, containing a detailed record of pertinent testimony before the subsequent congressional investigation (cf. Wells, *Congress and Phelps, Dodge and Company* [New York, 1875]). For an excellent review of Wells's position on the tariff and fiscal matters cf. his article "The Meaning of Revenue Reform," *North American Review,* LXIII (July, 1871), 104–53.

21. Statement of Mr. Jackson S. Schultz before the Ways and Means Committee in *Moieties and Customs Revenue Laws,* p. 106.

22. *Ibid.,* pp. 1–277.

23. In addition to recommendations in the various annual reports, the Secretary of the Treasury made a special statement, to be found in *Senate Miscellaneous Document No. 36* (43d Cong., 1st sess. [1874]).

24. 18 U.S. Statutes 186 (1874).

cials, and all proceeds thereof were directed to be paid into the Treasury. A special fund of $100,000 was appropriated for the next fiscal year to be used by the Secretary of the Treasury to make suitable compensation to informers. In smuggling cases only was any officer of the customs entitled to compensation as informer, and no informer's reward was to exceed one-half the net proceeds. Compensation to informers was to be paid only for original information and only when his claim was recognized by the court having jurisdiction of the case. Severe punishment was prescribed for officers of the customs who accepted any portion of an informer's compensation. Fraudulent or false invoices were punishable by fines of from $50 to $5,000 or a year's imprisonment, but only when falsified with intent to defraud. Any act subjecting an entire invoice to confiscation for containing fraudulent items was repealed. The omission of dutiable charges, regardless of their amount, was not to work forfeiture, but such charges were to be added to the appraised value in double their amount. *Intent to defraud* was to be found by a court or jury as a separate and distinct finding of fact prerequisite to forfeiture. Compromise or abatement by any officer of the United States except the Secretary of the Treasury of any claim was deemed a felony, punishable by a fine up to $10,000 *and* imprisonment up to ten years. The production of books, papers, and accounts was compulsory only upon court order after motion of a government attorney for suits pending, "particularly describing such book, invoice, or paper, and setting forth the allegation which he expects to prove," and custody of the papers in question was to remain with the owner. A three-year statute of limitation was placed on the commencement of suits, and the duty-free passage of any goods through the custom house was held conclusive after one year in the absence of fraud.

The passage of this act closed an important stage in the history of public administration in the United States. As was to be expected, the number of forfeitures declined rapidly, and complaints were frequently heard in the years following that the act had gone too far and that, with the removal of the chief incentive to detection and investigation, undervaluation was again on the increase. But the forward step made was not reversed, and further refinements in the law facilitated the development of effective customs administration without recourse to the cupidity of public officers.

Under the first regularly elected Democratic administration since 1861, Secretary of the Treasury Manning and his assistant and successor, Mr. Fairchild, set to work to remove as many as possible of the objectionable features of the tariff laws and tariff administration. Among the steps taken to determine the nature and extent of the existing shortcomings was the sending, in August, 1885, of a lengthy questionnaire, containing twenty-four questions or problems, to two hundred and twenty-seven local customs officers throughout the country. Replies of varying length and quality were received from all but nineteen of these and, together with a mass of other data, including reports by special Treasury agents, general appraisers, and a special report by the Secretary of the Treasury, were reproduced in a volume of nearly one thousand pages, issued as a supplement to the annual Treasury report to Congress for 1885. This volume and a similar but shorter special supplement to the annual report for 1886 furnish an excellent insight into the nature and problems of customs administration during the entire period under discussion. A substantial portion of the material directly or indirectly concerns valuation and is, in effect, a summary of valuation history and problems in the two or three decades leading up to 1890.

The making and certification of invoices abroad.—Mr. Manning found two stages in the execution of the customs laws which were notably weak. The first, and in his estimation the more important, was at the source of foreign-market valuation—namely, the making, certification, and authentication of invoices abroad. Under the provision of law that the invoice price became the dutiable value when it exceeded market value, the invoice became highly significant. On the one hand, there was the constant pressure upon importers and foreign exporters to keep the invoice price as low as possible; on the other hand, there was a reluctance on the part of appraisers to report appraised value as less than the invoice. Consequently, apart from other considerations tending to the same result, the invoice of purchased goods, when it appeared complete and free from fraud, became generally the practical basis for dutiable value. In the case of consignments, however, substantial difficulties were encountered, inasmuch as the law required the invoice to show, not a simple matter of fact, for example, price actually paid, but a matter of conjecture—"fair market price." The foreign manufacturer or shipper of consigned goods knew that if he "guessed wrong" and invoiced his goods above the prevailing market price, he would nevertheless be bound by his wrong estimate despite the elaborate appraisement machinery on both sides of the ocean for determining market price. He was therefore obliged, in self-defense, to shade the invoice price sufficiently to provide against contingent declines in market price or lower estimates thereof, but not beyond a figure which would subject him to penalty duties for the 10 per cent, or greater, excess of appraised over invoice value. The natural consequence was a general undervaluation of consigned goods, a practice encouraged by the liberality with which American consuls authenticated invoices as representing market price.

The consuls were subjected to considerable criticism for their inadequate knowledge and enforcement of the tariff laws. But, in undertaking any responsibility for the accuracy of invoices, the consuls worked at a disadvantage. Many of them were understandably unsympathetic with our tariff laws, inasmuch as a large part of consular duties consisted of furthering the American export trade, which has traditionally suffered from effects of the tariff.[25] Also, although consuls were officially serving the State Department, many of the regulations specifying their duties actually originated in the Treasury Department, and it was embarrassingly true that the whole consular system was supported mainly by the fees for authenticating invoices.[26] The result was not conducive to the best of feeling between State- and Treasury-Department personnel at the levels involved. This was

25. Apart from the effects of our tariff on the balance of payments and foreigners' ability to purchase, the inequity and sheer arrogance of United States tariff policy have not helped to make easy the consul's job of promoting American commerce abroad.

26. The fee for verification and authentication of triplicate invoices was $2.50. Secretary Manning, in expressing dissatisfaction with the consular service, cites annual data on consular receipts and expenditures: "Thus it will be seen that the cost of our imperfect Consular service to the Treasury was $78,837.55 in 1885 in excess of total receipts" (U.S. Treasury, *Annual Report, 1885*, II, xiv–xv). Actual figures are given in the accompanying tabulation.

Year	Total Consular Fees	Fees from Invoices	Total Consular Costs
1883............	$926,055	?	$870,291
1884............	908,932	?	872,345
1885............	791,345	$699,852	870,183

especially true after the appointment of the Treasury foreign agents, and consuls were loath to make any extended studies of foreign costs and market prices. Their disinclination in this respect was aggravated by the frequent ignoring or overruling, by the appraisers in the United States, of such consular studies as were made. The appraisers, it appears, felt somewhat hostile, with respect to both consuls and foreign agents, to "the removal of the appraiser's division to the other side of the ocean."

An indication of the divergence between cost studies furnished by consuls and final appraised values is found in the case of the silk trade from Horgen and Zurich through the port of New York in the last three months of 1884:

Total invoice value	Fr. 4,484,051.35
Importers' additions on entry	190,825.47
Appraisers' additions to make market value	198,369.01
Dutiable value	Fr. 4,873,245.83
Cost of labor and materials (consular est.)	Fr. 5,022,369.00
10 per cent overhead (waste, insurance, interest, etc.)	502,236.90
Total cost of production	Fr. 5,524,605.90

These figures show cost of production as exceeding appraised value by 13 per cent and as exceeding invoice value by 23 per cent. To the extent that this was typical of the entire silk trade, Secretary Manning estimated that total imports of silks at New York for 1884 escaped payment of duties on over $4 million in value, as represented by their cost of production. Since cost of production was, by the Tariff Act of 1883, for the first time made an alternative basis of dutiable value in the absence of foreign-market value, it appears that the appraisers failed to make adequate use of the data furnished by the consuls.[27]

Local appraisement problems.—The foregoing account leads to a consideration of the second major weakness alleged by Secretary Manning—the appraisement of merchandise at the ports of entry. The following were the chief defects cited: the accepted "doctrine" among appraisers that the invoice value, if correct, governed the dutiable value; the fact that examiners, whose salaries were $2,500 per year, were the *de facto* appraisers of merchandise paying duties, in the larger ports, of from $12 million to $15 million annually; the cost of

27. *Ibid.*, p. 43.

production formula in the 1883 act, which stimulated consignments and the concealment of market prices; the great increase in the use of *pro forma* invoices, permitting entry and clearance of goods subject to later production of the certified invoice; the uncertainty of the law on several important points, particularly with respect to the valuation of coverings; the prohibitive nature of the tariff itself, with rates so high that public sentiment was against strict enforcement.

Elaboration of one or two of the foregoing points is pertinent. The question of the valuation of coverings and containers, as well as of other charges, had been especially vexatious since the Civil War. Section 24 of the Act of June 30, 1864, made dutiable value the "actual value on shipboard at the last place of shipment to the United States," including all charges and "the value of the sack, box, or covering of any kind." Section 7 of the Act of March 3, 1865, made a blanket repeal of "all acts and parts of acts requiring duties to be assessed on commissions, brokerage, costs of transportation, shipment, transshipment, and other like costs and charges incurred in placing any goods, wares, or merchandise on shipboard." Section 9 of the Act of July 28, 1866, again made all charges dutiable, specifying nearly every conceivable charge that might be added, with the drastic provision that charges added by the appraiser were to be included in the determination of the application of the 20 per cent penalty. Also, this section required that all charges be distributed pro rata over all items of the invoice. This meant that an item dutiable under value brackets might easily be subjected to a substantial increase in duty if near the upper limit of its value class.[28]

Under this state of the law the value of boxes, cartons, coverings, and the like was added to the appraised value of the goods, regardless of whether it was already included, unless it was distinctly itemized

28. The Walker Tariff of 1846 abolished all minimum valuations and placed the tariff completely on an ad valorem basis. After the Civil War, instead of a revival of minimum valuations, specific and compound rates subject to value brackets were introduced and became increasingly common. The ad valorem equivalents of the duties for each of the several brackets for a given kind of merchandise were roughly the same or else increased with increasing value. Expressed in other terms, these taxes (whether at specific or compound rates) were generally proportional or, in some cases, progressive. The present tariff act, however, exhibits almost every conceivable type of eccentricity in behalf of special interests, including highly regressive rates, so that an increase in dutiable value could result in an actual reduction in duty (cf. *supra*, p. 6, n. 11).

in the invoice separately from the value of the goods per se. Because of frequent misunderstandings by shippers, invoices were often improperly made out and the consignee or importer was obliged to pay duty twice on the charges. Moreover, if these additions brought the appraised value to an excess over the entry of more than 10 per cent, the 20 per cent penalty duty on the whole applied. Furthermore, if the omission of charges from the entry could be attributed to fraud, the whole invoice was subject to forfeiture, and instances of such cases were cited in the various hearings already referred to. The Anti-Moiety Act, as observed above, provided for the addition of dutiable charges, when omitted from entry, in double their amount. Despite the more favorable penalty provisions of the Anti-Moiety Act, this was still a rigorous provision, and section 7 of the Tariff Act of 1883 contained the following modification:

> Hereafter, none of the charges imposed by said section or any other provision of existing law shall be estimated in ascertaining the value of goods to be imported, nor shall the value of the usual and necessary sacks, crates, boxes, or covering, of any kind be estimated as part of their value in determining the amount of duties for which they are liable: Provided, that if any packages, sacks, crates, boxes, or coverings of any kind shall be of any material or form designed to evade duties thereon, or designed for use otherwise, than in bona fide transportation of goods to the United States, the same shall be subject to a duty of one hundred per centum ad valorem upon the actual value of same.

Under this wording the Treasury was faced with the necessity of making many embarrassing administrative decisions. Did section 7 exempt from duty *all* containers, so long as they were filled, including such diverse items as cardboard shoe boxes, the tin containers of shoe blacking, glass jars containing preserved fruit worth less than the jars, elaborate candy boxes, or even plush-lined cases for musical instruments? These were all "the usual and necessary covering." On the basis of an opinion of the Attorney-General, dated January 11, 1884, the department continued to assess duty on coverings on the theory that the value of the containers was an integral part of the value of the goods. On January 25, 1886, the Supreme Court ruled in the important Oberteuffer case[29] that so long as the charges for coverings were bona fide, and separately shown on the invoice, they were deductible and duty free.

29. *Oberteuffer* v. *Robertson*, 116 U.S. 499 (1886).

It was estimated that this decision required the refunding of some one and one-half to two million dollars in duties covered by protests pending decision. The decision also, as subsequently interpreted by the Attorney-General, required the admission duty free of all filled containers, regardless of their value, so long as they met the test of *bona fides*. The result was wholesale confusion and differential treatment at the several ports of entry, as well as of different importers at the same port of entry. Exorbitant claims as to the cost of coverings and related charges were made in invoices. A typical example was that of matches imported from Sweden, costing £142 1s. 8d. per 2,500 gross. The following deductions were claimed and allowed as nondutiable charges:[30]

	£	s	d
Inside coverings and packing	54	11	8
Paper labels and putting up in dozens	7	2	1
Outside case and label zinc-lined	15	2	1
Inland transportation	4	1	3
Total deductions	81	7	1
Leaving, as dutiable	60	14	7

Instances in which the deductible value of the containers was greater than the value of the contents were legion. Shoe blacking invoiced at 11,000 francs claimed deductions of 7,000 francs. French violins, worth 5 francs, were imported in boxes valued at 7 francs and exempt from duty. Cartons covering Crefeld velvets, formerly stated in the invoice at 5 marks, were charged under the new law at 40 marks. Malaga grapes, packed in kegs with cork dust, uniformly shipped and sold as an entirety, claimed more than 50 per cent reduction in duty by virtue of the value of the kegs, without which the grapes would have no market value.

The Supreme Court, in rendering the Oberteuffer decision, had alluded to the desire of Congress to reduce duties by the 1883 act. But the confusion into which a complex and far-flung administrative organization can be thrown by an apparently innocuous change in the law and its interpretation is well expressed in the following words commenting on the law of coverings and containers:

30. Report of special agents A. K. Tingle and George C. Tichenor, November 4, 1886, in U.S. Treasury, *Annual Report, 1886*, II, 140.

The law, as interpreted by the Attorney-General and the courts, has added infinitely to the difficulties of the appraising officers, and has multiplied the inconsistencies and inequalities of the tariff to such an extent that regularity and uniformity in administration are impossible. It reduces the duties collected upon almost all imported merchandise subject to rates based on value, but in irregular, variable, and eccentric ways, the largest reductions being often upon goods dutiable at the lower rates.[31]

Despite the pleas of Secretary Manning and the introduction of several bills to remedy this condition, Congress took no definitive steps in the matter until 1890.

The problem of "pro forma" invoices.—The *pro forma* invoice has been mentioned as a source of difficulty in the proper appraisement of merchandise. This type of invoice was first authorized by the Act of March 3, 1863, which allowed the Secretary of the Treasury to permit entry of goods in the absence of the certified invoice where hardship would otherwise occur. Treasury regulations required that *pro forma* invoices be made by the shipper and in all respects correspond to the certified invoice, for the production of which bond was required to be given. Experience had demonstrated that in many cases it was difficult or impossible for the exporter to obtain and transmit to the importer a certified invoice by the time of arrival of goods shipped from points remote from consulates or agencies thereof, and the Anti-Moiety Act extended the privilege to any shipment upon importer's affidavit showing hardship. Four years later, the Attorney-General, in his opinion of October 4, 1878, decided that no penal duties for undervaluation were assessable on entries by *pro forma* invoices, so long as bond had been given for the production of the certified invoice, on the theory that the certified invoice was the original and legal document. This permitted importers and their correspondents abroad to experiment with low values in a *pro forma* invoice without fear of penalty. If the low valuation passed the appraiser, shippers were notified accordingly, and the certified invoices would correspond to the appraisement.

The use of the *pro forma* invoice became widespread in all the principal ports after the Attorney-General's decision. In 1884 there were nearly 30,000 such entries at New York, 7,266 covering goods valued at more than $100, with individual invoices covering merchandise as high as $18,000 in value. An analysis of such invoices revealed that the greatest part covered merchandise subject to high ad valorem

31. *Ibid.*

rates and that although the firms with the highest standing used regularly certified invoices, houses of less reputation with correspondents in identical cities abroad found it necessary to resort to *pro forma* invoices. There is no question that this practice developed into a substantial mechanism of undervaluation and that its use was facilitated by lax enforcement on the part of customs officers and government attorneys.[32]

Reappraisement at New York.—The port of New York in the last half of the nineteenth century had not only outstripped all others in the volume and value of imports but occupied a predominant place in the customs and revenue system of the entire United States. From two-thirds to three-fourths of all importations and customs receipts was supplied by that port. It is not surprising that the needs and problems arising out of this immense concentration of trade should require special treatment and that local practices should arise which were not always understood or appreciated by competing ports or Treasury officials. In reviewing the many documents, acts, controversies, and investigations in the history of customs administration in the nineteenth century, one is struck with the fact that conditions at New York were the focal point of virtually all customs legislation and that the "New York Custom House" was to a large extent synonymous with the United States custom system.

Perhaps the classic illustration of this influence and its bearing on subsequent legislation is the body of practices which had developed in the reappraisement of merchandise at New York. It will be recalled that the Act of March 3, 1851, which provided for the appointment of general appraisers, required that appeals to reappraisement at ports where a general appraiser was stationed, should be decided jointly by

32. Importers themselves were allowed to prepare *pro forma* invoices (a not unreasonable permission if properly controlled). But these were accepted without adequate, and in some cases any, explanation for the nonproduction of the certified invoice. The bonding procedure was most lax. An examination of the bonds for production of certified invoices at New York revealed that many were defective because of careless execution; that practically 90 per cent contained custom-house brokers as sureties, many of whom were said to be financially irresponsible but individually liable up to $150,000 on outstanding penal, warehouse, and other bonds; that, although 229 defaulted bonds had been presented to the federal district attorney for suit in 1884 and part of 1885, not one suit had been instituted. For a thorough discussion of the use of *pro forma* invoices cf. report of U.S. General Appraiser Combs and special agents Hinds and Lapp, August 5, 1885, in U.S. Treasury, *Annual Report, 1885*, II, 64–70; also pp. 111, 591, 675, and 824.

the United States general appraiser and "one discreet and experienced merchant" selected by the collector. The theory underlying this provision was that the general appraiser (although in the nature of the case and as implied by his title he could not be expected to have specific knowledge of the values of the myriad kinds of merchandise subject to reappraisement), by virtue of his intimate knowledge of valuation law and procedure, could, in conjunction with a merchant having specific knowledge of the kind of goods under review, render an intelligent and fair decision. The volume of appeals at the port of New York had grown so great by 1885, and the kinds of merchandise so varied, that recourse was had to procedures in reappraisement substantially different from those employed in local appraisement. Instead of the purely executive, unilateral, individual type of investigation and decision traditional to local appraisement, reappraisement at New York had developed into a kind of judicial proceeding in which importers, their attorneys, and expert witnesses were heard, cross-examination was permitted, and decision on the basis of the evidence thus submitted was jointly made by the general appraiser and the merchant appraiser. Apart from the convenience and even the necessity of freeing the reappraisement officials from the burdensome and time-consuming process of fact-gathering, this judicial type of procedure undoubtedly resulted in a more thorough disclosure and assimilation of facts and consequently sounder decisions.

Nevertheless, the apparent irregularity of this practice, and certain unfortunate by-products, led Secretary Manning to order its summary discontinuance and a return to the execution of reappraisement "in substantially the same manner as is pursued on original appraisement":

The law of reappraisement is precisely the same as that of original appraisement, and there is no authority or justification for the system which, it appears, has grown up in your office of treating a reappraisement as in the nature of a trial in a court of law, wherein the reappraising officers sit as judges and render decisions according to the preponderance of testimony adduced.

. . . .

I am informed that it is the practice to hold reappraisements on certain days of the week within the hours of twelve and three, and that, owing to the number of appeals pending, two or more cases are often heard at the same time by different merchant appraisers, all acting in conjunction with the general appraiser; that importers and witnesses are permitted to throng the general appraiser's office, in whose presence the conclusions of the appraising board are often announced; and that if such conclusions are not satisfactory to the importer, he is allowed to protest and reargue the case, with a view to a modification of the finding, in which he is often successful.

. . . .

The appraising officers are entitled to all information obtainable concerning the foreign market value of goods under consideration, but such information is not public property. It is due to merchants and others, called to give such information, that their statements shall be taken in the presence of official persons only. . . .

Article 1416 of the Regulations enjoins appraisers to give courteous and due attention to the explanations and statements of importers, in person or by representative . . . but they are to limit the privilege so accorded to one person. . . . There is no office here for the lawyer or custom-house broker, and such persons, as well as others not officially called before the appraisers, should be excluded.[33]

This ruling of the secretary elicited a storm of protest from importers and their counsel, who prepared elaborate written arguments citing judicial authorities and precedents in their behalf. The secretary concluded, however, to adhere to his ruling, holding that reappraisement was an executive and not a judicial function.

Whatever the merits of this position, there were a number of forces all demonstrating the need for more satisfactory machinery for the prompt disposition of customs litigation of all kinds and for a thorough revision and simplification of tariff and customs administrative laws. For a number of years the various secretaries had urged Congress to supply the necessary legislation, and, by the end of the 1880's, positive action had become imperative. Secretary Fairchild in 1887 gravely summed up the situation as follows:

The numerous ambiguities in the tariff schedules furnish constant means of evasion; disputes and litigation increase rather than diminish. The calendar of customs suits in the southern district of New York has grown so large that there is no reasonable prospect of disposing of them in this generation. A merchant who has suffered an illegal exaction of duties cannot hope for a speedy trial of his cause, and justice is practically denied him. The laws which were ostensibly enacted to prevent fraud by undervaluation promote rather than suppress that evil.[34]

33. Letter of Daniel Manning, Secretary of the Treasury, to Mr. A. J. Perry, U.S. general appraiser, New York, N.Y., June 9, 1885, reproduced in *ibid.*, II, 98–99.

34. U.S. Treasury, *Annual Report, 1887*, p. xxxiii.

The movement for the establishment of a special customs tribunal to clear up the tremendous backlog of customs cases and to provide speedy justice in the future, gathered strong support despite the initial opposition of Secretary Manning. This, and the various other pressures for reform, finally culminated in the passage of the Customs Administrative Act of 1890. This act, which is discussed in the following section, made far-reaching changes in the machinery and procedures for customs valuation. It may properly be said to have closed the post–Civil War period and to have effected the transition to the twentieth-century form of customs administration as we know it today.[35]

The Emergence of Contemporary Valuation Procedure—1890–1940

With the passage of the Customs Administrative Act of 1890, customs valuation reached—if not in substantive law, at least in organization and procedure—essentially the status it occupies today. It is the purpose of this section to review in broad outline the major legislative accomplishments of the final fifty years under observation, leaving the treatment of the judicial and administrative refinements to Part III, which examines the nature and significance of the current law of dutiable value.

THE CUSTOMS ADMINISTRATIVE ACT OF 1890

The Customs Administrative Act of 1890 was not a complete revision of all outstanding laws for the administration of the tariff, but it was a step in that direction, specifically repealing dozens of superseded and obsolete laws and all others inconsistent with itself. It redefined dutiable value to include the value of all coverings of any kind and "all costs, charges and expenses incident to placing the merchandise in condition packed ready for shipment to the United States." This disposed of the troublesome problems of containers and coverings which had grown out of their exclusion from dutiable value by the act of 1883. Unusual coverings, dutiable at 100 per cent ad valorem

35. During the period just discussed there were occasional references to home valuation but no important legislative attempts in that direction (cf. U.S. Tariff Commission, *American Valuation*, pp. 22–23; also *Report of U.S. Tariff Commission, 1882*, esp. I, 593–94; cf. also *House Executive Document 101* [48th Cong., 1st sess.] and *Senate Report No. 1990* [49th Cong., 2d sess.] for further data on undervaluation).

by the 1883 act, were made subject to duty at the rate to which they would have been subject if separately imported but not less than that applicable to the contents. Since this was in addition to the value of the coverings already included in the dutiable value of the goods, double duties on such coverings were the result. In most cases this was more favorable than the former 100 per cent duty, and no doubt was directed at reducing evasive practices to a minimum.

The penalty for undervaluation was placed on a sliding scale, beginning with 20 per cent for cases where appraised value exceeded entered value by more than 10 per cent and increasing thereafter 2 per cent for each additional 1 per cent of excess beyond 10 per cent. This was an increase over the old flat-rate penalty of 20 per cent, but the new penalty was subject to a maximum of 80 per cent. Beyond an excess appraised valuation of 40 per cent, the goods were presumed fraudulent and subject to seizure. The burden of rebutting the presumptive fraud was upon the claimant, and, if successful, remission was obtained. *Pro forma* invoices were made subject to the same penalties and forfeitures, thus removing all advantage and encouragement to undervaluation from their use. Affidavits showing necessity were prerequisite to the issuance of a *pro forma* invoice. Regardless of the invoice, any forfeiture for undervaluation applied to all merchandise in the case or package containing the undervalued articles.

As a check against undervaluation of consigned goods all invoices of goods consigned directly by manufacturers were to be accompanied by a statement of the cost of production, signed by the manufacturer and attested by the consular officer. For goods consigned by other than the manufacturer, invoices and accompanying statements were to declare in detail the prices actually paid by the exporter. No additions upon entry were permitted for goods obtained other than by purchase. Appraisers were directed, in the absence of an actual foreign-market value, to make use of the cost-of-production basis of dutiable value, "such cost of production to include cost of materials and of fabrication, all general expenses covering each and every outlay of whatsoever nature incident to such production, together with the expense of preparing and putting up such merchandise ready for shipment, and an addition of eight per cent. upon the total cost thus ascertained." In no case was appraised value to be below the cost of production so ascertained.

Prior to 1890, damage allowances had been made on goods damaged in shipment on the basis of a special examination and return made by the appraiser showing the percentage of damage sustained. No duty was collected on damaged goods to the extent of the damage thus certified. This had long been criticized as subject to widespread abuse, resulting partly from misrepresentation by importers, partly from collusion with appraisers, and partly because of the sheer difficulty of making an accurate estimate of either the physical or the pecuniary damage sustained by the goods, particularly those of a perishable variety or where inspection was difficult under the conditions of storage, packing, etc. It was reported that certain custom-house brokers became specialists in damage claims, virtually guaranteeing mitigation of duties in excess of any allowances obtainable by the importer.[36] It was alleged, also, that goods which had passed the custom house duty free or at large reductions as a result of such allowances were sold in the general market for a substantial portion, and in some cases all, of their normal value. The Administrative Act abolished all damage allowances but permitted abandonment of damaged goods to the United States. To discourage minor claims, abandonment was permitted only of quantities in excess of 10 per cent of the shipment. Since the owner was covered by insurance, he would not suffer from abandonment in genuine cases of damage. Proceeds of the sale of damaged goods were retained by the government.

Other changes effected by this act included the abolition of all custom-house fees and the substitution of an export declaration for the oath formerly required. The same penalties obtained for false declarations as for false oaths. Collectors and other officers of the customs were made nonliable to any owner, consignee, or other person for any moneys collected by them or for any decision or other acts against which appeal might be made under the act. In all seizure cases under the customs laws the burden of proof of absence of fraud was placed on the claimant so long as probable cause for prosecution was certified by the court. This overcame the practical inability of the government to recover successfully under the terms of the Anti-Moiety Act, since intent to defraud could rarely be proved in court.

36. Cf. Chamber of Commerce of the State of New York, *Report of Special Committee on Revenue Reforms* (New York, 1875). (Concerns undervaluation and damage allowance.)

The most important change made by the Administrative Act was the creation of a nine-man Board of General Appraisers, appointed by the President and having original jurisdiction of all protests of classification and appeals to reappraisement. Three members of the board were permanently stationed at New York: the others were to travel and sit at such ports or places as directed by the Secretary of the Treasury. Not more than five members were to belong to one political party, and permanent tenure of office was granted, subject to presidential removal for neglect, inefficiency, or malfeasance. The appraisers had the power to administer oaths, to compel attendance of witness, and to require the production of papers and accounts. Reappraisement cases were heard originally by a single general appraiser, subject to review—on appeal—by a board of three such appraisers, whose decision as to value was final. Classification cases and other "questions of law" were heard by a three-man board and were appealable to a federal circuit court[37] as formerly. Abstracts of all significant decisions in both reappraisement and classification cases were to be published under the supervision of the Secretary of the Treasury. The general offices at New York were to be furnished, under regulations of the Treasury, with samples and with abstracts of decisions for inspection by customs officers and the public.

Thus the time-honored system of merchant appraisement was abolished, after a century of operation, and a quasi-judicial organization and procedure established to perform the functions of a special customs tribunal. A moderate degree of supervision by the Secretary of the Treasury was deemed necessary for proper co-ordination with the general customs organization. The appraisers took office and began work almost immediately. The measure of their success after a year of labor may be inferred from the annual report of the secretary in 1891. Up to November 1, 1891, the board had received 2,107 appeals to reappraisement, of which 2,051 had been decided, leaving only 56 pending. On November 1, 1890, 996 protests of classification, etc., were on hand; by November 1, 1891, 41,557 additional protests had been received at New York, and 8,589 from all other ports, making a total of 51,142 cases. Of these, 33,897 involved the constitutionality of the Administrative Act and the later tariff act of October 1, 1890, and

37. At this time "circuit courts," as distinguished from "circuit courts of appeal," were the equivalent of the federal district courts of today.

would be decided by a single decision of the Supreme Court. Of the remainder it was estimated that nearly all would be decided by January 1, 1892. The secretary was highly gratified by the results:

This showing gives assurance that the Customs Administrative Act has realized the purpose of its enactment and afforded what was imperatively demanded—a speedy, just and efficacious means for the settlement of differences between the government and importers, both as to classification and values.

. . . It has demonstrated its value and efficacy in checking fraudulent undervaluations and securing uniform assessment of duties, and while in some details amendment is desirable, yet in its main features it should not be disturbed.[38]

CHANGES TO AND INCLUDING THE PAYNE ACT OF 1909

The Administrative Act freed the regular tariff acts of the necessity of including administrative matters for some time to come and only in those acts where changes were necessary or where the subject matter was closely related to the tariff schedules did such provisions appear. The McKinley Tariff of October 1, 1890, clarified the "chief value" provision by standardizing the phraseology throughout the schedules to read "component material of chief value." This phrase was defined in section 5 to mean "that component material which shall exceed in value any other single component material of the article; and the value of each component material shall be determined by the ascertained value of such material in its condition as found in the article." This act and its successors exhibited a considerable increase in the number of items subject to duties under the "chief value" and "value bracket" provisions, the latter becoming especially numerous.

The Wilson Tariff of 1894 contained no changes of interest for this study, but the Dingley Act of 1897 made several changes of note. It extended the undervaluation penalty by eliminating the penalty-free 10 per cent margin between entered and appraised value but reduced the penalty rate to 1 per cent for each 1 per cent of excess of appraised over entered value, subject to a maximum of 50 per cent. Excesses greater than 50 per cent were presumptively fraudulent, and forfeiture proceedings were required and rebuttable as previously. Entered value, as well as invoice value, was made the minimum dutiable value regardless of the appraiser's return, thus subjecting the importer

38. U.S. Treasury, *Annual Report, 1891*, p. xlii.

to another "administrative" basis for dutiable value, over and above the growing maze of economic or substantive valuation bases.[39]

The cost-of-production formula was changed by the Dingley Act to permit an addition of "not less than eight nor more than fifty per cent" to cover overhead. Of most significance for this study was the appearance for the first time, and in rudimentary form, of what has since become known as United States value:

> It shall become lawful for appraising officers, in determining the dutiable value of such merchandise, to take into consideration the wholesale price at which such or similar merchandise is sold or offered for sale in the United States, due allowance being made for estimated duties thereon, the cost of transportation, insurance, and other necessary expenses from the place of shipment to the United States, and a reasonable commission, if any has been paid, not exceeding six per centum.

This provision was contained in the same paragraph as the cost-of-production formula and afforded a basis to which to resort when no other alternative was available or when the cost-of-production data were questionable. In view of the wording as given above, it appears that the application of United States value was in no case mandatory and that even when used as a guide it established no necessary minimum valuation.

The Payne-Aldrich Tariff Act of 1909 is notable for its strengthening of the Board of General Appraisers and the creation of the United States Court of Customs Appeals.[40] The former was given by this act "all the powers of a circuit court of the United States" with respect to matters under its jurisdiction. The President of the United States was to designate one of the nine general appraisers as board president, who would be responsible for the constitution and disposition of the separate boards of three. The president was given charge of all fiscal and administrative affairs of the board, with authority to hire neces-

39. Admitting the enforcement difficulties involved, it is hard to comprehend the species of administrative and legislative ethics which compels, for duty purposes, the independent valuation of goods "any invoice or affidavit thereto to the contrary notwithstanding" and then about-faces and makes such invoice the basis for duties, only if it is *higher*. When there is added to substantive legislation which is itself of debatable justice, a superstructure of technical, exacting, and punitive administrative law, the possibilities of reforming the "dishonesty" of potential violators would appear to be beyond any reasonable expectation.

40. 36 U.S. Statutes 11 (Act of August 5, 1909). For a helpful account of the history and work of both courts cf. William H. Futrell, *The History of American Customs Jurisprudence,* esp. Parts III–V.

sary personnel and perform like functions. Any general appraiser or
board of three could permit, in his or their discretion, cross-examination of witnesses by importers or attorneys. The provision that the
general appraisers could use "all reasonable ways and means" of ascertaining dutiable value, involving "both judicial and inquisitorial powers" left the procedure open and unrestricted to the rules of evidence
binding regular trial courts. By the 1909 act the Board of General
Appraisers achieved virtually full judicial status and became independent of Treasury Department supervision.

The Court of Customs Appeals created by the same act consisted of
a presiding judge and four associate judges, with exclusive appellate
jurisdiction of cases decided by the Board of General Appraisers. The
court's headquarters were in Washington, D.C., but it could hold, in
its discretion, hearings in any judicial circuit. Appointments were non-
partisan and any three members constituted a quorum, the concur-
rence of at least three being necessary to any decision. In terms of
salary and in all other respects the status of the court was equivalent
to that of circuit courts of appeal, and its decisions were reviewable
only by the Supreme Court.

The Payne Act thus completed the reforms in customs jurisprudence begun by the Administrative Act of 1890. Although the Board
of General Appraisers had operated efficiently under the earlier act, it
only partially relieved the circuit (district) courts of the tremendous
volume of litigation, since the number of applications for review by
such courts was constantly increasing. The decisions of the circuit
courts in many cases could be appealed all the way up to the Supreme
Court. The congestion of court calendars was so great that the average
life of a customs appeal after leaving the Board of General Appraisers
was four and one-half years. The act of May 27, 1908, requiring the
review of all cases on the basis of the original record of the board,
reduced this to two and one-half years.[41] But, apart from the element
of delay, a fundamental defect in the procedure lay in the fact that
each of at least one hundred and twenty judges throughout the federal

41. U.S. Treasury, *Annual Report, 1908*, pp. 58–59. The procedure in reviewing the board's decisions under the 1890 act had permitted the referral to the
board by the court for the taking of such additional testimony as either litigant
chose to furnish. This amounted in most cases to a trial *de novo* by the circuit
court after the return of the additional evidence, since neither litigant was disposed to present his entire case initially before the board.

judiciary was a possible final arbiter of customs appeals. The impossibility of any uniformity in the interpretation of customs laws under these conditions is obvious. The raising of the Board of General Appraisers to the circuit-court level eliminated, in one step, more than half the number of judicial arbiters in customs cases. The creation of the Court of Customs Appeals removed all others but the Supreme Court and completed the task of concentration and specialization. The fruits of this legislation have been threefold: the speedier disposition of customs litigation; greater uniformity of decision; and the higher quality of decision made possible by the high degree of specialization on the part of the customs judiciary.

Along with the establishment of the Court of Customs Appeals the Payne Act, in section 28, created the office of assistant attorney-general in charge of customs. The assistant attorney-general and the deputy assistant attorney-general were to be appointed by the President at annual salaries of $10,000 and $7,500, respectively. Subject to the supervision of the Attorney-General, the assistant and his staff were given charge of the interests of the government in all customs litigation. They thus took over the functions of federal district attorneys in representing the government before the courts, as well as certain supervisory functions formerly handled by the solicitor of the Treasury.

The Payne Act made further changes pertaining to the administration of dutiable value. For the first time importers were permitted to make *deductions* from invoices, as well as additions, to make market value upon entry at the custom house. Although only a small percentage of entries was affected thereby, this was a belated recognition of the injustice which obtained in specific cases under the old law. Had this provision been in effect at the time of the Phelps-Dodge importations previously discussed, that whole unfortunate controversy would have been avoided. That it required nearly forty years thereafter for this legislative inequity to be corrected is a commentary on the relative weakness of importers as compared with other business groups in the American economy. That other legislative anomaly—the provision that, no matter what the market or otherwise dutiable value as determined by the appraisers, the invoice value, if greater, was to govern—was eliminated, leaving only entered value as the minimum.

Revision was again made in the penalty duty for undervaluation, raising the point at which presumption of fraud entered from 50 to 75 per cent excess in appraised, over entered, value. It was also specified that no penalty would ensue where the amount of duty would have been unaffected by the undervaluation. This relieved many cases of manifest injustice where penalties would accrue for technical under-valuation, although duties were unaffected, as in the case of goods covered by value brackets, specific duties, and the free list.[42]

The definition of United States value and the circumstances under which it was to be applied was significantly clarified by section 11. In brief, the section provided that consigned or other merchandise which was not "freely offered for sale in the usual wholesale quantities in the open market of the country of exportation to all purchasers" should in no case be appraised at less than the United States value, as defined. The definition made allowance for a deduction up to 8 per cent for general expenses and profits on purchased goods, the 6 per cent allowance for commission applying only to consigned goods. The mandatory use of United States value under these conditions resulted in its more frequent application, with a concomitant increase in duties resulting from the nature of the formula.

Before the Tariff Act of 1913 is considered, mention should be made of the intensive drive against customs frauds conducted at the port of New York by Collector Loeb, under the direction of Secretary of the Treasury MacVeagh. Undervaluation was a prominent target of this drive, which yielded a total of nearly six million dollars in fines, forfeitures, and compromises during the period from March 9, 1909, when Collector Loeb took office, to October 31, 1911. Together with payment of back duties, this brought into the Treasury a sum of over seven million dollars, as compared with a figure of slightly over nine hundred thousand dollars from similar sources over the entire fifteen-year period from 1894 to 1909.[43]

42. Cf. *Hoeninghaus* v. *U.S.*, 172 U.S. 622 (1898), in which the Supreme Court affirmed the penalty for undervaluation in the case of goods subject to value brackets even when duties were unaffected. One of the forfeiture cases investigated by B. G. Jayne and compromised for $50,000 involved, among other things, the undervaluation of sugar subject to specific duties. The sugar was improperly classified at a low rate, and, although there was apparently collusion between the importer and the sampler, Mr. Jayne testified that the undervaluation tended to deceive the appraiser and resulted in the lower classification.

43. Cf. I. Newton Hoffman, "Customs Administration under the 1913 Tariff Act," *Journal of Political Economy*, XXII (November, 1914), 853.

THE UNDERWOOD TARIFF OF 1913 AND THE EMERGENCY TARIFF OF 1921

Although a number of administrative changes were made by the Underwood Tariff, none of them concerned the substantive nature of dutiable value.[44] Nevertheless, some of the provisions are of interest. One of them was an exception to the requirement that the entered value should be the minimum dutiable value regardless of the appraised value. This provision permitted the importer, in relevant cases, to certify at the time of entry that his entered value was above foreign-market value and that the goods were so entered to meet advances by the appraiser in similar cases pending an appeal for reappraisement. If the importer's contention was subsequently sustained by a final decision on reappraisement and if it appeared that the action of the importer was taken in good faith and after due diligence and inquiry on his part, the Secretary of the Treasury could allow the duties to be levied on the lower basis claimed, in which case the Secretary of the Treasury was obliged to accompany his directions with a statement of his conclusions and the reasons therefor. This elaborate administrative maze through which the importer was compelled to run in order to become entitled to what the law purportedly forced upon him—namely, the payment of duty upon foreign-market value regardless of the price he actually paid—is an example of the *reductio ad absurdum* to which many tariff administrative provisions were rapidly coming in the latter days of protection in the United States. It was small comfort, therefore, for the importer to discover that, in addition to all the stated contingencies in this provision, the Treasury ruled that if the final appraisement sustained the importer only in part, he lost all the benefits of the provision and paid duty on the higher originally appraised, but officially repudiated, value. To add to his dismay, he was also forced to pay penalty duties for undervaluation, and the Court of Customs Appeals held that it was powerless to redress his wrong.[45] Even so, the 1913 act was an improvement over the old law.

---

44. Cf. James F. Curtis, "The Administrative Provisions of the Revenue Act of 1913," *Quarterly Journal of Economics*, XXVIII (November, 1913), 31–45.

45. *Mills and Gibb* v. *U.S.*, 8 C.C.A. 31 (1917). In this case the local appraisement was 20 per cent higher than the basis contended by the importer. Reappraisement reduced the difference to 5 per cent. The secretary stated that the importer's

Another concession to international trade made by the Underwood Tariff was the limitation placed upon protests of classification and other matters of law. Formerly an importer could protest any classification, favorable or unfavorable. An enterprising domestic manufacturer, deeming his protection against foreign competition inadequate, had imported a competing foreign product and promptly protested its classification as erroneous, claiming that it was subject to a higher rate. The Court of Customs Appeals sustained his right to do so.[46] In order to prevent the growth of this kind of harassing and potentially frivolous litigation, the Treasury Department prevailed upon Congress to limit protests to those claiming a lower rate.

By 1918 the necessity of revising customs administrative laws was again obvious, and the newly established Tariff Commission under the chairmanship of Professor Taussig, proposed an extensive revision.[47] Although no legislative action was taken at this time, the Tariff Commission's study became the basis for later recommendations, many of which were incorporated in the Tariff Act of 1922.[48]

The upheavals in world prices and monetary systems following World War I had important effects upon the history of customs valuation. Depreciated currencies abroad stimulated exports to this country, and, although devastated Europe was not in a position seriously to undermine American industry, additional protection was demanded. It was found that foreign goods were being sold for export to the United States in American currency. Because of the depreciating condition of foreign currencies the export price was frequently higher than the price for home consumption. The Supreme Court had ruled in 1898 that foreign-market value meant the price for home consumption and that the export price was to be ignored. Consequently, under the described conditions, importers could deduct upon entry to make market value and pay duties on less than the purchase price. This, of course, was highly displeasing to domestic producers, and, since there

---

contention had not been sustained, thus compelling him to pay duty on the original appraised value plus 20 per cent penalty duty for undervaluation. Judge DeVries of the Court of Customs Appeals rendered a vigorous and cogent dissenting opinion.

46. *U.S.* v. *Schwartz and Co.*, 3 C.C.A. 24 (1912).

47. U.S. Tariff Commission, *Report on the Revision of the Customs Administrative Laws* (1918).

48. U.S. Tariff Commission, *Tariff Information, 1921: Proposed Revision of the Customs Administrative Laws.*

was no judicial remedy for this consistent treatment of importers, resort was had to legislation.[49] The Emergency Tariff of 1921 incorporated a new alternative basis for dutiable value—"export value"—which was to govern in all cases where it was higher than foreign-market value. The definition of export value in this act was long and cumbersome, but, in brief, it was the price of the goods for exportation to the United States. In modified form this alternative basis for dutiable value has been retained in subsequent acts to the present time.[50] The Emergency Act also contained the antidumping law which is still in effect and the implications of which, for customs valuation, will be considered in a later chapter.

THE FORDNEY-McCUMBER TARIFF OF 1922[51]

After a year of lobbying, logrolling, debating, and high pressure the Republican majority in Congress passed the Tariff Act of 1922, establishing a new high level of protective and prohibitive duties and including a comprehensive revision of tariff administrative law, the net effect of which was to confer even further protection. Prominent among the new features of this act was the so-called "flexible" provision for the "scientific" adjustment of tariff rates. This provision (sec. 315) gave the President the power to "equalize" the domestic and foreign costs of production of any article of import by proclaiming, after investigation, such increases or reductions in rate, subject to a maximum change of 50 per cent, as he found necessary to effect the stated purpose. The general implications and ramifications of the flexible provision are beyond the scope of this study; the provision is, however, related to customs valuation by virtue of both its legislative history and certain of its administrative features.

The principle of home valuation, which had for the most part lain

49. It is not here intended to deny the reasonableness of appropriate tariff devices to offset currency depreciation, but it is perhaps not out of place to point out that export value (usually lower than when different from foreign value) was deemed an improper basis for dutiable value until it could be used when, and only when, advantageous to domestic producers (cf. discussion of the Passavant case, *infra*, pp. 158–62).

50. Cf. Benjamin Arthur Levett, *Through the Customs Maze* (New York, 1923), p. 38, for a brief discussion of export value in the Emergency Act of 1921. The application and consequences of export value today have much wider implications than the combating of the effects of depreciated currencies.

51. 42 U.S. Statutes 858 (Act of September 21, 1922).

dormant for many years,[52] was—like every other tool of administrative protection associated with the tariff—brought to the front and vigorously demanded by its exponents in the hearings on the Fordney bill in 1921. Many conflicting views were presented by the mutually opposing interests, and the conceptual as well as the terminological confusion between the various possible forms of home valuation— United States value, domestic value, and American selling price—did not help to raise the general quality of the debates.

While the hearings were in progress, the Tariff Commission made a brief study and report, resulting in the first published critical analysis of the nature of dutiable value and its possible alternative bases.[53] Although the commission pointed out the hazards of any change from the long-established procedure, the Ways and Means Committee in framing the bill made the American selling price "of comparable and competitive products of the United States" the primary basis of dutiable value. The bill passed the House in this form.[54]

The Senate Finance Committee had received many objections to this provision of the House bill. Moreover, it was working on the cost-equalization formula, first publicized as a plank in the Republican platform in 1904,[55] which it proposed to substitute for the American valuation principle. Nevertheless, the committee desired to investi-

52. Pleas for the establishment of home valuation had never entirely died out and can be found from time to time in the various tariff hearings and reports of customs officials. The subject was discussed at some length in the hearings on the Payne Bill: U.S. Congress, House Committee on Ways and Means, *Tariff Hearings, 1908–9*, VII, 7490–7515.
53. U.S. Tariff Commission, *American Valuation*, already cited. This little monograph is an excellent and concise introduction to the history of dutiable value in the United States.
54. Cf. Thomas Walker Page, *Making the Tariff in the United States* (New York, 1924), p. 54. An illuminating discussion of the House bill's definition of American valuation, and of the problems involved, may be found in Levett, *op. cit.*, pp. 123–41. Also, a document rich in information and sources, but likely to be misleading in matters both of fact and of interpretation, was prepared under the auspices of the Ways and Means Committee: *Tariff Information, 1921: Explanatory Notes with Information and Authorities Accompanying a Proposed Customs Administrative Act.* In addition to containing running comments on various administrative items in the proposed bill, it contains a number of appendixes: "Notes on American Valuation"; "History of Ad Valorem Valuation Provisions"; "Valuation Provisions in the Several Tariff Acts of the United States"; "Memorandum of Decisions of the Supreme Court on Uniformity and Preference under the Constitution"; "Statutes and Decisions of the Supreme Court on Delegation of Powers in Tariff Laws"; "Valuation Provisions in Foreign Customs Tariffs."
55. Cf. Taussig, *op. cit.*, p. 363.

gate thoroughly the matter of American valuation, and it obtained an appropriation of $100,000, which made possible the so-called "Reynolds Investigation." This was a study, based on actual entries at the New York Custom House, of importers' margins and the selling prices of imported goods in this country, with considerable attention to the problem of comparability. The findings revealed such wide variations in margins and prices, and such grave difficulties in the matter of comparability of foreign and domestically produced items, that Senator Smoot was convinced of the unwisdom of the American valuation plan as a general basis for dutiable value. In a prepared speech before the Senate he gave an able exposition of a few of the defects of both American selling price and domestic value for general application. But in the case of coal-tar products, and as an adjunct of the flexible provision, he was willing to use American valuation, "frankly" on the principle that rates based on foreign values would not afford the extreme protection needed in the cases indicated. When Senator Jones of New Mexico challenged that position, pointing out that it was merely necessary to raise rates on foreign values to a sufficient height to obtain the desired protection, it became obvious that the American-valuation plan was a device similar to the minimum-value provision of the early nineteenth century—a device to keep the American public from seeing in all its nakedness the exorbitant level of duties contemplated by rampant protectionism:

MR. SMOOT: I recognize, I think, what the Senator is getting at . . . no one is trying to deny it; in fact I will say to the Senator now that if . . . the article was transferred to American valuation, and the President exercised all the powers which he is authorized to exercise under this bill and increased the 60 per cent duty to 90 per cent, under the American valuation that would mean that there would be a 900 per cent duty on that article.

MR. JONES: I recall one particular class of main dyes, where the American manufacturer said that the reason why he did not want to have a tariff based upon the foreign valuation was because the rate would have to be too high . . . he said it would have to be 1000 per cent.

MR. SMOOT: Oh, I will go the Senator one better than that. There was one of them that said it would have to be 2000 per cent.[56]

Nevertheless, the provision of American selling price, for application to coal-tar products and as one of the tools of the flexible provision,

56. *Congressional Record,* LXII, Part VI, 5884, April 24, 1922. For Senator Smoot's general discussion of American valuation cf. pp. 5876–78.

was enacted into law, subject to the provision that in the latter case rates were not to be raised. The various issues in the application of the American selling price, and the manner in which it has been used subsequent to its achievement of legal status, are discussed in a later chapter.

Another victory scored by domestic interests was the creation of section 516, affording them the privilege—specifically denied them on policy grounds by the 1913 act—of appealing appraisements and protesting classifications of specific importations. In the case of objections to dutiable value on any importation, the domestic manufacturer, producer, or wholesaler was permitted to file a complaint with the Secretary of the Treasury, who would forward a copy of it to each port involved, whereupon the appraiser was required to report each subsequent importation of such merchandise with all pertinent facts and the reasons for the appraisement. If the appraiser thereupon advanced the value, and the importer appealed to the Board of General Appraisers, the domestic producer was entitled to appear before the board as a party in interest. If the appraiser did not advance the value, the domestic interest could make its own appeal to reappraisement in the same manner as an interested importer. Even if the lower value was ultimately sustained, the enforced litigation and suspension of liquidation on all such entries resulting from the domestic manufacturer's appeal would be vexatious and costly to the importer. A somewhat corresponding procedure was prescribed for matters of classification. Section 516 thus made it legal, if not respectable, for domestic interests to become the self-appointed custodians of law enforcement and to leave no stone unturned to insure that the full possibilities of the last technical exaction available by statute against importers be not overlooked by unwary customs officers.[57]

57. One of the most onerous, vexatious, and costly punitive provisions in the Tariff Act of 1930 was the complex of regulations for enforcing "marking requirements" upon importers. Unless specifically exempted by Treasury regulation, "every article imported into the United States, *and* its immediate container, *and* the package in which such article is imported, shall be marked, stamped, branded, or labeled, in legible English words, in a conspicuous place, in such manner as to indicate the country of origin of such article" (section 304, Tariff Act of 1930; italics added). Failure to have goods properly marked at the time of importation automatically imposed an additional 10 per cent penalty on the value of the goods. The Court of Customs Appeals held that a domestic producer who discovers an imported article which he feels is improperly marked may protest and be heard by the courts. This means that a domestic producer who detects a misspelled word or

In certain other matters the administrative provisions of the Ford-ney Act reduced the hardships upon importers. In the case of entries under protest, previously discussed in connection with the 1913 act, the importer was not to be penalized if his contention was upheld *either in whole or in part,* and he was permitted to pay duty on the final appraised value rather than on the higher value entered by him under protest, which so frequently subjected him to additional pen-alty duties. Forfeiture proceedings were not required until the excess of appraised value over entered value exceeded 100 per cent, instead of 75 per cent as formerly. It should also be observed that from the standpoint of clarity and orderly draftsmanship the Fordney Act was a marked improvement over previous general tariff acts.

DEVELOPMENTS IN THE PERIOD 1922–40

Two legislative items of interest appeared between the enactment of the two great tariff acts following World War I. One was the act of May 28, 1926, changing the name of the Board of General Ap-praisers to the "United States Customs Court." The other, in 1929, in view of the court's relatively light work load, transferred to the Court of Customs Appeals the jurisdiction of patent appeals formerly exer-cised by the Court of Appeals for the District of Columbia. The court's new name accordingly became the "Court of Customs and Patent

---

other minor irregularity in the marking of a competing imported article can run into court with his finding and very possibly obtain redress of the "wrong" done to him. The following examples of penalties actually levied for minor infractions were testified to by importers during the hearings on the Customs Administrative Bill: a $1,500 penalty for improper marking of bags of shelled nuts from Portugal: a *c* was erroneously substituted for *g,* making "Portucuese" instead of "Portuguese" product; a $12,000 penalty for failure to mark Argentine wool with the name "Argentina" instead of the name of the *estancia* where the wool was grown. In this case the wool was purchased by a domestic manufacturer before it left Argentina; the country of origin was perfectly well known to him; the wool would lose its identity in the process of manufacture; and the shipment was correctly marked at the owner's expense, but to no avail, before it left the bonded warehouse. The $12,000 fine in this case was, in reality, the penalty for not using wool grown on the backs of American sheep. Illustrations of this variety could be multiplied *ad nauseam* by referring to the records of the various tariff hearings. The foregoing appeared in *Hearings on H.R. 6738* (75th Cong., 1st sess.), pp. 41 ff., 194 ff. The Customs Administrative Act of 1938 made a number of substantial improvements, permitting the marking of goods in customs custody, or the exportation of goods improperly marked, without penalty. It also gave much needed flexibility to the administration of the marking provisions by increasing the latitude granted to the Secretary of the Treasury.

Appeals." By the Tariff Act of 1930, the judges of both courts were given life terms, subject to good behavior, thus finally rendering them independent of executive removal.

The hearings preceding the enactment of the Tariff Act of 1930[58] were remarkably similar to those of eight years before. The same groups and the same faces descended upon Washington with briefs, affidavits, and testimony to plead their special causes. Likewise the published hearings of both the relevant House and Senate committees contained thousands of pages of material of the same import, if not of identical content. Again the proposal for American valuation as the general basis of dutiable value was strongly urged by lobbyists for trade associations and, by this time, for agricultural and labor groups. The representative of the American Farm Bureau Federation indicated the interest which his organization was taking in the possibilities of administrative protection:

> Our membership in the Farm Bureau during the last two years has been more attracted to and interested in the flexible provisions than any other section that even might have included rates. . . . During the last two years the farmers have realized that some of their rates were not adequate, and to get the rates raised under the flexible provisions, such as the 50 per cent limitation feature, we have been interested before the Tariff Commission in cases on these commodities: wheat, corn, Swiss cheese, cherries, maple syrup, maple sugar, butter, milk, cream, flaxseed, fresh tomatoes, tomato paste, onions, peppers, eggs, and egg products.

Whatever the assistance bestowed upon them by the Fordney Tariff, the "interests" clamored for more, and ever more, protection. Even the privilege of interfering in appraisement and classification to the extent allowed them by section 516 was insufficient. The spokesman for the American Tariff League referred to 516 as "a hollow gesture," because it did not operate swiftly enough and because private attorneys of the domestic interests were not permitted to conduct the case against the importer on an equal footing with the Attorney-General before the courts.[59]

Despite all the representations, the valuation provisions of the Hawley-Smoot Tariff Act, as finally passed, were in substance the same as those in the 1922 act. Since these provisions and pertinent portions of the testimony preceding their enactment are discussed in

58. 46 U.S. Statutes 590 (Act of June 17, 1930).
59. U.S. Congress, Senate Committee on Finance, *Tariff Act of 1929: Hearings on H.R. 2667: Special and Administrative Provisions* (July 15–18, 1929), p. 24

later chapters, it is unnecessary to recount them here. Mention is made, however, of the incorporation into the act, in section 340, of a requirement that the Tariff Commission ascertain the changes in existing ad valorem rates which would be necessary to place the entire tariff upon the domestic-value basis. The President was charged, by section 642, with the investigation, by such agencies as he deemed appropriate, of the various alternative bases of dutiable value, and the submission to Congress of the results of such study with whatever recommendations he found advisable. Both these studies were made by the Tariff Commission and the reports duly transmitted.[60] A further detailed study, less directly pertaining to the general subject of valuation, was made by the Tariff Commission in 1932 in response to a Senate resolution calling for data relating to the effects of depreciated foreign currencies upon imports into the United States.[61]

The Reciprocal Trade Agreements Act of 1934, of epoch-making importance in the tariff history of the United States, did not affect the principles of valuation.[62] From then until the United States entered World War II the principal change in the law of dutiable value was made by the Customs Administrative Act of 1938. This act inserted the words "for home consumption" in the definition of foreign-market value, thus eliminating from consideration the value of exports to countries other than the United States. The words "for domestic consumption" were also inserted in the definitions of United States value and American selling price, for ostensibly parallel reasons.[63]

The foregoing history has attempted to portray the broad, general development of customs valuation in the United States and at the same time to present sufficient detail to permit a reasonably clear understanding of the major problems involved. The significant conclusions emerging from the historical survey are summarized in Part IV. Part III, following, treats in more detail the problems of contemporary valuation law and procedure.

60. Cf. U.S. Tariff Commission, *Domestic Value—Conversion of Rates: Report No. 45* (2d ser. [1932]); also *Methods of Valuation,* already cited.
61. U.S. Tariff Commission, *Depreciated Exchange* (1932).
62. I.e., in the law of dutiable value in the United States. It did accomplish very substantial and desirable improvements in Canadian valuation of United States exports (cf. *supra,* pp. 309–10).
63. This change permitted the American chemical and dye industry to dump its products abroad without jeopardizing its high tariff protection from the dutiable-value structure based on prices in the home-controlled market.

PART III

Contemporary Valuation Law and Procedure

CHAPTER V

Foreign and Export Value

General Valuation Provisions of the Statute

PART II of this study has traced the general development of dutiable value and the related problems of customs valuation in the United States up to the present. It is the purpose of Part III to examine in detail the several forms of dutiable value currently in effect, special problems in customs valuation, and the economic implications of the law and its administration. The focal point of observation will be the body of valuation law and procedure developed in recent years, principally by the Customs Court and the Court of Customs and Patent Appeals.[1]

The Tariff Act of 1930, as amended, is the current statutory expression of valuation law. Court decisions under prior acts are often controlling, however, either because the current statute did not change certain provisions of earlier laws or because the points of law in question have been omitted from the statutes and left to the courts to decide. From the inception of the Board of General Appraisers in 1890 to the present there has been a steady growth of an organic body of customs law filling many tens of thousands of pages and covering

1. Judicial decisions on customs matters are made by three tribunals: the Supreme Court, the Court of Customs and Patent Appeals (prior to 1929 the Court of Customs Appeals), and the United States Customs Court (prior to 1926 the Board of General Appraisers). Customs and patent decisions of the Court of Customs and Patent Appeals are contained in separate volumes; for convenience, the references contained herein will omit the designation "Customs." Since 1938, the decisions of the United States Customs Court have been separately published semiannually in bound volumes. These decisions are of three kinds, abbreviated as indicated: "C.D."—Customs Decisions, containing opinions in full and covering protests of classification and other "matters of law"; "Abs."—Abstracts of decisions in less important protest cases; "Reap."—Reappraisement decisions, covering reappraisements by a single judge or reviews of reappraisements by a division of three. Customs Court judges were known as "justices" between 1926 and the effective date of the Tariff Act of 1930. Abbreviations of judicial references contained herein are explained in detail in United States Treasury Department, *Digest of Customs and Related Laws and Decisions Thereunder* (1935), I, v–vi.

literally thousands of questions of fact and law. Because of the tremendous volume and the continuing growth of valuation law, as well as conflicting decisions therein, the following treatment is at best representative and tentative rather than comprehensive and definitive.

Section 402 of the Tariff Act of 1930 defines dutiable value as follows:

(a) BASIS.—For the purposes of this Act the value of imported merchandise shall be—

(1) The foreign or the export value, whichever is higher;

(2) If the appraiser determines that neither the foreign nor the export value can be satisfactorily ascertained, then the United States value;

(3) If the appraiser determines that neither the foreign value, the export value, nor the United States value can be satisfactorily ascertained, then the cost of production;

(4) In the case of an article with respect to which there is in effect under section 336 a rate of duty based upon the American selling price of a domestic article, then the American selling price of such article.

Section 503 states the administrative "general rule" concerning dutiable value:

Except as provided in section 562 of this Act (relating to withdrawal from manipulating warehouses) and in subdivision (b) of this section [relating to entries pending reappraisement of test cases], the basis for the assessment of duties on imported merchandise subject to ad valorem rates of duty shall be the entered value or the final appraised value, whichever is higher.

A number of preliminary observations should be made at this time and kept in mind during the following detailed analysis of the substantive law of dutiable value. First, it is evident that, before any decision can be made as to dutiable value, both foreign and export value must, if possible, be ascertained. If both can be ascertained, the higher applies; if only one is ascertainable, it applies; if neither can be found, resort must be had to the remaining alternates.[2] Thus, both

2. The appraiser frequently has great difficulty in discovering a value corresponding to any of the valuation bases specified. Nevertheless, he is technically prohibited from making an arbitrary valuation, i.e., every appraisement must be one of the forms specified in sec. 402 (C.R. 2931, 3090; Abs. 26863 [CC]). He may in fact, however, make an arbitrary valuation and label it as one of the statutory bases (e.g., foreign value) and it will stand before the courts unless the importer (a) overthrows the legal presumption of correct appraisement and (b) satisfactorily establishes a different value as correct (*Garbey* v. *United States*, 24 C.C.P.A. 48 [1936]). It is sometimes easy to show that the appraisement is palpably erroneous without successfully establishing another valuation. In such cases the appraisement stands.

foreign and export value have primacy in the ascertainment of dutiable value.

A second observation stems from the fact that the several substantive bases of dutiable value are "alternate" rather than "alternative"
bases. They do not provide a free choice among several alternatives;
they can be used only in the absence of the base or bases having
priority, as indicated, subject always to the general rule of making
the entered value the minimum. Also, from the standpoint of the
importer, the alternates are not equally desirable. As between foreign
and export value, it would be difficult to state a priori which of the
two would result in higher duties in a particular case. For reasons
which will appear later it is probable that where foreign and export
value diverge, export value is the lower of the two. United States
value, the next alternate, is usually higher than either of the foregoing, since the statutory deductions for approximating foreign value
are generally considerably less in the aggregate than their real counterparts. Cost of production, both as defined and as interpreted,
depends so largely upon the circumstances of individual importations that very little generalization can be made as to its relative
desirability to the importer. The American selling price, as specified
in subsection 4 above, applies only to coal-tar intermediates and
certain other special cases and need not be considered at this time
except to state that by its very nature it is substantially higher than
any of the other bases except in rare and unusual cases. Although
importers and foreign exporters cannot effect a choice among existing
alternates, they can often influence the basic commercial conditions
underlying their importations in such a manner as to throw dutiable
value into a desired category. All the statutory provisions, administrative regulations, and judicial findings pertaining to dutiable value
represent, from one point of view, an endeavor to minimize the freedom of importers to manipulate the conditions underlying the valuation of imports and to minimize all uncertainty in the administration
of dutiable value.

A third observation which should remain in the foreground in the
consideration of the details of the substantive law of dutiable value
is the significance of penalty duties for undervaluation. The importance to the importer of sustaining his contention as to dutiable
value is much greater than merely the saving of the difference in

duties upon the two values; in every case in which appraised value exceeds his entered value the importer must pay a penalty,[3] and this penalty may amount to more than the regular duties or even to more than the purchase price of the merchandise itself. Every issue connected with valuation procedure and law therefore assumes a significance for tariff or administrative protection seldom appreciated or contemplated in political and academic discussions of the nature and effects of the tariff.

Statutory Definition of Foreign and Export Value[4]

Subsections *c* and *d* of section 402, as amended, define foreign and export value in detail:

(c) FOREIGN VALUE.—The foreign value of imported merchandise shall be the market value or the price at the time of exportation of such merchandise to the United States at which such or similar merchandise is freely offered for sale for home consumption to all purchasers in the principal markets of the country from which exported, in the usual wholesale quantities and in the ordinary course of trade, including the cost of all containers and coverings of whatever nature, and all other costs, charges, and expenses incident to placing the merchandise in condition, packed ready for shipment to the United States.

(d) EXPORT VALUE.—The export value of imported merchandise shall be the market value or the price, at the time of exportation of such merchandise to the United States, at which such or similar merchandise is freely offered for sale to all purchasers in the principal markets of the country from which exported, in the usual wholesale quantities and in the ordinary course of trade, for exportation to the United States, plus, when not in-

---

3. This study departs from established customs terminology by referring to additional duties for undervaluation as "penalty duties." This is done both to distinguish from other types of additional duty (such as countervailing and dumping duties, to say nothing of the "additional duties" paid by the importer on the increase in valuation when his contention as to dutiable value is overruled) and to recognize, as did the Supreme Court in 1902 (cf. *infra*, p. 278, n. 2), the obvious nature of such duties. Penalty duties for undervaluation are 1 per cent of the appraised value for each 1 per cent excess of appraised over entered value. The penalty is automatic, regardless of whether the undervaluation be deliberate or unintentional. Remission is made, however, for clerical error or upon successful application to the Customs Court proving lack of intent to defraud and fulfilling other requirements specified in sec. 489. For further discussion of the remission feature cf. *infra*, pp. 277–83.

4. Foreign and export value together account for probably more than 95 per cent of all appraisements (cf. *infra*, p. 196, n. 2). Inasmuch as this chapter is devoted to foreign and export value, and to avoid confusion, the definition of the other bases is reserved for subsequent chapters.

cluded in such price, the cost of all containers and coverings of whatever nature, and all other costs, charges, and expenses incident to placing the merchandise in condition, packed ready for shipment to the United States.

It will be noted that except for the distinguishing phrases "for home consumption" (foreign value) and "for exportation to the United States" (export value) these two definitions are almost identical. Since the identical phrases which go to make up the respective definitions have the same meaning in law, it is possible to discuss both foreign and export value simultaneously. This is especially desirable in view of the intimate relationship between these two forms of dutiable value.

The Interpretation of the Statute

An examination of the foregoing definitions reveals a large number of individual factors affecting the existence or the amount of any valuation under the categories in question. A separate listing of these, in the order in which they appear in the definition, will serve to emphasize the nature of the problem and to prepare for the individual treatment of the points in question:

1. Market value or price
2. Time of exportation
3. Such or similar merchandise
4. Freely offered for sale
5. For home consumption (or exportation to the U.S.)
6. Principal markets
7. Country from which exported
8. Usual wholesale quantities
9. Ordinary course of trade
10. Cost of containers and coverings
11. All other costs, charges, etc.

This breakdown of the two definitions is not free from objection. It omits a number of important qualifying words which must be taken into consideration; moreover, it may not represent the most appropriate grouping of the wording under consideration. Nevertheless, it affords a starting-point for the analysis. It will shortly be seen that very few of these factors are independent in the sense that they may be interpreted without reference to the others. In fact a major difficulty in the analysis is experienced because of the permutations and combinations made possible when each of several different shades of meaning is applied to each of several factors. The resulting combinations make for many more possible conditions and elements of value than the number of individual factors to be considered.

For the purposes of analysis the factors listed above might be classified either as "conditions" or as "components" of value accordingly as they: (1) require the satisfaction of certain prerequisites legally essential to the existence of either foreign or export value; or (2) prescribe the inclusion of actual value ingredients or elements to make total dutiable value. Some of the factors, as will be seen, operate to accomplish both. Because of the difficulties of such a classification it is preferable to conduct the analysis on a step-by-step basis, discussing in turn each significant term or factor in its relation to the entire valuation problem. The order in which the several items are taken up differs from the order in which they appear in the definition; this is done to provide a sequence corresponding more closely to the logical primacy and closeness of relationship of the factors under consideration.

MARKET VALUE OR PRICE

The phrase "the market value or the price" presents a number of difficulties. In one sense, it is the ultimate objective or *quaesitum* of the whole appraisement process, representing the final dutiable value and comprehending all the elaborations and modifications of the various qualifying phrases. In another sense, it is the point of departure or foundation upon which dutiable value is erected by subjecting the putative basic price of the goods per se to the prescribed modifications. Further complications are suggested by the question of whether "market value" and "price" are construed to be synonymous, or alternative and distinctive, terms.

In economic theory, the terms "market value" and "price" are usually considered as synonymous and as representing the equilibrium of demand and supply under given market conditions, even though these conditions range from perfect competition to complete monopoly. Because of various requirements in the law, such as that of free offer, the terms "market value" and "price" in the law of dutiable value are narrower in this respect than is their connotation in theoretical economics. On the other hand, although the term "market value" in the law might seem to connote some kind of meeting of minds between buyers and sellers in the market, no such implication is necessary in the interpretation of the word "price." A "price" satisfying the requirements of the law of dutiable value might therefore be merely the seller's asking or announced price at which he is willing to offer his goods. As will be seen later, offered prices play a significant role in customs valuation, especially in the absence of actual transactions. Thus the inclusion of the word "price" in the statute has facilitated the treatment of many cases on a basis which might be dubious or impossible were the statute limited to the term "market value." In most cases, however, the courts have not found it necessary to treat "market value" and "price" as other than synonymous and interchangeable terms and have employed as a unit the phrase "the market value or the price" in the same manner as the statute.[5]

The major difficulties experienced in the past concern the interrelationships of the phrase "market value or price" with the various qualifying factors listed above. The effects of these interrelationships will be discussed under the heading of the most appropriate factor. For example, the question of what is the basic, substantive price of the merchandise per se is best treated in the discussion of "the usual wholesale quantities." The question of whether or not inland freight is legally included within the market price is best handled in the treatment of "principal markets." The question as to the existence or nonexistence of dutiable value on either the foreign- or the export-value basis arises frequently in connection with the interpretation of the phrase "such or similar" and is perhaps best discussed under that heading. The necessary interdependence of all the terms or factors and the consequent artificiality of their separate treatment must always be borne in mind. There still remain, nevertheless, a number of aspects of dutiable value which are best discussed under the heading of "market value or price." These include the treatment of cash discounts, commissions, and foreign drawbacks and taxes.

Cash discounts.—Assuming satisfactory evidence of their existence, cash discounts (not to be confused with the highly complex subject of quantity discounts) have always been allowable in the determination of market price. The rationale underlying this treatment is simple and best illustrated in the words of the Supreme Court in 1865:

The value means the cash value. The price at 30 days' credit might be different, and the difference would be greatly increased by a credit of six months or a year, but the value or cost would still be the same. The differ-

5. Cf. *United States* v. *Passavant,* 169 U.S. 16 (1898), which is fundamental to a long line of decisions pertaining to the nature of market value.

ence would be chargeable to the credit, and not to a difference in the value of the goods.[6]

It is not necessary that importers take advantage of the cash discount in order to maintain the lower foreign value.[7] It is possible for actual settlement prices to be always higher than foreign-market value for dutiable purposes. The position of the courts in this matter coincides with the economic view of the situation, since the failure to take advantage of a cash discount constitutes a short-term import of capital along with the import of the merchandise.

Commissions.—The question of whether commissions paid at any stage in the transfer of the merchandise are part of dutiable value turns upon whether they are a part of market price in the foreign market concerned. This in turn depends upon such other terms of the statute as "freely offered for sale," "ordinary course of trade," and so on. In practice, the question is usually resolved by the function performed by the commissionaire. If he represents the seller, the commission is dutiable; if he is an agent of the purchaser, it is nondutiable.[8] The difficult technical questions in such cases are usually questions of fact, and it is up to the courts to determine from the mass of testimony, affidavits, reports of Treasury attachés,[9] and other data, just whom the commissionaire represents. Since, in the nature of his occupation, he is a "go-between," he often represents both, or neither more than the other. But if the seller's freely offered price to all potential purchasers is at a level exclusive of the commission paid in a given case, the commission forms no part of market value and is therefore nondutiable.[10]

The shift over a hundred years ago from specific purchase price to market value as the basis of dutiable value led logically to the exclusion from dutiable value in specific cases of certain components of specific purchase price. Nondutiable commissions are in this class.[11] A good example of the possible substantial excess of specific purchase

6. *Arthur* v. *Goddard*, 96 U.S. 145 (1877).

7. *Ibid.;* also C.R. 2049.

8. *United States* v. *Case and Co., Inc.*, 13 C.C.A. 122 (1925); also C.R. 36051; C.R. 1531.

9. Sec. 649 of the Tariff Act of 1930 changed the name of all foreign customs agents from "customs attachés" to "Treasury attachés."

10. *United States* v. *Kohlberg*, 27 C.C.P.A. 223 (1940).

11. It will be recalled that in the early part of the nineteenth century the policy of including or omitting commissions from dutiable value varied from statute to statute (cf. *supra*, pp. 57–60, 99).

price over market value is found in the case of *American Express Company* v. *United States* (14 C.C.A. 53 [1926]), involving the dutiability of a 175,000-franc commission paid by the American purchaser to an employee of Sachs and Company, Paris, for his services in selecting and matching pearls. The report of the Treasury attaché abroad corroborated the importer's testimony that the commissionaire devoted a large amount of his own time to the project and that Sachs and Company received no part of the commission. The foreign agent's report stressed the point that the commission "unquestionably entered into the cost of the pearls to Mr. Swift." The court ruled that this cost had no relevance to the question of market value. In the same category fall various service items which do not alter the goods and which do not affect market value.[12]

Drawbacks.—The question as to whether foreign drawbacks and other abatements of either customs or internal taxes are properly an element in dutiable value has been resolved by the courts in the same manner as the larger question of the dutiability of any foreign tax, whether remitted or not. The general test is the statutory requirement that the dutiable value be "the foreign value or the export value, whichever is higher." In the interpretation of the general rule, the courts are not concerned with whether a drawback has or has not been allowed upon imported merchandise.[13] The relevant question, in satisfaction of the statute, is: "What is the market price in the country of export, both for home consumption and for export?" If by virtue of the drawback the price for export is lower than the price for home consumption, the latter price applies, not because a drawback has been paid but because the statute bases dutiable value on the higher of the two prices. If for some conceivable reason the export price, even with benefit of drawback, were higher than the price for home consumption, it would govern. Likewise, in the absence of foreign value, if export value exists, the question is again not one of drawback, if such

12. Such services may include inspection, comparison with samples, rejection, repacking, supervision of packing and shipping, etc. (cf. *Stein* v. *United States*, 1 C.C.A. 36 [1910]).

13. The treatment of foreign drawbacks for purposes of ascertaining dutiable value is not to be confused with their treatment in the application of countervailing duties. For an informative discussion of the history of United States' policy with respect to the latter problem cf. Jacob Viner, *Dumping: A Problem in International Trade* (Chicago, 1923), pp. 173–78.

has been paid, but of an export value meeting the various tests of the statute.

The Passavant case, already cited, laid down the basic principle for the treatment of foreign drawbacks and taxes with respect to dutiable value. This case involved German velvets which were subject to certain internal-revenue taxes in Germany unless exported. The export price was thus normally lower than the price for home consumption. At the time of importation (1890–92) there was no specific statutory provision for export value in the tariff laws of the United States. The appraiser added the amount of the tax to the export price to make market value "in the principal markets of the country of exportation" (the wording of the Administrative Act of 1890). The Supreme Court held that the German tax, even though none had been levied on the goods in question, was part of the dutiable value because it formed part of the market price in the country of exportation:

> This market value or price was the price in Germany and not the price after leaving the country, and the act does not contemplate two prices or two market values. . . . Doubtless, to encourage exportation and the introduction of German goods into other markets, the German Government could remit or refund the tax, pay a bonus or allow a drawback. . . . But the laws of this country in the assessment of duties proceed upon the market value in the exporting country and not upon the market value less such remission or amelioration as that country chooses to allow in accordance with its own version of public policy.[14]

Justices Brown and Peckham, dissenting from the majority opinion, pointed out that there were clearly two separate and distinct wholesale market prices—one for home consumption and one for export—and that so far as the evidence was concerned there was nothing to indicate that the export market in Germany was not ten times greater than the domestic market. The dissenting justices concluded that the court's construction was unnecessary and served to work a hardship upon American consumers by imposing an additional levy upon them.

Inasmuch as the Passavant decision has been followed in numerous subsequent court findings concerning the general nature of market value or price, in the treatment of foreign taxes and drawbacks, and in many related issues concerning dutiable value, it is well to examine it in the light of the history of dutiable value in this country, after first testing it in terms of the reasoning of the decision itself.

14. *United States* v. *Passavant*, 169 U.S. 16 (1898) at pp. 22 ff.

The court's unqualified statement that the act "does not contemplate two market values," in order to make sense, must be interpreted to mean that the act did not contemplate more than one dutiable value for a given article in the United States. Since an act of Congress cannot legislate out of existence two, or two dozen, market values, if such exist in a foreign country, the act obviously meant that only one market value, from among all those existing in a given country, can be selected as the basis for dutiable value in the United States. The question then resolves itself into "which market value is the most appropriate basis for dutiable value?"

The court may not have felt obliged (it did not, for all that appears in the decision) to state the reasons for its preference of the home-consumption price, rather than the export price, in Germany; but to state that "the market value or price was the price in Germany and not the price after leaving the country" was a patent misrepresentation of the conditions at issue. The export value was as much the market value *in Germany* as was the value for home consumption. It was even more so, if the not unlikely possibility suggested by the dissenting justices—that the export market might have been far larger than the home market—was a fact. In any event the court asserted no reason for its decision other than to repeat the formula that the law contemplated the assessment of duties on the market value in the exporting country.[15]

The contention of the dissenting justices that the majority decision was unnecessary is further corroborated by the history of dutiable value in the United States. The original basis for dutiable value was the specific purchase price. This basis was not finally changed until 1842, when the tariff act of that year resulted in the permanent adoption of market value. Two motives are apparent as the underlying

---

15. The only case cited by way of precedent was that of *Muser* v. *Magone*, 155 U.S. 240 (1894), which upheld an arbitrary method of appraisement of cotton embroideries from St. Gall, on which no market value was said to exist for the goods in the finished condition and for which the appraiser used a constructive formula in order to approximate market value. The only significant elements common to the two cases were the excess of appraised value over purchase price and the contested legality of the methods of appraisement used. The present statute specifically defines foreign value as the value "for home consumption." The point to be observed is that in the Passavant decision the court, in effect, performed a legislative act—the insertion in the statute, *de novo*, of the words "for home consumption."

reasons for this change: (1) the prevention of undervaluation; (2) the adoption of a single dutiable value for a given article of import. The history of customs valuation in the first half of the nineteenth century was in large part a search for a method of valuation which would "protect the revenue and the honest importer" from the competitive undervaluation of "foreign traders." At a time of relatively undeveloped and inadequate informational and communication facilities, business records and books of account, customs organization, etc., dependence upon invoices and affidavits for evidence of dutiable value was too uncertain and unreliable a basis for the assessment of duties. The adoption of market value gave to customs authorities a yardstick for the determination of dutiable value independent of the invoices and declarations of individual importers and at the same time provided for uniform duties per article of import, a type of uniformity not required by the specific-purchase-price basis.

But neither of these purposes—the prevention of undervaluation nor uniformity of dutiable value—required more than the selection of a single, appropriate market value. The value or price most accurately reflecting the actual value of the imported merchandise, if different from the price actually paid, would have been the price which was freely available to any importer for like merchandise in the relevant markets of the country concerned. Such markets were, by definition and by trade practice, the export markets in the various countries of the world.

The effect, if not the intent, of the majority decision in the Passavant case was the adoption by judicial interpretation of partial countervailing measures against direct and indirect subsidies of exports in the form of drawbacks and bounties, which had become more and more prevalent during the latter half of the nineteenth century and which resulted in an increasing divergence between export prices and prices for home consumption. But the question as to when export prices become dumping prices and therefore justification for appropriate countervailing measures is a separate question of policy not to be confused with the question of ordinary dutiable value. The arbitrary selection of home-consumption markets and the repudiation of the export markets of the world as the basis for dutiable value on goods shipped to the United States is an outstanding example of the raising of tariff duties by administrative and judicial decision.

The exclusion of export value as the basis for dutiable value resulting from the Passavant decision persisted until domestic manufacturers during the depreciated currency debacle following World War I discovered that its use would be to their advantage. As we have seen, export value was then hurriedly incorporated into the Emergency Tariff of 1921 but applicable only when it was higher than foreign value. In addition to currency considerations, this served to protect against the depressing of foreign-market prices under certain conditions to an artificially low level to minimize dutiable value on exports to the United States.[16] In some respects, however, export value has proved to be a boomerang by permitting a lower value than United States value—which would otherwise apply in the absence of foreign value—and, in addition, the frequent avoidance of foreign value itself. To the extent that export value is actually used, it is a restoration of the basis for dutiable value in large part applicable when market price was originally substituted for specific purchase price.[17]

Foreign taxes in general.—As in the case of drawbacks and tax abatements, the Passavant case has been controlling for many years[18] in the general treatment of taxes as part of foreign or export value. This has resulted in some curious conditions difficult for the layman to understand but having substantial validity independent of the Passavant decision.

All foreign taxes—customs, internal revenue, excise, production, consumption, and the like—so long as they are generally applied to

16. Perhaps the best example of this is the case of the Canadian ferrosilicon industry cited by Professor Viner, which prior to 1921 was able profitably to depress prices for the home market, which took less than 10 per cent of the output. Exports at substantially higher prices to the United States were legally entered at the Canadian home-market prices, which ran from 20 to 40 per cent below prices for export. Viner correctly points out that provisions in acts prior to 1913 making the invoice price the minimum dutiable value would have prevented a situation of this kind. Since invoice value, however, may or may not represent export value, the new export-value provision in the 1921 act was not the "reinsertion . . . of the old requirement that duties be levied on the current market value in the country of exportation or on the export value, whichever was higher" (Viner, *op. cit.*, pp. 7–8). Cf. also Abraham Berglund, "The Ferroalloy Industries and Tariff Legislation," *Political Science Quarterly*, XXXVI (June, 1921), 270 ff. Berglund made reference, without specifying, to other indications of this practice.

17. This follows from the relatively higher degree of uniformity in export prices. The export market deals with fewer purchasers and involves large wholesale quantities of merchandise sold under relatively uniform terms.

18. But cf. *infra*, p. 162, n. 21.

goods entering at wholesale into foreign consumption, are part of foreign value.[19] They are thus made a substantive element of dutiable value whenever goods are appraised at foreign value (i.e., whenever foreign value is higher than, or exists in the absence of, export value), even though they are not levied on the actual merchandise exported to the United States. But if there is no foreign value and the importation is appraised at export value, such taxes are not included in dutiable value.[20] This is a condition which could not have been foreseen at the time of the Passavant decision, since there was then no statutory provision for the export-value basis. This freedom from duties on foreign taxes makes export value a desirable category for importers in addition to the likelihood of its being lower than foreign value for other reasons.[21]

Export taxes have consistently been held not to be part of dutiable value since they form no part of market value in the country of exportation.[22] This is true whether the merchandise is appraised at foreign or export value and despite the fact that such merchandise in all cases pays the tax. Only in the case in which the export tax accrues prior to sale in the open markets of the country of export and therefore forms part of market value in the export market can it be considered an element of dutiable value. This condition is largely hypothetical in view of normal administrative procedure in the levy of export taxes, since any foreign government would partially defeat its own ends by writing an export tax law in a form which would thus needlessly handicap its foreign trade.

19. Cf. *Rheinstrom* v. *United States,* T.D. 20761 (1899); *Roger and Gallet* v. *United States,* 12 C.C.A. 201 (1924). These are important cases following in the Passavant tradition.

20. Cf. *United States* v. *F. S. Allenby and Co. et al.,* 20 C.C.P.A. 80 (1932). Foreign internal taxes are rarely levied or left unabated on export goods.

21. I.e., lower than foreign value would be were it found to exist for the merchandise in question. Because of various technicalities turning upon other phrases in its total definition, foreign value is often declared to be legally nonexistent even when there exists an actual foreign-market price for the merchandise, fulfilling all but perhaps one minor requirement of foreign value as legally interpreted. An important decision concerning the British purchase tax, going far toward offsetting the effects of the Passavant decision without specifically reversing it, has recently been made in *United States* v. *Wm. S. Pitcairn Corp.,* 33 C.C.P.A. 183 (1946). Because of its more intimate connection with the phrase "freely offered for sale," discussion of it is deferred until later (cf. *infra,* pp. 179–80).

22. T.D. 18950. The leading case on export taxes is *Sternfeld* v. *United States,* 12 C.C.A. 172 (1924); cf. also *United States* v. *Tadross et al.,* 14 C.C.A. 10 (1926).

Local taxes, whether or not levied on the shipment under appraisement, do not form part of the general market value abroad and are therefore excluded from dutiable value. Thus the *droit-de-ville* and *octroi* at Bordeaux were held in the Rheinstrom case to be excluded from dutiable value because they were not definitive of conditions in the principal markets of France. But, like all substantive provisions of law, the principle may be set at naught by technicalities.[23]

An illustration of the multiplicity of considerations surrounding the dutiability of foreign taxes is found in *Hughes Fawcett, Inc.* v. *United States.*[24] This case involved a number of importations of Czechoslovakian yarns from 1934 to 1937. The government contended that the 13 per cent "Pauschal" excise tax on all yarn was part of the foreign value of the merchandise. Testimony revealed that this tax was ultimately allowed as a credit to the purchasers of yarn against the tax on yarn products; the yarn tax was merely an indirect means—collectible at the source to prevent evasion by small purchasers and users—of taxing the finished product. Hence, the tax was held by the courts to be no part of the foreign-market value of yarn.

The foregoing discussion indicates some general principles attaching to the notion of market price in customs law and their application in representative cases. As indicated above, the comparative treatment of internal and export taxes levied by foreign countries affords a curious contrast to conclusions often reached with respect to the shifting and incidence of taxation. Under the law an importer is compelled to pay duty on Chinese taxes on someone else's goods that never leave China and is exempt from duty on Chinese taxes on his own goods which he must pay before they can leave the country for exportation to the United States.

SUCH OR SIMILAR MERCHANDISE

The phrase "such or similar merchandise" is one of the most important terms in the several definitions of dutiable value. The difficulties of establishing sound criteria of similarity, the even greater problems of practical application, and the far-reaching consequences of its ap-

23. An auction-sale tax levied by the Province of Quebec on certain horses was held to be part of the market value of the horses when exported to the United States in the absence of evidence as to whether the tax was levied in all the Canadian provinces. All presumptions are in favor of the appraisement (Reap. 4329).
24. 27 C.C.P.A. 372 (1940).

plication render it of profound significance to customs valuation. The problem of similarity for purposes of dutiable value is substantially different from that of similarity for purposes of classification, and the courts have properly ruled that the time-honored principles of similitude for determining rates of duty do not govern the question of similarity for value purposes.[25] An automobile worth $500 might reasonably be required to pay the same rate of duty as another worth $5,000, but it is obvious that there is no similarity with respect to value. It follows that reasonable and workable criteria of similarity for value purposes must be narrowly defined and applied and cannot hastily be adopted without danger of serious injustice. For this reason, although judicial interpretation of the "such or similar" provision is considerably further developed than that of some of the other phrases under consideration, the courts have not yet adopted a definitive set of rules in the matter. A further important preliminary observation should be made at this time, namely, that in some cases it is to the government's advantage to establish similarity and in others to the importer's. The question of advantage turns upon the facts in each individual case.[26]

The words "such" and "similar" have been construed to be distinctive and alternate terms. "Such" means "identical" and has priority of application over "similar."[27] In the absence of an ascertainable market value for identical merchandise the value of similar merchandise must be sought, and this applies to both foreign and export value. Since a good share of merchandise in foreign countries for the American market is differentiated to suit the tastes of American consumers, it often occurs that there is an export value but no foreign value for identical merchandise. If the statutory provision for "similar" merchandise did not exist, the importer could, by a slight product differentiation, escape the necessity of paying duty on the generally higher foreign-

25. *United States* v. *Morganite Brush Co.*, 18 C.C.P.A. 90 (1930); *United States* v. *Thomas and Co.*, 21 C.C.P.A. 254 (1933). In the Massin case, *infra*, the court used precedents in classification cases as a general guide in attacking the problem.

26. As will be seen later, the invoking of "dissimilarity" by the importer has served in many cases to exclude foreign value, leaving a lower export value as the dutiable basis. In other and probably less numerous cases, the importer has been able in the absence of foreign value to avoid the application of United States value by establishing the similarity of a competitor's products dutiable at export value.

27. *United States* v. *Johnson Co.*, 9 C.C.A. 258 (1919); *United States* v. *Irving Massin and Brothers*, 16 C.C.A. 19 (1928); *United States* v. *The American Bluefriesveem, Inc.* (*Van Houten Co.*), 22 C.C.P.A. 67 (1934).

market-value basis. But because of the essentially narrow limits to similarity for value purposes, there are numerous importations on the basis of export value and much vigorous litigation between the Attorney-General and importers on the question of similarity.

The Massin case sets forth the basic principles of similarity for value purposes:

> In view of the common meaning of the word "similar" and of the authorities cited, we are of the opinion, and so hold, that if goods are made of approximately the same materials, are commercially interchangeable, are adapted to the same uses, and are so used, ordinarily, they are similar within the meaning of section 402(b). The importer or foreign manufacturer may not, by making a few changes in structure, or in giving the product a new name, or by restricting its sale to the American purchaser only, *ipso facto* remove his merchandise from section 402(b), the foreign value provision.[28]

Three general tests of similarity are thus established: (1) similarity in construction (same materials); (2) commercial interchangeability; (3) similarity in potential and actual use. It will be observed that, so far as this decision is concerned, the several criteria are cumulative prerequisites and the insufficiency of any one might be fatal to similarity. The application of these principles to concrete cases is of course the final test of the principles involved, and an examination of the record indicates that the courts have, on the whole, used a high degree of circumspection in rendering judgments of similarity.

In the Massin case the government's claim of similarity failed on the issue of use. The importation consisted of black silk hatter's plush, invoiced, entered, and appraised at United States value of 2.18 and 3.50 gold marks, respectively, for two different widths. The government appealed to reappraisement, and the single justice[29] found a foreign value of similar merchandise at 3.00 and 4.80 gold marks, respectively. When the case reached the Court of Customs Appeals, that court found that, although the hatter's plush claimed as similar by the government was perhaps sufficiently similar in quality and construction, "the imported material is used for making blocked and men's silk hats, while quality 5400 is adapted to use for general millinery purposes, in

28. 16 C.C.A. 19, 25.
29. Between the time of the creation of the United States Customs Court in 1926 and the effective date of the Tariff Act of 1930 the members of the court were called "justices." Section 518 of the 1930 act specified that they should thereafter be known as "judges."

draping ladies' trimmed, loose hats, for which it is used, and that the goods are not interchangeable."[30] This decision not only emphasizes the use to which imports are actually put but, by implication, the cumulative effect of slight differences in similarity for each of the criteria mentioned. It also established the principle that the actual value of similar merchandise—not some proportionate part thereof representing an adjusted value for differences—must be taken as the dutiable value. This is obviously the correct interpretation of the statute, and hopeless administrative confusion would result from any other interpretation. This principle leads naturally to the use of value itself as a criterion of similarity for value purposes, since a wide divergence in price between two competing articles would presuppose some intrinsic dissimilarity, tangible or intangible.[31]

The Van Houten cocoa case furnishes an example of the establishment of similarity to the advantage of the importer rather than of the government and illustrates several important points in the economics as well as in the law of customs valuation.[32] This case emphasizes the criterion of commercial interchangeability. The importer and exclusive agent in the United States, Van Houten Company, was controlled by the foreign manufacturer and exporter. The importations consisted of chocolate liquor and chocolate powder consigned from Holland to the importer. Van Houten liquor and powder were not freely offered for sale in Holland whether for home consumption or for export to the United States. Thus there was neither foreign nor export value for "such" merchandise, and the importations were appraised at United States value.[33] The importer appealed to reappraisement, con-

30. 16 C.C.A. 19, 26.

31. Among instances of "intangible" dissimilarity are such differences as the existence of brand names, which may lead to substantially different prices for identical physical products. This leads to the difficult question of whether and to what extent monopolistic restrictions on sale, etc., resulting in price differentials above the prices of otherwise similar articles, should be treated as factors precluding similarity. In the Van Houten case, next discussed, the government unsuccessfully contended that such practices demonstrated dissimilarity since they prevented "commercial interchangeability" between monopoly-controlled and other merchandise.

32. *United States* v. *The American Bluefriesveem,* cited above.

33. It will be noted that United States value in this case was higher than foreign value, whereas in the Massin case it was lower. Although United States value is ordinarily higher than either foreign or export value, no necessary relationship exists when resort is had to *similar* merchandise, especially in cases in which the assumed similarity is not complete.

tending that there was a foreign value for chocolate powder and an export value for the liquor—namely, that of similar merchandise sold and exported by other manufacturers. The Customs Court sustained the importer and the government appealed, stating in its brief:

It would seem, therefore, that the court below had no competent legal basis or ground for finding and holding that the Van Houten (imported) cocoa was commercially interchangeable with other cocoas if the Van Houten cocoa was not sold in the home market (Holland), or was not freely offered for sale at wholesale for export to the United States. How can an article be commercially interchangeable when it cannot be purchased for consumption in the home market?

The appellate court held that commercial interchangeability need not be established by actual transactions but could be determined on other grounds:

If that [i.e., actual transactions] were required, there would seldom, if ever, be any occasion to resort to the market value of similar merchandise to determine the foreign or export value of imported merchandise, for, if the imported merchandise is freely sold in the country of exportation, there would be a foreign or export value of *such* merchandise, and resort to market value of similar merchandise would be unnecessary, and, in fact, improper.

The final decision held that there was commercial interchangeability between the Van Houten products and others and that the other criteria of similarity set forth in the Massin case were satisfied. This case presents the interesting phenomenon of an exclusive export-import agency taking advantage of the freely offered prices of competitors to establish a lower basis for dutiable value on its own products.

Commercial interchangeability has never been rigorously defined, nor has it been finally accepted as indispensable to similarity.[34] Nevertheless, a number of decisions have included it as a substantial element in the burden of reaching judgment. As indicated above, it has been declared by the court not to depend upon a seller's willingness to sell in the open markets; nor does it depend upon the buyer's willingness to accept the similar article as "good delivery," since this requirement might well demand identical merchandise.[35] Commercial value would seem to be preferable to commercial interchangeability inasmuch as it would supposedly reflect the net differences in similarity,

34. *Ibid.;* also, *United States* v. *Thomas and Co.,* 21 C.C.P.A. 254 (1933).
35. *United States* v. *Thomas and Co.*

of whatever kind; and since the Massin case the courts have recognized the criterion of commercial value or price in determining similarity for purposes of dutiable value.[36] But commercial value can be used as a deciding factor only when other factors are on balance; if taken independently, commercial value is meaningless, since, as the court in the Thomas case indicated, the value of a steam engine might be the same as that of an automobile, but it would hardly make the two similar.

The third general criterion of similarity advanced in the Massin case—composition or construction—was illustrated and amplified by the Kraft cheese case, involving the importation of cheese from Roquefort, France. The traditional and standard quality of Roquefort could not be cut without crumbling. To meet the demands of the American market a special quality was developed which could be sliced with a minimum of crumbling and sold or served in portions. Importations of the "portion" cheese, entered at their export value, were appraised at the higher foreign value of Roquefort "standard." The importer appealed and the case eventually reached the appellate court. The testimony showed that the portion cheese was developed after considerable experimentation by altering the process of growing the mold but that the actual ingredients were the same. There was some indication that the new process cost less. The court held that the difference in process, in addition to the undeniable difference in adaptability to use—the capacity for slicing without crumbling—rendered the two brands dissimilar.[37]

The foregoing examples represent the basic criteria of similarity which the courts have found for value purposes. Refinements have been superimposed upon these; but all of them fall into three categories roughly corresponding to the supply, demand, price categories of economic theory and their underlying conditions: (1) conditions prior to the entry of the goods into the market—materials, processes, and costs of construction; (2) essential utility—quality, form, adaptability to use and/or actual use, including to some extent the intangibles of consumer preferences; (3) conditions in the market place—commercial interchangeability or commercial value. The various sub-

---

36. Cf. *United States* v. *Vietor and Achelis,* 17 C.C.P.A. 412 (1930); also, the Thomas case, cited above.

37. *United States* v. *Kraft-Phenix Cheese Corp.,* 26 C.C.P.A. 224 (1938).

sidiary issues which go to make up the principal elements often become the deciding factors: hence the sole difference precluding similarity may be a brand name;[38] on the other hand, a distinctive and well-known brand may not preclude similarity.[39] It has been stated that the petty whims and caprices of consumers are not to govern the determination of similarity;[40] on the other hand it has been held, as expressed in the Massin case, that *adaptability* to use may not be sufficient; goods must actually be *so used* to constitute similarity. Each individual case must be interpreted on its own merits in the light of existing principles; and any individual case might furnish the occasion for the development of a new principle.

USUAL WHOLESALE QUANTITIES

The interpretation of the phrase "in the usual wholesale quantities" deals with the very essence of market value, since for most importations the basic unit price of the goods is related, directly or indirectly, to the quantity purchased. The economies of large production, purchasing, and distribution, which give rise to substantial trade or quantity discounts in domestic markets, are operative with perhaps even greater force in international markets. It is not uncommon for there to be as many as six or eight different unit prices for the identical article, varying inversely with the quantity purchased,[41] and the unit price for large quantities may run as low as 25 per cent of the price for small quantities.[42]

A number of questions arise in connection with the interpretation of the phrase in question. Are wholesale quantities those which are sold only to wholesalers, jobbers, commissionaires, dealers, or others

---

38. Swiss cheese bearing certain brands which were well known and advertised was held to have higher value than cheese not so advertised; brand held to be a factor in the value of goods (C.R. 2205).

39. Cigarette-paper booklets held similar to others sold in the foreign market; foreign value or expert value to apply instead of United States value (*United States* v. *R. J. Reynolds Tobacco Co.*, Reap. 3690 [1935]); government appeal denied (23 C.C.P.A. 391).

40. *Scharf Bros. Co. (Inc.)* v. *United States*, 16 C.C.A. 347 (1928).

41. Prices do not always vary inversely with the quantity purchased since trade discounts are frequently based on the wholesale classification or status of the purchaser. Over the long run, trade status and quantities purchased tend to be in agreement; at any given time a purchaser in a favored status may pay a lower unit price for smaller quantities than one not so favored.

42. E.g., *United States* v. *Minkus*, 21 C.C.P.A. 382 (1934).

for *resale?* Or does the term apply equally to sales to ultimate consumers or users? Must a wholesale quantity be a large quantity, or can
it be a small quantity such as one unit? Must it be a quantity which is
sold at a wholesale price or can a retail price be considered as "the
price . . . in the usual wholesale quantities"? If there are several classes
of wholesalers, each of which is allowed a different discount, i.e., is
charged a different price, which price is to be selected for purposes of
dutiable value? Is the term "usual" to have the effect of designating
for dutiable value the price at which the bulk of the manufacturer's
output is sold? Or is it to designate the price at which the majority of
the manufacturer's *transactions* are consummated? Must either of, or
both, these alternatives be extended to permit a selection from among
many resale prices at wholesale by intermediate wholesalers, jobbers,
and middlemen? What if there are a number of manufacturers of
similar merchandise and each sells at a different price or at the same
average price for all his output but at different prices for different
classes of wholesaler? Momentary reflection upon the nature of the
problem is sufficient to indicate the magnitude of the task of adopting
a set of consistent principles which will adequately cover all cases.

It is thus not surprising that the record of the courts in attempting to
define and apply the concept of usual wholesale quantity exhibits
perhaps more conflict and dissension than the treatment of any other
value factor. Some of the confusion is attributable to periodic overemphasis upon an individual word in the phrase, such as "usual" or
"quantities," to the neglect of other words; more often it is the overemphasis of other phrases in the total definition of dutiable value,
particularly the term "freely offered for sale to all purchasers." The
great practical difficulty is the lack of uniformity in the marketing
practices, business organization, and underlying trade conditions exhibited by the multiplicity of different commodities moving in international commerce. The consequence is that individual words or
phrases in the definition of dutiable value are frequently given differential significance in their application to different sets of conditions,
and an attempt to apply the meanings so determined results in the
practical cancellation of other terms of equal importance.

The Tariff Act of 1922 effected an extensive codification and simplification of customs administrative law, and in its simplified definition
of dutiable value the previous, long-established phrase "actual market

value or *wholesale price*" gave way to "the market value or the price
... in the usual *wholesale quantities*" (italics added). There is no evidence to indicate that Congress thereby intended to depart from the
use of wholesale price as the basis of dutiable value. Nevertheless, the
absence of the term "wholesale price," and the presence of the term
"wholesale quantities" has led to repercussions presumably unin-
tended by the framers of the statute.

A clear indication of the judicial attitude toward the use of wholesale versus retail prices for dutiable value prior to the enactment of
the Tariff Act of 1922 is found in a prominent decision that, even in
the absence of wholesale prices, retail prices may not be used and
that in such cases recourse must be had to one of the other forms of
dutiable value provided by law.[43] Without establishing general principles for distinguishing wholesale from retail prices, the court held
that the sale of an article direct to the user in unit quantities was a
retail transaction and that its price could not be used for purposes of
dutiable value. The repudiation of this principle in recent years is one
manifestation of an unfortunate trend away from the use—for purposes
of dutiable value—of basic manufacturer's wholesale price, toward
the adoption of final wholesale or even retail prices.

An important step in this direction was the decision in *United States
v. Richards*,[44] in which the court distinguished between sales to wholesalers and sales in wholesale quantities. The court stated that the law
was not concerned with the persons who buy but with the manner in
which they buy. In the case at bar the effect of the decision was to prevent the basing of dutiable value on lower prices granted to persons
and firms arbitrarily classified as wholesalers, regardless of the quantity purchased, instead of the higher price to the majority of purchasers who bought in the same quantities and who accounted for the
bulk of the manufacturer's output. The decision was perhaps appropriate to the circumstances at hand; but the pronouncement that "the
law is not concerned with the persons who buy" has been used repeatedly to further the trend of dutiable value away from price levels
in the basic wholesale markets of the world in which American importers actually do their buying.

43. *Keve and Young* v. *United States,* 11 C.C.A. 94 (1921).
44. 15 C.C.A. 143 (1927).

In the Riglander case[45] the court displayed an unusual degree of liberality. Trade discounts of 5, 10, and 15 per cent were allowed to three different classes of purchaser in the foreign market, and the court recognized the 15 per cent discount as the appropriate deduction from list price to make dutiable value. This was done on the showing that the 15 per cent discount was freely offered to all purchasers who would buy 200,000 francs worth of merchandise per year, that the bulk of the manufacturer's output was sold at the 15 per cent discount, and that all importers purchasing the merchandise received the discount. The court held that in the absence of evidence to the contrary it must be presumed that the purchases were made in the usual wholesale quantities, particularly in view of the actual allowance of the discount. This presumption, even though not necessarily inconsistent with the facts, hardly appears justifiable, since the quantities purchased might easily have been well above the "usual" in any one of several senses of the word.[46]

The Riglander decision had the effect in that particular case of adopting as dutiable value the wholesale price for the bulk of the output. This did not, however, become an established principle in the interpretation of usual wholesale quantity. The general position of the court for many years, and one which is still largely applicable, has been that the usual wholesale quantities are those involved in the "major portion of sales" (majority of transactions) at wholesale.[47] If, for example, a manufacturer distributes 90 per cent of his entire output through large wholesalers at 20 per cent discount and the remainder through small jobbers at 5 per cent discount, a larger number of sales to jobbers would nullify for purposes of dutiable value the lower price at which the vast bulk of the output was sold. Thus the American importer, who is usually a large wholesaler buying in large quantities at the lowest wholesale price, may be obliged to pay duty

45. *United States* v. *Hammel, Riglander and Co., et al.,* 16 C.C.A. 37 (1928).
46. It was not shown that the majority of the manufacturer's *transactions* with *all* purchasers allowed the 15 per cent discount; also, no quesion was raised about the freely offered prices of other manufacturers of similar merchandise, jobber's prices, etc.
47. *G. W. Pleissner* v. *United States,* 16 C.C.A. 507 (1929); *United States* v. *Minkus,* 21 C.C.P.A. 382 (1934); *United States* v. *Livingstone and Southard, Inc.,* 23 C.C.P.A. 214 (1935). The "major-portion-of-sales" doctrine also includes offers for sale, but the effect of such offers in conjunction with actual sales has never been clearly defined.

on the highest wholesale price resulting from the existence of small jobbers and commissionaires in foreign countries.

Judge Bland, in a separate opinion in the Minkus case, rejected the unqualified adoption of the "major-portion-of-sales" doctrine, showing its inadequacy or impropriety in a number of hypothetical cases. He held that Congress intended that dutiable value be based neither on the high price for small quantities involving expensive packaging or other costs nor on the low price for unusually large quantities; that the major-portion-of-sales (and/or offers) doctrine would result in anomalies where sales were approximately equally divided, in number of transactions, between large and small quantities with corresponding divergence in price; that it did not adequately consider the effect to be given to offers which did not ripen into sales; and that it afforded no satisfactory rule for weighting sales for the entire industry against those of the individual firm or for selecting a time period over which the majority of sales were to be computed. In short, he contended that the whole problem was so complicated that the adoption of a hard-and-fast rule would prove embarrassing to the court in dealing with types of cases which could not readily be foreseen and which would require discretion in order to be properly adjudicated. The Bland dissent raised a number of pertinent issues and afforded greater insight into the general problem. It made no attempt at their solution, but the point that the major-portion-of-sales doctrine should not be adopted as an inflexible rule was well taken. The rule has been far from inflexible and has frequently been supplanted by less fortunate interpretations, some of which were written by Judge Bland himself.[48]

The decision in the Faber pencil case[49] specifically reversed the Riglander decision already cited and began a line of decisions which have successively restricted the recognition of wholesale price as the applicable interpretation of price "in the usual wholesale quantities." The Faber case, like the Riglander, involved the issue of a lower price

48. E.g., the opinion in the American Shipping case, *infra*, p. 177. The problem of defining usual wholesale quantity illustrates the difficulty of weighing the various desiderata in the question of whether or how to formulate an inflexible rule. The advantages of the adoption of a rule which will be applied with certainty must be weighed against the disadvantages of its adoption should it prove to be inadequate, unjust, or administratively unworkable. The Bland objection to inflexibility appears to the writer to have been reasonable in view of the many aspects of the problem which had not been adequately considered or resolved.

49. *United States* v. *A. W. Faber, Inc.*, 21 C.C.P.A. 290 (1933).

for purchases in minimum annual quantities. The court held that, although the purchases were made in the usual wholesale quantities, the statute required a freely offered price to all purchasers in the usual wholesale quantities, not merely to those who agreed to buy a minimum amount per year. On the face of it this decision was reasonable, but it tended to overemphasize the term "all purchasers" at the expense of "usual wholesale quantities" and "ordinary course of trade." By shifting the emphasis, one could correctly point out that the statute does not prescribe as dutiable value the freely offered price to *all* purchasers, or even such price to all purchasers in the usual wholesale quantities, but limits its stricture only to all purchasers in the usual wholesale quantities *and in the ordinary course of trade*. A transaction might well be in usual wholesale quantity but be outside the ordinary course of trade because the trade is, by tradition, commercial practice and economical operation, geared to, and dependent upon, regular distribution through large wholesalers. To take the position that large wholesale distribution and the price terms accompanying such distribution are outside the ordinary course of trade when the vast bulk of commodities exchanged in many trades is so distributed is to do violence to the known facts of commercial practice.

In the Riglander case, which was reviewed at length in the Faber decision, much testimony was adduced showing the manufacturer's justification for the larger discount in terms of greater stability of factory operation, steadier employment, and the maintenance of a skilled-labor force resulting from, and dependent upon, the ability to plan production on the basis of the minimum annual guaranty by the large wholesalers. There were also economies in distribution resulting from the fact that the large wholesalers maintained a stock of merchandise, whereas the small jobbers, commissionaires, and other middlemen who accounted for a minor fraction of the output did not maintain stock, were under none of the expense connected therewith, and would have to be supplied *ad hoc* by the manufacturer at greater expense for each individual transaction. There was no element of contingency in the discount for any importation, since it was allowed on each invoice and not at the end of the year.

The decision in the Faber case had the effect of classifying a wholesale price normal to the regular and ordinary course of trade—a price at which both the bulk of the output and the majority of sales were

made and which was freely available to all past or prospective purchasers on the same terms—in the same category with large, sporadic,
individual transactions at depressed prices, the consequences of which
in terms of both economic effects and administrative problems are
quite different. Because of the increasingly restrictive effect which the
"freely offered" concept as interpreted by the courts has had upon the
notion of usual wholesale quantity, the discussion is continued in the
following section.

FREELY OFFERED FOR SALE

The term "freely offered for sale" historically grew out of the problems which arose very early in the nineteenth century in connection
with the importation on consignment by agents of foreign manufacturers. As indicated in Part II of this study, it became profitable for
foreign manufacturers to establish an agency in the United States, to
discontinue selling in the open markets abroad, and to consign all their
merchandise to agents on invoices at, or below, cost of production.
The result, even in the absence of fraudulent undervaluation, was a
substantial saving in duties to the detriment of American and other
importers who had to buy in the open markets abroad and pay duties
on the higher purchase price. As a remedy for this situation, consignments became the first class of importations required by statute to pay
duties on actual market value, and the invoices covering them were
eventually required to state the price which the exporter "would have
received or was willing to receive" as an indication of actual market
value. Later, after United States value had been introduced as a method of valuation for agency importations, the primary basis of dutiable
value, later known as foreign value, was made applicable only to goods
which could be procured by all purchasers on even terms. Hence, the
adoption of the phrase "freely offered to all purchasers."

But, whatever its historical origins, the "freely offered" proviso has
gradually come to embrace a number of meanings and to perform a
variety of functions in the administration of dutiable value. These may
be listed roughly as follows:

1. To facilitate the determination of dutiable value by the use of
   "offered" prices as evidence of value:
   a) In the absence of actual sales
   b) In conjunction with actual sales

2. To prevent the manipulation of dutiable value by nonrecognition of prices associated with departures from free competition in the form of:

   a) Buying limitations

      (1) Controlled market prices abroad

      (2) Price discrimination abroad

      (3) Tying of distributors to manufacturers abroad

   b) Selling limitations

      (1) Limitation of dealers

      (2) Resale price maintenance

      (3) Other restrictions on sale or disposition

The desirability, practical necessity, and legality of using offered prices in the absence of actual transactions as a method of determining dutiable value has long been recognized.[50] The statutes prescribing the competence of the Customs Court permitted, and the higher courts upheld, the use of price lists, catalogues, and similar evidence of market value.[51] Cases frequently arise in which the valuation of imports on any other basis than that of offered prices would be impossible or else arbitrary and inequitable for either the importer or the government. Instances have occurred in which an importer has received the benefit of a lower valuation than his purchase price by the showing that offers at a lower price were freely made at the date of exportation.[52] The question of the effect of offered prices in overriding or modifying actual prices has already been discussed in certain of its aspects in connection with variable discounts and appears again in connection with the following treatment of restrictions in general.

The use of free offers as evidence to afford a basis for dutiable value in the absence of actual sales performs a positive and constructive function quite different from the use of the "freely offered" proviso to reject a known market price as the basis of dutiable value because of the presence of restrictions of one kind or another. The latter use of the proviso appears far more frequently in the decisions of the courts and is of more significance in its effects upon dutiable value.

The Goodyear case, decided in 1922, is one of the leading cases on the effect of restrictive practices upon dutiable value. The Goodyear Tire and Rubber Company of Toronto manufactured tires in Canada for Canadian consumption as well as for export. The Canadian market

---

50. Cf. *United States* v. *Baldwin Universal Co.*, 18 C.C.P.A. 394 (1931), for rulings, prior authorities, and discussion of the issues.

51. *Ibid.*

52. Cf. *United States* v. *Briones and Co., Inc.*, 22 C.C.P.A. 245 (1934).

for the Goodyear product was completely controlled by the manufacturer and apportioned by districts among a limited number of selected automobile manufacturers, jobbers, and dealers. The export market was open to any exporter who agreed to ship the tires out of Canada. The manufacturer's price was graded for each of the four classes of purchaser, and strict resale price maintenance was required. On an importation of tires purchased by the Goodyear Company of Akron the appraisement was made on the basis of the highest of the graded prices—that to dealers and service stations in Canada. This price was apparently higher than either United States value or cost of production. The importer appealed, contending that there was no foreign value in view of the complete control by the manufacturer and the lack of a freely offered price to all purchasers. Counsel for the government contended that the manufacturer's control of prices, sales, and distribution was sufficiently well established to have become the ordinary course of trade in Canada. The court rejected this argument, stating that it ran counter to the whole development of statutory safeguards for the protection of the revenue against the making by a manufacturer of a market value to his liking, which might well operate not for the protection of jobbers, dealers, and others, as presumed in the case at bar, but to reduce duties on goods manufactured largely or wholly for foreign consumption.[53]

This construction of the "freely offered" proviso rests on substantial ground and is different in principle from the narrow construction which gears dutiable value to the highest wholesale price in existence, represented by a small fraction of either the total volume of business or the total number of transactions for the trade. In recent years the interpretations have been rigorously directed against minor deviations from unconditional offer while at the same time opening the way to removal of certain of the safeguards to dutiable value expounded in the Goodyear case. Whether this attitude of the courts is a simple manifestation of strict constructionism or whether it represents an undifferentiated bias in the direction of theoretically perfect competition is not evident.

In the American Shipping case[54] the court reached the remarkable

---

53. *Goodyear Tire and Rubber Co.* v. *United States*, 11 C.C.A. 351 (1922).
54. *American Shipping Co.* (*General Electric X-Ray Corp.*) v. *United States*, 29 C.C.P.A. 250 (1942).

conclusion, on the basis of the "freely-offered-to-all-purchasers" doctrine, that retail prices are to supersede wholesale prices when the same quantities are involved in both retail and wholesale transactions. This case involved the importation of scientific instruments. Such instruments were sold by the manufacturer in the English market either through dealers or direct to consumers. The dealers were charged the established wholesale price, which was 33⅓ per cent less than the retail price. The nature of the instruments was such that dealers ordered one unit at a time, and on the basis of the major-portion-of-sales doctrine this became the usual wholesale quantity. Since consumers also purchased from the manufacturer in the same quantity but were charged the full list price, the court concluded that the article was not freely offered for sale to *all* purchasers in the usual wholesale quantities at the lower price and sustained the appraiser's advances to the retail price.[55]

While thus reversing its former position[56] that retail prices are not to be considered the basis for dutiable value, the court in an earlier decision also substantially reversed its stand taken in the Goodyear case against the use of controlled prices. By a series of highly refined distinctions in the Diagonale case[57] the court concluded that although *resale* price maintenance in the foreign market was damning to freely offered price, the existence of *basic* price control, which directly and necessarily affects dutiable value, was no barrier to free offer. In this case the importer had paid 0.60 lira per gram for silver filigree in Campo Ligure, Italy, but was compelled by the court's decision to pay

55. It is interesting to note, in passing, the enormous increase in duties resulting from this example of administrative protection. The importer entered the merchandise at the wholesale price, which for the larger units was approximately $50. On the assumption that the rate of duty was 50 per cent for this class of merchandise, the importer expected to pay a duty of $25. Instead, he had to pay 50 per cent on $75 (the retail price) plus undervaluation-penalty duties of 50 per cent on $75 (1 per cent on appraised value for each 1 per cent excess of appraised over entered value), or a total of $75 in duties, which is 150 per cent on the wholesale price paid for the merchandise. Abstracting from transportation, etc., the landed cost (including duty) of this article would thus be raised from $75 to $125, or 250 per cent of the price paid by dealers abroad for the same article. This situation would be mitigated, of course, to the extent of remission of penalty duties if the importer were successful in prosecuting a remission case before the Customs Court.

56. Cf. the Keve and Young case, *supra*, p. 171.

57. *United States* v. *Michele Diagonale*, 22 C.C.P.A. 517 (1935), dissenting opinion by Judge Graham.

duty (and presumably additional penalty duties) on the 0.93 lira per gram price in the Genoese market, which was held to be the principal market. A report of the Treasury attaché stated that the Genoese market was tightly controlled by a syndicate embracing all dealers, who charged the price fixed by the syndicate although they "freely offered" the filigree to all purchasers at the high fixed price.

The court's principal contention was that, if competition in price were made an indispensable element in dutiable value, the finding of foreign or export value would be prevented in a great many cases, creating a very complicated administrative problem. The point was undoubtedly well taken, but it is difficult to square this reasoning with that found in the numerous other decisions strictly construing the "freely-offered-to-all-purchasers" phrase to prevent the use of normal wholesale price as dutiable value. Nor can it be deemed consistent with the vigorous position against price control taken in the Goodyear case or in others specifically requiring recourse to alternate forms of dutiable value when the statutory forms having priority were not completely satisfied.

A recent case provoking much interest both because of the issues and because of the large number of importations affected was the British purchase-tax case.[58] The British purchase tax, established in 1940 to raise revenue during the national emergency, was a general excise levy ranging from 16⅔ per cent to 100 per cent (depending on classification) on the wholesale value of goods in England. The question of the inclusion of the tax in the foreign value of all English goods imported into the United States appeared, at least superficially, to be governed by the fact that the British law specifically based the excise on wholesale prices and provided for the accrual of the tax prior to the actual movement of goods into retail establishments. For purposes of administration all British manufacturers and wholesalers of any consequence were required to register and were made responsible for collection of the tax whenever goods moved into the hands of an unlicensed retailer or dealer. Since this permitted tax-free transactions between registered manufacturers and/or wholesalers prior to the eventual accrual of the tax, American importers claimed that the tax did not form part of the freely offered wholesale prices "to all purchasers" and therefore was no part of foreign value. In view of its

58. *United States* v. *Wm. S. Pitcairn Corp.,* 33 C.C.P.A. 183 (1946).

many recent strict interpretations and applications of the "all-purchasers" doctrine, the court had no alternative but to sustain this
position. Although this had diametrically opposite economic effects
from those of the Passavant decision, the cases were distinguished
upon technical grounds.

The foregoing discussion and illustrations indicate the nature of the
problems and the administrative and judicial trends pertaining to the
application of the "usual-wholesale-quantity" and "freely offered"
provisos.[59] Before the remaining factors in the definition of foreign
and export value are considered, a word should be said in clarification
of a possible misconception concerning the selection of the appropriate market price in relation to appraisement procedure. In the Proctor
case[60] the court, in reaching its conclusion to reject the higher discount
allowed to the importer, made the following interesting statement:

> If there were other importers of this article whose aggregate sales did
> not reach the point where the 30 per centum deduction was applicable,
> the appraiser at the port of entry would necessarily have one value for one
> man's goods and another for another man's goods, both purchased in the
> same market, of the same individual, and on the same date.

If the court meant that the appraiser would be confronted with two
different invoice values for two different importations, that is obvious
and inevitable, whatever policy the court adopted. If it meant that
the adoption of the higher price would facilitate, or the adoption of
the lower price would hinder, the making of uniform appraisements,
it is palpably erroneous. If there can by law be but one dutiable value,
it is the task of the appraiser and the total machinery of appraisement to apply the legally adopted value uniformly. In the exigencies
of administration perfect uniformity is an unrealizable ideal, but it
certainly does not depend upon, nor would it be aided by, the adoption of the highest rather than the lowest of a series of prices as the
single, legally applicable dutiable value. There is the possibility that
the court had in mind the proviso making the entered value the
minimum dutiable value regardless of the appraised value. Since it
is the normal practice of the importer, in the absence of better information on dutiable value, to enter his merchandise at the invoice

59. For additional significant illustrations cf. *United States* v. *American
Glanzstoff Corp.*, 24 C.C.P.A. 36 (1936), and *United States* v. *Mexican Products
Co.*, 28 C.C.P.A. 80 (1940).

60. *United States* v. *Proctor and Co.*, 15 C.C.A. 373 (1928).

value, the importer with the higher entry would be precluded from enjoying the legally appraised dutiable value based on the lower price, if such should be adopted. In this sense only can there be two dutiable values, but the obvious remedy, and one which is highly desirable in any case, is the elimination of the entered-value-minimum proviso. There is no controlling or substantial reason in equity or in sound administration which justifies the exaction of a tax in excess of that defined by substantive law and officially recognized and adopted as correct by those responsible for its determination and collection. This applies with especial force in view of the undervaluation-penalty duties which apply automatically when the appraiser's return shows an excess over the entered value.[61]

OTHER FACTORS IN FOREIGN AND EXPORT VALUE

Ordinary course of trade.—The term "ordinary course of trade" is a modifying factor whose significance lies solely in its effects upon the other factors in the definition and not in any substantive or intrinsic content of its own. It therefore has never been rigorously or even specifically defined, and its consequences vary widely depending upon what factor or circumstance is subjected to the "ordinary-course-of-trade" test. It is most frequently applied to the concepts of "usual wholesale quantity" and "freely offered for sale," and illustrations of such cases have already been given. Important applications of it may, however, be made to the question of "principal markets,"[62] the dutiability of containers and coverings,[63] "all other costs,"[64] and elsewhere. As indicated above, its potentialities in offsetting the undesirably restrictive interpretation of the "freely offered" proviso have been overlooked or ignored. It is possible that with changing com-

---

61. The collection of the income tax in the United States faces difficulties at least equal in scope and importance to those of the customs revenue, yet there is no feature in the income-tax law comparable to the entered-value-minimum proviso. The writer has been informed by Lester M. Baker of the Internal Revenue Service at Chicago that refunds of excessive income-tax payments are made automatically by the government in cases of clerical error or in cases under investigation where the findings reveal over- instead of underpayment. In all other cases (including excessive withholdings) claim must be filed, but the taxable income shown in the original entry or return does not operate as a minimum.

62. *United States* v. *Traders Paper Co.*, 14 C.C.A. 293 (1926), and cases cited therein.

63. *United States* v. *Spingarn Bros.*, 5 C.C.A. 2 (1913).

64. *Ibid.*

mercial and trade practices the phrase will be invoked to modify existing interpretations of the various principles under discussion.

For home consumption.—[65] This phrase was added to the definition of foreign value by the Customs Administrative Act of 1938 and was sought partly as a result of the decision in the Livingstone case,[66] in which sales for export to countries other than the United States were held to determine foreign value. This was another case turning upon "usual wholesale quantity" and involved the attempt on the part of the government to use retail prices in finding foreign value where retail and wholesale quantity were allegedly the same. The merchandise consisted of twelve instruments known as "rotoscopes" purchased by the sole American agent at 40 per cent discount from the list price. Because of the sole-agency relationship there could be no export value and that question was not involved. The importer entered the instruments at the purchase price, claiming it as the freely offered foreign value in England. The evidence showed that no more than one rotoscope at a time had ever been sold in England for home consumption and that the price for single units to the user was the list price less 20 per cent, which was the value returned by the appraiser. The testimony also indicated that a 30 per cent discount was freely offered and allowed for wholesale quantities of from two to five instruments and 40 per cent for six or more. Several sales for export to China and Japan, as well as sales to the United States, were held by the court to indicate that the usual wholesale quantities were greater than one unit, and the sales to countries other than the United States were held to be adequate evidence of foreign value at the 30 per cent discount for usual wholesale quantities of greater than two units and less than six. In rendering its decision, the court established the principle, which had apparently never been specifically decided under the statute, that all unrestricted offers for sale in foreign markets, either for home consumption or for export to countries other than the United States, should be considered in the attempt to arrive at foreign value of imported merchandise.

Judge Bland delivered a vigorous dissent, maintaining, among other things, that the majority decision would enable foreign manu-

65. The distinguishing phrase "for exportation to the United States," contained in the definition of export value, has given no difficulty in application and requires no discussion.

66. *United States* v. *Livingstone and Southard,* 23 C.C.P.A. 214 (1935).

facturers of big machines, who sell them one at a time at a high price
for home consumption, to secure a low dutiable value for exportation
to the United States by merely showing offers or sales to other foreign
countries. Granting that such be true, it would merely recognize the
original and long-established position of the law that wholesale
prices, if genuine, should govern, rather than the higher retail prices
for single units sold to the user. In any event, the controversy was
settled by the statutory restriction of foreign value to sales and offers
for home consumption.

Principal markets.—Although a number of theoretical questions
arise in the interpretation of the phrase "principal markets," the term
has not been one of major difficulty in application. Its effect is twofold: (1) It establishes what is considered to be the "true" market
price among several which may exist in different cities or regions of
a foreign country. (2) It determines the inclusion or noninclusion of
inland freight charges in the value for dutiable purposes.

Logically the same kinds of questions can be asked concerning
"principal markets" as concerning "usual wholesale quantities." Can
there be more than one principal market? If prices differ in different
"principal" markets, does the selection of the market for dutiable
purposes depend upon the place of production (e.g., factory), place
of sale, volume of production and/or sales, number of transactions,
or some other criterion? These and other questions in the determination of the meaning and application of the phrase under consideration
have not been methodically answered in terms of carefully developed
and clearly enunciated principles.

Fortunately the facts in most cases are sufficiently simple and ascertainable to provoke relatively little contention, and, where disagreement exists, the presumption of correct appraisement often settles the
issue. In the Haviland china case, Limoges was selected rather than
Paris on the basis of relative volume of sales at wholesale.[67] In the
Diagonale case cited above,[68] the matter was decided on the basis of
the Treasury attaché's statement that Genoa was the principal market,
since "all the leading firms who sell this merchandise are situated in

---

67. *United States* v. *Haviland and Co.*, 167 F. 414 (1909), affirmed in 177 F.
175 (1910), certiorari denied, 216 U.S. 618. The real issues in this case appear to
have been the questions of free offer and market price, but the case was decided
on the principal-market issue.

68. *Supra*, p. 178.

Genoa." Had the principal-market question been the main issue in that case, it might have received different treatment, as indicated in Judge Graham's dissent. In most instances the principal markets are located, and construed to be, at the place of manufacture; and the issue is generally resolved on the weight of evidence affirming the status of the market selected.[69]

The question of inclusion or noninclusion of inland or other transportation charges prior to exportation arises much more frequently than that of the determination of the principal market per se. The question of the dutiability of freight charges is handled in a manner similar to the treatment of drawbacks and taxes already discussed in conjunction with "market value or price." Stated simply, the general rule is that market value is determined at the market place and, by assumption, includes all costs and charges essential to bring the goods to market. In theory the issue resolves itself into the determination of the true market price in the principal markets and the assessing of duties accordingly. In practice, however, both because of differences in the terms of sale and because of the existence of basing-point price systems in the country of exportation, certain problems arise. If the merchandise is sold f.o.b. the principal markets, no adjustments for transportation costs are necessary, since market price is represented by the invoice price, assuming the latter to be representative. If goods are sold f.o.b. the factory and the factory is not one of the principal markets, the prices in the latter apply. A common method of selling goods for export is to sell and invoice them f.o.b. the port of exportation, even though the factory or the principal markets are elsewhere. Since this price includes nondutiable items of freight to bring the merchandise from the principal market to the port of exportation, deductions from invoice prices are allowable in the determination of the market price in the principal markets.[70]

The leading cases on principal markets in recent years are the Heffernan and Traders cases, involving the open price policy of the

69. Cf. Benjamin A. Levett, *Through the Customs Maze* (New York, 1923), pp. 56–57.

70. If the price in the principal markets is uniform and known to appraisers and importers, such price is adopted without necessary recourse to that in the invoice. But for most kinds of merchandise, particularly in the determination of export value, the only practical way of determining true market value is to use representative invoice prices as the starting-point, making such additions or deductions as are contemplated by law.

German paper combine.[71] The combine controlled all internal sales of wrapping-paper in Germany, and a uniform domestic delivered price was charged regardless of destination. Berlin was conceded to be the principal market, and shipments were made from the plant nearest the point of delivery. In the Heffernan case, importations were made from a plant at Berlin via Hamburg. The importer claimed deduction of the freight from Berlin to Hamburg on the ground that the invoice price covered delivery f.o.b. Hamburg and that such deduction from the invoice was allowable under the accepted practice which recognized as nondutiable transportation charges from the principal market to the port of exportation. This claim was disallowed by the court on the ground that, although Berlin was the principal market and the goods were sold f.o.b. Hamburg, the deduction would reduce the dutiable value not only below the market value at the principal market, namely, Berlin, but below that at Hamburg or anywhere else in Germany. This ruling was affirmed in the Traders case, in which it was attempted to establish, by the manufacturer's testimony, that he would have been willing to make price allowances for freight in the event of factory delivery. This was rejected as purely hypothetical, in view of the control of the foreign market and the standard practice of uniform delivery price anywhere in Germany.

Because of the relatively small geographical area embraced by the typical exporting country and the consequent lack of great dissimilarities in price in different sections of such countries, the problem of principal markets in the application of dutiable value has not given much trouble. Were the foreign situation typically to be that which prevails in the United States, where internal freight costs between widely separated markets are often greater than ocean freight, the existing court interpretations of the term "principal markets" would be far from adequate to meet the requirements. For these reasons the problem for dutiable value is vastly different from that faced by the Tariff Commission in its cost studies under section 336 of the tariff law.

Country from which exported.—When the basis of dutiable value was changed from specific purchase price to actual market value, the problem of defining the market in which the valuation was made

71. *United States* v. *Heffernan Paper Co.*, 13 C.C.A. 593 (1926); *United States* v. *Traders Paper Co. et al.*, 14 C.C.A. 293 (1926).

became of significance. Not only is it necessary to ascertain the principal markets within the country of exportation, but the definition of the country itself is also significant. If the country were left unrestricted, it would become profitable in some cases to ship merchandise from the country of production to the United States via an intermediate country in which the prevailing market prices were lower because of negligible demand than in the country of origin. Thus, by means of purely nominal transactions in the intermediate country and reshipment at little or no additional transportation cost, dutiable value would be established at a lower level than that based on the economically significant markets contemplated by the framers of the law.

The problem was originally attacked by a provision that goods, the produce of countries other than the one of exportation, were to be appraised at their value in the country of origin. But this rule proved embarrassing in cases in which goods were altered or enhanced in value in the intermediate country or were difficult to identify as of the country of origin. The statute was therefore changed to base dutiable value for all goods on the "country-of-exportation" principle, leaving the determination of what constituted the country of exportation to the administration and the courts. The criteria of determination are largely matters of specific judgment appropriate to particular cases. The general rule in the case of goods reshipped from a third country is that the country of reshipment is considered the country of exportation unless the evidence indicates that the merchandise was destined for the United States at the time of original shipment.[72]

The case of *Stairs* v. *Peaslee* is one of the leading cases on the question of country of exportation.[73] It involved merchandise shipped from India to Halifax, Nova Scotia, and reshipped to the United States. The Supreme Court ruled that the market value in the principal markets of England governed, since the law no longer permitted appraisement on the basis of the country of origin and Canada was subject to English dominion. The court expressed the principle that the word "country" in the revenue laws had always been construed to embrace all the possessions of a foreign state, however widely separated, which are subject to the same supreme executive and

72. *Customs Regulations,* 14.3(d).
73. 18 How. 521 (1855).

legislative control. As late as 1891, long after Canada had been granted dominion status, the Board of General Appraisers held, on the strength of the Stairs case, that certain merchandise from Canada must be appraised according to the principal markets of the British Empire and not those of Canada alone.[74] In 1921, however, when the Stairs case was cited as a precedent for considering Canadian as English markets, the Court of Customs Appeals ruled that Canada was a separate nation for customs purposes. The court pointed out that the United States had separate treaty relations with Canada, that in various public documents relating thereto Canada was referred to as a "nation" and a "government," and that she had sufficient autonomy to levy tariff duties against the United States, Great Britain, and other countries. Goods from England which were re-exported duty free from bond in Canada were therefore held to have been exported from Canada and subject to inclusion of Canadian tariff duties as part of dutiable value in the United States.[75]

Normally, if goods are altered or sold to the American importer in the country of re-exportation, that country is considered the country of exportation.[76] On the other hand, a number of cases may be found in which for one reason or another—principally, original intent to ship to the United States, as indicated by the evidence—merchandise passing through, or re-exported from, a third country is considered as having been exported from the country of origin.[77]

Time of exportation.—The time of exportation as a factor in the determination of dutiable value is of substantial importance to im-

74. T.D. 12145. "The board expressed some doubt as to the correctness of this decision in view of the changed political status of the Dominion of Canada under the British North American acts, but it regarded the rule announced in the Stairs-Peaslee case as still binding upon it" (11 C.C.A. 115, 119).

75. *Maier* v. *United States,* 11 C.C.A. 115 (1921). The importer probably had little hope of winning his case on the ground indicated but appealed to the Stairs precedent as a last resort in an effort to escape the inexorable levy of additional duties for undervaluation. He had purchased some sixty thousand yards of textiles from a Canadian firm who had imported them from England. The Canadian tariff duties would have been $7,844.55 and were clearly shown on the invoice. The importer claimed that they were nondutiable and entered his goods at $27,807.24, their value in England. The appraiser advanced the value to $34,-759.05, which called for penalty duties of roughly 25 per cent of $35,000.00, in addition to the increase in regular duties. At this time there was no provision for remission of penalty duties except for manifest clerical error.

76. T.D. 12145; C.R. 29047; T.D. 42451; C.R. 2044.

77. T.D. 22338; C.R. 36357; T.D. 41622.

porters under actual conditions of import buying and delivery. Even
under the simplest arrangements for purchase and shipment there
may be a time lag between the date of purchase and the date of exportation. Under contractual arrangements, especially long-term con-
tracts requiring manufacture to order and later shipment in one or
more importations, there may be an interval of as much as two years,
or even more, between the date of purchase and exportation of the
final shipment. Such time differences may result in the doubling or
tripling of duties or in their substantial reduction, depending upon
the corresponding changes in prices and dutiable values. For example, screenings purchased in Canada for $5.75 per ton rose to
$15.00 current market value before actual exportation to the United
States, and duties were assessed accordingly.[78] Salted anchovies from
Spain purchased in June, 1932, at 240 pesetas per kilo had declined
in value to 205 pesetas by September, the time of exportation, and
were finally appraised at the lower price.[79] Prices of bags imported
from Calcutta dropped substantially in the foreign market between
May 1 and May 12, and the importer's entry based on the latter date
was sufficiently below the appraised value based on May 1 to require
the assessment of $3,000 in undervaluation-penalty duties.[80] The sig-
nificance of the time difference in question is also pointedly illustrated
by the Phelps-Dodge case discussed in chapter iv, above.

It is important to distinguish between periods of rising prices and
periods of falling prices so far as the practical consequences for dutiable value are concerned. The average time lag between the date of
purchase and the date of exportation increases substantially in periods
of rising prices because of the basic conditions underlying the price
situation. Rising prices are normally the result of a relative shortage
of goods, and in such periods orders must be placed well in advance
of delivery.[81] In periods of declining prices, goods are generally im-

78. Reap. 431.
79. *United States* v. *Briones and Co., Inc.*, 22 C.C.P.A. 245 (1934).
80. *Western Bag Co.* v. *United States*, 11 C.C.A. 220 (1922). On the importer's
showing that the entry was based on an erroneous date in the duplicate invoice,
the actual date of exportation having been May 1, the penalty was remitted.
81. The current (early 1947) price situation is much in point. The writer was
recently informed by one examiner that the market price of Canadian paperboard
has advanced within a six-month period from $85 per ton to $140, and deliveries
are difficult to obtain. Some 25 per cent of all entries are currently raised to meet
price advances.

mediately available from stock, and there is special incentive as well as opportunity for prompt shipment, resulting in a minimum interval between date of purchase and date of exportation. In actual practice, therefore, the date of exportation as the time basis for dutiable value results in a net increase in duties over and above the date-of-purchase basis.

The time element in the law of dutiable value thus adds substantially to the uncertainties of importing. When dutiable value was related to the date of purchase,[82] it was possible for an importer to base his calculations upon a known duty and make his decisions accordingly. Such decisions are not confined to simple purchase for resale at whatever the future market may bear but include the making of contractual resale prices, cost quotations, and many other kinds of business commitment requiring firm estimates of cost. From this point of view the law violates one of the established canons of sound tax policy—the laying of taxes with certainty and in such manner as to create a minimum of business dislocation. The introduction of speculative elements of this kind constitutes one of the important forms of administrative protection, or barriers to trade over and above the simple payment of duties, in the operation of the tariff.

Historically, the shift from date of purchase to date of exportation was the result of the shift from specific purchase price to market price; since actual transaction prices were no longer to be used, transaction dates lost their relevance and it became desirable to select a new time basis as close to the date of entry as feasible. The date of exportation was reasonably close to the date of entry, was easily ascertainable from ships' documents, and was compatible with the use of invoice consulation as evidence of market price. It thus appears that the time basis for dutiable value currently in effect is largely a function of more fundamental considerations as to the nature of dutiable value; its disadvantages, so far as business is concerned, stem from the same source as most of the difficulties observed in the course of this study—the departure from actual transaction prices as the basis for the levy of ad valorem duties.

A number of minor administrative problems are involved in the determination of the date of exportation. Normally the date of sailing, as indicated by the ship's documents or consular certification, is

---

82. Cf. *supra*, pp. 97–98.

taken as the date of exportation.[83] Shipments by land from interior countries or from countries contiguous to the United States are considered exported as of the day they cross the border.[84] Shipments by mail are legally exported the day the ship sails, not the date of mailing.[85] Importations on ships which have returned to port because of accident, and which have resailed, are considered to have been exported as of the original date of sailing.[86] But, in the case of an inordinately long delay, the original transaction is deemed to have been rescinded and the date of second sailing governs.[87] Likewise, in the case of wheat from Canadian lake ports carried in a vessel which had stopped at another Canadian port to discharge wheat that was no part of that destined to the United States, the date of second sailing was held to control.[88]

The factor of time works in a curious way outside of price fluctuations to complicate the problem of dutiable value. This occurs when shrinkage in quantity or weight common to certain classes of bulk goods, such as green sugars shipped in the raw state, takes place between the date of exportation and the time of weighing or gauging preparatory to appraisement. Since all appraisements are required by law to be made in unit quantities, the shrinkage results in an appreciation of unit values based on the invoice price for the total shipment. This unit value appreciation becomes of substantial significance when the merchandise is subject to duties by value brackets and also in connection with the application of penalty duties for undervaluation.[89]

In early instances of imported sugars that lost weight by virtue of shrinkage *en voyage,* the importer was assessed duties on the lower

83. T.D. 27995(D); *United States* v. *Lawrence,* 137 F. 466 (1905); *Masson* v. *United States,* 1 C.C.A. 149 (1911).

84. Levett, *op. cit.,* p. 56; T.D. 38097(D).

85. C.R. 30255.

86. C.R. 27894; C.R. 844.

87. C.R. 30299.

88. Reap. 4248. These were shipments of wheat "unfit for human consumption," dutiable at 10 per cent ad valorem, from Fort William, Ont., to Buffalo, N.Y. The vessel sailed from Fort William on July 28, 1936, but stopped at Port Colbourne, Ont., to discharge other wheat, sailing from Port Colbourne on August 1. The difference in the two dates raised the dutiable value from 78¾ cents to 85¾ cents per bushel.

89. Undervaluation-penalty duties are no longer applicable to undervaluation resulting from shrinkage (*Customs Regulations, 1943,* 14.3[e]).

weight with no change in unit values.[90] But as it became recognized that the shrinkage was an essential part of the preparation for refining and that the quality actually increased in the process, and commercial practice based the settlement price on the shrinkage factor, it became established policy to assess duties on the higher unit value yielded by settlement value divided by the weight at importation.[91] In the case of castile soap which had increased in quality during the shrinkage en route, the principle of unit-value appreciation was upheld, but the assumption that such appreciation exactly offset the shrinkage in weight was rejected for lack of evidence, and the importer paid duty on the original unit value at the time of exportation.[92]

Containers and coverings; all other charges.—The complexity of the problem surrounding the dutiability of containers and coverings, and of other "charges," has already been noted.[93] Since most of the problems affecting containers and coverings also pertain to the other charges, the subjects are discussed together. For convenience, the pertinent portions of the definitions of foreign and export value are quoted:

> Foreign value: . . . including the cost of all containers and coverings of whatever nature, and all other costs, charges, and expenses incident to placing the merchandise in condition, packed ready for shipment to the United States.
> Export value: . . . plus, when not included in such price, the cost of all containers and coverings of whatever nature, and all other costs, charges, and expenses incident to placing the merchandise in condition, packed ready for shipment to the United States.

The differences in wording between the two definitions arose out of the continuation, in the act of 1922, of the wording contained in the original definition of export value in the Emergency Tariff Act of 1921. The variation reflects the fact that goods for export are frequently sold in their "packed" condition for exportation, whereas similar goods for home consumption are sold only with their ordinary coverings. In both cases, the *cost,* not the *value*—namely, the specific price paid, rather than the prevailing market price for the services

90. *Marriott* v. *Brune,* 9 How. 619 (1850); *United States* v. *Southmayd,* 9 How. 637 (1850).
91. *American Sugar Refining Company* v. *United States,* 181 U.S. 610 (1900).
92. *Reiss* v. *Magone,* 39 F. 105 (1889).
93. *Supra,* pp. 59–61; 121–24.

rendered—of all dutiable charges is to be taken for purposes of dutiable value. This suggests that dutiable value is divided into two major parts—the "market value" of the goods per se and the "dutiable charges" to be added thereto. This distinction between market value and total dutiable value, in order to avoid confusion, has not heretofore been emphasized in this study; but it has been important for a number of reasons, most of which are now only of historical significance.

The high point of this distinction was reached in the elaborate opinion, with equally elaborate dissent, in the case of *United States* v. *Spingarn Brothers*.[94] This case grew out of the reliquidation by the collector, of an entry which had been liquidated a year previously, to include the value of packing charges alleged to have been fraudulently concealed by the importer. The Court of Customs Appeals affirmed the distinction between market value and dutiable value which was not observed under the existing administrative practice; the former was construed as an evaluation to be performed by the appraiser; the latter, a finding of fact to be made by the collector. The remedy for errors in the former was an appeal to reappraisement; for the latter a protest, having the same recourse to higher courts as classification cases.

There were a number of consequences resulting from this decision. It had the effect of excluding all dutiable charges from value for purposes of classification as well as for the computation of penalty duties. This was of course favorable to importers, especially for goods subject to rates by value brackets. The administrative results were important in many ways, largely because the appraiser would often include the cost of coverings in the market value of goods while the collector would interpret them to be dutiable costs to be added to market value to make dutiable value. This overlapping jurisdiction of the collector and the appraiser led to considerable confusion and frequently to double duties or complete exemption from duty on charges; moreover, since the remedy for an appraiser's action was an appeal to reappraisement and for an act of the collector a protest, the importer or the government, as the case might be, was often left without any remedy after exhausting the wrong one under an erroneous interpretation of the facts.

94. 5 C.C.A. 3 (1913).

The Tariff Act of 1922 resolved this question by its new definition of dutiable value which included all dutiable costs in the several forms of value as defined. This returned to the appraiser the complete and exclusive responsibility for the determination of all dutiable costs and charges and their inclusion in appraised value. It did not mean that costs and charges were to be *appraised* at their *value;* only their specific costs could be included, but the appraiser was made responsible for their correct "ascertainment."[95] It also followed from the new definitions of dutiable value that, both for the purpose of determining classification and for the assessment of undervaluation-penalty duties, all costs were to be included. That is the situation obtaining at the present time, with section 503 of the Tariff Act of 1930 specifically providing that the final appraised value determines the classification where the rate is in any manner based upon value.

An example of the operation of these provisions, as well as of the effects of a small item of dutiable charges upon total duties, is found in the case of an importation of imitation pearl beads. Such beads were dutiable under the 1930 act at the rate of 60 per cent ad valorem if not more than one-fourth cent in value per inch of temporary string. For value over one-fourth cent per inch, a compound duty of 60 per cent plus one-half cent per inch applied. The importation was made in a tin-lined wooden box costing $7.50. The collector added the cost of the box to the value returned by the appraiser, bringing the unit value barely above one-fourth cent, thus reclassifying the importation from the simple 60 per cent duty bracket to the compound rate, which at the lower margin of the new bracket represented an ad valorem equivalent of some 260 per cent. On appeal the importer showed that in the ordinary course of trade a plain wooden box costing $2.50 rather than $7.50 was used for shipment. The court sustained the importer under section 503, holding that the collector may not add dutiable charges to reclassify into a higher bracket. Had the higher classification been upheld, it would have increased regular duties from $180 to over $768, exclusive of the inevitable undervaluation

95. In *United States* v. *Woolworth and Co.*, 26 C.C.P.A. 33 (1938), the tenuous nature of the distinction between "appraisement" and "ascertainment" is made obvious. In this case the appraiser advanced the amount of packing charges from the invoice figures to an amount representing his estimate of their current cost. His action was sustained on the principle that authority to ascertain implied the exercise of judgment which could be overturned only by substantial evidence.

duties which would have accrued. In this case it appeared that the appraiser had *appraised* the dutiable charges at a lower value than the actual cost, which is the legal basis for estimating charges. The correct remedy for the collector would have been an appeal to reappraisement rather than the arbitrary reclassification of the merchandise.[96]

Dutiable costs and charges are usually not sufficiently large percentagewise to result in substantial increases in either ordinary ad valorem or undervaluation-penalty duties if the importer's contention as to their treatment is not sustained. But, when unusually large importations are concerned or where unusual charges are involved, the inclusion or noninclusion of such charges in dutiable value may result in very substantial differences in duty. In 1923 the city of San Juan, Puerto Rico, began construction of an aqueduct requiring large amounts of cast-iron pipe and fittings. The successful bidder for furnishing this material was awarded a contract ultimately running to nearly $950,000, and he imported all the pipe and fittings from Belgium. Included in the exporter's sale price were three items of charges which the government contended were dutiable. These included 6 per cent insurance against breakage, 6 per cent insurance against exchange fluctuations, and a 3 per cent commission. The testimony showed that the importer would assume no obligation to pay for goods broken in transit and insisted on a price in American currency although it was the exporter's practice to sell in Belgian currency. The 6 per cent charge for breakage represented self-insurance by the exporter, the ordinary rates by responsible insurance companies running from 5 to 10 per cent. No insurance company willing to assume

96. *L. Heller & Son (Inc.) v. United States*, 20 C.C.P.A. 257 (1932). This case forcefully illustrates the anomalous nature of duties based upon value brackets. The manifest absurdity of a law which makes the imposition of an increase of $600 in regular duties and even more in total duties depend upon the nature of a $7.50 box is one indication of the kinds of distortion to which the tariff has been subjected in the interests of protection. A distinction should be made between duties subject to value brackets where the mean ad valorem equivalent is roughly the same for each bracket and those duties for which the ad valorem equivalents change radically from bracket to bracket. Compound rates, as in the case above, are the chief offenders in this respect and generally represent successful lobbying by highly special interests. But even when the mean ad valorem equivalent is the same from bracket to bracket, substantial changes in duty result from minor differences in value at the class limits, especially when the classes are wide. The correction of value-bracket anomalies should receive high priority in any program of practical tariff reform.

the risk of exchange fluctuation was found by the exporter, and the commission was shown to be a purchasing commission. The court sustained the importer on all three items, totaling 15 per cent of the foreign value of the importation. It is obvious that the exclusion of such charges even under simple ad valorem rates of duty when applied to sums of the size in this case is a matter of importance to all concerned.[97]

The foregoing analysis has been concerned primarily with an exposition of the law of dutiable value with respect to its two most important bases in the United States—foreign and export value. Such an exposition reveals a substantial body of court-made law which has been developed to bridge the gap between the bare statute and the numerous administrative problems arising in the assessment of ad valorem duties. It is pertinent to ask, after a recital of the findings in the cases cited above, whether or not there has been an observable bias on the part of either the administration or the courts for or against the importer. Discussion of this issue is reserved, however, until consideration has been given to the remaining forms of dutiable value and to certain other provisions of the law, which will permit a more comprehensive view of the problem.

97. *United States* v. *Enrique Vidal Sanchez,* 15 C.C.A. 443 (1928). For other illustrations of the administration and effects of dutiable costs and charges cf. *United States* v. *Woolworth et al.,* 22 C.C.P.A. 184 (1934); *United States* v. *Richard and Co.,* 14 C.C.A. 120 (1926).

CHAPTER VI

United States Value; Cost of Production

United States Value

As ALREADY indicated, United States value was originally adopted as an alternate basis to provide for merchandise which was not generally offered for sale in foreign markets and which therefore had no foreign-market value. Such importations included consignments or actual sales to agents for sale at auction or through regular channels in the United States, to exporters' branch houses or sole purchasers, or from importers' plants located abroad to the home plant or distributing house in this country. United States value was originally conceived as an approximation of foreign value made possible by working backward from the selling price in the United States to a constructive foreign-market value by deducting expenses and profits incurred in importing the goods.

The term "United States value" is misleading and is often confused in substance with "domestic value," the full market value of the imported merchandise in the United States. The Customs Court once made the following statement:

What in subsection (d) of section 402 is called United States value is a misnomer. It is not the market value in the United States. It is that less very substantial deductions. It is in effect a foreign value as established by a market sale or offer to sell in the United States of such or similar merchandise.[1]

The number of importations which are appraised at their United States value is relatively small when compared to those appraised at foreign or export value.[2] Nevertheless, the importance of this form of

1. *United States* v. *Carbic Color and Chemical Co.*, T.D. 40859 (1925).

2. E. W. Camp, then commissioner of customs, testified before the Ways and Means Committee in 1929 that probably less than 1 per cent of all entries were based on either American selling price or United States value. U.S. Congress, House Committee on Ways and Means, *Tariff Adjustment, 1929: Hearings*, XVI, 9751. This was confirmed by William Hannan, appraiser at the port of Chicago,

dutiable value extends beyond its actual application in connection with section 402(e), since it has been included as a companion basis for the American selling price in determining dutiable value on coaltar products and has been vigorously urged along with American selling price and domestic value to take the place of prices in foreign markets as the primary basis of dutiable value. The following pages will attempt to indicate the significant problems in the application of United States value and to examine its economic implications.

Section 402(e) of the Tariff Act of 1930 defines United States value as follows:

UNITED STATES VALUE.—The United States value of imported merchandise shall be the price at which such or similar imported merchandise is freely offered for sale, packed ready for delivery, in the principal market of the United States to all purchasers, at the time of exportation of the imported merchandise, in the usual wholesale quantities and in the ordinary course of trade, with allowance made for duty, cost of transportation and insurance, and other necessary expenses from the place of shipment to the place of delivery, a commisson not exceeding 6 per centum, if any has been paid or contracted to be paid on goods secured otherwise than by purchase, or profits not to exceed 8 per centum and a reasonable allowance for general expenses, not to exceed 8 per centum on purchased goods.

In addition to the use of United States value as an alternate basis of valuation for ad valorem duties in general, it is also prescribed as an alternate to the American selling price in paragraphs 27 and 28, containing duties on coal-tar products. Because of the close administrative connection between United States value and American selling price in the treatment of coal-tar products, discussion of this aspect will be deferred to the treatment of American selling price. Also, since a large part of the definition of United States value consists of terms identical with those already discussed in detail in connection with foreign and export value, only the significant differences will be discussed in the present chapter.

The first observation to be made is that United States value divides imports into two classes: purchased goods and goods procured otherwise than by purchase. The former are more generously dealt with

---

October 9, 1946, as indicative of the current ratio. (Hereinafter, the tariff hearings before the respective House and Senate committees on the tariff bills in 1921 and 1929 will be referred to simply as "*House* [or *Senate*] *Hearings, 1921* [or *1929*]," with appropriate volume and page numbers; full titles may be found in the Bibliography.)

and are allowed deductions of a maximum of 8 per cent each for profits and for general expenses. Nonpurchased goods are allowed a maximum of 6 per cent for commissions, none for profits or general expense.[3] All deductions within the specified categories must be itemized and are disallowed or reduced if upon the evidence they appear to have been inflated.[4] Allowances for profits are to be the profits upon "such or similar" merchandise and not those for the firm or the industry as a whole.[5] The "principal market" of valuation, it will be noted, is in the singular and, in practice, is generally the principal port of importation.[6] Internal revenue taxes applicable to imports are included in the selling price in the United States and are not allowed as deductions to make United States value.[7]

A fundamental requirement of United States value which has been placed upon it by judicial interpretation is that a previous or "prototype" importation of such or similar merchandise must have been made before it can be applied.[8] In most cases this means that the prototype importation must be appraised on the basis of cost of production. The deductions allowable to make United States value have been held to be those incidental to the prototype importation and not to the merchandise under appraisement.[9]

The reasoning underlying the prototype requirement is that, since the statute requires the existence of a freely offered price in the United

3. This interpretation of the statute was forcefully made in *Johnson* v. *United States*, 13 C.C.A. 373 (1926). The court held that it was the intention of Congress to favor the American importer, who purchases goods outright and maintains an expensive selling establishment in this country, with greater deductions than the foreign consignor, who sells through a sole agent on a nominal commission basis.

4. *United States* v. *American Aniline Products, Inc.*, 22 C.C.P.A. 380 (1934).

5. *Ibid.*

6. A study of the Tariff Commission's findings in its report on domestic value (cf. *supra*, p. 145, n. 60) indicates that New York is the principal market and principal port of entry for the vast majority of all importations. In other cases the principal port of entry is likewise usually the principal market. Because of the relatively small number of entries under United States value and the limitation to one market, the principal-market provision has not offered much difficulty.

7. *Faunce* v. *United States*, 25 C.C.P.A. 131 (1937). This is an unnecessary construction of the law and departs from the original purpose of United States value, namely, to find foreign value by deducting all duties, costs, and other charges constituting the difference in selling prices in the two countries involved. For discussion of this issue cf. *infra*, p. 297, n. 51.

8. Leading cases on the prototype doctrine are *United States* v. *Sheldon*, 23 C.C.P.A. 245 (1935); *Stern Hat Co.* v. *United States*, 26 C.C.P.A. 410 (1939); *United States* v. *Collin and Gissel* (*Ludwig Baer*), 29 C.C.P.A. 96 (1941).

9. T.D. 40859 (CC).

States as of the date of exportation, it is *ipso facto* impossible to use the price of merchandise in the process of importation. For most goods the importer is not certain as to their ultimate selling price in the United States until after they have been imported and sold. Difficulties in determining beforehand consumer demand, especially for a new line of goods; seasonal changes in demand; domestic competition; unanticipated marketing costs: these, and many other, conditions make it impossible accurately to predict final selling prices. This uncertainty is multiplied by a basis of dutiable value which itself depends upon the ultimate selling price. When the ultimate selling price is uncertain, not only is there no dependable starting point for the computation of United States value, but the deductions for profits and, to less extent, for general expenses, are also indeterminate. Customs authorities and courts have logically taken the position that duties cannot be levied upon contingent and hypothetical future selling prices that may never materialize.

On the other hand, there are certain classes of importation—such as books or other articles which have been announced in advance to sell at a certain list price or which have actually been sold in advance by the importer or contracted for delivery at a definite selling price and which are freely offered to all purchasers at such price—where this objection does not apply. Not only is the application of United States value to such goods feasible from the standpoint of a satisfactory determination of the selling price of the goods in the United States at the time of exportation, but it would seem to be the clear mandate of the statute to make such application in view of the established construction of the words "freely offered for sale." The statute does not say that such or similar merchandise must already be in stock in the United States or that it must be available for instant delivery.[10] On the contrary, this point was specifically decided in the White Lamb Finlay case,[11] in which the court held that merchandise need not be in stock so long as reasonably prompt delivery may be made, and a period longer than from September 20 to October 25 was held to afford reasonably prompt delivery. Since the bulk of imported merchandise can be made available for delivery in the United States

10. Although the Customs Court so held in C.R. 17.
11. *White Lamb Finlay, Inc.* v. *United States,* 29 C.C.P.A. 199 (1942). This case concerned export value, but the requirements for free offer are the same as for United States value.

within a month or two after its date of exportation, the prompt-delivery test of the *bona fides* of a free offer does not preclude the basing of United States value on known or contracted prices in the United States of the merchandise undergoing appraisement. Nevertheless, the courts not only have steadfastly insisted on the prototype requirement for all imports, regardless of the certainty of the selling price, but have become increasingly severe in defining the requirements of acceptable prototype importations.

An illustration of the technicalities interposed in the way of establishing United States value, as well as the method used in determining it, is found in the Collin and Gissel case. This concerned the sale of beer-barrel washing machines to breweries in the United States. The importer and exclusive representative of the German manufacturer took orders from large breweries at the freely offered price of $6,000 in the early months of 1934 and of $5,500 after June 1. Altogether the importer sold eighteen machines in that year, and all of them he purchased outright from the exporter. The importation in question was exported on July 11 and entered at Houston, Texas, at the invoice price of $3,300. The appraiser ultimately returned an appraised value on the cost-of-production basis of 12,511.30 reichsmarks, which at prevailing exchange rates was slightly in excess of $5,000. The importer appealed to reappraisement, holding that United States value was applicable, based on the freely offered price of $5,500 after June 1, and showing that contracts had been made at that price for pending deliveries. The single trial judge of the Customs Court sustained the importer's contention and found a United States value of $3,529.92[12] (broken down as shown in the accompanying tabulation).

United States selling price	$5,500.00
Less 8 per cent each, general expenses and profits	880.00
	$4,620.00
Less ocean freight	100.53
	$4,519.47
Less insurance	18.82
	$4,500.65
Less customs duties—27½ per cent on United States value .	970.73
United States value ($4,500.65 ÷ 1.275)	$3,529.92

12. Reap. 4580.

The government appealed for a review, and the appellate division of the Customs Court sustained the findings of the trial judge.[13] The government then appealed to the Court of Customs and Patent Appeals on assignments of errors of law. The appellate court reversed the Customs Court on the ground that United States value was inapplicable for lack of a prototype importation. It was found that all the previous importations of identical machines had been sold at the former price of $6,000. The fact that prototype importations had actually been sold in the United States, although at a higher price, or that additional importations to make delivery under contract at the then current freely offered price of $5,500 were already en route to the United States at the date of exportation of the merchandise in controversy carried no weight with the court in sustaining the existence of United States value. The court's decision turned on the fact that, since all the previously imported machines had already been sold and those en route had not yet arrived, "no imported machine was in the United States available to be offered for sale by the importer at $5,500, or any other price, on July 11, 1934, the date of exportation."

The foregoing is perhaps an extreme case, but it indicates the court's reluctance to apply United States value in the absence of definitive and unequivocal selling prices of prototype importations. The necessity for such importations for most kinds of merchandise is in itself demonstrative of the confusion which would obtain if United States value were made a major basis of valuation. Nevertheless, the American Tariff League in 1929 urged its adoption in a more severe form[14] as the primary basis for dutiable value, claiming that it would reduce undervaluation, afford greater certainty in appraisement, produce greater revenue, and provide greater protection to American manufacturers. Reply briefs by the National Council of American Importers and Traders made an excellent analysis of the difficulties for both importers and the government in the administration of United States value in any form and effectively refuted the Tariff League's

13. Reap. 4723.

14. The Tariff League advocated the elimination of all deductions except the duty and proposed American selling price, and an "Americanized" cost-of-production formula, as first and second alternate value bases (*Senate Hearings, 1929: Special and Administrative Provisions,* pp. 50–51).

contentions.[15] Since the claims of the League and the replies of the importers furnish a convenient point of departure for further analysis of the economic and administrative aspects of United States value, they are recapitulated and discussed along with other issues in the following paragraphs.

It is generally conceded that the selling prices of imports in the United States fluctuate much more rapidly and widely than the basic wholesale prices abroad.[16] Importers' sale prices for large classes of goods are geared to seasonal demand and changes in styles and fashions. The existence of wide margins or markups for many imports permits much greater variation in price in countries of importation than in the basic international wholesale markets. But, even if such prices were stable, the difficulties of ascertainment would present an insuperable task for both appraisers and importers, and, under the general undervaluation penalty provisions which automatically apply when there is a difference of opinion between the appraiser and the importer, the latter would inevitably suffer. An importer has forty-eight hours after the entry of the importing vessel in which to enter his goods, and the impossibility of estimating the final selling prices and computing deductions for ocean freight, insurance, general expenses, duty, and profits—much of which is dependent upon the final selling price—for a multiplicity of articles in large invoices, sometimes running to a hundred or more pages, is obvious. Under foreign valuation the invoice price is generally the prevailing foreign-market value, and entries can usually be based thereon. Under United States value, or any basis using selling prices in the United States, invoices become of little use so far as valuation is concerned, and importers and appraisers alike have no conveniently available starting point in their estimate of dutiable value. The appraisers, however, are under no compulsion of time and may take weeks or months to complete their investigation and render an appraisement. If the appraiser's return is greater than the entry, undervaluation-penalty duties accrue; if it is less, the importer must pay on his entered value anyway.[17]

15. *Ibid.*, pp. 94–125.   16. *Ibid.*

17. It should here be stated that the law permits the importer to amend his entry prior to the time that it has come under the observation of the appraiser for purposes of appraisement. While this permits an informal consultation with the appraiser, it does not bind the appraiser or remove the importer's legal liability for entering the correct value.

But there would be other difficulties in the general application of United States value. It would not provide for the large class of importations made by chain stores, department stores, and others who sell directly at retail and have no wholesale selling price. Nor does it provide for goods not sold in their imported condition in the United States, such as unbound books, raw materials, or many components of manufactures in this country, all of which may possess a foreign value as currently defined in the statute but no United States selling price.

Not only do the complications of United States value at the appraising and selling end of import transactions preclude its satisfactory use as a general form of dutiable value, but it proves embarrassing to buyers of merchandise abroad. A buyer's success in procuring foreign merchandise often depends upon his ability accurately to estimate his landed costs. This is easily done on the basis of foreign prices, but the uncertainties of duty when dependent upon an uncertain selling price (to say nothing of the difficulties of computing duties on the United States value basis even when the selling price in the United States is known) would add substantial difficulties to the task of purchasing abroad. A change in the definition to provide for valuation as of the date of importation rather than of exportation would further complicate matters. Such a change would still not permit a dependable estimate of the selling price in the United States and would further disturb the estimates of buyers in purchasing. A price increase between the date of exportation and that of importation—a period varying with the distance of the country of exportation—might easily result in an increase in duties sufficient to wipe out the bulk of the importer's margin. In any case, the speculative element in the importing business would be greatly increased. Likewise, it has been urged by both importers and domestic producers that combinations of importers would depress prices for a few days before arrival of large importations, to the detriment of both revenue and tariff protection.[18] This, however, is an argument against United States value in general rather than against a change in the date of valuation, since the same tactics could be used with respect to the date of exportation. There is undoubtedly basis for the contention of selling-price manipulation by importers, especially in the case of goods with limited markets, since the courts

18. Cf. *House Hearings, 1921*, VI, 4211–13; also discussion of "home valuation" in 1832, *supra*, pp. 78–82.

have ruled that a single purchaser may make a market,[19] and offers in the absence of sales may establish a market price.[20]

The Tariff League's contention that domestic producers would receive additional protection by the general adoption of United States value is susceptible of several interpretations. Some additional protection would be afforded if United States value were generally adopted without a conversion of rates. This is true of its existing form because of the statutory limitation on deductions of general expenses and profits, and because of court decisions on internal-revenue tax additions; it would be true a fortiori if the version of United States value offered by the league were adopted. Such additional protection would be fortuitous and eccentric, falling with differential weight on different classes of imports and serving to tax wages and to some extent profits spent in the United States. But, since changes in rates, not valuation methods, are the established and recognized method of conferring protection, even the League admitted elsewhere that "minor" changes in rates would be necessary to prevent disturbance of established protective-duty levels.[21]

The only other meaning which can be attached to the Tariff League's statement on protection is that the adoption of United States value would reduce undervaluation. Neglecting the fact that the league's representative grossly misrepresented the nature and significance of undervaluation, failing to distinguish between fraudulent and purely technical undervaluation, his claim of additional protection is totally incompatible with that of increased revenue to the government, except in cases of revenue inelasticities certainly not contemplated by the Tariff League.[22]

19. E.g., *Lloyd* v. *United States,* 9 C.C.A. 280 (1919).

20. *Sandoz Chemical Works* v. *United States,* 13 C.C.A. 466 (1926).

21. The League's spokesman glibly used the illustration of a commission merchant operating on a margin of 1 to 5 per cent as representative of the importing business. He made the even more remarkable statement that the entire tariff could be converted by the Finance Committee in "a couple of weeks." It took the Tariff Commission approximately sixteen months with a staff of up to one hundred and forty persons and a total expenditure of $250,000 to perform the task of converting to the domestic-value basis, essentially a much simpler task than conversion to United States value.

22. The concept of "revenue elasticity" is here used to differentiate from elasticity of demand. It is possible that a reduction in imports consequent upon an increase in tariff levies would be accompanied by an increase in revenue. But this assumes existing levies to be lower than those which would yield maximum rev-

Another criticism of United States value is its alleged tendency to rise ad infinitum with any increase in either selling price or dutiable value. It is contended, in brief, that an increase in duties is added to the selling price, which in turn results in a further increase in dutiable value, which must be compensated by a still higher selling price, and so on.[23] Since this process must soon result in prohibitive prices, it has been intimated that the use of United States value is tantamount to price- and profit-fixing by the government: " 'If you are buying the goods do it on a 16% gross profit or quit,' says the government, and 'if you are an agent working on commission don't let your principal pay you over 6%.' "[24]

There are several objections to this analysis. Assuming that it is possible to pass successive increases in duty on to the consumer in successive price increases, the pyramiding process would stop even in the absence of allowable deductions for duty in the case of all rates of less than 100 per cent at a point at which further increases in duty and price became negligible.[25] But the pyramiding tendency in the case of United States value is arrested, for all practical purposes, after the initial price increase by an increase in the deduction from selling price to make United States value. This increase in the deduction is substantially equivalent to the increase in duty, thus offsetting the increase in duty. The effect is perhaps best illustrated by an arithmetical example (Table 4), which shows the consequences of adding the increase in duty to the selling price. As indicated, the illustration assumes a unit

---

enue. Such duties under the present tariff are probably exceptional, and, in any case, the "revenue standard" is neither desired by the Tariff League nor could it be achieved by the fortuitous method of generally increased valuations.

23. Benjamin A. Levett, *Through the Customs Maze* (N.Y., 1923), pp. 50–53; also, *Senate Hearings, 1921*, VII, 5109(6).

24. Levett, *op. cit.*, p. 52.

25. This is the general case, applicable to domestic value (which allows no deduction for duty) rather than to U.S. value. Let A = initial increase in selling price and R = rate of duty. Then, for successive importations, the sum, S_n, of the several increases in price is equal to

$$A + AR + AR^2 + AR^3 + \ldots + AR^{n-1} = \frac{A(R^n - 1)}{R - 1}.$$

But when $R < 1$, $\lim S_n = A/(1 - R)$, which for a rate of 50 per cent would therefore yield a total increase in selling price of, at most, double the initial increase; a rate of 100 per cent would yield constant successive increases, or a total increase of nA; rates over 100 per cent would produce a rapid, upward, inverted pyramiding effect, resulting in increases without limit.

cost or purchase price abroad per article of $0.50; transportation, etc., of $0.05; a 50 per cent rate of duty; and general expenses and profit of $0.10 each.[26] A prototype importation is assumed to have been made, dutiable at statutory "cost of production" equal to the purchase price abroad. In addition to illustrating the complications encountered in applying the United States value formula, the example reveals that:

TABLE 4

ITEM	SUCCESSIVE IMPORTATIONS DUTIABLE AT U.S. VALUE (AMOUNTS IN DOLLARS PER UNIT OF IMPORT)					
	0	1	2	3	4	5
S_p		1.0000	1.0133	1.0192	1.0187	1.0186
D		0.4733	0.4748	0.4818	0.4816	0.4815
U	0.50	0.5267	0.5385	0.5374	0.5371	0.5371
RU	0.25	0.2633	0.2692	0.2687	0.2686	0.2686
C	0.50	0.5000	0.5000	0.5000	0.5000	0.5000
T	0.05	0.0500	0.0500	0.0500	0.0500	0.0500
G	0.10	0.1000	0.1000	0.1000	0.1000	0.1000
P	0.10	0.1000	0.1000	0.1000	0.1000	0.1000
S_c	1.00	1.0133	1.0192	1.0187	1.0186	1.0186

S_p = selling price in U.S. of previous importation.
D = deductions from S_p to make U.S. value: $T + .16S_p + RU$.
U = U.S. value: $(S_p - T - .16S_p)/(R + 1)$.
R = rate of duty: 50 per cent. RU = amount of duty.
C = cost of article abroad (importer's purchase price).
T = transportation, insurance, etc.
G = general expenses.
P = profits.
S_c = selling price in U.S. of current importation.

(1) the initial increase in selling price results from the insufficiency of the statutory deductions to equal their real counterparts—no change in duty or price would result if deduction of actual profits and expenses were permitted; (2) the selling price is practically stabilized at the level reached by the first importation under the United States value basis—with negligible adjustments for several importations thereafter; (3) if the importer absorbs the initial increase in duty, his

26. Monopolistic control is assumed, compatible with the legal necessity for application of the United States value basis for duty. Note that if the importer chooses to absorb the initial increase in duty his profit is reduced to $0.0867 per unit.

profits are reduced, but neither his profits nor his general expenses are limited to the statutory 8 per cent figure.

Without entering upon a detailed discussion of the various possibilities depending upon differing cost- and demand-functions, we may say that the importer will stabilize his price at the optimum level, absorbing the higher duty to the extent necessary to maximize profits, under the same principles which he would use in responding to a simple increase in rate or valuation on the foreign-value basis. The chief disadvantage of United States value lies in the greater complication in estimating both duties and selling price and the inconvenience and confusion of experiencing a change in dutiable value every time the selling price changes, from whatever cause. Such disadvantages may be minimized by absorption by importers of initial changes in duties or by establishing low selling prices in the United States market during "out-of-season" periods in anticipation of large importations prior to the following season.

For the various reasons indicated, United States value would not be suitable as a primary basis of valuation. This is quite different from saying that the place now given to it in the dutiable-value provisions in section 402 is inappropriate. Its present use as an alternate basis of secondary importance fulfils a definite need for a valuation base to provide for consignments and similar importations for which a foreign value does not exist either by exporter's intent or as a by-product of export-import organization. Except for its limitation of deductions,[27] it furnishes a reasonable approximation of legitimate foreign value,[28] and, as long as the proportion of total importations requiring its application is low, it can be administered without the hopeless confusion which would ensue were it to be made general.

27. There appears to be no justification for the retention of the limitations in question. Since the end in view is the approximation of foreign value, any such limitation defeats, *pro tanto*, the achievement of such purpose. Not even administrative simplification can be urged in defense of such limitation, since the importer must produce and appraisers and judges must evaluate documentary evidence as to the actual figures involved, whether they be higher or lower than the statutory limits.

28. United States value is also occasionally used unofficially by appraisers as a cross-check against undervaluation even when foreign value exists. A substantial difference between values on the two bases, with due allowance for actual costs of importation and sale, would arouse the appraiser's suspicions (cf. testimony of Otto Fix, former examiner of merchandise at New York, in *Senate Hearings, 1929: Valuation*, p. 58).

Cost of Production

Cost of production was first made a statutory basis for dutiable value in section 9 of the Tariff Act of 1883, which authorized appraisers, in the absence of a satisfactory market value—whether by reason of consignment or otherwise—to ascertain the cost or value of the materials at the time and place of manufacture, together with the expense of manufacturing, preparing, and putting up for shipment, and to use this estimate as the minimum dutiable value. Cost of production thus historically preceded United States value as an alternate basis directed against consignments. The Administrative Act of 1890 carried a somewhat stronger definition of cost of production, requiring a flat addition for profit of 8 per cent upon total cost as previously ascertained. The Dingley Act of 1897 increased the addition for profit to "not less than eight nor more than fifty per cent" upon total cost and also provided that United States value, in a rudimentary form, could be "taken into consideration" by appraisers. Section 28(11) of the Payne Act of 1909 included a minimum of 10 per cent for general expenses, in addition to the 10 to 50 per cent for profit. The same section made United States value the minimum for consigned goods and for purchased goods not freely offered for sale.

This recapitulation indicates a close relationship between cost of production and United States value as alternate bases in the absence of freely offered market prices abroad. Cost of production not only preceded United States value in time as a legal valuation base but was prior to it in application after the latter had been introduced. This priority was reversed in the Tariff Act of 1922 largely because of the difficulties of gathering cost data. The principal use of the cost-of-production formula at present is its application to merchandise sold under restrictive agreements both abroad and in this country and to unfinished goods imported for further processing and hence not sold in the United States in their imported condition.

Section 402(f) of the Tariff Act of 1930 carries the following definition:

(f) COST OF PRODUCTION.—For the purpose of this title the cost of production of imported merchandise shall be the sum of—

(1) The cost of materials of, and of fabrication, manipulation, or other process employed in manufacturing or producing such or similar merchandise, at a time preceding the date of exportation of the particular

merchandise under consideration which would ordinarily permit the manufacture or production of the particular merchandise under consideration in the usual course of business;

(2) The usual general expenses (not less than 10 per centum of such cost) in the case of such or similar merchandise;

(3) The cost of all containers and coverings of whatever nature, and all other costs, charges, and expenses incident to placing the merchandise under consideration in condition, packed ready for shipment to the United States; and

(4) An addition for profit (not less than 8 per centum of the sum of the amounts found under paragraphs (1) and (2) of this subdivision) equal to the profit which is ordinarily added, in the case of merchandise of the same general character as the particular merchandise under consideration, by manufacturers or producers in the country of manufacture or production who are engaged in the production or manufacture of merchandise of the same class or kind.

It will be observed that the upper limit of 50 per cent for profits, contained in definitions prior to 1922, does not appear in the current act. There is a rough parallelism between the additions imposed by the cost-of-production formula and the deductions allowed in finding United States value: ceilings are placed on the deductions to make United States value, and a comparable floor is placed on the additions to basic costs of production.

The principal technical requirement in the application of the cost-of-production formula, assuming the absence of prior bases, is the formal itemization of the four separate classes of cost indicated by the subdivisions in the statute.[29] This is important, as a purely arbitrary appraisement will stand in opposition to an importer's unitemized showing. Such a breakdown is, of course, necessary to a satisfactory evaluation of the cost figures as well as to judgment of the respective merits of opposing claims of importers and the government during litigation. From the standpoint of an intelligent estimate of cost, a breakdown of subdivision 1, showing the respective costs of materials and fabrication, would seem to be equally important, but the court in the Wirth case held this not to be required under the statute since Congress could easily have specified such a requirement had it felt it necessary.[30]

29. *Philip Wirth et al.* v. *United States,* 23 C.C.P.A. 283 (1936); *Mrs. G. P. Snow* v. *United States,* 24 C.C.P.A. 319 (1936); *United States* v. *Malhame and Co.,* 24 C.C.P.A. 448 (1937).

30. But in the Cottman case (*infra,* pp. 253–57), the court rejected cost-of-production data which did not include an allowance for cost of raw materials in the

The great practical difficulty in appraising merchandise on the cost-of-production basis is that of procuring reliable information independent of the evidence submitted by the importer. For this purpose appraisers must rely almost exclusively upon investigations by Treasury attachés abroad made while the merchandise awaits appraisement.[31] It is usually many months, and frequently years, before duties on such importations can finally be liquidated, especially if there is disagreement and litigation. The Treasury attachés often take the deposition of the foreign manufacturer but, in any case, request permission to examine his books. If the manufacturer refuses to permit inspection of his books, his affidavit, unless executed in the United States, is not admissible in evidence, thus effectively precluding overthrow of the presumption of correctness of any appraisement made.[32]

The theoretical barriers to accurate cost-of-production estimates are well known to economists and need no elaboration at this point. Considering the purpose for which such cost data are required, extended cost analysis would be inappropriate as well as administratively unworkable.[33] But even under the seemingly simple formula prescribed by the statute, cost determination for valuation purposes cannot escape the theoretical difficulties implicit in the problem. It will be noted that subsection 4 of the cost definition requires the addition of profit, not that of the manufacturer whose goods are under appraisement but that which is representative of the industry. This re-

---

case of a government-owned phosphate mine. It would thus appear that the separate costs under subdivision 1 can be impeached although they are not required to be itemized.

31. Ordinarily only 10 per cent of imported merchandise is designated for examination and appraisement. The remainder is released to the importer immediately after payment of estimated duties and giving of bond. But if the importer wishes to re-export the merchandise in the event that final assessed duties are so high as to preclude importation without a loss, he must leave the shipment in customs custody.

32. Under section 510 of the 1922 act refusal by a foreign exporter or manufacturer to open his books to a Treasury agent was punishable by refusal to admit into the United States any merchandise manufactured or exported by him; delivery of any such merchandise was withheld from the consignee and the merchandise sold at auction unless such refusal was withdrawn within a year. This harsh provision was omitted from the 1930 act.

33. The attainment of precision in cost-of-production estimates is of much greater significance for rate-making, such as done by the Tariff Commission under section 336, than for purposes of dutiable value and should not be confused with the latter.

quirement was designed to prevent manipulation of cost figures by
individual exporters; but does it mean that the costs of other firms
must be ascertained and "averaged" before an appraisement of any
importation can be made? The Customs Court, in contemplating the
futility of such a construction when this was urged by government
counsel, became more outspoken than usual:

> Every manufacturer's manufacturing costs, for a variety of reasons, are
> different from those of his competitors. As the costs of each differ, the indi-
> vidual profits thereby differ. By which is the importer to be bound, and by
> which is the ad valorem for his taxes to be ascertained—those who have low
> costs and therefore higher profits, or those who have high costs and there-
> fore lower profits? Any application of the new words quoted above, would
> therefore be a mere arbitrary guesswork process. They are consequently un-
> workable. Unworkable words in any statute should be ignored in apply-
> ing it.[34]

The appellate court did not subscribe to this doctrine for disposing of
unworkable statutory provisions but resolved the problem by stating
that if the profits of other firms were "readily ascertainable" they were
to be taken into account.

Even when confined to the individual manufacturer or exporter of
the goods in question, the use of the cost-of-production formula frequently runs into endless complications, expense, delay, and frustration for all concerned. An illustration which is perhaps typical of
much that takes place in routine customs administration throughout
the country concerns an importation of unbound books by the University of Chicago Press. The books consisted of some three hundred
copies of a three-volume set pertaining to land utilization in China,
printed by the University of Nanking as the outcome of a number of
years of research conducted by Dr. J. Lossing Buck. The project was
financed jointly by several philanthropical foundations which contributed amounts totaling some $140,000 for general agricultural re-
search in China, including the training of Chinese students of agron-
omy. The volumes in question were published to acquaint agricultural
economists and others with the findings, and distribution in this country was to be made by the University of Chicago Press, which appeared as publisher.

The importation, consisting of two shipments, was entered early in
1938 at the Chicago custom house at the value specified in the invoice

34. *United States* v. *Henry Maier*, 21 C.C.P.A. 41, 44 (1933).

prepared by the University of Nanking. Because of the prototype requirement and the fact that the books would not be sold in their imported condition (unbound), United States value was inapplicable and appraisement was withheld pending investigation of the cost of production. The Treasury attaché in China was ordered to make a cost study, and the University Press was requested to obtain and present complete figures of all financial contributions to the research project and all expenses incurred in connection with the publication of the book. The Press entered upon protracted and voluminous correspondence with the University of Nanking and the Secretariat of the Institute of Pacific Relations to obtain an itemized statement of all donations, expenses, and other financial transactions in any way associated with the project. Unfortunately, because of the Sino-Japanese war, the University of Nanking had moved to Chengtu, some twelve hundred miles from Nanking, where the records were stored. By the summer of 1941 the customs examiner in Chicago had uncovered sufficient evidence to notify the Press, through its customs broker, that his investigations had revealed that "almost a quarter of a million dollars had been used in the production of these volumes" and that there "would be a heavy penalty at final appraisement." The Press was allowed another month in which to amend the entry, and another appeal was accordingly sent to the various foundations and the New York offices of the University of Nanking to furnish all information in their power. The only available cost information appeared in the accompanying summary, expressed in Chinese dollars. This was sub-

Receipts		C$292,687.55
Expenditures:		
Salaries:		
Experts from abroad.............	C$ 30,001.13	
Staff, clerks, etc.................	150,276.69	
Travel to secure data..............	27,496.72	
Equipment—calculators, etc.........	4,450.19	
Books and maps..................	2,188.47	
Supplies, schedules, and charts	19,625.57	
Office expenses and supplies........	7,499.33	
Special trip to U.S.A.—Dr. Buck......	6,962.30	
Printing of books:		
Printing and expense.............	38,705.86	
Transportation, packing, etc.......	2,152.28	
		289,358.54
Balance on hand for completion of printing account......		C$ 3,329.01

mitted to the customs authorities, but still they were not satisfied. The examiner, in scrutinizing reports from the Treasury attaché, discovered that the cost of half-tones reproduced in the books had been charged by the University of Nanking at 15 cents per square inch; this appeared to him to be deliberate undervaluation in view of his knowledge that commercial firms in the United States (with the highest-paid photoengravers in the world) charged 28 cents per square inch for small, and 70 cents for large, half-tones. Also, the examiner discovered a letter in the importer's files, written from China by Dr. Buck in November of 1941, indicating that an additional $22,000 (Chinese) had been received by the University of Nanking to publish Volume I in the Chinese language. On the basis of this casual statement and with no knowledge of the proposed Chinese format, projected number of copies, or other information, the examiner contended that Dr. Buck's statement was an "admission" that the costs of the English edition had been understated.

The next step in the proceedings was for the local custom house to secure a ruling from Washington on the question of what items of expense in the list given above were to be imputed to the cost of the books. Counsel in the Treasury Department ruled, early in 1942, that "only such portion of the cost of research as may be directly attributable to the publication of the books should form a part of the cost of production thereof" but that "under the principle stated above . . . in addition to the cost of printing the books, items such as travel, books and maps, salaries of experts from abroad, and salaries of the staff and clerks engaged directly in the preparation and editing of the manuscript for the book should also be included in the cost of production thereof." As a general principle of equitable apportionment this ruling was unobjectionable. In practice, however, the task of ascertaining what portion of the total cost of research, as well as of the other cost items, should be allocated to the cost of producing the book and what portion to the training of students, the conduct of a university, etc., poses the same insoluble problems which are associated with joint costs wherever they are found. The case was finally settled on the basis of a reasonable interpretation of the facts, as well as the law, but only after years of annoyance, worry, expense, and loss of time by many individuals and organizations, some of whom were only remotely connected, or acquainted, with the circumstances involved. Similar experience with some half-dozen other scholarly publications from abroad has resulted in such excessive duties and cumulative litigation that the University Press has been all but forced to abandon collaboration in this type of importation and distribution.[35]

Further indication of undesirable trends in the application of the cost-of-production formula has appeared in a number of decisions which have included in foreign cost of production certain items, intangible or otherwise, which were not true cost items to the foreign manufacturer. Since the statute does not distinguish between materials produced in the United States and foreign materials, customs officers have no explicit authority for the omission of the costs of American materials purchased by a foreign manufacturer in the ordinary course of trade and incorporated in his finished product for exportation to the United States. But, when American materials are shipped abroad cost free to a foreign processor for completion and reimportation by the original shipper in the United States, it would seem to be an unreasonable construction of the law to include in the dutiable value the cost of such material. This, however, appears to be the practice.[36] What is more difficult to understand, in terms either of equity or of statutory interpretation, is the incorporation into the foreign cost of production of intangible costs incurred in the United States. Thus the cost of plans of imported mosaic pictures and windows was included in dutiable cost of production even though the plans were made in the United States.[37] To be sure, the statute does not specifically distinguish between "foreign" and other costs; but, taken *in pari materia* with the other forms of dutiable value as well as with provisions elsewhere in the tariff act for the free reimportation of American-made goods and for the reimportation of American goods repaired abroad duty free except for the value of the repairs, the wording of the cost-of-produc-

35. The author is indebted to Professor Viner for supplying this illustration and to the University of Chicago Press for making all information available. Inasmuch as this case was reconstructed from correspondence and other data in the files of the importer, it does not present the point of view of the customs officials. Since customs officers are also human beings, they, like importers, occasionally reach a state of desperation in attempting to satisfy all the requirements of the law. It is believed, however, that the two University of Chicago Press cases cited herein indicate typical problems faced by both importers and customs officials in the application of the cost-of-production formula.

36. Cf. *Stirn* v. *United States*, 12 C.C.A. 42 (1924); also *Austin* v. *United States*, 7 C.C.A. 186 (1916).

37. T.D. 42113.

tion provision hardly warrants the interpretation which prevailing administrative, as well as judicial, practice appears to have made.

The absurd lengths to which the inclusion of intangible items in cost is carried, and the consequences of such administrative intransigence, are illustrated by the recent appraisement of another importation of books by the University of Chicago Press. A number of years ago a $50,000 grant was made available to the Humanities Division of the University of Chicago for research in Greek philology. The bulk of the grant was devoted to the preparation of an exhaustive index of Greek-word terminations, alphabetized in reverse order to enable papyrologists and epigraphers to reconstruct Greek words and phrases from fragmentary manuscripts and other archeological remains. After years of exhaustive and scholarly research, typewritten copy running to nearly a thousand pages was ready for printing. Because of the highly specialized nature of the job, requiring a large supply of Greek type and compositors specializing in Greek material, the Chicago Press decided not to do the printing itself but to have it done by the Oxford University Press in England. Arrangements were made for Oxford to print one thousand copies, and shortly before the job was completed the Chicago Press requested shipment of some four hundred and fifty copies and announced the book to the trade in the United States at a list price of $10. It was anticipated that the books would be duty free, in view of their foreign-language nature, but they were classified as dutiable and the problem of valuation arose.[38]

The book had been announced for sale to the trade in England by the publisher's agent prior to exportation. The customs authorities, however, found neither foreign nor export value to exist, apparently on the ground that the research donation of $50,000 for preparation of the manuscript placed the book outside "the ordinary course of trade" —clearly an unnecessary interpretation. United States value was also ruled out for lack of a prototype, although a freely offered price in the United States existed at the time of exportation, and, abstracting from custom-house delays, prompt delivery could be had. Conse-

---

38. Paragraph 1630 provides for the free importation of "books and pamphlets printed wholly or chiefly in languages other than English." Except for infrequent passages of English, the book was composed primarily of Greek word terminations, with cross references and notes largely in Latin. Although the customs authorities had considerable difficulty in reading it, they concluded that the book was not chiefly in languages other than English.

quently, it was decided that the book was to be appraised at "cost of production." But the authorities were not content to ascertain cost of production in terms of the statute as ordinarily understood. They insisted that the $50,000 research grant, made and spent in the United States long before printing, was part of statutory cost of production. The Oxford Press was the manufacturer or producer of the imported article. The costs of preparing the manuscript on this side of the ocean formed no part of "the cost of materials of, and of fabrication, manipulation, or other process employed in manufacturing or producing such or similar merchandise," etc., as defined by law. The imported article was a printed and bound book—not a scholarly manuscript which had been previously produced in the United States at substantial cost over a period of years. Nevertheless, after much controversy and communication with Washington, the book was finally appraised at approximately $50 per copy. Since the applicable 20 per cent rate would produce a duty of $10 per copy, which was greater than the wholesale selling price in the United States, the Press decided to send the books back to England and receive a 99 per cent drawback. Interested libraries in this country could import the book duty-free under paragraph 1631, and the Press could later import a few volumes for test purposes without the risk of liability for enormous aggregate duties should the suit ultimately be lost after years of litigation.

Cost of production for purposes of customs valuation is thus seen not to be the kind of cost conceived by the businessman, which in relation to selling price determines profit. So far as the wording of the statute is concerned, it is somewhat akin to the economist's notion which includes profits in the form of a representative rate of return. From the administrative point of view, as originally intended by Congress, it is a constructive basis of valuation which, like United States value, attempts to reach a hypothetical foreign value but which does so by working forward from basic material costs instead of backward from selling price. This is fairly evident when it is considered that the addition for profit normally brings the total cost into equality with selling price.[39]

39. Perhaps the classic illustration of this equality is found in the Cottman case, in which the court, in order to determine the profit under the cost-of-production formula, deducted other costs from the selling price of $6.00 per ton, added the profit back to the other costs, and concluded that the total cost of production under the formula was $6.00 per ton (cf. *infra,* p. 256).

Although the cost-of-production formula in itself is not unreasonable, its actual application almost inevitably imposes a heavy burden of administrative protection in addition to the duties collected under it. The expense and delay attendant upon securing cost information both here and abroad are only part of the administrative difficulties encountered. The tendency for customs authorities to include every conceivable item of expenditure in cost estimates is partly the result of the insoluble nature of the problem of cost apportionment and partly the result of the lack of administrative discretion permitted and/or assumed by customs administrators. The exercise of discretion in the direction of reasonableness would seem to be especially necessary in applying the residual form of dutiable value which is all that remains after every other basis has failed and where concessions to reality are therefore the more imperative.

CHAPTER VII

American Valuation: Domestic Value and American Selling Price

THE term "American valuation" is the loose general expression which has been employed more or less indiscriminately by its exponents to mean any method or combination of methods of valuation which bases dutiable value upon selling prices or costs in the United States. It has thus included various modifications and combinations of United States value, domestic value, American selling price, and even American costs of production.[1] United States value, because of its deductions and fundamental purpose of affording an approximation to foreign-market value, is more properly classified with the various forms of foreign valuation; its use of selling price in the United States as the basis for computation has, however, afforded an entering wedge to the proponents of American valuation.

The circumstances surrounding the limited adoption of American valuation proposals in the 1922 and 1930 tariff acts have been briefly recited.[2] The following pages present an analysis of the respective merits of domestic value and American selling price as bases for dutiable value, as well as a discussion of the actual operation of the latter since 1922.

Domestic Value

One response made by Congress to the American valuation proposals during the 1929 hearings was the provision, in section 340, for a fact-finding study to be made by the Tariff Commission to convert all existing tariff rates, based in any manner upon value, to their ad

1. The cost of production of comparable American-made goods was advocated by the American Tariff League in 1929 as the residual alternate basis for dutiable value under American valuation (cf. *Senate Hearings, 1929: Special and Administrative Provisions,* pp. 50–51).
2. *Supra,* pp. 139–42.

valorem equivalents on the domestic-value basis. Section 340 specified that actual imports during the two-year period, July 1, 1927–June 30, 1929, be taken as the basis for calculation; actual dutiable values and selling prices for such imports, together with rates under the 1930 act, were the factors to be used in determining the converted rates.

Domestic value is defined in the act as follows:

(1) The term "domestic value," applied with respect to imported merchandise, means

(A) the price at which such or similar imported merchandise is freely offered for sale, at the time of exportation of the imported merchandise, packed ready for delivery, in the principal market of the United States to all purchasers, in the usual wholesale quantities and in the ordinary course of trade, or

(B) if such or similar imported merchandise is not so offered for sale in the United States, then an estimated value, based on the price at which merchandise, whether imported or domestic, comparable in construction or use with the imported merchandise, is so offered for sale, with such adjustments as may be necessary owing to differences in size, material, construction, texture, and other differences.

Subdivision A, above, is the usual definition of domestic value. However, in anticipation of the widespread absence of such selling price at the date of exportation (the "prototype" problem discussed in connection with United States value), it was necessary, in order to cover the bulk of the importations during the period under study, to include subdivision B. The phrase "comparable in construction or use" has a much broader connotation than "such or similar" and may include articles differing substantially in value from those actually imported. Since these differences were to be compensated by "such adjustments as may be necessary," the selection of domestic value under B would not result in the application of American selling price unless the domestic article were in all respects identical to the imported article.

Early in 1931 the Tariff Commission set up field headquarters in New York and began its study. Data were obtained from importers' records and custom-house entries. Every attempt was made to select importing houses which, as a whole, would yield representative data from the standpoint of variety of imports, countries of origin, volume of business, completeness of records, and channels of distribution. Likewise, representative samples of merchandise, in terms of variety of grades, quality, color, design, etc., were selected from the invoices of each importer. Numerous difficulties were presented, including the linking of purchases and sales of given importations, the averaging of data, the selection of markets, the weighting of classes or subclasses of merchandise, and the compensating for changes in classification as between the 1922 and the 1930 tariff acts.[3] A factor of substantial importance for the ultimate validity of the converted rates was the difference in duties between the two acts, since the selling prices of the goods in question were largely dependent upon actual duties under the 1922 act.

Despite all the difficulties, the commisson completed its task in sixteen months and published the results in a volume of over eight hundred pages.[4] The report consisted of some thirty pages of introductory material, explaining the plan of investigation, the problems encountered, and the methods of solution, followed by the detailed conversion figures by tariff paragraphs for each ad valorem rate. Supporting the converted rates were summary figures of such data as total importations by commodity, by principal market or port of entry, and by individual importer (unidentified), dutiable values, unit prices, and existing rates of duty. The study was duly transmitted to Congress with the intimation that the adequacy of the results was questionable but that Congress could judge for itself the significance of the study from the review of the methods of investigation and a consideration of the nature of the problem.[5]

Only very general statements can be made concerning the equivalent rates found by the commission. On the whole, they were, as expected, substantially lower than the existing statutory rates primarily applied to foreign value. As far as can be estimated by a random perusal of the nearly eight hundred pages of tabulations, a high percentage of the total number of converted rates would be included in a range of from 45 to 65 per cent of the corresponding statutory rates. Wide variations are found for articles dutiable under a single existing rate; this obtains not only for different commodities under one rate but for different importers dealing in similar merchandise under the same paragraph. The accompanying extract (Table 5), for a minor portion

---

3. The actual importations studied were made under the 1922 act, whereas the rates to be converted were those in the 1930 act.

4. *Domestic Value—Conversion of Rates* (1932).

5. *Ibid.*, p. 14, "Plans versus Accomplishment."

of the silk articles, knit or crocheted, which are dutiable at 60 per cent under paragraph 1208, gives some indication of the difficulties involved in the conversion of the tariff to another value basis. It is evident that if the tariff were to be converted on the basis of a single "average" rate for an entire paragraph, a real and in many cases substantial change in effective duties would result; on the other hand, the attempt to minimize such changes by further subdivision of each paragraph and subparagraph to correspond to the variation by individual commodities would multiply the size and complexity of the tariff beyond recognition.

No legislative action was taken as a result of this study since obviously none was desirable. The commission's report effectively dem-

TABLE 5[3]

Article	Converted Rate (Per Cent)
Women's hose	25.8
Men's underwear	28.7
Women's sweaters	23.6
Women's suits	17.9
Women's silk and wool suits	18.3
Women's silk and wool skirts	19.6
Men's mufflers	23.4
Weighted average	25.8

onstrated the complex nature of any attempted conversion of rates and the impossibility of obtaining any realistic "equivalents." Moreover, in exhibiting the many problems encountered by the commission in its field work, the study clearly implied the confusion which would attend the actual administration of the tariff on the domestic-value basis. Many of the problems which the commission was obliged to resolve more or less arbitrarily, such as finding a comparable article, interpreting and adjusting for comparability once such an article was found, selecting the appropriate wholesale selling price, etc., would have to be dealt with *ad hoc* by the appraiser for individual entries in a large percentage of total importations.

Other problems which would have to be faced by both importers and government in the application of domestic value are those which obtain in the case of the United States value and which have already been discussed. The problem of deductions would not be involved for

6. *Ibid.*, p. 566.

domestic value as for United States value, but the necessity for conversion of rates would be imperative because of the great divergence between domestic value and the existing basis. Any such conversion would result in wide and accidental changes in effective rates of duty for many commodities and would probably open up the whole tariff question anew. At the present time, some fifteen years since the commission's study, the rates found by the commission are, for all practical purposes, obsolete.

American Selling Price

American selling price is defined in section 402(g) as follows:

(g) AMERICAN SELLING PRICE.—The American selling price of any article manufactured or produced in the United States shall be the price, including the cost of all containers and coverings of whatever nature and all other costs, charges, and expense incident to placing the merchandise in condition packed ready for delivery, at which such article is freely offered for sale to all purchasers in the principal market of the United States, in the ordinary course of trade and in the usual wholesale quantities in such market, or the price that the manufacturer, producer, or owner would have received or was willing to receive for such merchandise when sold in the ordinary course of trade and in the usual wholesale quantities, at the time of exportation of the imported article.

There are two categories of merchandise which are appraised under this definition: (1) articles whose basis of valuation has been changed to American selling price by presidential proclamation under section 336; (2) coal-tar intermediates under paragraphs 27 and 28 of the tariff schedules. The operation of the American selling price for these two categories is discussed in the pages immediately following; a subsequent discussion deals with the arguments which have been advanced for and against this basis of valuation.

PRESIDENTIAL PROCLAMATIONS UNDER SECTION 336

Section 336 of the Tariff Act of 1930 (section 315 of the 1922 act),[7] containing the so-called "flexible provisions," provides that the Tariff Commission upon request of the President or either house of Congress,

7. The complex array of problems encountered in making the cost studies under section 336 is beyond the scope of this study. It is sufficient to state that the "flexible provisions" in the 1922 act and its successor caused a major rift in the Tariff Commission and came near to scuttling the whole commission. Perhaps the

upon application of an interested party,[8] or on its own motion, shall investigate the difference in production costs of any domestic article and of any like or similar foreign article and report to the President the rate of duty necessary to equalize such costs. If the President approves, he may proclaim such rate of duty, to take effect thirty days thereafter. No rate of duty may be increased or reduced more than 50 per cent. Subsection *b*, however, provides that, if the cost difference cannot be equalized by this procedure, the American selling price may be adopted as the basis for the existing rate or such rate reduced by not more than 50 per cent. No rates can be increased when the change to American selling price is made.[9]

During the nearly twenty-five years which have elapsed since the enactment of the flexible provisions of the tariff, ten proclamations involving American selling price have been made, and two of these were reductions of duty on coal-tar products already on the American selling-price basis.[10] The remaining eight included taximeters, rag rugs, diethylbarbituric acid, sodium silicofluoride, optical fire-control instruments, rubber-soled and rubber footwear, canned clams, and wool-knit gloves and mittens. Although the proclamations involving American selling price constitute roughly only 10 per cent of the total which have been made under the flexible provisions, they have been important in terms of controversy and dissension within the Tariff Commission and in subsequent litigation.

The taximeter investigation resulted in one of the early proclamations involving the change to American selling price.[11] It illustrates the enormous increase in protection afforded by this basis of valuation even when actually reducing the rate of duty. The investigation was ordered as the result of an application by the Pittsburgh Taximeter Company, looking to an increase in duty. Only two other competing

---

best available insight into the administration of the flexible provisions is to be found in the fifteen-hundred-page volume: U.S. Senate, Select Committee on Investigation of the Tariff Commission, *Investigation of the Tariff Commission* (1926).

8. Subject to the approval of the Tariff Commission.

9. Rates on coal-tar products under pars. 27 and 28 likewise may not be increased under sec. 336.

10. Cresylic acid and phenol were reduced from 7 cents per lb. and 40 per cent to 3½ cents per lb. and 20 per cent on American selling price by proclamations of July 20 and October 31, 1927, respectively.

11. U.S. Tariff Commission, *Taximeters* (1926).

concerns in the United States were in operation at this time, and one of these was absorbed by the other during the course of the investigation. The commission found that Germany was the principal competing country and that the imported article sold for a unit price of $135 singly or $130 in quantities. Invoice prices f.o.b. the German manufacturer's plant averaged about $35. The domestic article sold for $150. Because of the confidential nature of the material, neither the foreign nor the domestic costs were revealed in the commission's published report. The commission majority recommended an increase in duty by reduction of the rate from 45 per cent on foreign value to 27.1 per cent on the American selling price, continuing the specific-duty component of $3.00 per meter. The net results are illustrated in Table 6. This tabulation reveals that an increase in duty of 133 per cent

TABLE 6

Basis	Value	Rate (Per Cent)	Ad Va-lorem Duty	Specific Duty	Total Duty	Effective Rate (Per Cent)	Increase (Per Cent)
Foreign.........	$ 35	45.0	$15.75	$3.00	$18.75	54	....
American........	150	27.1	40.65	3.00	43.65	125	133

was effected by shifting the basis of valuation while actually reducing the rate of duty by 40 per cent.

Commissioner Costigan wrote a strong dissenting statement indicating that the majority had yielded to political pressure and had demonstrated bias by forwarding its report to the President against the recommendation of the commission's advisory board of experts.[12] The dissenting statement concluded as follows:

1. The present record is in essential respects so deficient, insufficient, out of date, and otherwise unsupported by recent data that, on the basis of that record, no change in the present rate of duty on Taximeters can be justified under the provisions of section 315.

2. If further proceedings in the taximeter investigation are deemed desirable, the investigation should be reopened by the Commission, with instructions to its staff properly and adequately to supplement and complete the present record.

12. Both foreign and domestic cost data were from two to three years old, and changes in currencies and general economic conditions indicated the necessity of an up-to-date investigation (*ibid.,* pp. 6–11).

Nevertheless, President Coolidge, on December 12, 1925, proclaimed the change in duty recommended by the majority, and it became effective thirty days later. The Tariff Act of 1930 raised the rate to 75 per cent and restored the foreign-value basis.

The rag-rug case was economically much more significant and affected a much larger segment of the consuming population in the United States. The rag rugs for which the duty was increased as a result of the investigation were of the "hit-and-miss" variety—colored cotton rugs without any systematic color pattern and widely used in American bath- and bedrooms. Japan was the principal competing country, and the foreign value ranged from thirteen to fifty-one cents apiece, as contrasted with American selling prices ranging from thirty-six to ninety cents, depending on sizes, etc., which were not altogether comparable with the Japanese product. Imports from Japan had risen from over a half-million yards valued at $214,000 in 1924 to nearly four million yards valued at $1,100,000 in 1926. As in the taxi-meter case, it was found that an increase in duty by 50 per cent would be inadequate to "equalize" the costs of production, so the existing rate of 35 per cent was transferred to the American selling price. Although this had the effect of raising duties by over 100 per cent, it was still inadequate to equalize the cost differential, since the commission's report indicated that this would require a duty of 125.5 per cent on foreign value or 57.9 per cent on American selling price. Again Commissioner Costigan dissented from the majority recommendation, principally on the ground that the commission had performed no field studies of costs in Japan and had based its estimates on inferences from invoices.[13] It was his contention that whenever the American selling price was prescribed the commission was under a double obligation to secure actual cost figures through field studies, since the legislative history of the American selling-price provision indicated that it was to be used only rarely and in strict conformity with the cost-equalization formula.[14]

13. The use of invoices is permissible under sec. 336 if cost figures are not readily ascertainable or as supplementary to cost figures. The commission declined to investigate foreign costs although it had agents in the Orient during the investigation and was invited by the importer to inspect several of the leading Japanese firms.

14. United States Tariff Commission, *Rag Rugs* (1928), pp. 32–33. It should not be overlooked that the cost-equalization formula, in theory at least, sets an upper limit to tariff rates.

Probably the most important example of rate increases under the American selling-price provision, from the standpoint of subsequent litigation, grew out of the investigation of "optical fire control instruments." The Senate resolution requesting the investigation was introduced by Senator Reed of Pennsylvania, who was influential in expediting the taximeter investigation.[15] It was passed after some debate in which national defense was stressed.[16] Actually, the descriptive terminology, "optical fire control instruments," represented a thinly disguised request for additional protection on commercial prism binoculars in behalf of the sole domestic manufacturer who already enjoyed a 60 per cent rate. In order to minimize hostility to it, the resolution as finally amended specified "optical instruments of a class or type used by the Army, Navy, or air force for fire control." The commission duly found that commercial prism binoculars were the only significant class of the optical instruments described which were not made in government ordnance plants or for which costs were ascertainable. It made a recommendation to the President, and, on December 14, 1932, Mr. Hoover proclaimed the rate of 60 per cent to apply to the American selling price on all binoculars greater than five-power and valued at more than twelve dollars each.

In due time an importation of 6×30 prism binoculars manufactured by Carl Zeiss, Incorporated, in Germany, was entered at the New York custom house and appraised on the basis of American selling price. The importer protested on the ground that the Tariff Commission in its investigation had not given fair notice of public hearing and that it did not confine itself to instruments actually *used* by the armed forces but predicated its findings upon a class or type "suitable for use" as such. The lower court overruled the importer's contention, but the Court of Customs and Patent Appeals found the point well taken. It held that, for the purposes of the provisions of section 336, the President is the agent of Congress and that he may not act under these provisions until a legal investigation has been made by the Tariff Commission. One of the statutory requirements of such investigation is a public hearing for which "reasonable public notice" has been given. The court found that the description of the merchandise used by the commission in announcing the hearing was not such as

15. *Taximeters*, pp. 6–7.
16. *Congressional Record* (72d Cong., 1st sess. [June 1, 1932]), pp. 11710–12.

would "fairly, adequately, and reasonably" acquaint interested parties that a hearing covering fire-control instruments "suitable for use" rather than "used by" the armed services was to be held. The presidential proclamation contained no finding that prism binoculars were of a class or type "used by" the services and, in view of the findings of the court, was "without authority of law, illegal, and void." The case was remanded for an appraisement of dutiable value under the original terms of the tariff act.[17]

It is clear that the American selling-price provision under section 336 has not been of great practical significance. This has been, in large part, because of the failure of the flexible provisions in general to provide a satisfactory means of adjusting tariff schedules. The serious difficulties and expense of making cost studies which are at best of dubious and temporary value have condemned the section as a whole, apart from any consideration of the nature of the equalization principle itself. Those rates under the 1922 act which were transferred to American selling price were appropriately raised and again placed on the foreign-value basis in the 1930 act. Of the four which have since been proclaimed, only three remain in effect. But even the limited experience with American selling price indicated above has been sufficient to indicate the substantial increase in protection which it makes possible.

THE COAL-TAR PRODUCTS

American selling price under paragraphs 27 and 28 (the coal-tar schedules), containing compound duties on intermediates and finished dyestuffs, has been of considerably greater importance than that under the flexible provisions of the tariff. The avowed policy of building an American dye industry after World War I required for its implementation substantial protection without effecting a complete embargo. Inasmuch as chemical-using and -processing industries required essential chemicals not available in this country, the valuation methods adopted made it possible to import the items listed in paragraphs 27 and 28 on the basis of United States value in the absence of comparable domestically produced products. As soon as a comparable American product appeared on the market, American selling price automatically went into effect and protection was doubled or tripled.

17. *Carl Zeiss, Inc.* v. *United States,* 23 C.C.P.A. 7 (1935).

Subsection *c* of paragraphs 27 and 28 reads as follows:

(c) The ad valorem rates provided in this paragraph shall be based upon the American selling price (as defined in subdivision (g) of section 402, Title IV), of any similar competitive article manufactured or produced in the United States. If there is no similar competitive article manufactured or produced in the United States then the ad valorem rate shall be based upon the United States value, as defined in subdivision (e) of section 402, Title IV.

It was not long after the passage of the Tariff Act of 1922 that difficulties and litigation in the administration of the coal-tar provisions developed. The question of which dyes were competitive and therefore dutiable on the basis of American selling price rather than United States value was handled largely by the issuance and posting in the custom house of lists of competitive and noncompetitive articles. These lists were made up by the chemical and dye section of the Treasury Department on the basis of investigations, price lists, and of specific data furnished by manufacturers. An importer might look in vain on either list for information as to his importation and, finding none, would make his entry at United States value. But, frequently, by the time the appraiser was ready to make his return, a domestic manufacturer had appeared on the scene with proof that he had "offered" a comparable article for sale at the date of exportation of the imported merchandise, thus resulting in an advance in value with the usual consequences of undervaluation, penalty duties, and litigation.

The first significant case to reach the Court of Customs Appeals challenged the constitutionality of the American selling-price provision. The importer contended that the law violated due process by imposing a duty not on the value of the property imported but upon the value of property belonging to another; that the power to fix the amount of the tax had been delegated to domestic manufacturers, who could increase or decrease such tax without limit; and that the coal-tar paragraphs were not designed to raise revenue "to pay the debts, provide for the common defense and general welfare of the United States" but were designed for the purpose and had the operation and effect of granting a monopoly to certain persons or classes of persons in the manufacture and sale of commodities in the United States and in the importation and sale of similar commodities imported from abroad, by delegating to such persons the power to fix the "taxes" payable by themselves and others.

The court upheld the validity of the law, stating that constitutionality does not depend upon the wisdom of the laws, their economic soundness, or their effects upon the people, but rather upon the power which Congress is authorized to exercise under the organic law of the land. The court added that appraisers have long been authorized to take into consideration the wholesale price at which similar or comparable merchandise is offered for sale, and that "there is nothing in paragraph 28 and section 402 which would justify even an inference that they were designed for any purpose but that of imposing duties on imported merchandise for revenue." As to control by domestic manufacturers, the court stated that it was the freely offered price, not the controlled price, which was to determine the basis of dutiable value.[18]

Having thus affirmed the constitutionality[19] of the American selling-price basis of dutiable value, the court proceeded to extend its scope. In a second Kuttroff case[20] the court held that the words "based upon" do not mean that the American selling price is to be taken as dutiable value but merely as a basis of calculation and that if the appraiser deems an imported coal-tar product to be of greater strength than a comparable domestic article, the selling price of the domestic article multiplied by the strength factor shall be the dutiable value. Paragraph 28 provided that "the specific duty of 7 cents per pound herein provided ... shall be based on standards of strength which shall be established by the Secretary of the Treasury," but no such proviso was made for the ad valorem component of the duty. Nevertheless, one short year after declaring in the first Kuttroff case that "there is nothing in paragraph 28 ... which would justify even an inference that [it was] designed for any purpose other than that of ... revenue," the court reached the conclusion that "it seems incredible that Congress, with the intention of encouraging the development of the dye industry in the United States, should require that such industry should be developed and its products actually sold in the United States in competi-

18. *Kuttroff, Pickhardt and Co.* v. *United States*, 12 C.C.A. 299 (1924). For the practical effect of "freely offered" price in the application of American selling price see *infra*, pp. 231–32.
19. Cf. *infra*, p. 246.
20. *Kuttroff, Pickhardt and Co.* v. *United States*, 13 C.C.A. 203 (1925).

tion with imported dyes, before adequate protection would be afforded." It therefore held that the ad valorem component of the duty, like the specific component, was subject to increase in ratio to strength.

An illustration of the working of this interpretation is found in another Kuttroff case.[21] An importation of "benzo red" was entered at its United States value of 79½ cents per pound. The appraiser advanced the value to $2.00 per pound. On appeal the single general appraiser sustained this value, but on further appeal the board advanced the value to $7.00 a pound. This was done on the representation of the Du Pont Company that it sold a comparable article for $2.00 per pound which was only two-sevenths as strong as the imported article. The government's case was ultimately rejected by the Court of Customs Appeals for lack of evidence that the domestic manufacturer was able to deliver in sufficient quantity to satisfy the requirements of a bona fide offer; had it been sustained, the increase in duties would have been nearly 800 per cent, with a like assessment of penalty duties recoverable, if at all, only after the expense and trouble of further litigation.

The doctrine of reasonably prompt delivery as a prerequisite of American selling price was established in another case involving the same principals. In that case the court said:

> Whether or not merchandise is freely offered for sale to all purchasers must depend upon the demand therefor and the number of purchasers thereof . . . . To freely offer an article for sale within the contemplation of subdivision (f), it should, at least, appear that some reasonable quantity of the offered article was ready or could be produced for reasonably prompt delivery. The existence of the article should be so advertised, mentioned, made known, or called to the attention of potential customers that they might or could learn that it was possible to procure the same. . . . It would be natural to expect also that customs authorities would be informed of its existence. . . .
> The assembling of the sales agents of the Du Pont Co., as shown by the testimony, the information given them that the domestic article was available with the direction that they should go forth and offer it for sale, in view of what was done and what was *not* done as a result thereof, is equally unconvincing. It tends to show that there was no real intent on the part of the Du Pont Co., and that it did not possess the ability to offer the new dye for sale to all purchasers before May 4th, 1923.[22]

21. *Ibid.*, 13 C.C.A. 17 (1925); for final decision cf. 14 C.C.A. 381 (1927).
22. *Ibid.*, 14 C.C.A. 176 (1926).

The possibilities of price-fixing by domestic monopolies behind the protective barrier of American selling price operating under ordinary rates of duty are evident from the Sandoz chemical case. The Sandoz Chemical Works had imported five shipments of a coal-tar product known as "pyrazolon." The importer's entries showed United States values ranging from $0.96 to $1.104 per pound. The local appraiser returned a value of $4.00 as the American selling price of a comparable domestic article. Among the statements in the importer's brief on appeal were the following:

It is admitted that pyrazolon is not a finished dyestuff but is an intermediate useful only in producing a finished dyestuff. It is admitted that the domestic manufacturer of the finished dyestuff on whose testimony the Government relies, never sold a pound of his intermediate pyrazolon and never offered it to any actual user. .... The domestic manufacturer furthermore admitted that the price of $4 was so high as to make it impossible for any prospective user to buy it and use it to make a finished dyestuff.[23]

The court in ruling against the importer, although stating that domestic prices which are unreasonably high and have no just proportion to costs of production will be subject to close scrutiny, also affirmed that "neither the law nor reason requires that the American producer shall fix such a selling price upon a coal-tar intermediate produced by him that his competitors may buy it on the market, use it in the manufacture of a completed dye, and profitably undersell the completed product of the American producer on the open market." It would appear to the observer that if a competitor in this country could buy an intermediate from a manufacturer, convert it into a finished product, and still "profitably undersell the completed product of the manufacturer," either the latter's selling price of the finished product would be at a high profit level or he would be operating inefficiently. In any event this case illustrates not only the ability of domestic manufacturers to fix prices but court approval of such price-fixing despite its earlier protestation that only "freely offered" prices are to be used for duty purposes.

The most ironical feature of the application of the American selling-price provisions to imported merchandise is the effect of the court's interpretation of "usual wholesale quantities" and "freely offered for sale." It will be recalled that in the application of foreign value the

23. *Sandoz Chemical Works* v. *United States*, 13 C.C.A. 466 (1926).

court's emphasis upon free offers to all purchasers, regardless of the implications of "ordinary course of trade," led to the establishment of dutiable value on the basis of a few sales by a minority of jobbers or commissionaires at final wholesale or even retail prices. The same interpretation has been applied to American selling price but with far graver consequences in terms of either protection-fostered monopoly or the administration of elemental justice. In the Gennert case the court held that lower wholesale prices to favored classes of purchasers do not constitute the freely offered American selling price.[24] This is to hold, in effect, that an American manufacturer may establish a "freely offered" list price as high as may be necessary effectively to keep out imports and may sell at such lower prices as he sees fit to large dealers, users, and others without disturbing the higher dutiable-value basis. This naturally follows from the doctrine that no price which is not "freely offered" to 100 per cent of all potential customers is admissible for the purpose of establishing dutiable value. Thus the American manufacturer, individually or in association, can so classify his distributive outlets and so arrange his schedule of trade discounts that he can establish the dutiable value without any of the limitations implied by the wording of the statute as ordinarily understood. It is doubtful that the court was fully aware of the fundamental difference in principle between the application of the "all purchasers" doctrine to foreign value and its application to American selling price. In both cases the results are unfortunate and inequitable; in the latter the inequity is compounded by the fact that the power to levy taxes on a competitor's merchandise is given in such manner that the court's constitutional pronouncement that it is "the freely offered price, not the controlled price," which establishes dutiable value is rendered an absurdity.

The Issues in the American Valuation Controversy

"Home valuation" made its earliest controversial appearance in the United States around 1831, when the general issue of tariff protection was at its height.[25] At that time the concept vaguely connoted either or both of two ideas: (1) landed cost *ex* duty at the port of entry;

24. *G. Gennert, Inc.* v. *United States*, 18 C.C.P.A. 12 (1930).
25. Cf. *supra*, pp. 78–82.

(2) the selling price in the United States of the imported article. Only occasionally and by implication was reference made to the selling price of the domestically produced article. The twentieth-century versions of "American valuation," on the other hand, are represented principally by American selling price and domestic value and reached their controversial zenith in the 1921 tariff hearings, with a resurgence during and shortly after the framing of the 1930 act.[26]

The claims and counterclaims concerning the nature and consequences of American valuation have been many and varied, but for purposes of analysis and appraisal they may be classified into some half-dozen major categories. The following classification has been made primarily for the discussion of American selling price, but, since much of the discussion pertains likewise to domestic value or any method of valuation based on selling prices or costs in the United States, the term "American valuation" is used where appropriate.

ADMINISTRATIVE ISSUES

The initial claim of the proponents of American valuation is its alleged administrative superiority over foreign valuation. The argument, in brief, runs that American valuation is easier of ascertainment, since all the facilities for its determination are on this side of the ocean: price lists, catalogues, trade journals, and other relevant information are all in this country where the applicable prices obtain; records and accounts can be inspected, subpoenaed, and introduced in evidence, and the attendance of witnesses compelled, all with a minimum of effort and delay. Litigation would be expedited and reduced; the need for foreign Treasury agents would be eliminated, with consequent saving in expense, elimination of friction with foreign exporters and governments, and disposition of difficult questions of the accuracy and weight of foreign agents' reports.

26. Cf. hearings before House Ways and Means Committee and Senate Finance Committee on Tariff Acts of 1922 and 1930 and hearings published in the U.S. Tariff Commission, *Methods of Valuation* (1933). Numerous short articles and editorials on the American valuation proposal appeared in trade papers, magazines, and similar periodicals while the controversy was at its height in 1921. Since they add little or nothing to the issues as presented in concentrated form in the hearings already cited, it is not thought profitable to include them in the Bibliography herein. Access to all these may be had by consulting references under the heading "American Valuation" in U.S. Tariff Commission, *A Tariff Bibliography* (1934).

On the surface, all these arguments appear to establish a prima facie case for American valuation. They are especially plausible when advanced individually without reference to the total problem of valuation and on the assumption that it is intrinsically as easy to use American prices as prices abroad. When examined critically, however, these arguments are revealed as essentially negative and as offering very little constructive advice as to how specific importations can be entered, appraised, and cleared through the custom house in an orderly, efficient, and equitable manner under American-valuation provisions.

Since the major problems of the importing business are those connected with the tariff and its administration, it is proper to begin the administrative discussion with the consequences of American selling price upon the purchasing of imports in foreign markets. The same kinds of uncertainties which have already been discussed in connection with United States value[27] would exist on a larger scale for foreign buying under the application of American selling price. If it is difficult or impossible for an importer to estimate in advance the final selling price of his own merchandise, or that of such or similar imported merchandise, how will he be able to predict the future selling price of the goods of somone else when he very likely knows of neither the existence, the nature, nor the price of the goods to be compared to his own? Businessmen and firms actually engaged in importing, who are familiar with custom-house hazards under existing valuation procedure, universally testify that the general application of American valuation in any form, and especially American selling price, would reduce foreign buying to "guesswork, speculation, and gambling."[28]

The same conditions apply a fortiori to the actual entry of goods when they reach the custom house. How will the importer know which wholesale price in what market of the United States for which American-made goods to select in making his entry? The importer

27. Cf. *supra*.
28. Cf. the cogent "Brief of the Italian Chamber of Commerce of New York" in *Senate Hearings, 1921*, VII, 5108 ff. Similar testimony was made during the various hearings by representatives of Marshall Field & Co., the National Retail Dry Goods Association, the National Council of American Importers and Traders, and other substantial importing organizations.

knows that if he guesses wrong, whether too high or too low, he will be penalized. If he enters his goods too high, he can never recover duties on the excess of his entered value over appraised value; if the entry is too low, he is immediately assessed a heavy fine for undervaluation. It does not squarely and honestly face the issue to reply glibly, as the proponents of American valuation frequently do, that the importer knows full well the prices of his competitor's products or he could not long remain in business. There is little relationship between the kind of competitive knowledge required to stay in business and the compulsion of having an accurate, intimate, and detailed knowledge of the complex of wholesale prices of the goods of all one's competitors on a certain day for the purpose of paying a heavy tax and avoiding, in addition, a heavy fine. Nor does it face the issue to state that the nature and operation of the penalties could be modified. The basic problem of entering and appraising merchandise at proper value would still remain.

The focal point of the administrative difficulties surrounding the application of American selling price is the problem of comparability and all that it implies. Virtually every new entry and appraisement would require both the importer and the appraiser to embark upon an extensive research project, first, to find the most comparable domestically produced article; second, to ascertain its "freely offered price," with all the qualifications in the definition; and, third, to decide whether it is really sufficiently comparable to warrant the use of its price to determine the dutiable value of the imported goods. The term "similar competitive article" used in connection with the application of American selling price is a much broader term than the narrowly construed "such or similar" phrase in the foreign-valuation provisions and opens the field to a much larger class of goods. On the one hand, this tends to multiply the confusion in determining comparability; on the other, there would still be numerous importations where no comparable domestic article existed or where the domestic article nearest in comparability would be so substantially different that its use as a basis for value would be a manifest absurdity. Not only importers and customs officials but even Senator Smoot, who defended the American selling-price principle in the Senate hearings early in 1921, reached the conclusion that, regardless of all other considerations,

American valuation is not adaptable as a general valuation basis because of its administrative unworkability.[29]

But what of the claims of the supporters of American valuation made during the 1929 and later hearings that this basis has had a number of years of successful operation on coal-tar products? The following is a representative statement, made by a former government attorney who was, at the time of the hearings, a lobbyist for the chemical industry:

> MR. LERCH: One of the objections of previous witnesses, as I understand it, to the American selling price is the claim that it will not work. As I have previously stated, I personally tried all of the cases under that section of the law as it is now applied to paragraphs 27 and 28, and I can testify, gentlemen, of my own knowledge that it has worked beautifully. . . . There has not been a single case that has been lost in the Court of Customs Appeals, with one exception. . . .[30]

It is evident from the court cases already cited that the importers entertained other opinions; but in the face of the national policy of building up a dye industry in this country they took it for granted that they would be forced to retire from the scene:

> REP. CROWTHER: I understand that there are a great many cases pending in the chemical schedules that the complainants have not forced the issue, because they practically know they are beaten on "comparability" before they start.
>
> MR. LERCH: There are now pending in New York, to my knowledge, at least 300 cases involving the value of coal tar products under 27 and 28, that have been there since 1923, and they will probably stay there until 1963 unless the government calls them out.[31]

The simple fact of the matter, apart from the question of duty levels, is that, the greater the administrative confusion, delay, and chaos in the custom house, the more "beautifully" the American selling-price plan "works" from the standpoint of the domestic producer.

Nevertheless, assuming that the plan as applied to coal-tar products has become administratively feasible after years of trial and

---

29. Cf. *infra*, p. 245. For an excellent statement by an experienced customs officer cf. testimony of George C. Davis, special agent in charge, port of New York, in *Senate Hearings, 1921: American Valuation*, pp. 85–123.

30. *House Hearings, 1929*, XVI, 10196.

31. *Ibid.*, pp. 10199–200. Trial of protest cases may, in the discretion of the trial judge, be postponed indefinitely by stipulation of opposing counsel. Since the importers "with one exception" were defeated in the coal-tar cases, they felt it useless to bring further cases to trial.

error, there can be little realistic analogy between the administration of provisions relating to a relatively limited number of chemical products subject to precise definition, laboratory analysis, and scientific tests of comparability, and the administrative problems associated with the sum total of imported merchandise ranging from the crudest of raw materials to antique furniture. How, for example, would a customs examiner determine the comparability of *Lady Chatterley's Lover* and *Forever Amber?* But, even if the qualitative difficulties in the matter of comparability were identical as between coal-tar products and all other imports, it does not follow that because the customs administrative machinery did not break down as a result of the limited application of American selling price to one class of imports constituting a minor fraction of all importations, it would not do so if the plan were made universal. An indication of the administrative expense resulting from the coal-tar provisions is found in the following statement:

With probably several thousand kinds and classes of imported dyes, which under these paragraphs had to be rated for dutiable purposes to comparable American dyes, the task was no easy one. In fact it presented a crucial test of the successful operation of American valuation. Intensive work of all those interested, however, and wholehearted and active cooperation by the Government officials resulted in the setting up of a bureau of standards and information, in which American industries cooperated with the Government, resulting in complete success without any unreasonable disadvantage to importing industries. The unquestionable result was the collection of the duties levied by Congress and the upbuilding of the American dye industry, so that today, instead of being a weakling industry of its kind and class in the world, it is one of the foremost, competing in all fields, and if I am correctly informed, exporting to other countries.[32]

One may well imagine the cost of administering the American selling-price plan if it were applied with the same assiduity to all imports.

UNIFORMITY OF DUTIES

Much time was spent in tariff hearings on the virtue of American selling price in assuring the levy of uniform duties on like products

---

32. *Ibid.,* p. 10209, statement of Judge Marion DeVries, formerly judge of the Court of Customs Appeals and later customs attorney for domestic chemical interests. The judge was correctly informed in the matter of exports, but he neglected to add that the dye industry was actually exporting to other countries at lower prices than it charged to consumers in the United States (cf. p. 10266).

from all countries.[33] The argument runs that foreign value, by the levying of unequal duties, discriminates against high-cost countries in favor of low-cost countries. For example (abstracting from transportation and similar charges), if the rate of duty is 50 per cent and foreign values for a given article are $1.00, $2.00, and $3.00, respectively, in Japan, Germany, and England, then the duties will be, respectively, $0.50, $1.00, and $1.50. Japan, which offers the most severe competition, "pays" the least duty; while England, initially in the most disadvantageous position, has her disadvantage increased. Under American selling price, like imported goods from all countries, regardless of their foreign values, would pay the same duty. The proponents of American valuation urged that the "discrimination" under foreign valuation is not "fair" to the high-cost country, that it violates most-favored-nation agreements, and that it also raises the price of goods to the American consumer, since "the high cost country sets the price."[34]

Little need be said about the alleged "unfairness" to competing foreign countries. No evidence was introduced by the proponents of American selling price, nor has this study been able to discover,[35] that any representations, official or unofficial, have ever been made by foreign countries that the basing of American ad valorem duties on foreign value was discriminatory or violated the most-favored-nation principle. Manifestly, neither charge is valid, since like goods of like foreign value are equally treated regardless of the exporting country. Nor does the levy of ad valorem duties on foreign value change the relative competitive position of competing countries. The levy of *any* duty tends to exclude the high-cost countries first of all from the pro-

33. *Senate Hearings, 1921: American Valuation*, pp. 284–88; Tariff Commission, *Methods of Valuation*, p. 57.

34. *American Valuation, 1921*, p. 192, testimony of J. F. Zoller, representing the American Valuation Association of New York City. Mr. Zoller's testimony, like that of most American valuation adherents, is replete with the crudest and hoariest of economic fallacies.

35. E.g., cf. *Senate Hearings, 1921: Foreign Communications;* out of nearly two hundred pages of foreign requests and recitals of unsatisfactory tariff treatment, none deals with the American valuation proposal. It would be reasonable to suppose that if any foreign country had felt aggrieved under foreign valuation it would have made its preference known at a time when it appeared that American valuation would be adopted.

tected market; but this is not peculiar to ad valorem duties or to the method of valuation.[36]

The whole issue concerning high-cost and low-cost countries is largely spurious and is based on a naïve conception of the nature of costs and price determination. Under foreign valuation, dutiable value is based on market price, not costs. Price differentials for identical goods (again abstracting from transportation and similar costs), as contemplated by the illustration given above, cannot long persist in competitive world markets. Under equilibrium conditions the marginal costs of all countries and of all firms within each country will be equivalent. Those who propose to remove the alleged discriminations are obviously interested in excluding low-cost as well as high-cost foreign goods from whatever source and would do so with the same Procrustean exactitude as the exponents of the "scientific" tariff would systematically eliminate all competition from abroad.

Foreign countries are concerned with the opportunity profitably to export goods. If it could be shown that the American selling-price plan would reduce either duties or administrative protection or both, they would undoubtedly favor it. Since importers and others who are interested in maximizing the economic and profitable flow of goods in international commerce are to that extent appropriate spokesmen for the trading interests of other nations, it may reasonably be inferred that such interests and the governments representing them do not wax enthusiastic over this proposal to free them from "discrimination."

Another argument alleging uniformity of duties under American selling price is based on the claim that it would result in nondiscriminatory treatment of different importers and different ports in the United States. But foreign valuation, as such, makes no such discriminations, and it was partly for this reason that it was preferred to landed cost by Calhoun and others in the nineteenth-century debates.[37] In actual administration it is possible for the appraisement of similar, if not identical, merchandise to vary from port to port and conceivably for different importers at the same port. This, however, is

36. The argument under discussion refers to differential costs of production in competing countries and should not be confused with the argument that a landed cost basis of value is theoretically superior to foreign value in the treatment of transportation charges (cf. *infra*, pp. 316–18).

37. Cf. *supra*, pp. 85–86.

the problem of obtaining and disseminating perfect knowledge and inducing perfect uniformity of action on the part of personnel throughout the entire customs organization. Enough has already been said about the difficulties of ascertaining American selling price and the problems of comparability connected therewith to indicate that little would be gained in the direction of uniformity by the adoption of this species of valuation.

UNDERVALUATION

It should be clear at this stage of the discussion that the term "undervaluation," by definition, means an excess of appraised, over entered, value. *Fraudulent,* as distinguished from *technical,* undervaluation, involves both the deliberate intent to defraud and the commission of an overt fraudulent act resulting in an undervaluation. Such an act may be the wilful falsification of an invoice, of an import declaration, or of any matter of fact pertaining to the value of an importation. Technical undervaluation involves a matter of interpretation, and such undervaluation represents a difference of opinion between the importer and the appraiser—a difference which is subject to appeal and judicial review.

At every hearing involving customs valuation, from the early part of the nineteenth century down to the present, American valuation proponents have brought forth exaggerated claims of undervaluation, invariably couching their argument in such terms as to leave the impression that all reported undervaluation, or the bulk of it, is of the fraudulent variety.[38] Customs officials and others have testified repeatedly that fraudulent undervaluation is negligible,[39] and official reports of undervaluation statistics confirm this position.[40] It is true that the amount of undetected fraudulent undervaluation is by nature not capable of ascertainment. But, in view of the long history, tradi-

38. For a brief but pertinent discussion cf. John Day Larkin, *The President's Control of the Tariff* (Cambridge, Mass., 1936), pp. 88–89.
39. E.g., testimony of Tariff Commissioner Page in *Senate Hearings, 1921: American Valuation,* pp. 5–7, and of George C. Davis, former customs official, in *House Hearings, 1929,* XVI, 9805–6. Similar testimony may be found in all the major hearings on valuation proposals.
40. A recent report, covering the year 1939–40, shows that less than 10 per cent of all investigation of alleged infractions of the customs laws pertained to undervaluation and less than 13 per cent of all collections for violations are represented by all types of fraudulent invoicing, including undervaluation (U.S. Treasury, *Annual Report, 1939–40,* pp. 289, 292).

tion, and techniques of the customs service in combating fraudulent undervaluation, the deterring effect of the heavy criminal and civil penalties for such fraud, the damaging effects upon business and personal reputations resulting from discovery and attendant publicity, compared with the probable pecuniary gain to be realized from the kind of fraudulent undervaluation not liable to detection, it is not unlikely that the customs revenue ranks among the most highly protected of revenue systems.

Opponents of the American selling-price plan admit the probable existence of a certain amount of fraudulent undervaluation without conceding that it is sufficient to justify a revolution in valuation procedure. They would probably agree that fraudulent undervaluation by importers would be completely eliminated by the adoption of American selling price, since the importer would presumably have no hand in its ascertainment. He would be in no position to falsify relevant facts, and his entry would represent only his guess as to dutiable value. But there is every reason to believe that there would be more, not less, disagreement between importers and appraisers and that litigation on the comparability issue alone would far exceed the total arising out of foreign valuation. Moreover, it is doubtful that American manufacturers, as a class, are substantially more honest than American importers.[41] The shift to American selling price, so far as fraudulent valuation is concerned, would probably mean only a shift from undervaluation to overvaluation, with a substitution of the *participia criminis*. In just what way fraudulent overvaluation by American manufacturers would be dealt with by law is uncertain.[42]

41. The following copy of a sworn affidavit by an American chemical processor appears in *Senate Hearings, 1929: Valuation*, pp. 49–50: "I hereby make affidavit that an American manufacturer of a coal-tar derivative was asked by an appraiser as to his selling price. He replied, '$7.50 per pound.' The appraiser thus fixed $7.50 per pound as the American valuation upon which I had to pay 45 per cent and 7 cents per pound. I have evidence that he was selling at $6 per pound—in fact, have a letter from him agreeing to sell to me at $6 per pound. I was thus forced, simply on his say so, to pay 45 per cent on $7.50 instead of 45 per cent on $6.00, thus causing me to pay on an importation of 100 kilos (220 pounds) 67½ cents per pound in excess of the actual dutiable American selling price. . . . I was thus forced to pay in excess of honest duty, and simply because of the verbal statement of a competitor, $148.50." For testimony concerning the giving of rebates by domestic chemical manufacturers cf. Tariff Commission, *Methods of Valuation*, pp. 87–88.

42. Sec. 14.5(h) of *Customs Regulations, 1943*, states: "When the appraising officer shall be satisfied after investigation that a similar competitive domestic

THE NATURE AND EFFECTS OF MANUFACTURERS' PRICE CONTROL

This study makes no attempt to estimate the extent of monopolistic and quasi-monopolistic price control exercised by producers in the American economy. That such control is substantial is common knowledge; instances of its actual or potential use in connection with the application of American selling price have already been cited,[43] and discussion in congressional hearings by all concerned have proceeded upon the assumption that such control exists and would be exercised by domestic producers in order to manipulate dutiable value under the American selling-price plan. The differences of opinion have lain chiefly in the conclusions as to the consequences upon dutiable value and the effects upon importations.

The opponents of American selling price generally rest their case on the statement that, since the domestic producer can control dutiable value by price manipulation, he can raise or lower duties at will, thus effectively excluding imports.[44] The supporters of the "American" plan counter by stating that the American producer will not raise his price because he would thereby exclude himself from the market; this follows from the fact that, assuming duties to be less than 100 per cent, the American selling price would always rise more rapidly than the duty and hence than the importer's costs and selling price.

---

article is offered for sale at an arbitrary and unreasonable price not intended to secure bona fide sales and which does not secure bona fide sales, such price shall not be considered as the American selling price, and such officer shall use all reasonable ways and means to ascertain the price that the manufacturer, producer, or owner would have received, within the meaning of Section 402(g), Tariff Act of 1930, as amended." Thus the law (cf. definition of American selling price, *supra*, p. 222), instead of penalizing the American manufacturer for non–bona fide price offerings designed to manipulate dutiable value, rewards him by granting the same protection which he would receive were he to act in good faith. It would appear that the minimum appropriate sanction against such fictitious price offerings would be to conclude that there was no freely offered price and to allow United States value to apply.

43. Cf. the circumstances in the cases of taximeters and prism binoculars, *supra*, pp. 223–27, and the price policies referred to in the Sandoz case, *supra*, p. 231.

44. Cordell Hull, a member of the House Ways and Means Committee in 1921, made the following remarks during the valuation hearings at that time: "Were we to adopt that policy in this country it would simply place the whole tariff laws in charge of the business interests to the extent that business organizations, trusts, or organizations of that kind, could raise or lower the prices, or influence prices, and run them up and down, and they could either increase or lower the tariff rates" (*House Hearings, 1921*, VI, 4183).

But the point at which the American producer would thus exclude himself from the market by such manipulation depends upon the rate of duty and the cost and price ratios concerned. If a given rate of duty provides more protection than a bare equalization of costs, the domestic manufacturer can, without fear of foreign competition, raise his price to the point at which the excess protection disappears (Table 7). Thus, if case 1 illustrates the initial position, the domestic manufacturer can raise his price 33⅓ per cent before further increases will exclude him from the market. Only in the improbable event that all tariff rates based on American selling price were no greater than necessary to equalize the cost differentials would there be any assurance that domestic manufacturers would not profit at the expense of

TABLE 7

Example	Foreign Value	American Selling Price	Rate of Duty (Per Cent)	Duty	Domestic Value (Foreign Article)
Case 1............	$1.00	$1.50	50	$0.75	$1.75
Case 2............	1.00	2.00	50	1.00	2.00
Case 3............	1.00	2.50	50	1.25	2.25

consumers by price increases or price maintenance in the face of declining costs.

The greatest danger of price control by domestic interests under American selling price would probably not result from manipulation in the crude form contemplated in the illustration shown above and frequently set up as a straw man by exponents of American valuation.[45] It would be rather in the establishment of a high "freely offered" list price, at which all purchasers could buy, with appropriate differential discounts to capture the bulk of the business. Under the court's interpretation of the "freely offered" provision, no falsification of price lists would be necessary to permit complete control of the market. In any case, it seems clear that the change to American selling price would confer a substantial and for many classes of merchandise a decisive power upon domestic manufacturers to manipulate tariff levies to their advantage.

45. E.g., testimony of John G. Lerch, representing various domestic manufacturers, in U.S. Tariff Commission, *Methods of Valuation*, pp. 54–55. Mr. Lerch's statement is probably the best explicit illustration of the argument in question.

THE HISTORICAL ARGUMENT

Our first tariff law, signed by George Washington on July 4, 1789, contained one provision the importance of which has been overlooked in much subsequent legislation. That stipulation was that ad valorem rates of duty be levied upon imported merchandise according to "the value thereof at the time and place of importation." The intent was based upon the principle that the administration of the tariff be entirely within our own jurisdiction. The low duties of that law proved satisfactory and effective because of this method of assessing duties upon the American value.[46]

The foregoing is a typical example of the "historical" type of argument used by the exponents of American valuation. In this particular case the proponent had apparently read the first tariff act of the United States and therefore concluded or maintained that it provided a species of home valuation. It is believed that sufficient quotation and documentation has been made in Part II, above, to indicate that the first tariff act was administered not on home or American valuation in any sense of the term but upon a hypothetical landed cost based on specific purchase price.[47] The low rates of duty in this tariff were levied not only on a foreign basis but on actual transaction prices, which gave full scope to low prices for large quantity purchases and carried none of the rigorous limitations now existing in connection with the interpretation of foreign value.

The "historical" or "patriotic" approach to the subject takes other forms, chiefly that of quoting eminent Americans reputedly in favor of American valuation. There is little point in collecting the names of distinguished citizens who have expressed an opinion or whose eminence has been used in one way or another in the American valuation controversy. But, because of fairly persistent misconceptions which have been disseminated or which have grown perhaps innocently out of partial knowledge, it might be well in passing to lay a few American valuation "ghosts" which rise repeatedly from the pages of tariff hearings and which lend themselves especially to *argumentum ad ignorantiam*.

Apart from the misconception surrounding the nature of the first

46. "Brief of the Home Market Club," Boston, Mass., *House Hearings, 1929*, XVI, 10267. Thomas O. Marvin, who left his position as general manager of the Boston Home Market Club in 1921 to become a member and later chairman of the Tariff Commission, was a strong advocate of American valuation.

47. Cf. *supra*, chap. ii, esp. pp. 39–40.

tariff act, perhaps the most frequently used "historical" argument is the supposed attitude of certain early nineteenth-century Americans—principally John Quincy Adams and Henry Clay—on the subject of home valuation. Both these statesmen are cited with respect to their initial or temporary espousal of the cause and without reference to their subsequent change of mind. It will be recalled that Mr. Adams, when he learned the true nature of home valuation, repudiated it, stating that he "must therefore vote against it," since a duty upon a duty was "a thing unknown in any country in the world."[48] As for Henry Clay, also cited by the Home Market Club, it has been indicated previously that his sponsorship of home valuation in the compromise bill was an act of diplomacy without any real conviction of its intrinsic merit and that subsequently, at the time of the rejection of home valuation in 1842, he went on record as preferring ad valorem duties and the dangers of undervaluation to the inequities and fraud resulting from the application of specific duties.[49] Daniel Webster referred to home valuation as "impracticable, unprecedented, and unknown in any legislation."[50] John Calhoun's position in the matter has already been made explicit and needs no reiteration.[51]

In a more recent generation, it is of interest to observe that the two great tariff leaders of their respective political parties, Senator Smoot and Cordell Hull, both disavowed American valuation. Mr. Hull's remarks have already been quoted.[52] Mr. Smoot's position may be summed up in his own words before the Senate:

A bill based upon American value was drawn on the basis of this calculation, but after due consideration it was abandoned. . . . I am convinced of the wisdom of the decision reached by the committee on the subject of valuation. Nothing would be more disturbing to business than a revolutionary change in valuation.

American valuation has made a peculiar appeal to many people who do not understand it because it carries the label, "American." Naïvely, many persons have assumed that if it is a choice between something "American" and something "foreign" they, of course, prefer the former. This distinction has nothing whatever to do with the merits of the controversy and should have no weight in the final decision.[53]

48. *Supra,* p. 80.
49. *Supra,* pp. 84–85, 96.   51. *Supra,* p. 85.
50. *Supra,* p. 86.   52. *Supra,* p. 242, n. 44.
53. *Congressional Record,* LXII, Part VI, 5878, April 24, 1922. Compare Mr. Smoot's treatment of the term "American" valuation with that in the jingoistic testimony of Matthew Woll before the Tariff Commission: "American labor be-

It also appears that the defeat of the American valuation plan as adopted by the House bill in 1921 was at least in part the result of the opposition of President Harding, who feared that manipulation by domestic interests would get out of hand.[54]

Another appeal to history which was occasionally made before the partial adoption of American valuation in 1922 was the reference to the short-lived trial of home valuation in 1842, and its constitutionality as declared by the Supreme Court in *Aldridge* v. *Williams*.[55] Inasmuch as the record of that experiment with home valuation hardly constitutes a recommendation in its favor and since the constitutionality of American selling price has been specifically established in recent years, this argument has been rendered obsolete.

OTHER ISSUES

Various other claims of minor import have been made for American valuation, but the majority of them are merely a reiteration of the age-old arguments for protection and constitute no distinctive contribution to the subject matter under discussion. Reference should be made, however, to the fact that during the 1921 hearings American valuation was urged as a foil to dumping and depreciated currencies. So far as the problem of dumping is concerned, the Antidumping Act of 1921 provided the most direct and effective solution; in any case, American valuation has no direct relevance to the problem and could accomplish nothing toward a solution except possibly to raise protection in general and/or in a hit-and-miss manner depending upon the extent to which rates were converted and upon the different and varying price policies of domestic producers. With certain qualifications, much the same shortcomings apply to the currency-depreciation argument; this, however, is examined in more detail in the following chapter.

One other issue, the "statistical" argument, should be dealt with briefly at this point. Matthew Woll, in his testimony before the Tariff

---

lieves that American valuation, or American selling price, as the basis for the establishment of tariff rates, is more easily ascertainable and certainly more American-like than our present system of basing duties on foreign value. . . . There is no valid reason why we should humble ourselves before any alien people in an effort to secure information on which to act pertaining to our own domestic affairs" (U.S. Tariff Commission, *Methods of Valuation*, p. 57).

54. *Senate Hearings, 1921*, VII, 5110(10); *House Hearings, 1929*, XVI, 10203.

55. Cf. *supra*, pp. 92–93.

Commission,[56] maintained that American valuation would "eliminate the unsound and unwarrantable statistics issued from time to time by the Commerce and Treasury Departments as to the value of our imports and exports," and that it would "make it possible for Government agents to know what is the value of American products displaced by the entry of foreign products into the American markets." The implications are obvious. Mr. Woll, who by his own testimony regarded the importation of goods as on a par with the importation of strike-breakers, convicts, and coolie labor, was interested not in the intrinsic reliability of foreign-trade statistics for reflecting as nearly as possible foreign-trade transactions but rather in their maximum inflation as an ideological weapon with which to further economic isolationism. Since American valuation would very substantially, although erratically, increase the dollar estimate of a given physical volume of imports, it would tend, *pro tanto*, to alarm all latter-day mercantilists into a stampede in the direction of a general import embargo. It is hardly necessary, in a work of this kind, to refer to the general economic relationship between exports and imports and the implications of that relationship for protectionist theory. In connection with the statistical argument, however, it should be stated again that export statistics of the United States represent, on the whole, transaction prices, whereas import statistics, so far as appraised merchandise is concerned, are derived from dutiable values which as a whole are in excess of transaction prices.[57] Thus United States import statistics are already inflated relative to export statistics by the aggregate excess of dutiable values over transaction prices. Moreover, it should not be overlooked that the export statistics of the United States understate the ratio of exports relative to domestic consumption to the extent of the difference between export dumping prices and prices for home consumption in the United States. The statistical "alarmists" might therefore find considerable solace in contemplating the "replacement"

56. U.S. Tariff Commission, *Methods of Valuation*, pp. 59–60.

57. This should be clear from previous discussions of the various requirements of foreign value as well as of the nature and application of the several alternate dutiable-value bases. The excess of dutiable value over transaction prices is especially large in the case of consignments and branch-plant importations, whether by domestic or foreign interests; in the case of American valuation, dutiable values are on the whole in excess of final selling prices of the merchandise in the United States, to say nothing of the relationship to import transaction prices.

of a given volume of American exports by a smaller volume of relatively overvalued imports, instead of the "displacement" of hypothetical high-cost domestic goods.

It should be clear from the foregoing discussion that the American valuation issue is inseparable from the larger issue of tariff protection. The same motives, the same economic and political alignments, and to a large extent the same lines of reasoning and argument which characterize the general issue of protection are reflected on a smaller scale in the valuation controversy. Nevertheless, the specific and detailed issues arising in the American valuation controversy are highly technical and have many ramifications not ordinarily understood even by many of those who are most active in promoting this form of valuation. The interesting and significant fact, however, is that American valuation need not be a success in the manner claimed by its promoters in order for it to achieve the consequences considered by them as desirable.

CHAPTER VIII

Dumping and Currency Conversion in Relation to Valuation

Valuation for Dumping Duties

THE administration of the Antidumping Act of 1921 is carried out by the operation of the regular appraisement and collection machinery of the Bureau of Customs under the supervision of the Treasury Department. Valuation procedures and problems under the dumping law are therefore an integral part of the general field of customs valuation.

The basic provisions of the Antidumping Act require the Secretary of the Treasury to make public a finding whenever, after investigation, he finds that a class or kind of imported merchandise is being sold or is likely to be sold in the United States or elsewhere at less than its "fair value," and that an industry in the United States is being or is likely to be injured or is prevented from being established by the importation of goods of the class being dumped. A finding of dumping by the secretary must specify the class or kind of merchandise to which it applies, and in practice all findings limit their application to the country from which the dumped merchandise is exported. After such a finding has been made, a special dumping duty, equal to the difference between the "foreign-market value" (in its absence "cost of production") and the "purchase price" (in its absence "exporter's sale price"), is levied on all importations of the described class which have not previously been appraised.

The definitions of foreign-market value and cost of production in the Antidumping Act are, respectively, with certain exceptions substantially the same as those of foreign value and cost of production for ordinary duties. The major difference for foreign-market value is that it provides that the value shall be taken as of the date of purchase, or agreement to purchase, if such precedes the date of exportation. This protects the importer from the levy of dumping duties merely because of an increase in market value subsequent to purchase. A second difference is that the antidumping law reads, in part, "the price ... at which such or similar merchandise *is sold* or freely offered for sale," etc. (italics added). This would appear to permit the use of actual transaction prices—whether or not "freely offered"—in the establishment of foreign-market value. But, as will be seen later, this difference in wording has been given no effect. A third difference is that foreign-market value for dumping duties is based on the price for home consumption but, failing this, on prices for export to countries other than the United States. In addition, there is a sentence at the end of the definition of foreign-market value in the dumping law excluding fictitious sales and offers from consideration. The only significant difference between the two cost-of-production definitions is that for ordinary duties the cost of "such or similar" merchandise is to be used, whereas for dumping duties the cost is restricted to "identical or substantially identical" merchandise.

In the administration of the Antidumping Act it is necessary to afford a proper comparison between foreign-market value and the price actually paid for the merchandise. "Purchase price" is therefore carefully defined, the intention being to arrive at the net price actually paid for the goods in their packed condition in the foreign market prior to exportation to the United States. Purchase price, as defined, covers imports for which a fixed price has been paid, or agreed to be paid, by the importer prior to exportation; in the absence of such price—e.g., for consignments and similar shipments—a constructive purchase price, namely, "exporter's sale price," is computed by working backward from the selling price of the merchandise in the United States. For both purchase price and exporter's sale price, additions or deductions are allowed for foreign taxes and tax abatements, expenses of bringing the merchandise to the place of delivery in the United States, including United States customs duties, or other adjustments appropriate to the basic purpose of rendering genuinely comparable the comparison between the selling price of the imported merchandise and its "fair value."[1]

1. The "fair value" of an import is nowhere defined in the statute. The Secretary of the Treasury has interpreted it to mean the foreign-market value or the cost of production as defined in the act, and the courts have upheld this interpretation (*Kleberg and Co.* v. *United States*, 21 C.C.P.A. 110 [1933]).

In terms of the objectives of the antidumping law, the valuation provisions are on the whole carefully drawn.[2] The treatment of foreign drawbacks, whether of internal or of customs duties, is such as to prevent the application of dumping duties as a result of such abatement. Price differentials resulting from tax abatements or from bounties are subject to elimination by countervailing duties under the basic tariff law and are not considered as evidence of dumping in customs terminology and administration. Also, and of substantial importance, "due allowance" must be made by the terms of section 202 for differences in price wholly or partly due to differences in quantities sold.

In order that dumping may be detected at its inception, so far as customs administration is concerned, the appraiser is required by regulation as well as by statute to make a preliminary investigation whenever he suspects imported merchandise of being sold at dumping prices. This procedure involves an interview with the importer of the merchandise in question, in which the importer makes affidavits as to various questions of fact on blanks prepared for the purpose. The courts have held that this procedure is mandatory and constitutes a substantial right of the importer.[3] On the basis of the information thus obtained and from other sources the appraiser may conclude that no dumping exists: the price differentials may result from large-quantity buying, or perhaps the merchandise may not be for resale in the United States and therefore not subject to dumping duties. On the other hand, if the appraiser is not satisfied, the matter is referred to the Bureau of Customs for further investigation, which may eventually result in the issuance of a dumping finding by the Secretary of the Treasury.

The administration of the Antidumping Act is subject—except for

2. Professor Viner in *Dumping: A Problem in International Trade* (Chicago, 1923) paid tribute to the draftsmanship of the Antidumping Act. On p. 264, however, he adverted to an apparent slip in draftsmanship in the definition of purchase price, which adds to the price paid (if not included in such price) the amount of foreign export tax. Viner contended that the amount of the export tax should be deducted, rather than added. Actually, this addition is necessary to prevent payment of dumping duty by an importer in those cases where the price for export is less than foreign-market value by an amount no greater than the export tax. E.g., suppose the foreign-market value to be $30 and the export tax $10. A sale for export at a price of $20 before tax should not be regarded as dumping, since the subsequent payment of the tax will bring the cost to the purchaser for export to the United States into equivalence with foreign-market value.

3. *Vulcan Match Co., Inc.* v. *United States*, 5 C.D. 188 (C.D. 398).

the secretary's actual findings of fact—to review by the Customs Court and the Court of Customs and Patent Appeals.[4] Although many dumping cases have been before the courts, relatively few of them have turned on the issue of valuation. A number of dumping appraisements have been voided by the courts on technical grounds. The assessment of dumping duties on several entries of Canadian wheat imported at Buffalo was prevented by an invalid appraisement which resulted from failure by the appraiser to take samples and to examine one in every ten packages in accordance with the statutory requirements of appraisement.[5] An importation of matches through the port of Los Angeles was relieved of dumping duties because of a voided appraisement which resulted from the failure of the appraiser to take affidavits as described above.[6] Appraisements under the antidumping law, like those under the tariff act, must be made in unit quantity.[7]

An outstanding example of the role of legal technicalities in deciding whether or not dumping duties are collectible, even when there is no question as to the existence of dumping, is found in a case decided by the Court of Customs and Patent Appeals in 1927.[8] As a result of a strike in January, 1921, the rug and carpet industry in the United States suspended operations for several months, and dealers were unable to meet the demand. An arrangement was made to import from Canada until the industry could get back into operation, and some $350,000 worth of rugs were purchased for American dealers from the Toronto Rug and Carpet Company at a price 23.2 per cent below the Canadian market value. Although this still gave the manufacturer a profit, due to the large quantities involved, the importer clearly acknowledged the existence of dumping by entering the merchandise at 24 per cent above the invoice price under the heading: "The fair market value for home consumption. . . ." The appraiser at Black Rock, New York, withheld appraisement and notified the Secretary of the Treasury of suspected dumping. Some eight or ten months later a finding of dumping was issued by the Treasury Department. The pertinent portion of the dumping order read as follows:

4. Cf. *Kreutz* v. *Durning*, 69 F. (2d) 802 (1934).
5. *C. J. Tower and Sons* v. *United States*, 21 C.C.P.A. 417 (1934). The "packages" in this case appear to have been carloads.
6. Cf. n. 3 above.
7. *United States* v. *Manahan Chemical Co., Inc.*, 24 C.C.P.A. 53 (1936).
8. *United States* v. *Tower and Sons*, 14 C.C.A. 421 (1927).

After due investigation I find that the rug making industry in the United States is being or is likely to be injured by reason of the importation into the United States of rugs from Canada, and that such merchandise is sold or is likely to be sold in the United States at less than its fair value.

For any further description of this particular merchandise, appraising officers will communicate with the special agent in charge at New York.

In addition to attacking the dumping appraisements, the importer contested the legality of the dumping finding on a number of grounds, the significant one for the decision being the secretary's action in delegating to the special agent at New York the authority to designate the kind or class of merchandise to which the dumping duty should apply. The court held this to be contrary to the requirement of the statute on the principle of *delegata potestas non potest delegari:*

If the Secretary of the Treasury had said "all rugs from Canada" we would have a different question before us, but in the case at bar he referred to "rugs from Canada" and left the description of the particular merchandise to the special agent. The necessary implication from the language used is that some rugs from Canada might not be subject to such duty since it was necessary for the appraising officers to see the special agent. Appraising officers, therefore, in performing their duties under the finding, could not perform under the act of the Secretary but must be limited to the kind and description of the merchandise which the special agent chooses to indicate. The statute under consideration does not by express terms or by fair implication authorize the delegation of such discretionary powers. It follows that all acts of customs officials growing out of the attempted levying of anti-dumping duties were invalid and void.

Thus it was not possible to implement the dumping law despite the manifest existence of dumping.

In contrast to the foregoing is the much-litigated Cottman case,[9] which not only is the leading case on the valuation provisions of the Antidumping Act, but which has been cited repeatedly as a precedent in cases involving the valuation provisions of the general tariff law. The importations in question consisted of phosphate rock from Casablanca, French Morocco, and were made in 1927 and 1928 at the port of Baltimore. Although the article was duty free under the Tariff Act of 1922, the appraiser, suspecting dumping, withheld appraisement and notified the Secretary of the Treasury. On February 9, 1928, a finding of dumping was issued, and the appraiser found the purchase price of the various importations to range from $4.00 to $5.00 per ton

9. *J. H. Cottman and Co. v. United States,* 20 C.C.P.A. 344 (1932).

and the foreign-market values from $7.52 to $7.58. This resulted in the levy of dumping duties equivalent to from 50 to 75 per cent ad valorem on an article ordinarily free of duty.

The importer appealed to reappraisement, and there followed in succession an application for review to the appellate division of the Customs Court, an appeal to the Court of Customs and Patent Appeals, a remand for a new trial by the single judge, a second review by the appellate division, and another appeal to the Court of Customs and Patent Appeals. The second decision of the appeals court was the final decision on the issues, although a further series of appeals on technical grounds was again carried all the way up to the C.C.P.A.[10]

The facts in the case were complicated and posed a number of widely divergent issues. The foreign exporter was the Office Cherifien des Phosphates, a governmental monopoly of the French protectorate in Morocco, organized for the mining and sale of raw phosphate rock. Sales of this product for home consumption in Morocco were made at two prices: $3.98 per ton to a superphosphate factory partially controlled by the government, and $3.50 per ton to local farmers. Both classes of sale were made with the restriction that the phosphates were to be consumed at home and not exported. The O.C.P. sold phosphates for export to various countries at varying prices and subject to restrictions on resale. In substance the restrictions precluded resale on sales to Europe and re-export on sales to the United States and far eastern countries. The f.o.b. price at Casablanca to European countries during the period in question was approximately $6.00 per long ton, to the United States $4.95, and to Japan $4.50.

The single judge in the initial reappraisement trial found a foreign-market value for home consumption of $3.98, namely, the price to the superphosphate works in Morocco, which in 1927 purchased 12,760 tons as compared with purchases of 501 tons by farmers. No dumping duties were assessable on this finding. On appeal by the government, the Third Division of the Customs Court affirmed this decision, but the C.C.P.A. reversed the decision and remanded the case for a new trial because of error in the trial court in refusing to admit certain evidence.[11] On retrial the single judge again found a foreign-market value of $3.98. The Third Division of the Customs Court on the second

10. *United States* v. *J. H. Cottman and Co.*, 23 C.C.P.A. 378 (1936).
11. *Ibid.*, 18 C.C.P.A. 132 (1930).

appeal, however, held by a thin majority[12] that there was no foreign-market value established as defined by statute, that no cost of production was shown by the record, and that the initial appeal to reappraisement "might well have been dismissed" for failure to make sufficient proof. Upon the importer's appeal from this decision, the C.C.P.A. made an extensive review of all the facts and issues.

The court first of all pointed out that section 205 of the Antidumping Act provides two bases for foreign-market value: (1) the freely offered price for home consumption; (2) in the absence of basis 1, the freely offered price for export. The court then reviewed its various decisions in which it had found free offer to be defective and cited the reasons therefor: in the Goodyear case it was complete control by the manufacturer, including price-fixing, limitation of dealers, and resale price maintenance; in the Richards and Company case it was price discrimination between wholesalers and nonwholesalers; in the Meadows case[13] it was resale price maintenance; etc. However, the court had never ruled precisely on the point as to whether a limitation on the use after sale constituted a barrier to free offer. In the case at bar the only limitation upon sales for home consumption was that the product be used for home consumption. This would appear to meet the literal requirements of the statute, but the court insisted that the price which constituted foreign-market value for home consumption must be a price which permits the consumer to export if he chooses to do so. Apparently counsel neither for the importer nor for the court observed that a strict construction of the wording of the Antidumping Act, as indicated above,[14] permitted the use of either the freely offered price or the price at which merchandise *is sold* to determine foreign-market value. After rejecting both the home-consumption prices as being no evidence of foreign-market value for home consumption, the court then turned to export prices. The court found all these to be controlled in one way or another, including the price to Japan, which apparently was restricted only by a verbal understanding not to re-export.

Having eliminated both alternate forms of foreign-market value,

12. The appellate divisions of the Customs Court consist of three judges. In this decision there were three separate opinions, including one dissent and one special opinion concurring in the result, but for different reasons, of the court's decision.
13. *Meadows, Wye and Co.* v. *United States*, 17 C.C.P.A. 36 (1929).
14. Cf. *supra*, p. 250.

the court looked into cost of production. An affidavit of the director and the chief cashier of the O.C.P. was placed in evidence by the importer, and the director testified in person. The government contended that no cost of production had been established, since no cost of materials or allowance for profit had been specifically shown. The importer contended that the material cost nothing and that the addition of the statutory 8 per cent minimum for profit would still leave the cost below the alleged dumping price.

The court upheld the contentions of the government, stating that no individual could do business on that basis:

> Whether the lands and mines constituted a part of the public domain or whether they were taken by the government after payment to the owners thereof does not appear. *Certainly the product of these mines has a value, for it finds ready sale.* . . . There was no cost of material shown by collective Exhibit 5, and this we hold must be done. If it be said that the cost of material is incapable of ascertainment under such conditions, then no cost of production can be shown under the statute because of the absence of this statutory element therein [italics added].

As a final illustration of its reasoning and as a revelation of the possibilities of the cost-of-production formula for either dumping or ordinary duties, the court stated that the statutory profit, i.e., that "ordinarily added," could be estimated by deducting the other costs of production from the representative sale price—the $6.00-per-ton price for Europe f.o.b. Casablanca.[15] The court was thus able to demonstrate that any price below the monopoly price to European countries was a dumping price and "such as to justify the antidumping finding here complained of."

The net result of all this litigation—the appeals, the dissenting and specially concurring opinions, the petitions for rehearing, etc.—was that the importer was obliged by the court's final ruling to pay a dumping duty on the appraiser's original finding of foreign-market values of from $7.52 to $7.58 per ton after the court had solemnly declared that no foreign-market value existed.[16] The court found that dumping

---

15. Sales to Europe constituted over 80 per cent of the total.

16. The importer later took the case to the federal district and circuit courts in an unsuccessful attempt to restrain the collector from collecting the dumping duties on the ground of illegal assessment. Both these courts held that all judicial remedies had been exhausted (cf. *Cottman Co.* v. *Dailey*, 20 F. Supp. 142 [1937]; affirmed 94 F. [2d] 85 [1938]). The author has been informed that the Treasury Department subsequently withdrew its finding of dumping *ab initio*, thus remov-

existed not because of dumping prices as defined by the statute but because of the limitation requiring home consumption on sales for home consumption and notwithstanding the clear wording of the statute, which states that the foreign-market value shall be the price at which such or similar merchandise *is sold* to all purchasers in the principal markets of the country from which exported, etc. In rejecting the cost-of-production formula on the ground that no cost of materials was shown, the court went beyond the requirement of the statute, holding in effect (cf. italicized portion of court's reasoning, above) that under the cost-of-production provision the *value*, not the *cost*, of product components is the criterion of dumping behavior. In view of a subsequent decision, presently to be discussed, it does not appear that the court was aware of this inconsistency in its decision in the Cottman case.

In the European Trading Company case,[17] several years after the Cottman decision, the court specifically ruled upon the question of whether the *value* of cost components has any bearing on the validity of cost-of-production estimates under the valuation provisions of the Antidumping Act. This case involved the importation of wire fish netting from Germany in 1934. The foreign manufacturer and exporter purchased his chief raw material, wire rods, from the Krupp works in Germany. He was allowed an export rebate by Krupp for exportation of the finished product. The appraiser included the rebate in the cost of production, and dumping duties were assessed, a finding having previously been issued. The importer appealed to reappraisement, and when the case reached the Court of Customs and Patent Appeals the government contended that the amount of the rebate must be included in the cost of production since it was not allowable "at a time preceding the date of shipment of the particular merchandise ... which would ordinarily permit [its] manufacture." The court found no evidence that the rebate was not allowable until after the date of exportation, since the product was especially made for export and had no foreign value and since the manufacturer had a long-standing, "most-favored-purchaser" agreement with Krupp under

---

ing the necessity of payment (cf. T.D. 49964[D] [1939] vacating T.D. 42577[D]).

17. *United States* v. *European Trading Co.*, 27 C.C.P.A. 289 (1940).

which he was at all times to receive the benefit of the lowest price charged anyone else. Counsel for the government then urged that the *value* of the rods in Germany be taken as the cost of the materials, but the court overruled this contention:

> The government insists, in effect, that, while the *finished netting* had no foreign value, the rods *per se,* did have and that the per se foreign value of the rods, instead of their actual cost, must be taken as the element in determining the cost of production of the finished netting.

> It would seem that to sustain the government's position here would require the combining of the foreign market value section (205) with the cost of production section (206) of the antidumping act. That is, it would require the foreign value of one of the materials (iron rods) to be determined and that value substituted for the actual cost of such iron rods in arriving at the cost of production of the completed netting. It is clear that under the statute this theory is untenable.

> The Antidumping Act provides two bases for determining dumping duties, and each is independent of the other.

Thus the court recognized the impropriety of confusing considerations of value with those of cost under the cost-of-production formula. If it be assumed that the export abatement permitted low prices which were dumping in the economic sense, they were correctible by the countervailing provisions of the tariff. In the Cottman case, however, no such remedy was available, and the principle was quite different. The low prices in the Cottman case, so far as the record was concerned, were the result not of any abatement of money costs but of an abundant supply of natural resources which had been preempted for exploitation. In so far as the construction of the statute is concerned, it would appear to the observer that if raw materials are available at their costs of extraction—whether from the public domain or from land grants obtained cost free by private individuals—their costs of extraction (including overhead) are *ipso facto* their costs of production. From the standpoint of the larger question of tariff policy, the differential distribution of natural resources throughout the world constitutes a basic ingredient in comparative advantage long recognized as a principal foundation of international trade. To label as dumping the natural consequences of such advantage, is to place the bulk of all international and interregional trade in the same category.[18]

18. The author is well aware that this cursory treatment of the problem of the imputation of costs is hardly adequate to dispose of the subject, and it is not impossible that the application of the cost-of-production formula for both ordinary and dumping duties to imports from governmental monopolies and controlled

Whatever the vagaries of court decisions, the basic purposes of the Antidumping Act appear thus far to have been fulfilled. Between its enactment in 1921 and 1935 approximately one hundred and twenty-five investigations were made and about half of them resulted in the issuance of dumping findings.[19] Few have been issued since, and at the present writing there remain in effect only nine such findings, four of which represent one article—ribbon fly-catchers—from Germany, Japan, Belgium, and the United Kingdom.[20] Unlike such administrative provisions as the flexible provisions of the tariff, the dumping law can accomplish its purpose by its mere presence in the statutes as a preventive weapon to be invoked only where essential.

Valuation and Currency Problems

HISTORY AND OPERATION OF CURRENCY CONVERSION RULES

The history of the legislative, administrative, and judicial treatment of the problem of the conversion of foreign currencies into their value equivalents in the money of the United States for the levy of ad valorem duties is a long and interesting one. Such history is closely connected with the life-histories of the numerous foreign coins, currencies, and moneys of account which have appeared, flourished, and disappeared or remained in modified form during the more than one hundred and fifty years since the beginning of United States customs administration. Only the barest outline of this history can be given here but it will serve to state the nature of the problem and the more important considerations involved.[21]

---

economies will give rise to perplexing problems in the future. But it would seem to be highly undesirable from both the administrative and the larger economic point of view to go behind the yardstick of money costs in the implementation of the cost-of-production formula for tariff purposes. To do so would result in hopeless administrative confusion as well as inconsistent and erratic economic consequences.

19. U.S. Treasury, *Digest of Customs and Related Laws and of Decisions Thereunder* (1935), II, 1845–47.

20. U.S. Treasury, *Customs Regulations, 1943*, as amended, sec. 14.7. The remaining five commodities on the dumping list are wool-knitted berets from France; glass frostings and fencing and netting from Germany; and electric-light bulbs and canvas-topped, rubber-soled footwear from Japan.

21. A useful text on the legal aspects of monetary problems is Arthur Nussbaum, *Money in the Law* (Chicago, 1939). For its treatment of currency conversion cf. "Valuation of Foreign Money," pp. 125–31.

The problem of currency conversion in connection with the levy of ad valorem duties arises out of the fact that imported merchandise traditionally has been purchased and invoiced in terms of the currency of the country of exportation. The value found by the appraiser (except for United States value and American selling price) is the value in the foreign currency, and it is the collector's responsibility before liquidation to convert the value found by the appraiser into United States money and to apply the rate of duty to the converted value. For obvious reasons definite, precise, and standardized regulations governing such conversion are essential. Although currency-conversion problems are normally not problems of appraisement, they form part of the larger problem of customs valuation.

The original currency-conversion rules were found in statutory enactments, fixing the values in United States money of the principal coins of foreign countries and directing in general terms that coins of other denominations were to be valued according to the ratio of their value to that of the principal coin in the foreign money concerned. Thus the first collection act in 1789 established the conversion rates of some thirteen principal coins "in value as near as may be to said rates."[22] The rates established by Congress were ostensibly based on assays regularly made by the director of the mint, and an act of Congress was required in order to effect a change.[23]

Almost immediately the problem of depreciated currencies arose to complicate the conversion problem. We have already seen that as early as 1792, consequent upon the status of the French assignat, Alexander Hamilton in the absence of any statutory provisions discussed at some length the problem of determining the value equivalents of depreciated currencies and allowed collectors to use their discretion in making conversions.[24] In order to standardize the treatment

22. Cf. *supra*, p. 43. It should be borne in mind that at this time most monetary systems were on a metallic basis and that the term "principal coin" meant the monetary standard.

23. The act of February 9, 1793 (1 U.S. Statutes 300), provided that no foreign coin issued subsequent to January 1, 1792, was receivable as legal tender until samples conformable to standard had been assayed at the mint and its value proclaimed by the President. Although conversion rates for duty purposes were separately enacted, they tended in the long run to conform with the rates proclaimed for tender purposes and were completely merged with the latter by the act of March 3, 1873 (cf. *The Collector* v. *Richards*, 90 U.S. 246 [1874]; *United States* v. *J. Allston Newhall*, 91 F. 525 [1899]).

24. *Supra*, pp. 44–45.

of depreciated currencies and to provide legislative approval there-of, the comprehensive collection act of 1799 gave the President author-ity to cause the adoption of appropriate regulations for the determina-tion of the value of goods invoiced in a depreciated currency "issued and circulated under the authority of any foreign government."[25] Under this provision, which remained in force for nearly a hundred years, the practice was to require upon entry a consular certificate of the value of the depreciated currency in terms of the standard.[26]

With the gradual disappearance of foreign coins from circulation in the United States and the standardization of the monetary systems of the world in terms of accurately defined mint parities, it became desirable as well as practicable to discontinue the cumbersome meth-od of statutory enactment based upon coins in actual circulation. The act of March 3, 1873,[27] adopted the general principle of determining the value of foreign money for all purposes in terms of mint ratios of pure metal. Under this act the director of the mint was required an-nually to determine the value of the standard coins of the various nations, and the values so found were to be proclaimed on January 1 of each year by the Secretary of the Treasury.

Since the act of 1873 there have been progressive refinements in the law of currency conversion. In 1890, by section 52 of the McKinley Tariff Act, provision was made for quarterly proclamations. In 1894 section 25 of the Wilson-Gorman Tariff Act gave the Secretary of the Treasury authority to reliquidate any entry upon receipt of satisfac-tory evidence that the value of the currency in the invoice had varied from the proclaimed rate by more than 10 per cent. This state of the law continued until the passage of the Emergency Act of 1921, which made further refinements and placed the currency-conversion rules for tariff purposes in virtually the condition existing today. Section 403 of the 1921 act provided for the conversion of currencies at their proclaimed values, except that, in the absence of a proclaimed rate or in the event of a variation of the proclaimed rate by more than 5 per cent from the buying rate for cable transfers in the New York market at noon of the day of exportation, the latter rate was to be used. The

25. *Supra*, p. 48.
26. Cf. *United States* v. *J. Allston Newhall*, 91 F. 525 (1899). Consular certifi-cates, expressing the value in standard gold dollars of the United States, were likewise acceptable in the case of currencies where no value had been established.
27. 17 U.S. Statutes 602.

Federal Reserve Bank of New York was required to determine and to certify such rates daily to the Secretary of the Treasury and was given discretion to take into consideration the last ascertainable transactions and quotations, whether direct or through the exchange of other currencies, and, in the absence of a market buying rate for cable transfers, to calculate such rate from actual transactions and quotations in demand or time bills of exchange. The Emergency Act, passed during a period of currency upheaval, practically completed the transition from mint parities to foreign-exchange rates as the measure of foreign-currency values and provided a highly responsive and simple administrative procedure for determining and publishing to all concerned the rates in question.[28]

In order to obtain an adequate understanding of the application and significance of the statutory provisions just described, it is necessary to review the more important currency conversion cases coming before the courts. With the passage of the mint parity act of 1873 there began a series of court decisions of substantial importance to the law of currency conversion, the significance of which has continued on up to the end of World War II.

The first of these was *The Collector* v. *Richards*,[29] in which the importer challenged the applicability of the 1873 act to dutiable value. This case arose out of the situation familiarly obtaining under duties subject to value brackets—the substantial increase in duties resulting from a minor difference in dutiable value at the dividing line between brackets. The importation consisted of woolen dress goods from France, subject to a rate of 35 per cent plus 6 cents per yard if valued at less than 20 cents, or 40 per cent and 8 cents if valued at more than 20 cents per yard. For many years, under the act of May 22, 1846, the French franc had been convertible at 18.6 cents. The proclamation of the Secretary of the Treasury based on mint parity valued the franc at 19.3 cents, which carried the dutiable value of the importation in question into the higher bracket. The importer protested on the ground

28. It is of interest to note that the statute speaks of the *variation* of the *proclaimed* (fixed) rate from the (fluctuating) *market* rate as defined. This makes the market rate the basis (denominator) for the purpose of computing the percentage of variation, a requirement recognized in *Customs Regulations*, 16.4(a), which provides that the difference between the two rates shall be divided by the Federal Reserve (market) rate instead of by the proclaimed rate.

29. 90 U.S. 246 (1874).

that the 1873 act did not repeal the act of 1846 and kindred acts governing conversion rates for duty purposes but was designed for, and limited to, other purposes, mainly concerning payment of debts and calculation of accounts. Although the appeals court in a lengthy opinion upheld the importer, the Supreme Court reversed the decision, holding that neither the principles of statutory interpretation nor a consideration of the merits required such a decision. With respect to the latter the court stated:

> In making the comparison of the moneys of different countries, their gold coins, if they have such, are employed for the purpose, gold having become the general medium of international exchange, whilst silver is regarded more as a domestic coin, and is usually made legal tender for only limited amounts. This practice, together with the rejection of the alloy from the estimate, is in accordance with the rule laid down on the subject by the most enlightened economists.[30]

. . . .

> Those values are now to be carefully ascertained and publicly announced by the proper officers of the government. This method will insure the greatest accuracy, and will be attended with many public benefits. It is just, both to the government and the importer because it is founded on truth; and it will be a great convenience to all persons who have any transactions in which the value of foreign moneys is in any way involved.[31]

The complications resulting from bimetallism and the use of silver as the standard coin in many countries in the latter part of the nineteenth century, as well as the divergence between foreign-exchange rates and mint parities,[32] were a frequent source of difficulty and litigation in the matter of currency conversion. But the Supreme Court was averse to the ad hoc settlement by court action of each and every importer's grievance in the matter of currency technicalities. The important consideration in the eyes of the court, within the limitations of the statute, was reasonable justice and administrative feasibility.

30. *Ibid.*, pp. 259–60.
31. *Ibid.*, p. 261.
32. Although this divergence was normally limited by the "shipping points" of the metal concerned, it was greater at times as the result of manipulation of foreign-exchange rates or for other reasons. Even within the limitations of the shipping points, the difference between mint parities and foreign-exchange rates often resulted, where value brackets were concerned, in substantially higher or lower duties on the legally applicable mint par basis than called for by actual market prices in terms of prevailing foreign-exchange rates, e.g., *U.S. v. Hirschbach and Smith*, 15 C.C.A. 44 (1927).

In *Cramer* v. *Arthur*[33] the court, in words which have often been quoted, denied the importer's contention for the use of the prevailing foreign-exchange rates instead of the proclaimed rates in determining the value of the Austrian paper florin:

> This we think the plaintiff cannot be allowed to do. The proclamation of the Secretary and the certificate of the consul must be regarded as conclusive. In the estimation of the value of foreign moneys for the purpose of assessing duties, there must be an end to controversy somewhere. When Congress fixes the value by a general statute, parties must abide by that. When it fixes the value through the agency of official instrumentalities devised for the purpose of making a nearer approximation to the actual state of things, they must abide by the values so ascertained. If the currency is a standard one, based on coin, the Secretary's proclamation fixes it; if it is a depreciated currency, the parties may have the benefit of a consular certificate. To go behind these and allow an examination by affidavits in every case would put the assessment of duties at sea. It would create utter confusion and uncertainty.

The finality of the secretary's proclamation was further upheld in *Hadden et al.* v. *Merritt*,[34] in which the high court stated:

> No errors alleged to exist in the estimate, resulting from any cause, can be shown in a judicial proceeding, to affect the rights of the government or individuals. There is no value, and can be none, in such coins, except as thus ascertained.

In some instances it would appear that the court's insistence upon establishing the validity of secretarial proclamations and actions of collectors thereunder led to misapplication of the act of 1873 with apparent injustice. Perhaps the best illustration is the case of an increase in duties by 100 per cent, turning upon the conversion rate of the Russian ruble.[35] The firm of Heinemann, Payson, and Morgan made an importation of colored carpet wools, invoiced at 41,975 rubles, from Taganrog, Russia, in the autumn of 1873. Since the act of March 3, 1843, the value of the ruble for custom-house purposes had been fixed at 75 cents. The merchandise was exported from Russia in October, 1873, and entered at New York on January 5, 1874. On December 20, 1873, in accordance with the act of March 3 of that year, the secretary proclaimed the value of the ruble, effective January 1, 1874, to be 77.17 cents. This difference in conversion rates raised

---

33. 102 U.S. 612 (1880).
34. 115 U.S. 25 (1885).
35. *Heinemann et al.* v. *Arthur's Executors,* 120 U.S. 82 (1886).

the value of the wool above 12 cents per pound and increased the duty from 3 cents to 6 cents per pound. The importer contended that the proper conversion rate was that in effect on the date of exportation, rather than the date of entry, since the date of exportation had for many years been the legal date for valuation. The Supreme Court held that the proviso of the governing act making the invoice value the minimum "made it imperative on the collector to compute the value of the silver rouble at the time of entry, according to that value as determined in accordance wtih the act of 1873, which was 77.17 cents. . . . The statute as to computation applied as of the date of entry, to such entered value." Just what provision of what "statute as to computation" the court had in mind is not known, since there does not appear to have been any statutory provision prior to the act of 1894 governing the date of conversion. Inasmuch as the entered value purported to show the value of the merchandise as of the date of exportation, the only reasonable and proper procedure would have been the taking of the value of the foreign currency as of the date of exportation.[36] The court's arbitrary ruling cost the importer approximately eight thousand dollars in increased duties.

Because of the wide fluctuation in the value of silver during the early 1890's, quarterly proclamations of mint ratios were deemed inadequate, and the reliquidation proviso already mentioned was added to the Tariff Act of 1894. The specific wording follows:

> Provided, that the Secretary of the Treasury may order the reliquidation of any entry at a different value, whenever satisfactory evidence shall be produced to him showing that the value in United States currency of the foreign money specified in the invoice was, at the date of certification, at least ten per centum more or less than the value proclaimed during the quarter in which the consular certification occurred.

Much controversy centered about the interpretation of this proviso, particularly in connection with the conversion of the silver rupee of India. Following the repeal of the Sherman Act and the closing of the mints of India to the free coinage of silver in 1893, the value of silver declined substantially. The exchange value of the rupee did not decline in proportion to the drop in its bullion value because of its rela-

---

36. The act of 1894 specifically made the date of exportation, as indicated by consular certificate, the governing date for currency conversion. Current regulations define the date of exportation for conversion purposes to be the same as that for appraisement purposes (cf. *Customs Regulations,* 16.4).

tionship to the English pound.[37] It thus developed that the proclaimed value of the rupee, based upon its metal content, was considerably below its exchange value, which represented the price paid by importers for Indian currency in settlement of their import obligations. By 1898 the bullion value of the rupee, and hence its proclaimed value, had fallen to 19 cents, or less than two-thirds of its normal exchange value of 32 cents. Under the proviso quoted above, the Secretary of the Treasury directed reliquidation on the basis of exchange rates as indicated by consular certificate attached to the invoice. The importers protested on technical grounds, claiming that the proviso was limited in application to fluctuations in bullion values and that it did not cover departures from proclaimed values by foreign-exchange rates. The circuit courts upheld this position for several years on the basis of certain principles of statutory construction, observing that the use of foreign-exchange rates was a radical departure from traditional currency-conversion rules and that it "would result in the introduction of those elements of uncertainty and confusion which the law had aimed specifically to prevent."[38]

The effect of these decisions was the use of converted dutiable values widely divergent from the actual market values and, in the case of the rupee, conferred substantial reductions in duty. The situation was finally corrected in 1905 by a decision of the Supreme Court handed down by Justice Holmes. In approaching the problem, Mr. Holmes used the following significant language:

> On the other side we start with the consideration that to an ad valorem tax it must be an object to ascertain the true value of the thing taxed at the time as of which it is taxed, and that the invoice price is referred to only to that end. The history of the statutes shows a series of continually closer approximations to it, and to our mind helps the contention of the Government, not that of the other side.

Reviewing the monetary history of the times and the legislative history of currency conversion, Mr. Holmes held that there was nothing in the proviso of the 1894 act to prevent its application to other than

---

37. The rupee was supported by the pound and officially placed on a 15-to-1 basis on the gold standard in 1898. This made the rupee a token coin worth 1*s.* 4*d.*, or about 32 cents in exchange (cf. case cited and references therein; also article, "Rupee," in *Palgrave's Dictionary of Political Economy* [London, 1910]).

38. *United States* v. *J. Allston Newhall*, 91 F. 525 (1899); cf. also *United States* v. *Beebe*, 117 F. 670 (1902).

bullion fluctuations and that the secretary's action was conclusive.[39] From this time on, prevailing foreign-exchange rates, whenever they departed from the proclaimed rate by more than the latitude permitted by statute, were recognized as the appropriate measure of the value of foreign currencies. As already indicated, the cumbersome method of reliquidation was abandoned in 1921, the margin of permissible variation reduced from 10 to 5 per cent, and a specific and carefully defined foreign-exchange market selected in order to prevent ambiguity and multiplicity of alternatives.

Numerous cases since have appeared before the courts on currency-conversion issues, but none of major significance for the present study until the departure of the various nations from the gold standard in the 1930's and the introduction of exchange controls as a measure of national defense or wartime policy. Reference is made, however, to certain cases as being of interest for their informative value or as illustrating curious or anomalous consequences attendant upon currency conversion. Among these are *Cablat* v. *United States*,[40] indicative of the complicated questions of fact sometimes associated with currency conversion; *United States* v. *Parkhurst*,[41] in which a currency-conversion reliquidation cut the Gordian knot of technical estoppel and permitted free entry of nondutiable goods; and *J. K. Clarke* v. *United States*,[42] illustrating the divergence of foreign-exchange rates for the same currency in different markets.

The departure of England from the gold standard in September, 1931, and the passage of the Gold Reserve Act in the United States early in 1934 gave rise to test cases attempting to impeach either the secretary's proclamations or collectors' decisions thereunder. In *Amalgamated Textiles, Ltd.* v. *United States*,[43] the merchandise involved was woolen cloth imported from England in the summer of 1933. The proclaimed rate for the pound sterling as of the date of exportation was $4.8665 as against the foreign-exchange rate of $4.77875 certified

---

39. *United States* v. *Whitridge*, 197 U.S. 135 (1905).

40. 11 C.C.A. 304 (1922).

41. 12 C.C.A. 370 (1924).

42. 17 C.C.P.A. 420 (1930). For an informative discussion of the use of foreign-exchange markets in the United States vis-à-vis those abroad prior to the Emergency Act of 1921 cf. letter of Acting Attorney-General John W. Davis, dated September 1, 1915, to the Secretary of the Treasury, reproduced in T.D. 35951.

43. 24 C.C.P.A. 74 (1936).

by the Federal Reserve Bank of New York. Since the variation, as defined, was less than 5 per cent, the proclaimed rate was adopted by the collector. The importer protested, contending that the collector, when confronted by two alternative rates furnished by officials in the executive branch of the government, adopted the wrong alternative, based upon the gold sovereign, a coin no longer in circulation. The court held, on the basis of earlier cases already discussed, that the correctness of the proclamation could not be impeached in a judicial proceeding and that it was binding upon the collector.

In *J. S. Staedtler, Inc.* v. *United States*,[44] following the devaluation of the dollar and the withdrawal of gold from circulation in the United States, the importer challenged the legality, not the correctness, of the secretary's proclamation on the ground that the governing statute called for proclamation of foreign-currency values in terms of the money of account of the United States and that gold was no longer the money of account of the United States, its use as the medium of circulation having been specifically prohibited by the Gold Reserve Act of 1934. The importer argued that the proclamation was void since it was based on gold ratios, the new conversion rates being merely a pro rata increase in the value of foreign currencies based on the old and new definitions of the gold content of the dollar. The court ruled that there was nothing in the form of the proclamation which indicated illegality; that only deductions from calculations respecting gold values were used to challenge it; that the money of account of the United States was defined by statute in terms of dollars and fractions thereof, making the question of monetary gold irrelevant; and that, in any case, the decision of the Supreme Court in *Hadden* v. *Merritt*[45] precluded any review of the secretary's finding.

After the declaration of war between Germany and Great Britain, the British government adopted a number of exchange-control measures, including the regulation of foreign-exchange rates. The official dollar rate for English pounds sold by authorized dealers in England was established in January, 1940, at $4.035. Effective March 25, 1940, a governmental order was issued providing that whiskey, furs, tin, rubber, and jute might not be exported to the United States unless payment were made in specified currencies to persons resident in the United Kingdom. Such currencies included United States dollars, and

44. 25 C.C.P.A. 136 (1937).   45. Cf. *supra*, p. 264.

English pounds purchased in the United Kingdom after September 3, 1939. The Federal Reserve Bank, faced with both a "free" and an "official" rate in the New York market for cable transfers, certified both rates to the Secretary of the Treasury—the official rate as noted above and a free rate of $3.475138. The Secretary of the Treasury, on April 15, 1940, notified collectors that he would publish only the official rate thereafter and directed them to liquidate duties at the official rates.

On May 13, 1940, an importer of woolen goods exported a shipment from England purchased with "old" sterling acquired at the free rate in the New York market, and he subsequently entered it at the custom house. The importer protested the collector's liquidation at the official rate and was upheld by the Customs Court. The Court of Customs and Patent Appeals reversed this decision on the basis of the numerous cases holding to the conclusiveness and nonreviewable nature of the secretarial proclamations. So far as the economic and administrative issues were concerned, the court pointed out that the official rate was the single, all-inclusive rate at which anything could be purchased in Great Britain, whereas such was not the case with the free rate. The court further stated that, if any number of exchange rates could be certified, the result for tariff administration would be "confusion worse confounded."[46]

In view of the importance of the case, the Supreme Court granted a petition for review and heard the detailed arguments of opposing counsel. On February 5, 1945, the high court handed down a decision sustaining the importer, with Justices Frankfurter and Black dissenting.[47] The majority opinion, reviewing the Whitridge case, reiterated the position that the ascertainment of the true value of an importation was the basic assumption upon which the currency-conversion rules were founded and that the history of legislation subsequent to the Whitridge case continued the trend toward a closer approximation of such value. Pointing out that the importer had acquired pounds at the lower rate[48] and that he had bought woolens—not one of the specified commodities subject to the official rate—the court continued:

---

46. *United States* v. *John Barr,* 32 C.C.P.A. 16 (1944).

47. *Barr* v. *United States,* 324 U.S. 83 (1945).

48. The free rate stated above was that prevailing on the date of exportation; actually, the importer acquired his sterling funds at an even lower rate.

If the higher "official" rate is used in the valuation of the woolens, the cost of the goods will be distorted and an inflated valuation for customs purposes will be placed upon them. Such a result would be quite out of harmony with the history of the statutes and should be avoided unless the result is plainly required by the statute.

The court found no merit in the contention that the application of the lower rate ran counter to the provision that the value of imported merchandise shall be "the foreign value or the export value, whichever is higher." With respect to the nonreviewable nature of the secretary's proclamation the court held that in the publication of the rates found by the Federal Reserve Bank the secretary's action was purely ministerial and that the doctrine of nonreviewability applied to the action of the bank, not to that of the secretary.

The minority opinion, in addition to defending the authority of the secretary to select a single appropriate rate, stated that the existence of multiple-valued currencies had far-reaching implications for international trade and that the decision of the majority might well lead to impairment of the regular valuation provisions of the tariff, to the possible abrogation of trade agreements,[49] and to the necessity for the application of bounty countervailing duties.

A review of some of the circumstances surrounding the secretary's decision in 1940 to ignore the free rate is of interest in furnishing background material for a consideration of the court's decision and as indicating the intricate relationship between customs valuation and international trade and finance in general. At the time of the disparity between the two rates, the existence of the low free rate was feared by domestic interests in the United States as leading to a "flood of imports,"[50] since "the low rate, if recognized for customs purposes, would tend to encourage British imports because they would be obtainable at a lower price in dollars."[51] Although the supply of free sterling in the United States was becoming increasingly thin,[52] the

49. Agreements under the Reciprocal Trade Agreements Act regularly contain a proviso permitting their denunciation under conditions of currency depreciation.

50. Cf. *New York Times,* April 17, 1940, p. 4, col. 5.

51. *Commercial and Financial Chronicle,* CL (April 20, 1940), Part II, 2479. Note the ambiguity of the quoted material: British imports bought with free sterling would be obtainable at a lower price in dollars regardless of valuation procedures.

52. *Ibid.;* cf. also *Federal Reserve Bulletin,* XXVI (July, 1940), 638.

demand for it was likewise low in view of the fact that the restricted commodities, exportable from England and the colonies only at official rates, normally constituted a major source of the demand for sterling. The unofficial rate was technically "free"; its depreciation was nevertheless a consequence of British exchange-control policy as well as of the prevailing abnormal conditions. Secretary Morgenthau, announcing the selection of the higher rate for customs purposes after a conference with the Attorney-General, the Secretary of State, and the Secretary of Agriculture, indicated that although he had no evidence that the British deliberately sought to gain trade advantage by currency depreciation, the Treasury policy was designed as a preventive measure. The result of the Treasury ruling was a further decline in the free sterling rate, an increase in the effective rates of duty on relevant imports of some 15 per cent, and a similar addition in the amount importers were required to post in cash or bonds upon entry. Commenting upon the situation, the *Commercial and Financial Chronicle* editorialized:

> In some quarters it is confidently believed that the British authorities will see the wisdom of maintaining the harmonious relations with the United States established by the tripartite monetary agreements and by the Hull trade agreement by extending the official London rate for sterling to the major part of the items which have hitherto been available for purchase with free market sterling.[53]

The official rate was, in fact, extended to all English exports in June, 1940, thus ending the controversy so far as international monetary policy was concerned. The interesting facts for the present study are the use of customs valuation as a partial weapon against a depreciated segment of the foreign exchange of a given country[54] and the consequences of such use in further depreciating the value of such exchange.

The decision of the Supreme Court has been criticized on a number

53. *Commercial and Financial Chronicle*, p. 2479.

54. This comparatively mild treatment of the British free rate contrasts with the more severe Treasury policy of assessing countervailing duties against the depreciated German registered mark. The issues were quite different, however, since the registered mark derived its bounty status from its value relationship to the free mark, purchases in which received the benefit of a direct export bounty. Cf. *F. W. Woolworth* v. *United States*, 28 C.C.P.A. 239 (1940), for a brief but valuable summary of certain aspects of the history of the mark since World War I, and the circumstances surrounding the application of countervailing duties.

of grounds:[55] that it represented undue judicial interference in executive matters; that substantial discretionary power is needed by the Treasury in dealing with unusual and complicated international monetary and economic conditions; that a single rate of exchange not only is contemplated by the statute but is administratively essential;[56] and that the theory of "inflation" of values propounded by the court was untenable in view of the unrealistic and speculative nature of the "free" rate, which was not to be compared to traditional free-market rates of exchange. In behalf of the court it should be stated, on the other hand, that there is merit in the position that currency-conversion procedures should be restricted to their fundamental purpose of converting values; that other and more effective measures were available and could be made available by Congress for providing weapons of economic warfare; and that, however described, the application of a conversion rate substantially higher than that actually in effect and available to all purchasers in the market described by the statute for conversion purposes does result in an inflation of the actual or "true" exchange values of goods.

DEPRECIATED EXCHANGE AND CUSTOMS VALUATION

A detailed consideration of the subject of depreciated currencies and their effects upon international trade is much beyond the scope of the present study.[57] Likewise, even the limited subject of tariff protection against such depreciation is substantially broader than the relationship of customs valuation to depreciated currencies.[58] It is

55. Apart from the criticisms of the minority cf. Arthur Nussbaum, "The Pound-Dollar Ratio before the Supreme Court: *Barr* v. *United States*," 45 Columbia Law Review 412 (May, 1945).

56. The administrative problem was complicated by the fact that multiple rates existed for the Canadian dollar and the Argentinean and Uruguayan pesos; it was feared that recognition of multiple rates for customs purposes would, in addition to complicating administration, confer tacit approval upon currency-depreciation devices in general.

57. Inasmuch as this study abstracts as far as possible from theoretical issues only indirectly related to valuation, the term "depreciated currency" is used synonymously with "depreciating currency." The crux of the depreciated-currency problem for international trade is the lag or disparity between the external and the internal purchasing power of the currency concerned. The existence of such disparity is assumed herein in connection with the use of the term "depreciated currency."

58. For an early review of the subject indicated cf. Walter Muhlbach, "Tariff Devices To Meet a Problem of Depreciating Currencies," *Journal of Political Economy*, XXXIII (June, 1925), 293–317.

pertinent, however, to indicate herein what valuation techniques can or cannot do in connection with protection against currency depreciation and to clarify certain misconceptions which have appeared in various tariff hearings during periods of popular clamor on the subject.[59]

Inasmuch as the levy of ad valorem duties in the United States is based upon the converted values for foreign currencies (except for imports purchased at dollar prices), it is true that the amounts of duties, and hence of tariff protection, varies with fluctuations in the exchange rates of such currencies. If it be assumed that tariff rates which are established under given exchange parities are nicely adjusted to afford the "proper" degree of protection, it follows that any appreciation of a foreign currency which is reflected in the actual conversion rate for customs purposes will result in overprotection and that any depreciation will result in underprotection. With minor exceptions in the history of the United States, there has been little concern in this country over the appreciation of foreign currencies;[60] for practical purposes the problem of fluctuating foreign currencies is therefore confined to conditions of depreciation.

In a consideration of the effects of depreciation upon tariff protection it should be observed that the resulting decline in protection occurs coincidentally with the decline in foreign selling prices measured in terms of United States dollars; it therefore takes place at a time when—other things being equal—protection is most needed. The currency problem has therefore been urged as an important weakness of foreign valuation, and the proponents of American valuation have been quick to assert that duty levels under their proposal are not affected by currency depreciation. They frequently go further and as-

59. The principal published hearings and Tariff Commission studies on the subject of depreciated exchange are U.S. Congress, House Committee on Ways and Means, *Equalization of Tariff Duties by Compensating for Depreciation of Foreign Currencies, 1932* and *ibid., 1933* (hereinafter cited as "Equalization of Tariff Duties"); U.S. Tariff Commission, *Depreciated Exchange and International Trade, 1921; Depreciated Exchange: Report No. 44* (2d ser., 1932); *Depreciated Currencies and Pulpwood: Report No. 43* (2d ser., 1932).

60. Foreign-currency appreciation has, of course, been of concern to importers in connection with currency conversion for tariff purposes. In *United States* v. *J. Allston Newhall and Co.*, 91 F. 525 (1899), the importer was relieved of a higher valuation resulting from appreciation of the rupee partly on the ground that the conversion rules then in effect permitted the use of foreign-exchange rates only for depreciated, not for appreciated, currencies.

sume that the adoption of American valuation would solve the problem.[61]

This position is untenable for a number of reasons. First of all it should be stated that of the various forms of American valuation only American selling price (or cost) completely insulates tariff duties from foreign-currency fluctuations.[62] Since American-valuation proposals customarily contain some form of domestic value as a necessary alternate to American selling price, the maintenance of protection would be only partial and irregular. But the fundamental weakness of American valuation in any form for maintaining protection in the face of currency depreciation lies in the fact that the problem is not susceptible of solution by valuation techniques. Valuation procedures are by definition limited to goods subject to ad valorem duties, in the broad sense, and would afford no relief to commodities subject to specific duties. Moreover, during the major depreciation debacles in which counteracting tariff protection has been sought in this country it was observed that imports on the free list caused virtually as much concern to domestic manufacturers as did dutiable imports.[63]

This leads to a consideration of the basic weakness of ordinary tariff duties for dealing with what is essentially a dumping problem.[64] The problem, from the standpoint of the interests desiring protection, is not one of maintaining *existing* duty levels but of providing a variable tariff levy which will automatically extinguish the decline in protection by an equivalent increase in duties. Abstracting from changes in American selling prices, valuation upon the basis of such prices would be no more adequate than specific duties in the face of

61. E.g., in the 1933 House hearings on tariff bills to offset currency depreciation, Representative Crowther made the following statement: "If we had had sense enough to adopt American valuation or landed values for the determination of duties we would never have been in this pickle" (*Equalization of Tariff Duties, 1933*, p. 19).

62. United States value presents the curious possibility that duties would be *increased* by foreign-currency depreciation to the extent that cost items subject to deduction were incurred in terms of foreign currencies.

63. The most hotly discussed item in the House currency hearings in 1933 was pulpwood and similar paper components which have been on the free list for many years (*ibid.*, pp. 86, 205–8, 255–56, 287–329, 435–39, 507–17).

64. Exchange dumping has been logically excluded from dumping proper as ordinarily defined because of the lack of price discrimination by individual exporters and different practical and theoretical problems which it poses (cf. Viner, *op. cit.*, pp. 15–16).

depreciated foreign exchange. Those who urge valuation methods as the appropriate method of attack on dumping of any kind fail to distinguish between the level of duties and total landed costs, including duty;[65] the latter only are conclusive in determining the competitive effectiveness of imports against domestically produced goods at given prices, and for ad valorem duties equivalent to less than 100 per cent of purchase price plus cost of freight the duty component of landed cost is less than the price component. During currency depreciation, the decline in purchase price is therefore much more significant for domestic competition than is the accompanying decline in the specific equivalents of ad valorem duties.

It may be urged, despite the foregoing, that, although valuation methods do not offer a satisfactory solution to the problem of depreciated currencies, there is no reason for failing to utilize them to the extent that they do aid the situation. Such use was indeed demonstrated by the Secretary of the Treasury's repudiation of the "free" sterling rate noticed above, and, although there were other and perhaps more important reasons for his action, it was assumed in commercial circles that his action was partially effective in reducing imports under the low free rate. But the effectiveness of such action lay in its indication of the official attitude of the United States and as foreshadowing other more direct steps to counteract the low rate; by itself, under an estimated 20 per cent average ad valorem duty on the traffic concerned,[66] it would have been quite inadequate to afford compensatory relief.

The permanent adoption of a wholly inadequate and inappropriate valuation remedy for currency depreciation such as contemplated by the American valuation plan, with all its permanent defects as already outlined, has little to recommend it. If valuation methods were the only available instrument for dealing with the problem and if they involved less than offsetting disadvantages, their use, despite their inadequacy, might be said to be justified. But there have been prepared and introduced into Congress far more pertinent and effective meas-

65. A related but less naïve confusion often in evidence before the enactment of the Antidumping Act of 1921 was the belief in the effectiveness of undervaluation penalty duties as an antidumping measure (*ibid.*, p. 268).

66. This appears to be a low estimate but is the figure cited by Nussbaum (in 45 Columbia Law Review, *loc. cit.*), as used in government briefs in the Barr case.

ures specifically addressed to this problem, which themselves failed of adoption because of the major objections to tariff devices of any kind for dealing with an international monetary problem which can be successfully resolved only by enlightened international co-operation.[67]

67. Perhaps the best insight into the types of tariff device proposed in the United States in recent years for dealing with currency depreciation, and the underlying reasons for their nonadoption, are to be found in *Equalization of Tariff Duties, 1933;* cf. esp. the testimonies of John J. Hopkins, special assistant to the Secretary of the Treasury, pp. 4–31; Robert L. O'Brien, chairman, United States Tariff Commission, pp. 447–83; Thomas Walker Page, commissioner, United States Tariff Commission, pp. 483–507; and E. Dana Durand, chief economist, U.S. Tariff Commission, pp. 330–69. The significant feature of the principal bill under consideration was the use of parity or undepreciated conversion rates for the levy of ad valorem duties, plus, if found necessary by the Tariff Commission, a surtax upon all imports equal to the difference between the value converted at the undepreciated exchange rate and the value at current exchange. Some fourteen or fifteen bills had been introduced in the House, but all were defeated, partly because of their administrative complexity but principally because of recognition that unequal and anomalous results would obtain with respect to different countries and different commodities; that the world depression was primarily responsible for abnormally low prices; that countries still on the gold standard exhibited prices almost as low, if not as low, as those in depreciated-currency countries; and that the increasing agitation as well as economic pressure might soon drive the United States itself off the gold standard, thus rendering any such legislation superfluous.

CHAPTER IX

General and Miscellaneous Aspects of Valuation

Remission of Undervaluation Penalty Duties

THE automatic levy of additional duties for an excess of appraised value over the value declared in the entry by the importer is of such importance in customs valuation that a consideration of the terms of remission is essential to the present study. The nature and effects of such duties in specific cases have already been indicated;[1] the purpose of the present discussion is to portray the principles which have been established by the courts in granting or denying petitions for remission.

The pertinent portion of the statute (Tariff Act of 1930, section 489) follows:

> Such additional duties shall not be construed to be penal and shall not be remitted nor payment thereof in any way avoided, except in the case of a clerical error, upon the order of the Secretary of the Treasury, or in any case upon the finding of the United States Customs Court, upon a petition filed at any time after final appraisement and before the expiration of sixty days after liquidation and supported by satisfactory evidence under such rules as the court may prescribe, that the entry of the merchandise at a less value than that returned upon final appraisement was without any intention to defraud the revenue of the United States or to conceal or misrepresent the facts of the case or to deceive the appraiser as to the value of the merchandise.

The language quoted above establishes the legal character of the additional duties as well as the basic conditions of remission: the additional duties are not to be construed as penal; the Secretary of the Treasury may make remission in cases of clerical error; and the Customs Court may make remission for any type of case under the prescribed conditions.

1. Cf. *supra*, pp. 97, 137–38, 178, 187, 188.

The statutory declaration that additional duties for undervaluation shall not be construed as penal is a matter of legal significance arising out of a long history concerning the secretary's powers of remission, the jurisdiction of various courts of record in the recovery of such duties, the distribution of forfeitures, and the civil and criminal liabilities of individuals. The issues are not germane to the purposes of this study; but it may here be remarked that the term "undervaluation penalty duty," though technically incorrect in terms of the statute, may be used with propriety in distinguishing from other types of additional duty so long as the purely legal distinctions, now largely historical, are kept in mind.[2]

The term "clerical error" represents an administrative improvement over "manifest clerical error" as contained in the 1922 tariff act. Since the courts had long interpreted the term "manifest clerical error" to mean only such errors as were obvious from an inspection of the invoice and entry papers, the secretary was unable to make remission even when collateral evidence clearly proved the error to be routine or clerical in nature.[3] Prior to the 1922 act even the courts were unable to remit penalty duties for other than manifest clerical error, and severe hardship was often experienced by importers.

The basic criteria of eligibility for remission as developed by the courts are perhaps best recapitulated in the Wolf case:[4]

Summarized, these adjudged cases announce certain fundamental facts which the petitioner must establish if he is to obtain relief: First, he must show that in undervaluing his goods he was acting in entire good faith; second, that there were no facts or circumstances known to the petitioner when he made his entry which would cause a prudent and reasonable person to question the correctness of the values given by him; third, that he has made to the collector in making his entry, a full and candid disclosure of all the material facts in his possession bearing upon the value of the merchandise imported.

2. Cf. *Helwig* v. *United States,* 188 U.S. 605 (1902), which is perhaps the leading case on additional duties for undervaluation and which presents an informative account of the history and nature of such duties. In this case the court remarked: "Whether the error is repaired by imposing a sum named as an additional duty, is not material in the consideration of the nature of the imposition. It is still a punishment and nothing else. . . . Congress may enact that such a provision shall not be considered as a penalty . . . but the intrinsic nature of the provision remains."

3. E.g., *Thomsen & Co.* v. *United States,* 5 C.C.A. 69 (1914); *DeLiagre* v. *United States,* 6 C.C.A. 470 (1915).

4. *Wolf and Co.* v. *United States,* 13 C.C.A. 589 (1926).

These three criteria are not mutually exclusive, since failure to make full disclosure is often difficult to reconcile with good faith; likewise, good faith is likely to be inconsistent with failure to make inquiry as to market values in the face of circumstances indicating the purchase price to be a special price below the market. In reviewing the courts' application of these three principles, it is not always easy to determine the factors influencing the decision, inasmuch as each case poses its own peculiar problems of the weight and significance of the evidence, the credibility of witnesses, and differing objective circumstances; hence, any pronouncement as to the degree of consistency or inconsistency of the various decisions is likely to be inaccurate. Some indication may be had, however, of the practical application of the remission feature from the instances cited in the following paragraphs.

Good faith.—It is the importer's responsibility under the statute affirmatively to prove good faith; the absence of any indication of bad faith does not constitute such proof.[5] Where the evidence is as consistent with an attempt to defraud as it is with good faith, remission may be denied.[6] On the other hand, mere carelessness has been held insufficient to deny remission. Thus when the Customs Court refused remission with the statement: "The most that can be said about the importer is that he was very careless. Sometimes neglect is as bad in law as acts of commission," it was overruled by the appellate court on the ground that this basis for denial was not sufficient.[7] In this case the importer could hardly be said to have affirmatively established good faith, but, since the case was an early one in which the question chiefly at issue was an important matter of jurisdiction, it is perhaps not representative of the court's position on the question of proof.

Special circumstances.—The most common indication of lack of complete good faith and the most frequent basis for denial of remission is the failure to make proper entry in the face of special circumstances known to the importer which should have made him question the correctness of his declaration in the entry. The class of cases appearing most frequently under this heading involves a close or special relationship between the importer and the foreign ex-

5. *Kachurin Drug Co.* v. *United States,* 26 C.C.P.A. 356 (1939).
6. T.D. 41099(CC).
7. *Fish* v. *United States,* 12 C.C.A. 307 (1924); affirmed in 268 U.S. 607 (1925).

porter where lower prices or greater discounts are granted to the importer than to the majority of purchasers abroad. In *Gresham* v. *United States*[8] the parent-company imported from a Canadian subsidiary during a strike in its own plant in Cleveland and entered the goods at the invoice value. The appraiser raised the value in amounts varying from 47 to 73 per cent, and there was no appeal to reappraisement. The testimony showed that the Canadian company had two selling prices, one for its own agencies and one for general distribution. The court denied remission, stating that inasmuch as the purchasing transaction was virtually a mere bookkeeping entry the parties concerned must have known that it did not reflect true market value. In the Bolinders case[9] the Swedish exporter owned all the stock in the American importing firm and made good any losses incurred by it. The court in denying remission stated that the existence of the agency relationship should have been sufficient to cause the appellant to make inquiry as to whether the invoice values were lower than the foreign value.

Other special circumstances held to have put the importer on inquiry have been his apparent knowledge that goods were bought at a bargain or below market price,[10] a substantial lapse of time between purchase and shipment in a rising market,[11] and knowledge that his declared values were being questioned.[12] Carelessness, negligence, and indifference have all been held as sufficient indication of lack of good faith and prudence prerequisite to remission,[13] even though at other times they have not operated as a bar to remission. It is obvious that very little generalization can be made concerning the kinds of acts or omissions determining eligibility for remission without a consideration of their relationship to the total set of circumstances involved.

Full Disclosure.—This is often a deciding factor in determining good faith and absence of intention to deceive the appraiser. If an importer frankly and openly discloses all relevant knowledge in an endeavor to

8. 27 C.C.P.A. 106 (1939).

9. *Bolinders Co., Inc.* v. *United States*, 28 C.C.P.A. 40 (1940).

10. Cf. *Lee and Co.* v. *United States*, 13 C.C.A. 269 (1925); *Wolf and Co.* v. *United States*, 13 C.C.A. 589 (1926).

11. *Finsilver et al.* v. *United States*, 13 C.C.A. 332 (1925).

12. *Kachurin Drug Co.* v. *United States*, 26 C.C.P.A. 356 (1939).

13. *Stone* v. *United States*, 13 C.C.A. 649 (1926); *Hensel* v. *United States*, 13 C.C.A. 498 (1926); Abs. 29058(CC).

arrive at a valid estimate for his entry, he can usually later succeed in obtaining remission of additional duties. If he follows the appraiser's advice or suggestion, he is reasonably sure of remission,[14] even though the appraiser is not responsible for the correctness of the information thus given. But if he ignores such advice and makes a lower entry, he seriously jeopardizes his chances of remission.[15] Likewise, if he fails to supply any information or knowledge in his possession tending to show a higher value than the entry, remission will almost certainly be denied if the facts are subsequently developed. Such withheld information may pertain to the strength of coal-tar dyes;[16] it may be a declaration of value to a foreign government prior to exportation;[17] it may be the subsequent arrival of a revised invoice or cost-of-production estimate from the exporter;[18] or it may be the existence of an agency or other close relationship with the exporter.[19] Because of the complexity of the laws governing dutiable value and the necessity for complete and accurate information as the first and most important prerequisite of appraisement, the government does not take lightly any indication of duplicity or reservation on the part of the importer. On the other hand, there may be an honest difference of opinion as to the relevance of particular information for appraisement purposes, especially in connection with the cost-of-production formula. Cost-of-production investigations are notoriously time consuming for all concerned on both sides of the ocean, and the compulsion to suspend normal business activity in order to supply additional information capable of being distorted into material for padding appraisement esti-

14. E.g., *Rosenbloom and Co.* v. *United States,* 17 C.C.P.A. 45 (1929); also T.D. 44539(CC).

15. *Kachurin Drug Co.* v. *United States,* 26 C.C.P.A. 356 (1939), in which the importer's broker told the appraiser: "Go ahead. Do your worst." Nevertheless, if there is an honest difference of opinion, and other circumstances are in his favor, the importer may still secure remission, particularly if he informs the appraiser of his intention to make a test case and follows through with a reappraisement appeal; cf. U.S. Treasury Department, *Digest of Customs ... Decisions Thereunder,* II (1936), 1429(qcp): "Remission of additional duties granted where it appeared that the importer notified the appraiser that he was going to make a test case and he entered the goods at what he believed was the correct value, the result of the whole proceeding being that not only his goods were advanced, but those of other importers, to the great advantage of the Government."

16. Abs. 49289.

17. *J. Benitez Cintes* v. *United States,* 16 C.C.A. 88 (1928).

18. *Celanese Corp. of America* v. *United States,* 18 C.C.P.A. 417 (1931).

19. *Bolinders Co., Inc.* v. *United States,* 28 C.C.P.A. 40 (1940).

mates is provocative of a kind of reluctance to make full disclosure which has no necessary relation to the question of good faith.

It is again pertinent to point out the incompatibility of the provision for penalty duties for undervaluation with the proviso in section 503 making the entered value the dutiable value even when final appraised value is lower.[20] "Final appraised value" may be the value found in the initial appraisement, in reappraisement, in review by a division of the Customs Court, or as the result of an appeal to the court of last resort where questions of law are concerned. For anyone unschooled in the nature of customs law it would be natural to suppose that, after the final wisdom of examiners, appraisers, individual judges, and courts had established the correct dutiable value, the government would be satisfied to collect duties on that basis. Even the levy of additional penalty duties for undervaluation, in the event of an excess of final appraised value over entered value, is at least understandable as part of enforcement machinery. But to include a provision in the law that the government's well-considered and officially adopted valuation is to be set at naught if it turns out to be less than the entered value, and the importer compelled to pay gratuitously higher duties, would seem to be impossible to reconcile with the canons of fair and enlightened government. The absurdity of this "heads I win, tails you lose" provision has been repeatedly called to the attention of Congress in an effort to secure its removal, but that body has not seen fit to eliminate it.[21] The importer in making entry is thus perpetually between the two millstones of final appraised and entered value: If he enters his goods too low, he pays not only duty on the higher appraised value but penalty duties in addition. If he enters his goods too high, he pays duty on his excessive entry. It seems fairly clear that a provision of this kind, which had its origins at a time when undervaluation-penalty duties either did not exist or did not apply in the absence of a 10 per cent, or greater, excess of

20. Except for "duress entries," i.e., those entered at a higher value under protest to meet additions by the appraiser on previous similar entries under appeal at the time of the duress entry cf. *supra*, pp. 137, 143, 150.

21. An illuminating exposition of this and other inequities of customs administrative laws may be found in the brief of Frank Lawrence, former government attorney and customs lawyer, in *House Hearings, 1929*, XVI, 9753–61; cf. also *Senate Hearings, 1929*, XVII, 572–77, for discussion of undervaluation penalty duties. A number of these anomalies were corrected by the Tariff Act of 1930 and the Customs Administrative Act of 1938.

appraised over entered value, and when appraisement was done by merchants, has no continuing place in intelligent customs legislation.[22]

Some Realities of Appraisement Practice

Thus far this study has been primarily concerned with what might be called the theory of dutiable value. The exposition of the gradual evolution of the statute from the simple concept of specific purchase price to the present complex definition of dutiable value and of the elaboration of the statutory principles by the courts into a refined and balanced doctrine, is likely to leave the student with the impression that apart from certain objectionable features of the statutes and of court interpretations, the problems of appraisement from the standpoint of the government have been practically solved. But the difficulties faced by customs examiners in their daily responsibility of accurately determining the values of merchandise varying almost infinitely in kind, class, description, quality, and utility are of a species which does not permit final solution. In the nature and difficulty of the appraisement process is to be found at least partial explanation of the rigor with which statutory valuation law has been drawn and the reasons why all presumptions are made in favor of the appraiser.

The fundamental question pertaining to practical appraisement of interest for a general study of customs valuation is one which is often raised, at least by implication, in tariff hearings and discussions on the subject of valuation: How wide a gap exists between the theoretical principles of dutiable value, as enunciated by Congress and the courts, and the actual findings of appraisers at the custom house? In the nature of the case this question is answerable only in a general way on the basis of inference from a wide variety of considerations. The following paragraphs consider briefly some of the major problems faced by appraising officers, the manner in which they attempt to

---

22. Actually the hardships of the entered-value-minimum provision have been substantially reduced by Treasury regulations based on other provisions of law. *Customs Regulations*, 14.3 and 14.4, permit amendment of entry and the giving of information by appraisers upon written request at the time of entry. Most importers familiar with these provisions protect themselves by filing such written request with each importation. To this extent the entered-value-minimum provision is either inoperative or serves to penalize those importers who are less well informed in the intricacies of the law.

meet such problems, and some general conclusions respecting the outcome.

The problems faced by the examiner[23] include the complexity of the value situation in terms of the infinitude of individual items with which he must deal;[24] price fluctuations; the relative inadequacy and potential unreliability of his information as to values; difficulty and delay in securing such information; such issues as the determination of usual wholesale quantity; the existence, nature, and amount of foreign taxes; questions of exporter-importer relationships; and all the related problems of valuation implied in previous chapters herein. Without further elaboration it is apparent that the specific problems faced by the examiner place him in a difficult position and that the measure of his success in resolving them depends to a large extent upon the quality and quantity of his sources of information.

A highly informative and concentrated discussion of appraisement problems is to be found in a one-hundred-and-twelve-page report to the Secretary of the Treasury by a specially appointed appraisement commission in 1912.[25] Although reflecting conditions which existed over thirty years ago, this document furnishes unusual insight into many aspects of appraisement which are by their nature permanent. The report divides the informational facilities utilized by appraisers into nine general categories, which are briefly discussed below.

1. *The consular invoice.*—The nature and importance of the invoice have already been indicated. It is the importer's primary evidence as to dutiable value. Certain issues concerning the use and validity of the invoice will be discussed after a consideration of other sources of information on values.

23. Examiners have been for many years the *de facto* appraisers of merchandise at large ports (cf. *supra,* p. 120). At such ports the appraiser's division is organized into a number of departments, each specializing in certain classes of merchandise, with an examiner or assistant appraiser in charge. The examiner's report of value, when signed by the appraiser or his deputy, becomes the appraised value. For a description of appraisement organization and procedure at New York cf. John Hedley Higginson, *Tariffs at Work* (London, 1913), pp. 47–65.

24. An investigating commission once found some twenty-five hundred separate items of chinaware alone in an attempt to ascertain foreign-market values in the Limoges manufacturing district in France (cf. discussion in *Appraisement Report* [cited in following note], pp. 11–14).

25. *Report of the Appraisement Commission of the Treasury Department, December 31, 1912* (reprinted by the Tariff Service Record, Washington, D.C.; hereinafter referred to as *"Appraisement Report"*). The author is indebted to William Hannan, appraiser at Chicago, for this valuable reference.

2. *The merchandise.*—The necessity of inspecting at least one in every ten packages (with certain specified exceptions) of imported merchandise brings to the examiner an intimate knowledge of the physical characteristics, nature, and quality of a wide variety of merchandise under his jurisdiction. Taken in relation to invoice descriptions and values, this firsthand acquaintance with the character of the merchandise gives the appraiser substantial, definitive, and unique knowledge in his profession and is an important integrating factor in the classification and assimilation of all value information.

3. *The local trade.*—Dependent upon the size and practice of each port, examiners are in a position to derive much valuable information in discussion or conference with importers or their representatives or through documentary evidence and other data furnished by importers. Despite the necessity for reasonable skepticism toward information furnished by importers, the appraiser over a period of time can learn much from this source.[26]

4. *The foreign trade.*—Although now chiefly restricted to proper "channels," direct contact or correspondence with foreign exporting firms, especially in the case of appraisers along the Canadian border, has frequently provided valuable information.

5. *Official information.*—Under this heading come special consular reports;[27] consular notations on the original or triplicate invoice (depending on whether the consul wishes the information to be seen by the parties to the importation); reports of special and confidential Treasury agents, chiefly upon specific request, of foreign-market values or cost of production; and various other more or less standard reports issued by various customs or consular officials. Among the latter there have appeared at one time or another the report of the collector of customs at Honolulu (miscellaneous information covering the value of Chinese merchandise); reports of the confidential agent in Japan (monthly report on Japanese food products; periodic reports of value of Habutai silk); report of the consul-general at Liverpool

---

26. As an indication of divergent attitudes at different ports at the time of the report, the appraiser's division at New York arranged for examiners to spend a portion of each day in direct contact and conference with importers; at San Francisco, on the other hand, a regulation of the appraiser forbade any such intercourse except in the presence or with the specific permission of the appraiser (*ibid.*, p. 38).

27. Cf. *supra*, pp. 119–20.

(weekly report of values for certain dates of selected lines of English merchandise shipped from the Liverpool area); periodic reports of consuls at Calcutta, Palermo, Milan, and others. In recent years the Customs Information Exchange, an office of the Bureau of Customs, has taken over a large part of the task of disseminating value information to the various ports. The C.I.E. reports are based largely on changes in values on specific merchandise reported by appraisers at the various ports. The work of Treasury attachés abroad, in addition to conducting specific investigations upon request, has been valuable in recent years in furnishing general information concerning foreign-exchange controls, unusual monetary conditions, and special commodity tax laws in foreign countries.

6. *Trade publications.*—For a number of staple lines of merchandise the standard trade publications afford accurate and up-to-date information as to values and are acceptable sources for appraisement purposes. The probability of divergence between such published prices and market prices depends upon the nature of the market, the frequency of publication, and other factors taken into consideration in the use of such price data.

7. *Conventional prices.*—There have on occasion developed within the appraisement system, with the approval of the Treasury Department, conventional prices for certain classes of merchandise arrived at through cost studies, conferences, and agreements with importers and foreign exporters. Such conventional prices or series of prices have generally applied to consignment goods where no adequate basis for dutiable value existed. Probably the best known of the conventional systems was the St. Gall stitch rate, applicable to cotton embroideries and oriental and Egyptian laces from Switzerland. This system originated in 1878 as a result of a cost-of-production investigation abroad. The values of goods in the unfinished condition were estimated on the basis of a stitch count plus 10 per cent for manufacturer's profit plus actual finishing costs. Experts to count stitches were placed in the office of the United States consul at St. Gall. In 1885 this basis was denounced as too low by reputable merchants, and an industry-wide conference of importers, exporters, and appraisers was held at New York. A new basis using stitching costs as of the day of shipment instead of purchase was recommended and adopted. The 10 per cent addition for profit was added after, instead of before, the addition of

finishing costs, thus increasing the dutiable value to conform more nearly to presumptive foreign value. Also a committee of seven merchants and manufacturers was selected to confer with the consul from time to time to adjust the stitch rates to seasonal or other variations. Inasmuch as the annual importation of such goods amounted to some $8,000,000 in the late 1880's, this conventional system was of substantial importance.[28]

Similar conventional systems included the "1908 rate list" on French chinaware from the Limoges district,[29] the Nottingham net schedule, and at New York an apparently unauthorized schedule for fresh tomatoes from Cuba. The conventional systems evidently worked well for a number of years, simplifying administration and promoting uniformity at different ports; they have, however, all been abandoned in favor of appraisement methods less likely to get out of touch with actual market prices. Such systems represent a kind of halfway house between ordinary appraisement techniques and the systems of proclaimed or official values of varying flexibility used by a number of foreign countries as a standard part of valuation procedure. The legal justification for the use of conventional prices in the United States was the statutory direction to the appraiser to use "all reasonable ways and means in his power" in the execution of his duties "under such rules and regulations as the Secrtary of the Treasury may prescribe."

8. *Judicial and quasi-judicial determinations.*—All reappraisement decisions of the United States Customs Court—as well as all other court decisions affecting the collection of duties—are regularly published and distributed in the weekly *Treasury Decisions.* Court decisions as to value are binding upon all subsequently imported merchandise, as well as on entries pending reappraisement, and therefore play a part in fixing dutiable value. The Appraisement Commission of 1912 in its report indicated that when the Board of General Appraisers was originally established its decisions were probably intended to have no further operation than upon the shipments actually appealed. Since the right of appeal existed for all shipments and the

28. *Ibid.*, pp. 13–14. A more detailed account of this system may be found in U.S. Treasury Department, *Annual Report, 1885,* II, 61–63, 70–74.

29. *Appraisement Report,* pp. 12–13. Undervaluation of china from Limoges once attained the proportions of a national scandal, culminating in the Haviland and Company case, 177 F. 175 (1910), certiorari denied, 216 U.S. 618.

board would probably follow its previous decisions, a given decision came to be regarded as binding upon all identical merchandise. The chief difficulty, so far as dissemination was concerned, was the inadequacy of the descriptions of merchandise. This has been at least partially resolved by the collection and filing of samples at New York. As to strict adherence to board decisions, the Appraisement Commission cited a disadvantage in the fact that many cases were decided by fixing of the dutiable value just below the statutory forfeiture point—then 75 per cent, now 100 per cent, above entered value—apparently to prevent the automatic forfeiture of the goods under appeal. In instances in which this was lower than the presumably correct value, subsequent shipments were appraised at a lower value than they should have been. In view of the later increase of the forfeiture point to 100 per cent, this situation is undoubtedly rare.[30]

9. *The examiner's knowledge.*—The expert knowledge of examiners is often referred to not only as the embodiment or repository of specific information as to values gleaned from the foregoing sources but also as an independent tool in the determination of dutiable value:[31]

Through the operation of these influences the examiner becomes a sort of clearing house of commercial and technical information, which has a bearing upon his work of classification and valuation. Without actual experience abroad he comes into possession of facts bearing upon market points, manufacturing districts, transportation routes, freight charges, manufacturing methods, material costs, trade customs, industrial organizations, market supplies, movements and prices, industrial processes, labor conditions and hundreds of other influences that . . . enter into his conclusions in his everyday work. . . . From the examiner's constant contact with means of information such as suggested, there results a certain trained sense of values which enables him to reach his determination in the major part of his everyday work by a mere inspection of merchandise and the formation of an opinion as to values based upon such inspection and an inspection of the invoice to determine whether or not such opinion is in accord with the invoice value.[32]

30. Except for frequent cases involving coal-tar products under the American selling-price provision. In most such cases forfeiture can be avoided by the proof of good faith by the importer before the courts. This litigation, in addition to that separately required to obtain remission of additional duties for undervaluation, is an added factor in the burdensome and restrictive nature of American selling price as the basis of dutiable value.

31. John H. Higginson, *Tariffs at Work* (London, 1913), pp. 57–59; Percy W. Bidwell, *The Invisible Tariff* (New York, 1939), p. 46; Tariff Commission, *Methods of Valuation*, pp. 21, 31.

32. *Appraisement Report*, pp. 19, 37.

There is no doubt that the experience and skill of individual examiners is one of the most important factors in the appraisement process. Yet the examiner's knowledge does not necessarily qualify him as an expert in the eyes of the court, and a common complaint of examiners before the inclusion in section 489 of the provision for the presumption of correct appraisement was that their testimony was rejected as hearsay because they had not personally been abroad and acquired first-hand knowledge in foreign markets of merchandise under appraisement.[33] Often an examiner receives reliable information in confidence, and divulgence of the source not only would be of embarrassment but would prevent the acquisition of further information. While the provision which sets forth the presumption of correct appraisement may frequently work hardship where definitive proof of dutiable value by either side is difficult or impossible, it is undoubtedly an essential element of sound customs administration.

Despite the multiplicity of his sources of information, there is no assurance that the examiner will have in his possession the precise information necessary for the correct ascertainment of dutiable value on the specific merchandise under consideration. So difficult is this problem that it is generally conceded by those experienced in customs matters that the vast majority of entries—perhaps as many as 90 per cent—are liquidated on the basis of invoice values.[34] The high degree of correspondence between invoice and appraised values has been held in some circles to indicate a flagrant departure from the principles of the law; in others it is taken as an indication of the normal identity of invoice values with market values; and by still others as an inevitable and not undesirable concession to administrative necessity. The crux of the discussion of the relationship between the theory

33. *Ibid.*, pp. 82–85.

34. Benjamin A. Levett, *Through the Customs Maze* (New York, 1923), p. 17; Tariff Commission, *Methods of Valuation*, p. 31; Tariff Commission, *American Valuation*, pp. 5–6; Bidwell, *op. cit.*, p. 46; *Appraisement Report*, p. 5. In recent years, however, this high correlation has tended to diminish because of court decisions on wholesale quantity, etc., the proliferation of foreign home-consumption taxes, and increases in price between date of purchase and date of exportation. Mr. Hannan, appraiser at Chicago, estimates that currently (1947) some 50 per cent of all importations are appraised at invoice (export) value, 25 per cent at export value higher than the invoice by reason of price increases prior to exportation, and 25 per cent at foreign value higher than the invoice because of foreign taxes, differences in wholesale quantity, etc.

and the practice of appraisement therefore becomes the relationship between invoice prices and dutiable value as defined by law.

It is appropriate at this point to distinguish between the significance of specific purchase price as the legal basis of dutiable value and the significance of its correspondence with dutiable value based upon general market price under a successful system of appraisement and enforcement. As indicated in Part II of this study, specific purchase price failed as the basis for dutiable value in the early nineteenth century because appraisers had no authority to appraise at other than the "true cost" of the article of importation. Such true cost was impossible of ascertainment when the only parties possessing evidence of such cost were those who profited by undervaluation and falsification of invoices. But when general market value was made the basis of appraisement and penalty duties were assessed for entries at less than market value, undervaluation was made less likely to succeed and more costly with failure. Coincidentally with the refinement of the definition of dutiable value, appraisement organization and techniques were elaborated, and a body of civil and criminal penalties perfected, all calculated to raise and to protect the integrity of the invoice. The equivalence of liquidated and invoice values for the preponderance of importations today therefore has widely different significance from such equivalence one hundred and fifty years ago.

In view of all the correlated influences brought to bear upon the accuracy of invoices in terms of prices actually paid, it is not unreasonable to conclude that the system is adequately controlled by a method of spot-checking involving perhaps less than 10 per cent of all entries. It is common knowledge that such procedure is a general characteristic of revenue systems of any magnitude anywhere.[35] So far as systems of customs valuation are concerned, the United States unquestionably brings more supplementary and independent investigation to bear upon the value problem than any other country in the world. From the study reported in the following chapter it appears that few foreign countries place any significant reliance, even in theory, upon sources of value information other than invoices and sworn declarations.[36]

35. Cf., e.g., the methods of internal-revenue collection and enforcement, especially for the income tax.
36. This, of course, is not relevant to systems of proclaimed valuations. Such arbitrary valuation foregoes considerations of accuracy in favor of general ad-

The general equivalence of invoice prices and market prices used as the basis of appraisement[37] is thus to be viewed as the necessary corollary of successful operation of an ad valorem system of duties. Indeed, to the extent that a market price is some kind of average representation of individual prices actually transacted, that is the result normally to be expected. Those who cite such equivalence as evidence of widespread undervaluation are stating in effect that in some mysterious way market prices are normally, or in the majority of cases, different from and higher than true specific purchase price, a position which does violence to the basic concept of market price.[38]

Customs Valuation and the Courts

A consideration of the general effects and tendencies of court decisions with respect to valuation is significant both for furnishing additional insight into appraisement standards, as discussed in the preceding section, and for independently indicating court attitudes toward importers and the government, respectively. The courts having cognizance of customs matters are in large degree the formulators as well as the custodians of the law of dutiable value. Court acceptance, rejection, or modification of initial appraised values upon appeal may be expected therefore to indicate the extent to which the terms of the law are satisfied in appraisement.[39]

---

ministrative simplicity and convenience in altering effective rates of duty by administrative action.

37. Appraised value may not *equal* invoice value, even when appraisement is *based* on the invoice. Additions or deductions for foreign taxes, subsidies, dutiable or nondutiable charges, etc., usually account for differences (cf. *supra*, p. 289, n. 34).

38. The equivalence in question is consistent with the theory of widespread undervaluation only on the assumption of general collusion among importers in addition to general ignorance or dishonesty on the part of customs officers. Entries below the general level are easily detected and offer no significant threat to the system.

39. A word at this point is perhaps desirable in explanation of the mechanism of appeals to reappraisement. Section 501 of the Tariff Act of 1930 provides that the collector must give written notice to the consignee or his agent whenever the appraisement (*a*) is higher than entered value or (*b*) results in a change in classification. The consignee has thirty and the collector sixty days from the date of such notice in which to file an appeal to reappraisement. Such appeal is tried before a single judge of the Customs Court, and his decision is final unless an application for review is made by either the collector or the consignee within thirty days thereafter. Such review is made by a division of three judges of the Customs Court,

For purposes of this discussion it is desirable to treat separately reappraisement proceedings before the Customs Court—including re-reappraisement before a division of three judges—and cases coming before the Court of Customs and Patent Appeals. The latter court ordinarily reviews only questions of law[40] and will not reverse a decision of the Customs Court unless that body has ostensibly proceeded upon a wrong theory of law or has made a decision unsupported by substantial evidence.[41] The Customs Court still retains certain of the quasi-judicial characteristics of the earlier Board of General Appraisers in the sense that it actually appraises or finds value.[42] The Court of Customs and Patent Appeals does not appraise but in its decisions either confirms or reverses the decision of the lower court. In the case of a reversal the C.C.P.A. may allow a prior judgment to stand (e.g., that of the single judge below or even the original ap-

and their decision (formerly termed a "re-reappraisement") is final except on questions of law only, which are appealable to the Court of Customs and Patent Appeals in the manner prescribed by sec. 198 of the Judicial Code.

In practice most importers employ customs brokers to transact all their custom-house business, and such brokers usually exercise the initiative in making appeals. The actual conduct of an importer's case before the Customs Court must, however, be done by a customs attorney. Brokers and attorneys generally operate on a contingent-fee basis (commonly dividing 50 per cent of the refund) and therefore possess a strong incentive to initiate appeals having some likelihood of success. Appeals by the government, technically instituted by the collector, are in most cases actually initiated by the appraiser, who has no authority to revise an appraisement and must therefore resort to appeal if additional evidence convinces him that his original appraisement was erroneous. Other government appeals result from investigations of supervising agents in the customs district concerned.

An important feature of customs litigation is the consolidation of numerous suits on a particular issue into one case, the decision of which simultaneously disposes of all the associated suits. While this is a logical procedure, it should be observed that it has a tendency to result in postponement of trial as long as possible in order to permit the inclusion of suits covering additional importations, thus maximizing refunds and contingent fees.

40. It will be recalled that whereas all classification questions are considered to be "questions of law," reappraisement proceedings may or may not be confined to questions of fact. If the interpretation of the law of appraisement is involved, a valuation case is eligible for appeal to the C.C.P.A., after initial trial before a single judge and review by a division of three. Classification cases, on the other hand, are initially tried before a division of the Customs Court and then may be taken to the C.C.P.A.

41. Cf. *Metz and Co.* v. *United States*, 13 C.C.A. 412 (1926), and *United States* v. *Rodier, Inc.*, 23 C.C.P.A. 336 (1936), for discussion of the cognizance by the C.C.P.A. of issues of fact. The "substantial-evidence" doctrine affords the appellate court some measure of latitude in reviewing questions of fact.

42. Cf. *United States* v. *F. W. Woolworth Co. et al.*, 22 C.C.P.A. 184 (1934).

praisement), or it may remand the case for a retrial at which additional evidence may be presented to permit a decision consistent with the findings of law laid down with the decision to remand. Since practically all significant questions of law reach the C.C.P.A., the decisions of that body may be taken as definitive of the law of customs valuation.[43]

So far as reappraisement proceedings before the Customs Court are concerned, there is some indication that importers emerge slightly more favorably than the government. This is to be expected in view of the strict construction of the law and regulations followed by appraisers and the tendency to resolve any doubt in favor of the revenue. The Tariff Commission, in a sample study of reappraisements,[44] analyzed all reappraisement appeals decided by the Customs Court during 1931. The commission found that, of the two hundred and sixty-six cases decided during that year, only eighty-six, or slightly less than one-third, resulted in decisions affecting unit values to an important extent. But a substantial percentage of these were cases in which the important change was made upon original appraisement, not by the court on reappraisement. A further breakdown of these eighty-six cases shows that for 44 per cent the court sustained the appraised value, for 38 per cent it reduced appraised value (usually to the level of entered value), and for 18 per cent it increased the appraised value. Assuming the court's decisions to have represented the correct interpretation of the facts and the law, it would appear that local appraisers made more than twice as many appraisements which were too high, as those which were too low. For those decisions of little importance in affecting unit values, initial appraisements were sustained in much greater proportion; but the ratio of "high" to "low" initial appraisements was almost two to one.[45]

To what extent court corroboration or modification of initial appraisements on appeal is indicative of the relative strictness of appraisement of the great bulk of merchandise which remains unappealed is a moot question. It is probable that the majority of appraisements are reasonably satisfactory to both government and importers,

---

43. Except in the infrequent cases reaching the Supreme Court.

44. *Methods of Valuation*, pp. 21–30.

45. *Ibid.*, p. 25, Table 6b. This, however, is too small a sample to afford a reliable conclusion.

or appeals by one or the other would be instituted. This is especially true of the staple lines by regular importers. The area of chief dissatisfaction undoubtedly concerns new lines of merchandise or unusual or irregular importations, particularly those not falling into the category of either foreign or export value; these are most likely to be subject to delay, investigation, and frequently excessive appraisement resulting in a test case for adjudication by the court.

Turning to the decisions of the Court of Customs and Patent Appeals it becomes apparent almost immediately that a statistical enumeration of cases "won" or "lost" by importers or the government can afford no indication either of court partiality in one direction or the other or of the consequences of the court's decisions in general for either side. Individual cases involving principles of law vary so widely in scope and importance that no common denominator is available for a comparison of effects. The following are a few of the respects in which decisions differ in significance.

1. Their effects upon the amount of dutiable value
2. The volume of imports affected
3. The number of issues decided
4. Their effects upon subsequent decisions
5. The "unilateral" or "bilateral" nature of their effects

These are not mutually exclusive considerations, but their distinctive importance is clear. A decision resulting in a shift of appraisement to an alternate basis of value with a consequent increase or reduction in dutiable value by perhaps 50 per cent or more obviously cannot be equated with one involving a 2 per cent commission. A decision concerning the dutiability of a particular type of royalty will concern only a small fraction of the number of importations affected by a decision on the dutiability of a general purchase tax in a principal country of exportation. Some cases are confined to a single narrow issue; others, like the Goodyear and Cottman cases, involve a number of important issues. A "leading case," such as the Passavant and Massin cases, may profoundly influence the course of subsequent decisions for many years, whereas the significance of others often ends with the disposition of the particular case. Decisions in a large class of cases are unilateral in effect, i.e., the principle established can be of advantage only to the importer or only to the government regardless of particular circumstances. Such, for example, would be a decision confined to the dutiability of an element or component of value. Probably more important as a class are those decisions of bilateral effect, the principles of which may be used to advantage by either the importer or the government, depending upon the facts of individual cases. The construction of "such or similar," "freely offered for sale," and similar terms may be of advantage to one side in the case at bar and perhaps for a number of successive cases, only to be turned to advantage by the other side in an equally important line of cases.

Since it is impossible to reach any conclusion concerning court attitudes by the statistical approach, it is necessary to resort to other criteria. Perhaps the most appropriate yardstick would be a review of court treatment of important areas in the application of dutiable value where there are substantial gaps in statutory coverage of the issues or where court interpretation is otherwise necessary and important. One such area is the interpretation of "usual wholesale quantity" as discussed in chapter v herein. Court decisions in that area appeared to be almost uniformly to the disadvantage of the importer, resulting in a departure from the use of ordinary wholesale price presumably contemplated by the statute because of overemphasis of the words "all purchasers" to the neglect of other terms of the statute.[46] Yet there is no evidence to indicate that in reaching this conclusion the court exhibited bias against the importer. The wording of the statute is such as to pose a difficult problem, and in reaching its decision the court was forced specifically to reverse itself. In any event the "100 per cent" doctrine has since been used by the court in exempting foreign taxes from dutiability and in upholding the application of export value when the foreign market could be shown in some small degree to have been controlled.[47]

46. The most extreme statement of the "all-purchasers" or "100 per cent" doctrine, and one which has been frequently quoted in support of subsequent decisions, is to be found in *United States* v. *American Glanzstoff Corp.*, 24 C.C.P.A. 35 (1936): "The expression 'all purchasers' does not mean . . . 99 per centum of the purchasers of such goods . . . but all of those who cared to buy such goods in such markets." Although the quoted material poses a qualitative distinction between actual transactions and the terms of offer, its principal use has been to accentuate the "all-purchasers" limitation to the neglect of the qualifying terms "usual wholesale quantities" and "ordinary course of trade."

47. The most notable case is the recent decision in *United States* v. *Wm. S. Pitcairn Corp.*, 33 C.C.P.A. 183 (1946), requiring the refund of an estimated $1,500,000 in duties collected on the British purchase tax. Certain classes of purchasers were exempt from the tax.

Another important area of interpretation concerns the words "such or similar." The narrow construction of this phrase has been of major advantage to importers in permitting the use of export value, but it has also been applied to prevent the establishment of a favorable basis of value by importers on the claim of similarity. But there is perhaps even more intrinsic reason for a narrow interpretation of this phrase than of the one just discussed. A substantial widening of the limits of similarity for value purposes would result in the denial of the ad valorem principle and the basic concept of appraisement. In the search for a basis of appraisement the further the departure from the kind and quality of the merchandise under consideration, the less likely is customs valuation to serve the purposes of the statute by an accurate estimate of value and the greater the danger of resort to arbitrary speculation.

Turning to the group of decisions on American selling price, which were generally to the interests of domestic manufacturers, we have a somewhat different situation. Ordinarily, customs administration proceeds upon the theory that valuation issues are solely the concern of the revenue versus the importer. As indicated elsewhere, in the case of American selling price this obvious fiction was eventually abandoned by the court and major doubts were resolved in favor of the domestic industry.[48] But such treatment was in keeping with the underlying purposes of the American valuation provisions in the statute and can hardly be a matter of substantial complaint against the court. Even in this area, when it developed that domestic producers took unfair advantage of the law, the court did not hesitate to afford the importer relief.[49]

It is probable that analysis of other areas of interpretation would lend further support to the conclusion that no general or persistent tendency to favor either the government or importers is evident in court decisions on valuation matters. The most that can be said on the basis of this study is that on certain issues or in particular cases the court has manifested a singular determination to reach a particular conclusion[50] and that in a number of others, as might be expected in

48. Cf. *supra*, pp. 229 ff.
49. *Supra*, p. 230.
50. Such as in the Diagonale and Cottman cases (*supra*, pp. 178, 253–57). The singular tendency cited refers to the written controlling opinion, not the opinion of all members of the court.

terms of human fallibility, the court has handed down decisions which might appropriately be called "sour"[51] rather than biased.

51. Although inelegant, this term apparently finds useful employment in the informal vernacular of the legal profession. Subject to the qualification that its use often reflects the biases of the critic, it signifies a decision which is unnecessary in terms of the phraseology and wrong in terms of the underlying logic of the law undergoing interpretation. A good illustration of this type of decision is *Faunce* v. *United States,* 25 C.C.P.A. 131 (1937), which resulted in the addition of United States internal revenue taxes to United States value. The history and theory of the United States value provision make it clear that the end in view is the approximation of foreign value by the deduction from domestic value of all charges (subject to statutory maximums for profits, etc.) accruing between the foreign and domestic markets. Evidence of the intention of Congress to achieve the objective in view is the provision in the law for the deduction—in addition to duty and other specific items—of "other necessary expenses from the place of shipment to the place of delivery." No maximum or other limitation is placed upon this deduction. If an internal revenue tax is not a "necessary expense" accruing prior to the place of delivery, it cannot form part of the delivered price and therefore of United States value. On the other hand, if it is a necessary expense it is *ipso facto* subject to deduction. By a narrow interpretation of the word "expense" the court frustrated the obvious intention of the law and required in all such cases the payment of a duty upon a tax whose presumptive and sole justification was to compensate domestic manufacturers for similar taxation on their own products. It is difficult to assess such psychological states as "motive," "intent," etc., but the author is inclined to believe that the court's decision in this case reflects principally an inadequate understanding of the economics of taxation and insufficient appreciation of the history and fundamental purpose of the United States value provision.

CHAPTER X

Methods of Valuation in
Foreign Countries

BEFORE the conclusion of this study of customs valuation it is pertinent to make a brief inquiry into valuation methods in foreign countries in order to view the operation of alternative systems and the administrative problems connected therewith. Many important countries, including Germany, Austria, Hungary, Spain, and Switzerland, make little or no use of ad valorem duties and are therefore not confronted with a significant valuation problem.[1] The majority of countries, however, use ad valorem duties to a significant or substantial extent and have adopted various methods and procedures for dealing with them.

The most common basis of dutiable value in foreign countries is some variety of c.i.f. or landed cost. The Tariff Commission in a fairly recent study found that, of forty-eight representative foreign countries, fourteen used foreign valuation while thirty-four employed landed cost.[2] Included in the latter group are a number of countries who have used official or proclaimed valuations either as the principal or as a supplementary basis of valuation and either for administrative simplicity or for increased protection by administrative action. These countries include Argentina, Brazil, Chile, Egypt, India, and Uruguay.[3] Czechoslovakia and Hungary use proclaimed "average" values

1. Cf. U.S. Tariff Commission, *Basis of Value for the Assessment of Ad Valorem Duties in Foreign Countries*, p. 3. For a convenient outline of valuation systems in various countries cf. also League of Nations, Economic and Financial Section, *International Economic Conference, Geneva, May, 1927*, Documentation, C.E.I. 28: "Methods of Assessment for the Application of Ad Valorem Duties" (Geneva, 1927).

2. *Basis of Value for the Assessment . . . in Foreign Countries*, p. 3. With the exception of the Union of South Africa all the countries using foreign valuation are in the Western Hemisphere.

3. Although not so indicated in the Tariff Commission study, possibly because of abandonment of the practice, Brazil and India are cited by Gregory as having

for certain commodities as an optional basis which may be rejected by the importer in favor of landed cost or specific duties set forth as alternatives. Canada, although using foreign valuation as the principal basis, has adopted proclaimed values, principally for agricultural products, as a supplementary means of affording seasonal or arbitrary increases in protection or for assisting industries subject to "prejudicial or injurious" foreign competition.

The principal countries making wide use of ad valorem rates are the United States and the British Empire. In order to furnish a more detailed survey of selected foreign systems, three of the most important countries within the British Empire—the United Kingdom, Canada, and Australia, each exhibiting a different basis of valuation—have been chosen for special study. Such study is necessarily brief and is confined largely to the statutory provisions.

The United Kingdom

From the middle of the nineteenth century until 1932 England was essentially a free-trade nation. Prior to World War I her customs duties were a revenue measure and consisted principally of specific duties on such staples as coffee, tea, sugar, tobacco, and a limited number of other commodities. In 1915 the so-called McKenna duties of 33⅓ per cent ad valorem were adopted principally for three groups of manufactures: (1) automobiles, motorcycles, and parts or accessories thereof; (2) musical instruments, parts and accessories; and (3) clocks, watches, and parts thereof. The McKenna duties were repealed in 1924 but were re-enacted in 1925 and still remain in effect. The Safeguarding of Industries Act of 1921[4] provided protection for a small group of key industries. The protected list was somewhat expanded by the Finance Act of 1926, but the combined McKenna and

---

used a valuation tariff in the latter part of the nineteenth century (cf. T. E. G. Gregory, *Tariffs: A Study in Method* [London, 1921], pp. 306–8).

4. Part II of the Safeguarding of Industries Act provided measures against dumping and depreciated currencies but was repealed on August 1, 1930 (cf. A. S. Harvey, *The General Tariff of the United Kingdom* [London, 1933], p. 52). This conveniently arranged little volume furnishes a concise exposition of the principal statutory provisions of the British tariff system as of 1933. For further material, and references, on the British tariff system cf. Carl Kreider, *The Anglo-American Trade Agreement* (Princeton, 1943).

key-industries duties were relatively so few that for all practical purposes England was still on a free-trade basis.

After much internal debate Great Britain finally abandoned her traditional free-trade status by the passage, on February 29, 1932, of the Import Duties Act, the essence of which was the levy of a general ad valorem duty of 10 per cent on all imports except for goods otherwise subject to duty, goods on a small free list (principally raw materials), goods for re-export, empire goods, and certain other minor exemptions. The general ad valorem duty was supplemented by additional duties to be ordered by the Treasury after appropriate investigation by the Import Duties Advisory Committee established by the act. Provision was also made for duties on goods from countries with tariff discriminations against English and empire goods.

The adoption of the general ad valorem duty made necessary a definition of dutiable value more detailed and comprehensive than the relatively simple provision applicable to McKenna duties and the Safeguarding of Industries Act. The definition of dutiable value in the McKenna act was as follows:

> Where the rate of duty of Customs imposed by this Act on any article is a percentage of the value of the article, that value shall be taken to be the price which an importer would give for the article, if it were delivered, freight and insurance paid, in bond at the port of importation, and duty shall be paid on that value as fixed by the Commissioners.[5]

This definition established a simple c.i.f. or landed-cost basis of value, subject to such administrative control as deemed necessary by the customs commissioners in order to prevent undervaluation. Provision was made for the handling of disputes as to value by referral to a specially appointed referee, whose decision would be final.[6]

The basic definition of dutiable value in the Import Duties Act is substantially the same as the foregoing but is supplemented by the following terms and alternates to landed cost:

> (2) In determining the value of any goods for the purposes of this Act the Commissioners may have regard not only to the value of the goods as declared by the importer, but to all relevant considerations and in particular—
> > (a) to the price which at the time of importation of the goods of

5. *Great Britain Statutes,* 15 and 16 George V, c. 36, "Finance Act, 1925," sec. 10(1).
6. *Ibid.,* Sec. 10(2) and (3).

which the value is to be ascertained (in this subsection referred to as "the said goods") is being paid by other importers for goods of the like class or description and quality; or

(b) if the price aforesaid cannot be determined to the satisfaction of the Commissioners, then to the price at which the said goods or imported goods of the like class or description and quality are being offered for sale in the United Kingdom to purchasers in the ordinary course of trade, less an allowance in respect of duties of Customs and reasonable merchanting expenses and profits incidental to the marketing of the goods after importation; or

(c) if the last-mentioned price cannot be determined as aforesaid, then to the price at which goods of the like class or description and quality wholly or partly manufactured or produced in the United Kingdom are being freely offered for sale in the United Kingdom to purchasers in the ordinary course of trade, less an allowance in respect of duties of Customs which that price would include if the goods had been imported and in respect of reasonable merchanting expenses and profits incidental to the marketing of the goods.[7]

It will be observed that the foregoing definition is far less precise and in principle allows customs officers much more latitude than the complex, rigorously defined system of alternates found in the tariff laws of the United States. There are rough similarities to American provisions, either current or at some period in the past. The phrase "the Commissioners may have regard not only to the value as declared," etc., is reminiscent of the rudimentary provision in the Dingley Act of 1897 permitting appraisers "to take into consideration" United States value as a check upon entered values. Subdivision *a*, above, represents a form of landed cost based upon foreign-market values rather than upon specific purchase price. Subdivision *b* is analogous to United States value except that it does not permit deduction for the c.i.f. components. Subdivision *c* is akin to the American selling-price provision, except that it permits the specified deductions as an approximation to landed cost.

In the administration of dutiable value the primary evidence of value is the exporter's invoice. No consular or other certification abroad is required, but the importer, as in the United States, must certify in writing the truth of the invoice at the time of entry. The formal entry is known as a "bill of entry" and normally must be supported by the invoice and bill of lading. In the absence of an invoice, a "bill of sight" may be executed comparable to the traditional *pro*

---

7. *Great Britain Statutes*, 22 George V, c. 8, "Import Duties Act, 1932," sec. 15.

forma invoice in the United States. Such entry must be "perfected" within a certain period either by production of the original invoice or satisfaction of all requirements for complete information. Different types of importer's declarations are required for purchased goods and for consigned goods, and detailed information is required as to commissions, royalties, insurance, carriage, freight, foreign-customs duties, and other charges to the port of importation. The currency of purchase must be shown, together with the conversion terms agreed upon, namely, whether at a fixed rate or at current rates. For duty purposes, values are convertible into sterling at the rate of exchange current on the date of the report of the importing ship, which date is also the date governing the valuation of the goods.

Disputes as to value are settled administratively in the manner provided by the McKenna duty act. The referee is appointed by the Lord Chancellor and may not be an official of any government department. His decision is final, and all procedures in the handling of the appeal are determined by him.[8] False and fraudulent entries are punishable according to the nature of the offense by penalties ranging from £20 and forfeiture of the goods to £500 or imprisonment for two years with or without hard labor.[9] There are, however, no undervaluation penalty duties in addition to the civil and criminal penalties as in the United States.

A feature designed for the simplification of the administration of dutiable value is contained in section 17 of the Import Duties Act. This gives the Treasury the power to convert ad valorem rates into specific equivalents whenever, after consultation with the appropriate department,[10] such conversion is deemed advantageous and convenient for the levy of duties. The basic criterion of the conversion is substantial ad valorem equivalence, and, when imports are subject to seasonal variations in value, the conversion is to consist of a sepa-

8. It is of interest to note the parallelism between British and American treatment of protests of classification and appeals as to value. Both countries have traditionally considered the former as justiciable matter, while appraisement or value questions have traditionally been an executive or administrative problem (cf. Great Britain, *Customs Consolidation Act, 1876*, secs. 30–31). But in the United States, as already indicated, appraisement remedies have become almost entirely judicial in nature.

9. Harvey, *op. cit.*, p. 24.

10. The Treasury is the arbiter of what constitutes "the appropriate department."

rate rate for each part of the year which manifests an essential variation. After such conversion has been ordered, no change may be made
for a period of six months; but Treasury regulations may prescribe
further variation in rate thereafter in order to maintain the basic ad
valorem equivalence.[11]

Relatively few conversions have been made under this provision.
Its possibilities for simplification of customs procedures are evident
by reference to the first substitution order under the act, which became effective shortly before Thanksgiving of 1933. This order applied
to dead turkeys and provided a duty of 1*d.* per pound as the 10 per
cent ad valorem equivalent.[12] The substitution orders, as the conversion orders are called, are in fact the result of recommendations of the
Import Duties Advisory Committee. Since the bulk of the work of the
committee has been that of recommending increases or reductions of
duty, the extension of drawback privileges, and other substantive
changes in duties, the relative lack of attention to conversion is understandable.

Three years of extended experience with the problems of customs
valuation led Great Britain to make certain refinements in the valuation provisions of the statute. The Finance Act of 1935[13] made a number of modifications, designed chiefly to protect against undervaluation by means of agency or branch-house relationships. This act
changed the wording in the definition of value from "the price which
an importer would give for the goods on a purchase in the open
market" to "the price which they would fetch on a sale in the open
market." It also specified that the computation of such price should
be based on the assumption that the (foreign) price is the sole consideration for the sale of the goods, that the seller (exporter) has no
direct or indirect interest in the subsequent disposal of the goods,
and that the seller and the buyer are in no way affiliated. This is a
roundabout way of expressing the notion that the landed cost shall

11. An example of such change made necessary in order to preserve the 10 per
cent ad valorem equivalence was the increase in the specific duty of 5*s.* 6*d.* per
cwt. on peppercorns, established early in 1934 by Substitution Order No. 1 of
that year, to 7*s.* 3*d.* per cwt. by Substitution Order No. 2 of November 1 of the
same year (cf. Great Britain, *Accounts and Papers, 1934–35,* XII, Cmd. 4753;
also *ibid., 1933–34,* XVI, Cmd. 4578).

12. *Ibid., 1932–33,* XVI, Cmd. 4454.

13. *Great Britain Statutes,* 25 and 26 George V, c. 24, "Finance Act of 1935,"
sec. 10.

be computed on the basis of the "fair market value" of the goods abroad. Additional paragraphs cover the handling of patented and trade-marked imports.

So far as the statutes are concerned, the English system of valuation presents an apparent simplicity and flexibility as compared with that of the United States. This simplicity is partly a reflection of British preference for administrative latitude in contrast to statutory detail, partly the result of the recency of Britain's adoption of protection, and partly the logical accompaniment of the lowness of her protective duties. A country the majority of whose tariff duties fall in the 10–25 per cent range should hardly find it necessary to adopt the complicated machinery inevitably associated with a long tradition of tariff protection and a scale of protective duties ranging largely from 50 to 100 per cent.

On the other hand, there are indications that already British customs authorities are following the lead taken by the United States in adopting restrictive procedures and interpretations of the law, especially with respect to consigned goods for which the value basis is somewhat comparable to "United States value."[14] During the negotiations leading to the Anglo-American Trade Agreement, American exporters, especially those with branch plants in England, complained against the general uncertainty experienced in the determination of dutiable value and the refusal of British customs authorities to allow what they held to be proper deductions from the domestic value to make dutiable value.[15] As a result of the complaints against the valuation methods of both countries, an exchange of notes recognizing the desirability of further consultation on the valuation problem was appended to the Anglo-American agreement, and a number of British duties were changed from ad valorem to specific.[16] Whether any appreciable modification of valuation procedures will result from this expression of intent remains to be seen.

14. Kreider, *op. cit.*, pp. 141–51.

15. *Ibid.* Kreider cites a complaint against refusal to deduct a special discount granted by the American exporter at the same time that the importer was requested by the Board of Internal Revenue to include it as profit for income-tax purposes. This, of course, would happen in the United States not only because the income- and customs-tax systems are unrelated but because the concept of market value in customs valuation excludes any consideration of special price reductions.

16. *Ibid.*, pp. 148–49.

Canada

The closest approximation to the United States system of customs valuation is found in that of Canada.[17] The Canadian system is based upon foreign valuation and contains numerous procedural and organizational features common to those of the United States either in the past or in the present. Among these are standardized invoices and consular certification,[18] foreign customs agents,[19] reappraisement procedure utilizing merchant appraisers, heavy penalties for fraudulent invoicing, and distribution of forfeitures to informers.[20] There are, however, features of the Canadian system which have no counterpart in the United States; these include the use of official or proclaimed valuations as a device for conferring additional protection, special provisions for depreciated currencies, a flexible method of appraising unusual importations which do not easily fall into the basic value categories, and the absence of undervaluation penalty duties.

Section 35 of the Canadian Customs Act[21] initially defines dutiable value as follows:

Whenever any duty ad valorem is imposed on any goods imported into Canada, the value for duty shall be the fair market value thereof, when sold for home consumption, in the principal markets of the country whence and at the time when the same were exported directly to Canada.

By the terms of section 36, dutiable value is in no case to be below the actual cost of production of similar goods at the time of exportation, plus a reasonable advance for selling expense and profit. Like-

17. For a concise presentation of the development of Canadian statutory valuation law cf. Manitoba, *Manitoba's Case: A Submission Presented to the Royal Commission on Dominion-Provincial Relations* (Winnipeg, 1937), Part IV: "The Effects of Federal Tariff Policy on Western Canadian Economy." The author wishes at this time to express his indebtedness to Professor G. A. Elliott of the University of Toronto for a number of helpful comments on this section of the study.

18. Except for the territory under the jurisdiction of the Canadian consul-general in New York City, export invoices from the United States are to be consulated at the appropriate British consular office.

19. *Appraisement Report*, pp. 104–5. The author has been informed by Professor Elliott that a staff of some twenty-five to thirty foreign customs agents was maintained by Canada prior to World War II but was disbanded during the war.

20. *Revised Statutes of Canada, 1927*, c. 42: "Customs Act," sec. 140.

21. *Ibid.* A convenient reproduction of the most pertinent valuation features of current Canadian customs laws may be found in *Exporters' Encyclopaedia, 1946* (41st ed.; New York, 1945), pp. 401–32.

wise, the dutiable value is to be not less than the invoice value, with the important exception of allowance for price declines before exportation.[22] The fair market value includes the amount of all foreign drawbacks; any privately paid export subsidy, bonus, special discount, or other consideration; and any royalty, rent, or other charge ordinarily made for like merchandise.[23] Consigned goods which have been sold by the exporter to persons in Canada prior to shipment are to be valued at not less than their invoice value exclusive of charges after shipment.[24]

Section 41 provides special consideration for importations difficult of appraisement:

41. Whenever goods are imported into Canada under such circumstances or conditions as render it difficult to determine the value thereof for duty because,—

(a) such goods are not sold for use or consumption in the country of production; or

(b) a lease of such goods or the right of using the same but not the right of property therein is sold or given; or

(c) such goods having a royalty imposed thereon, the royalty is uncertain, or is not from other causes a reliable means of estimating the value of the goods; or

(d) such goods are usually or exclusively sold by or to agents or by subscription; or

(e) such goods are sold or imported in or under any other unusual or peculiar manner or condition:

the Minister may determine the value for duty of such goods, and the value so determined shall, until otherwise provided, be the value upon which the duty on such goods shall be computed and levied.

The Minister of National Revenue is the sole judge as to the existence of the contingencies cited above. They are the familiar conditions which are for the most part provided for in the United States by the several alternate forms of dutiable value and the interpretations of the courts. The Canadian method of administrative settlement of these difficulties is undoubtedly more expeditious; whether or not it affords the same degree of equity as the American judicial process is a matter of conjecture.

22. *Revised Statutes of Canada, 1927,* "Customs Act," sec. 38(5). Invoices of exports to Canada must show both the fair market value for home consumption in the country of export and the actual transaction price.

23. *Ibid.,* secs. 39–40.

24. *Ibid.,* sec. 38(2).

The basic Canadian currency-conversion rules are similar to those of the United States, making use of proclaimed rates based on mint parities as the basis of conversion. In the absence of such a rate, or in the event of appreciation or depreciation, a consular certificate or its equivalent is required to be attached to the invoice showing the rate of variation from parity or the true value in terms of the standard Canadian dollar. In order to maintain protection in the face of depreciated currency, a series of curious provisions is contained in section 35. In brief, imports from a depreciated-currency country shall not be valued at less than similar goods manufactured in Great Britain. If no such goods are produced in Great Britain, then the comparison is made with similar goods produced in any European country whose currency is not substantially depreciated. In any case, until otherwise provided, the minister may determine the value of such goods.

Reappraisement is provided for in section 52, following written notice of dissatisfaction presented within six days after appraisement. One "disinterested and experienced person familiar with the character and value of the goods in question" is chosen by the importer, another by the collector, and a third is appointed from among the Dominion appraisers by the minister of revenue. The majority decision of these three is reported to the collector and is final and conclusive. Reappraisement personnel are compensated at the rate of fifteen dollars apiece, to be paid by the dissatisfied person if the reappraised value is equal to or greater than the appraised value or is greater than 10 per cent above the invoice value; otherwise the expense of reappraisement is borne by the government.[25]

For the purposes of standardizing appraisement policy as well as of protecting the general interests of the government, the Tariff Board may review the decision of the appraiser or collector as to principal markets or fair value in the country of export in any case or class of cases, and its decision, when approved by the minister, is final.[26]

An important feature of the Canadian tariff is found in section 43(1):

25. Professor Elliott states that reappraisement by a board of three is seldom resorted to. Appeal to the chief appraiser's office at Ottawa is quicker and cheaper and usually results in agreement between importers and authorities.

26. The Canadian Tariff Board consists of three members appointed for a period of ten years each. It was created in 1931 and replaced the former Board of Customs.

If at any time it appears to the satisfaction of the Governor in Council on a report from the Minister that goods of any kind are being imported into Canada, either on sale or consignment under conditions as prejudicially or injuriously to affect the interests of Canadian producers or manufacturers, the Governor in Council may authorize the Minister to fix the value for duty of any class or kind of such goods, and notwithstanding any other provision of this Act the value so fixed shall be deemed to be the fair market value of such goods.

This provision for arbitrary official valuation for protective purposes was originally confined to "natural products of a class or kind produced in Canada."[27] The extension to all products was added by an amendment in 1930. All proclaimed valuations are to be published in the *Canada Gazette,* and appeals therefrom are reviewable by the Tariff Board, which is obliged to hold a public hearing and to make a finding as to the proper value required to prevent importations prejudicially or injuriously affecting Canadian producers. If no fixed value, or a lower value, is found adequate by the Tariff Board, such finding becomes effective immediately. In the absence of a finding after appeal, the proclaimed value ceases to have effect three months from the date of the appeal.[28]

Numerous valuation proclamations have been issued under this provision, chiefly for fruits and vegetables, livestock, meats, sugar, eggs, poultry, and other agricultural products.[29] Most proclamations on agricultural products are issued in order to provide for seasonal low-price conditions and are usually canceled within a period of nine months or less. This affords the greatest protection when the potential volume of imports is greatest, as well as when Canadian production is highest, thus tending to reserve the home market for domestic producers at favorable prices at the time when competition is heaviest. There have also been a number of proclamations covering fairly important raw materials and manufactured products, including bituminous coal, lime, ferromanganese, brass and copper products, cotton and artificial silk fabrics, and various articles of clothing.[30]

The adoption of arbitrary valuations represented an important step

27. *Ibid.,* sec. 43.
28. *Ibid.,* sec. 43(3).
29. A comprehensive list of official values proclaimed in 1931 and in the first half of 1932 may be found in U.S. Tariff Commission, *Methods of Valuation,* pp. 16–20.
30. *Ibid.*

in the steady increase in Canadian tariff protection by administrative action subsequent to World War I. Even more significant than the arbitrary valuation provisions themselves were the revised dumping-duty provisions included in section 6 of the Canadian Tariff Act in 1930. Previous to this time Canadian antidumping legislation had, like that of the United States (which, in fact, drew from earlier Canadian experience), required dumping duties equal to the excess of fair market value for home consumption in the country of export over the actual selling price to the Canadian importer. The dumping duty was not, in any case, to exceed 15 per cent of the appraised value, nor was it to apply unless the appraised value exceeded the purchase price by more than 5 per cent. The 1930 amendment provided that if the selling price to the Canadian importer were *less than the arbitrary valuation proclaimed by the minister,* a dumping duty would be assessed equal to the difference between the arbitrary valuation and the selling price.[31] Although it was subject to a maximum of 50 per cent of the proclaimed value, the dumping duty could thus be raised to any desired height merely by raising the arbitrary valuations. This completely changed the nature of the dumping law from a genuine antidumping provision to an arbitrary weapon of economic warfare and, together with the effects of the arbitrary valuations themselves, resulted in enormous effective rates of duty.[32] A still further extension of administrative protection, although not without some justification, was made in 1933 by the granting of unlimited power to the governor-in-council to establish arbitrary conversion rates for depreciated currencies.[33]

Despite the fact that these arbitrary measures were directed primarily at United States exports,[34] it is probable that Canadian consumers—especially the farmers in the prairie provinces—were the chief sufferers. In any case, an important object of United States tariff negotiations with Canada under the Reciprocal Trade Agreements pro-

31. Manitoba, *op. cit.,* pp. 11–12.
32. Cf. *Report of Royal Commission on Dominion-Provincial Relations, 1940,* I, 158: "Prior to the Trade Agreement with the United States in 1935, arbitrary valuations were regularly applied to such important items as textile fabrics, rubber footwear, wearing apparel, fruits and vegetables, automobiles, and electrical apparatus which, in many cases, raised the real rates to fantastic heights."
33. Manitoba, *op. cit.,* p. 13.
34. Cf. U.S. Tariff Commission, *Second Trade Agreement between the United States and Canada* (1938), I, 3.

gram was relief from the Canadian valuation feature. The first agreement, effective January 1, 1936, was successful in obtaining a substantial measure of such relief, resulting in material reductions in effective duties on fresh fruits and vegetables; hardwood doors and flooring; electric-light fixtures and lamps; automobiles; various kinds of electrical apparatus, including radios; and a number of textile items.[35] The second trade agreement three years later secured still further reductions, especially for fresh fruits and vegetables, the principal overvalued items prior to the first agreement.[36] Together with the reduced rates, these modifications have restored the Canadian tariff in many respects to its condition prior to 1930.

With the advent of World War II and its problems of domestic supply and internal price control, the minister of national revenue was authorized, on the recommendation of the Wartime Prices and Trade Board, to determine the value for duty on the basis of invoice values instead of fair market values.[37] This accomplished the double purpose of expediting appraisement and reducing duties and therefore prices for consumption. A similar wartime measure permitted blanket disregard of all foreign duties and taxes of any kind in estimating dutiable value.[38] A third measure suspended dumping duty except on fresh fruits and vegetables, a highly desirable step which might well be generalized and made permanent in view of the distorted nature of the Canadian antidumping provision under arbitrary valuation.

Many of the basic Canadian valuation provisions were evidently borrowed from the experience of the United States. The earlier establishment of United States customs procedure and the existence of a common frontier several thousands of miles in length, with close working relations between customs officials of both countries, have been naturally conducive to such a result. The use of foreign valuation by both countries, in contrast to the use of landed cost by virtually all

35. *Ibid.*, p. 34.
36. On the basis of certain assumptions as to invoice values, Tariff Commission estimates reveal effective ad valorem equivalent duties in excess of 200 per cent on fruits and vegetables prior to the first agreement. These have all been brought below 100 per cent and in some cases the new equivalents are as low as one-tenth of their former level (*ibid.*, pp. 91–92). For details of the reductions in arbitrary valuations in the 1936 agreement cf. U.S. Tariff Commission, *The [First] Trade Agreement with Canada: Report No. 111* (2d ser.), pp. 94–102.
37. Cf. *Exporters' Encyclopaedia*, pp. 406, 409.
38. *Ibid.*, p. 413.

nations outside the Western Hemisphere, is partly the result of tradition and association and partly the natural consequence of widely separated ports of entry and a two-ocean approach to the various trading areas of the world.[39]

Australia

Australia's statutory provisions for customs valuation reveal similarities to those of both Canada and the United States. Australia uses a system of foreign and export values as a basis, subject to a 10 per cent addition—similar to the early 10 and 20 per cent differentials of the United States—to afford a simple approximation to landed cost. An examination of the wording of the Australian act is pertinent:[40]

(1) When any duty is imposed according to value, the value for duty shall be the following:—
   (a) (1) the actual money price paid or to be paid for the goods by the Australian importer plus any special deduction, or
       (2) the current domestic value of the goods, whichever is higher;
   (b) all charges payable or ordinarily payable for placing the goods free on board at the port of export; and
   (c) ten per centum of the amounts specified under paragraphs (a) and (b) of this sub-section.

The term "current domestic value" is defined as the price at which the seller in the country of export is selling or would be prepared to sell identical goods to all purchasers for home consumption. Current domestic value is therefore the rough equivalent of foreign-market value and is not to be confused with domestic value as defined in the tariff act of the United States. The "special deduction" referred to in

39. Professor Elliott points out an important difference between Canadian and United States treatment of manufacturers' prices based on quantity considerations. Whereas dutiable value in the United States is based on price "in the usual wholesale quantities," Canadian practice uses actual selling price if the foreign manufacturer charges the same price in the domestic market for substantially similar quantities. This prevents the basing of dutiable value on higher prices for irrelevant smaller quantities. Another factor of substantial advantage to Canadian importers is the fact that a firm decision pertaining to classification and appraisement can be secured from Ottawa prior to shipment, upon presentation of information and samples. It is Professor Elliott's view that the highly restrictive Canadian valuation practices which grew up in the 1930's were largely a symptom of the depression, and that their subsequent modification under trade agreements and during the war represents the normal condition.

40. Australia, *Customs Act, 1901–35*, sec. 154.

(a)(1) is defined as "any discount or other deduction allowed to the Australian importer which would not ordinarily have been allowed to any and every purchaser at the date of exportation of an equal quantity of identically similar goods." What therefore at first sight appears to be specific purchase price turns out to be a specification of manufacturer's export value or price to all purchasers. In practice individual manufacturer's export value is likely to be the same as general export value because of product differentiation between exporters and the general reliability of the invoice as representing the market value of the kind of goods under consideration. Consigned goods are dutiable at "the amount which would be the value for duty if the goods were at the date of exportation sold to an Australian importer instead of being consigned to Australia." This is similar to the early American practice of defining the value of consigned goods as the amount which the manufacturer "would have received" had the goods been sold in the open market. Unlike the Canadian and United States systems, foreign drawbacks of both import and internal duties are nondutiable.

The Australian system of valuation is reinforced by a very carefully designed export invoice required for all importations.[41] The invoice contains separate columns for current domestic value and the money price actually paid with all additions or deductions made in the transaction under consideration. Transportation, packing, and other charges to the port of shipment, including export taxes, are dutiable and are required to be shown in detail. Port and wharf charges, marine insurance, and ocean freight need not be shown inasmuch as they are nondutiable—the 10 per cent addition for landed cost being substituted for them. Like all systems of customs valuation the Australian system relies heavily upon the invoice; but so concerned are the Australian authorities over the validity of the invoice that, in addition to the statutory penalties for fraudulent invoicing, they also impose a fine of £100 upon any person who "shall have any blank invoice in his possession capable of being filled up and used as a genuine invoice."[42]

The appraisement of merchandise in Australia is thus largely a matter of verification of the statements in the invoice. For special difficul-

41. Complete details of the Australian invoice, as well as a detailed description of the components of dutiable value, may be found in the *Exporters' Encyclopaedia*, pp. 234–37.

42. Australia, *op. cit.*, sec. 159.

ties the statute carries a provision almost identical with that of Canada already discussed:

Whenever it is difficult to determine the value of goods for duty either because the goods are not sold for use or consumption in the country of production or because a lease of the goods or the right of using the same is sold or given but not the right of property therein, or because the goods have a royalty imposed thereon and the royalty is uncertain or is not a reliable means of estimating the value of the goods, or because the goods are usually or exclusively sold by or to agents or by subscription or are sold or imported under any other unusual or peculiar manner or conditions (of all which matters the Minister shall be the judge) the Minister may determine the value for duty of the goods.[43]

Closely associated with this section is the provision for reappraisement "by experts in the manner prescribed" whenever the owner of the goods objects to an assessment of the value of the goods by the collector following the collector's suspicion of the declared value.[44] Instead of additional duties as penalty for undervaluation, the Australian law gives the government the right of pre-emption of any goods at a price 10 per cent above the declared value.[45]

Several other features of the Australian tariff system are of interest in connection with the valuation problem. Under the Canadian preference tariff[46] no greater amount of inland freight is included in value for duty than the actual amount of the freight charges that would have accrued if the goods had been forwarded from the point of origin to the nearest point of exit from Canada. This enables Canadian carriers to compete with those of the United States in furnishing transcontinental rail or other hauls to the port of exportation. Another special provision arises out of New Zealand's re-export status with respect to Australia. Under the terms of the New Zealand Re-export Act of 1924 the value for duty of goods re-exported from New Zealand to Australia is the higher of two alternates: (*a*) the value which would

43. *Ibid.*, sec. 160.

44. *Ibid.*, sec. 158.

45. This procedure has been aptly referred to as "hoisting a man by his own petard" (cf. Gregory, *op. cit.*, p. 320). Gregory, quoting others, criticizes pre-emption on the grounds of clumsiness, potential fraud, and injustice. If the customs officials misjudge the value, the merchants and the government or both are likely to suffer. The government may fail to realize on resale, and resale is prejudicial to the merchant community. Cf. *supra*, p. 81, for reference to proposals to introduce pre-emption into the United States.

46. Australia, *Customs Tariff (Canadian Preference), 1931.*

have applied had the goods been exported directly to Australia or
(*b*) the landed cost to New Zealand (using the 10 per cent addition as
a substitute for ocean shipping to New Zealand) plus 10 per cent additional on the total New Zealand landed cost as representing the final
landed cost at Australia. In the absence of an invoice (and the maximum in any case) the value shall be the current domestic value in
New Zealand at the date of export plus all charges to the port of export
plus 10 per cent of the sum of the foregoing.

By the Tariff Board Act[47] a four-man board appointed by the governor-general was established to investigate and report on "any dispute
arising out of interpretation of any Customs Tariff or Excize Tariff, or
the classification of articles in any tariff in which appeal is made to the
Minister for the decision of the Controller General." This would appear to provide the basis for revision of either statutes or regulations
in cases of important questions or difficulties in the administration of
the tariff.

Some Observations on Alternative Systems

Certain conclusions may be drawn from an observation of the procedures and experiences of foreign countries with respect to valuation.
One of these pertains to the contentions which have been set forth by
protectionists in the United States alleging the administrative superiority of landed cost as the basis for dutiable value. The argument is
best expressed in the words of a lobbyist appearing before the Tariff
Commission during the valuation hearings in 1933:

> For more than 100 years our tariffs have been written on that antiquated
> system of "foreign value." It has been discarded practically by all of the
> leading commercial nations of the world that have tariffs, but few remaining, as shown by a recent report of this commission, on that basis of valuation, and they being inconsequential countries for the most part in South
> America.[48]

47. Australia, *Tariff Board Act, 1921–34*. The provisions for the protection of
consumers are more strongly stated in the Australian Tariff Board Act than in the
Canadian act. The Australian act provides that the board shall investigate the
taking advantage of the tariff by manufacturers who charge unnecessarily high
prices, or act in a manner which results in unnecessarily high prices, or act in
restraint of trade.

48. U.S. Tariff Commission, *Methods of Valuation*, p. 51: testimony of John G.
Lerch on behalf of the American Tariff League.

Apart from the fact that there is no evidence that any of the countries now using landed cost were ever on any other basis or that they ever had occasion to "discard" foreign valuation, the implications of this quotation (later made explicit in the testimony cited) are totally misleading. The argument runs that it is impossible, even with a large corps of investigators throughout the world, to combat undervaluation under any system based on foreign values, and the alleged abandonment of that system by other nations is cited as evidence in support of this position. This argument is fallacious and, when used by those who know better, is insincere. Virtually all landed-cost systems are based on foreign valuation of one kind or another. The only difference between such systems and that used by the United States is that the latter does not require the addition of ocean freight, insurance, and other charges between the foreign market and the port of entry. The valuation problem, so far as the authenticity of invoices and entries is concerned, is identical for both types of system. Most foreign countries, regardless of their basis of dutiable value and with certain notable execeptions such as England, require the same general procedure of invoice consultation prior to exportation as does the United States and in many cases insist upon even more elaborate invoices and charge higher consular fees.[49]

Much of the confusion between landed cost and various forms of American valuation implicit in many discussions and statements in tariff hearings arises out of the early association of landed cost with "home valuation" and out of the place connotation often given to it as "the value in the country of importation."[50] But landed cost should not be confused with selling price in the country of importation; the latter includes widely varying profit margins depending on the vicissitudes of the domestic market. Landed cost, on the other hand, is directly

49. E.g., Brazilian consulates charge a minimum of $8.00 for each consular invoice certification plus $4.00 for certifying the required commercial invoice plus a sliding-scale addition for shipments of greater value than $1,000 (cf. *Exporters' Encyclopaedia*, p. 335). South American countries in particular make wide use, as an additional revenue measure, of high consular fees in the form of a flat rate or sliding scale or as a percentage of value (cf. U.S. Tariff Commission, *Basis of Value . . . in Foreign Countries*, esp. discussion of individual Latin-American countries; cf. also Gregory, *op. cit.*, p. 317).

50. E.g., "stated in other terms, the distinction between foreign valuation and landed cost lies between value in the country of exportation and value in the country of importation" (U.S. Tariff Commission, *Methods of Valuation*, p. 14).

linked to foreign prices, and all the administrative problems of foreign valuation are necessarily associated with landed cost. Realistically, landed cost breaks down into many subspecies, often taking as its basis specific purchase price, often foreign-market value, and sometimes either of these with flat-rate percentage additions in place of actual charges for ocean freight and insurance.[51] Only in rare instances, and usually as a last resort, do any of the tariff systems of foreign countries utilize domestic prices as the basis of dutiable value.[52] It is thus clear that those who cite the successful use of landed cost in foreign countries as an argument for the abandonment of foreign valuation by the United States either on the ground of administrative simplicity or as a safeguard against undervaluation are merely refuting their own case.

A different argument in favor of landed cost as against foreign valuation, as practiced by the United States, rests upon more valid theoretical ground. This is the argument that, by failure to include the costs incidental to the conferring of place utility upon imported goods by their transportation to the country of destination, the normal competitive position of different exporting countries under economic equilibrium is disturbed, thus resulting in the uneconomic production and transportation of goods. This is illustrated by arithmetical examples reproduced in Table 8 from a note on the subject by Carl Kreider.[53] Assuming a 10 per cent ad valorem duty, and foreign-market prices and transportation costs as indicated, Australia undersells Canada when foreign value is the dutiable basis. With landed cost as the basis, the competitive position is reversed. Thus foreign valuation, which ignores an important portion of the economic costs of bringing the goods to market, favors distant countries or those otherwise less advantageously situated with respect to transportation, and the

51. U.S. Tariff Commission, *Basis for Value . . . in Foreign Countries*, for specific forms of landed cost in individual countries.

52. Other than the final alternate provision for dutiable value in the United Kingdom, this study has not encountered any other instance in which the equivalent of American selling price is in use in any foreign country. Moreover, careful analysis reveals that what appears to be domestic value (the selling price of the imported merchandise) in such countries as Austria, Belgium, the Irish Free State, the Netherlands, and Siam turns out to be delivered cost less import duty (cf. definitions reproduced *ibid.*, pp. 4, 5, 11, 12, and 16).

53. Carl Kreider, "Valuation for Customs," *Quarterly Journal of Economics*, LVI (November, 1941), 157–59.

buyer's choice is changed by virtue of the use of one basis of dutiable
value rather than another.

That this result is practically, as well as theoretically, possible is
evident from figures supplied by the Tariff Commission in a study of
the relation of transportation costs to total landed costs (ex duty) for
specific kinds of merchandise from various sources of supply to the
United States.[54] These figures show a ratio of transportation costs to
duty-free landed costs running up to 40 per cent. The ratio of transportation costs to dutiable values is of course much higher; the 40 per
cent factor just mentioned would represent 66⅔ per cent of dutiable
value (assuming this to equal purchase price), and tariff levies would

TABLE 8

ITEM	CASE 1 (FOREIGN VALUATION)		CASE 2 (LANDED COST)	
	Australia	Canada	Australia	Canada
Foreign-market value...	50	88	50	88
Freight..............	50	10	50	10
Duty................	5	8.80	10	9.80
Delivered cost.......	105	106.80	110	107.80

be raised by this amount if landed costs were to be used by the United
States with unconverted ad valorem rates.

Despite the reasonableness, on theoretical grounds, of the landed-
cost basis of dutiable value, there are sound objections to its adoption
by the United States. Classifications and rates of duty have already
been established on the basis of foreign valuation, and the change to
landed cost would involve a differential increase in tariff levies against
goods in all ad valorem categories. Presumably reductions in all ad
valorem rates could be made to compensate for the increased valuation; but this would require different reductions for different commodities depending upon the transportation-cost factor for each.
Apart from the tremendous investment of research and calculation
necessary in order to determine the "proper" percentage reduction for
each and every rate in the tariff schedules, the results would still be inaccurate and inequitable as between different items contained in a

54. U.S. Tariff Commission, *Methods of Valuation*, pp. 32–33.

single paragraph but subject to substantially different transportation costs. Moreover, the result would be different duties not only for different countries but for different ports of entry in the United States. So far as differentials between countries are concerned, they are the desired end under the argument in question; this aspect of the matter has been said, however, to raise some question as to discrimination between countries or to violation of most-favored-nation agreements.[55] With respect to the latter, we have already seen that the constitutionality of differential duties at the various ports of entry has been challenged; but it does not appear that this would represent a serious obstacle.[56]

55. This has been stated by the Tariff Commission (*ibid.*, p. 34). It is not known on what ground the commission took this position, but it may have reasoned as follows: the most-favored-nation principle calls for the same duty for a given article regardless of origin; specific duties conform most perfectly to the principle by ignoring transportation costs; foreign value ignores transportation costs and therefore conforms more closely to the principle than does landed cost which "favors" near, as against distant, countries.

But this argument overlooks the essential difference between specific and ad valorem duties. Specific duties, by "ignoring" transportation costs, maintain neutrality with respect to competitive equilibrium. Ad valorem duties, by virtue of their dependence upon *value*, cannot ignore transportation costs even when superficially appearing to do so, as in the case of foreign value. Since the value equivalent of "place utility" is an element in total value in any market, a tax which specifically exempts the "place-utility" component does not operate with neutrality but with discriminatory effect upon sources of supply subject to transportation differentials. This is precisely the point made by Kreider and already discussed.

To restate the proposition in other terms: A tariff duty may or may not *exempt* transportation costs, but no duty, whether ad valorem or specific, can or does *ignore* them. Specific duties, so far as the economics of the situation is concerned, are the specific equivalent of ad valorem duties upon landed cost, since landed cost under competition is equal for identical commodities regardless of origin unless the equality is perversely offset by taxation. Both specific duties and ad valorem duties based on landed cost tax all economic value components from all nations equally and therefore conform more closely to the spirit of the most-favored-nation principle than do duties based on foreign value.

56. The Constitution requires duties to be uniform throughout the United States (Art. I, sec. 8, cl. 1) and prohibits preference of ports of one state over those of another (Art. I, sec. 9, cl. 6). These clauses have been construed to require geographic, rather than absolute, uniformity, i.e., that they operate throughout the United States "in the same way whenever the subject matter is found" (*Billings* v. *United States*, 232 U.S. 261, 282 [1914]; cf. *Aldridge* v. *Williams*, 3 How. 9 [1845]). No elaborate or definitive conclusion by the Supreme Court on differential customs duties resulting from valuation procedures appears to have been made. It is to be observed that the modified form of landed cost first used in the United States avoided discrimination between ports by the use of flat-rate additions to foreign cost; also, that such discrimination exists in the use of United States value.

Perhaps the most practical objection to a change to landed cost, unless made as part of a more fundamental revision of the entire tariff structure, is the fact that it would accomplish little in the desired direction in view of the nature of world trade and the realities of tariff-making. An examination of the items shown by the Tariff Commission to have the highest transportation-cost factors (greater than 15 per cent of delivered cost) reveals that virtually all of them are bulky or perishable commodities subject to specific duties.[57] Most of the commodities imported under ad valorem rates are goods of relatively high value and small bulk, for which the transportation-cost factor is not of much relative significance. In view of these considerations and the important role played by product differentials as the basis of much international trade, together with the basic cost advantages, including transportation costs (as distinct from *duties* on transportation costs), usually enjoyed by the principal competing country, it is doubtful that the noninclusion of transportation costs in dutiable value makes much difference in the competitive situation.[58]

Moreover, it should not be overlooked that the practical application of landed cost would have much different significance for large countries such as the United States and Canada from that for small countries such as England and the majority of those which use landed cost. The former are faced not only with widely separated principal domestic markets and heavy internal transportation costs but with alternative and competing transportation agencies and routes from the various ports of entry to the principal markets. If ocean freight, but not competing internal transportation, costs were made subject to duty, a shipment, for example, from Vera Cruz to New York normally moving by water might conceivably be shifted to less economical rail transportation at New Orleans in order to reduce the duty. Or perhaps such a situation might obtain on goods from Vera Cruz to San Fran-

57. These include pig iron, granite, fluorspar, lumber, window glass, and fresh vegetables. Crude petroleum, shown as having a transportation-cost factor between 20 and 30 per cent, is on the free list.

58. Note the difference between the two propositions: (*a*) the change to landed cost from foreign value would result in significant changes in duties, and (*b*) such change would result in significant differences in the relative competitive position of foreign countries. For *b* to obtain there must be competition not only between foreign countries on substantially identical articles but between different countries with widely differing transportation costs to the United States. The satisfaction of both these conditions is likely to be limited to staple or standardized commodities subject to specific duties.

cisco if not on goods to New York. Imported merchandise from Denmark to Chicago via the St. Lawrence Canal would be subject to duty on total transportation costs to Chicago, while the same merchandise entered at New York would be duty free for part of its transportation costs. Such anomalies would perhaps be of relatively minor significance, but similar considerations were deemed of sufficient importance for Australia to exempt a large portion of Canadian internal transportation costs from dutiable value.[59] To the extent that duties on transportation costs are unimportant, the original argument for landed cost loses much of its significance.

One or two other observations may be made as a result of a brief survey of foreign valuation systems. The use of proclaimed valuations for certain kinds of imported merchandise has occasionally been suggested as a measure of administrative simplification and means of combatting undervaluation in the United States. The best discussion of the merits and demerits of this system encountered in the course of this study is that by Gregory concerning the Indian and Egyptian systems.[60] The Indian official valuations were adopted every three years by the Tariff Committee in consultation with the mercantile community. Two consequences were observed: the larger and more influential merchants generally succeeded in obtaining the most favorable valuations; and the periodic revisions were accompanied with much the same kind of wrangling and debate, though on a smaller scale, as is experienced in the course of a major tariff revision. In Egypt a more flexible method was used under which the customs administration together with the principal merchants adopted valuations for certain articles on the basis of current prices. The valuations were fixed for periods of a maximum of twelve months and were renewed from month to month thereafter unless denounced by either party fifteen days or more before expiration. In Canada, on the other hand, the avowed purpose of proclaimed values has been not administrative simplicity but additional protection. Appeal to the Tariff Board is allowed, however, and to that extent importers enjoy some voice in the proceedings.

The satisfactoriness of official values either for the mercantile community or for domestic producers depends, of course, upon their pur-

59. Cf. *supra*, pp. 313–14.
60. Gregory, *op. cit.*, pp. 307–8, and references cited therein.

poses and their approximation to current prices. Where administrative simplicity is the sole objective, the use of proclaimed values may achieve its end without any substantial sacrifice of the ad valorem principle, since a marked divergence of actual and official prices is presumably rectified without objection and without undue delay. When additional protection is the purpose in view, the ad valorem principle is subordinated, if not lost altogether, and the official values become a device for the double concealment of protection. On the one hand, like the minimum-value provisions of early American tariffs, they do not on their face enable detection of the degree of protection afforded; on the other hand, by using the proclaimed or administrative method, changes can be made much more quietly and unostentatiously than by the legislative method. Whether this concealment results in greater or less protection is a matter of policy on the part of the government in power.

In many respects the use of official values is equivalent to the use of specific duties and entails the advantages and disadvantages of such duties. From the standpoint of application, the use of official values and specific duties is substantially the same inasmuch as the whole problem of appraisement is eliminated. From the standpoint of their selection and adoption, the use of proclaimed values poses serious problems of itemization in the tariff schedules corresponding to the problem of classification in customs administration. In shifting from a system of appraisement to one of official values, if the latter are to result in an approximation to actual values, each tariff class or paragraph formerly covered by an ad valorem rate must be subdivided into as many units as there are grades of merchandise of different value contained in the class. Since most tariffs using a mixed system of rates, including the tariff of the United States, have to a large extent already adopted specific duties wherever feasible from the standpoint of the itemization problem, there are definite limits to the practical possibilities of adopting proclaimed values. Nevertheless, because of changes in the character of imported merchandise over a period of years, many tariff paragraphs become obsolete, and new possibilities appear for the itemization of important selected commodities in connection with either specific rates or proclaimed values.

Should the principle of special protection in the United States at some future time give way to a national policy of the expansion of total domestic and international trade and the efficient administration of the tariff as a revenue measure, the use of either an adjustable system of proclaimed valuations or a flexible system of conversion to ad valorem specifics, similar to that in England, might reasonably be given a place in the tariff system of the United States.

International Efforts To Standardize Principles of Valuation

Early in the 1920's, the newly formed International Chamber of Commerce undertook to interest the League of Nations in the simplification of customs procedures. This led to the adoption by the League, in 1923, of the International Customs Convention,[61] an agreement pledging its signatories to modify or eliminate administrative protection along the lines indicated in the various articles of the convention. No specific reference was made therein to methods of valuation, but closely related subjects such as consular fees and the clearance of goods through the customs were dealt with. Eventually all but four or five of the League's members subscribed to the convention, and periodic reports were made of action taken by the individual signatories to effectuate the purposes of the agreement.

The first specific attention to valuation methods on a broad international basis was given in 1926 by the International Chamber of Commerce in preparation for the International Economic Conference to be held at Geneva the following year. In November, 1926, the Trade Barriers Committee of the I.C. of C. reported that specific duties were in principle preferable to ad valorem duties, which "give rise to continual difficulties of application, and . . . facilitate covert discrimination and certain fiscal ruses to increase indirectly official customs tariffs."[62] Shortly before the conference convened, the Economic and Financial Section of the League prepared a brief outline of valuation methods currently in use in various nations, of declarations and documents required to be submitted to the customs, and of legal and administrative

61. Cf. International Chamber of Commerce, *The Customs Convention and Its Benefits to Trade* (Brochure No. 33 [November, 1923]).

62. International Chamber of Commerce, *Report of Trade Barriers Committee* (Brochure No. 44 [November, 1926]), Sec. IV: "Customs: Technical Questions," p. 4.

means used in various countries for checking value declarations.[63] This study was too brief to do more than indicate the wide variation in valuation methods used by the different nations. The International Economic Conference went on record as expressing no opinion as to the respective merits of specific and ad valorem duties but recommended that any system of value investigations be administered with full regard for the maintenance of commercial good will among nations,[64] that importers be afforded access to special or regular judicial tribunals, and that the several states by specific stipulation in internal legislation and commercial treaties endeavor to limit the practical difficulties in applying duties.

The next gesture in the direction of multinational improvement of valuation procedures was made at the Second International Economic Conference at Geneva in 1930. The question was briefly considered by the League's economic committee:

> The Secretariat prepared for the Economic Committee an account of the different methods at present in the countries which employ ad valorem duties.
>
> The Economic Committee noted this but was of opinion that it should be supplemented by a further inquiry into the effects in actual practice of the application of the different methods.
>
> It seems very difficult to consider the possibility of establishing uniform methods for assessing value more particularly where this is the most necessary—namely, in the big overseas countries.[65]

The last sentence, above, succinctly expressed the futility of any attempts at substantial improvement of the situation since the nation which made the greatest use of ad valorem duties (1) was not a member of the League; (2) had in general the highest tariff rates; (3) manifested by far the most complex valuation procedures; and (4)

63. League of Nations, Economic and Financial Section, *International Economic Conference, Geneva, May, 1927*, Documentation, C.E.I. 28: "Methods of Assessment for the Application of Ad Valorem Duties" (Geneva, 1927), pp. 20–30.

64. During this period the activities of United States customs agents in Europe in connection with value investigations had been the subject of much international irritation and diplomatic representations (cf. *supra*, pp. 21–23). For the recommendations cited cf. League of Nations, *Report and Proceedings of the World Economic Conference, Held at Geneva, May 4–23, 1927* (Geneva, 1927), II, 115.

65. League of Nations, *Proceedings of the Second International Conference with a View to Concerted Economic Action, Geneva, November 17–28, 1930* (1st ser., 1931), p. 251.

was the nation whose trading relationships were the most important for the world at large. No further efforts in this direction appear to have been made by the League. The passage of the Hawley-Smoot tariff, the ensuing world depression, and the gradual involvement of European nations in international conflict required the League's attention to graver issues in the final years of its existence.

The formal establishment of the United Nations following the end of World War II made possible the revival of efforts in the direction of multinational formulation of trade policy along lines designed for the promotion of world prosperity and peace. Among the steps in this direction have been the plans for an International Trade Organization. Article 35 of the charter for the I.T.O., as finally adopted by the Havana Conference, contains the following proposals with respect to valuation: [66]

1. The Members shall work toward the standardization, as far as practicable, of definitions of value and of procedures for determining the value of products subject to customs duties or other charges or restrictions based upon or regulated in any manner by value. With a view to furthering co-operation to this end, the Organization may study and recommend to Members such bases and methods for determining value for customs purposes as would appear best suited to the needs of commerce and most capable of general adoption.

2. The Members recognize the validity of the general principles of valuation set forth in paragraphs 3, 4 and 5, and they undertake to give effect, at the earliest practicable date, to these principles in respect of all products subject to duties or other charges or restrictions on importation based upon or regulated in any manner by value. Moreover, they shall, upon a request by another Member directly affected, review in the light of these principles the operation of any of their laws or regulations relating to value for customs purposes. The Organization may request from Members reports on steps taken by them in pursuance of the provisions of this Article.

3. (a) The value for customs purposes of imported merchandise should be based on the actual value of the imported merchandise on which duty is assessed, or of like merchandise, and should not be based on the value of merchandise of national origin or on arbitrary or fictitious values.

(b) "Actual value" should be the price at which, at a time and place determined by the legislation of the country of importation, and in the ordinary course of trade, such or like merchandise is sold or offered for sale under fully competitive conditions. To the extent to which the price of such

66. United States, Department of State, *Havana Charter for an International Trade Organization, March 24, 1948* (Department of State Pub. 3117, "Commercial Policy Series," No. 113), pp. 28–29.

or like merchandise is governed by the quantity in a particular transaction, the price to be considered should uniformly be related to either (i) comparable quantities, or (ii) quantities not less favourable to importers than those in which the greater volume of the merchandise is sold in the trade between the countries of exportation and importation.

(c) When the actual value is not ascertainable in accordance with sub-paragraph (b), the value for customs purposes should be based on the nearest ascertainable equivalent of such value.

4. The value for customs purposes of any imported product should not include the amount of any internal tax, applicable within the country of origin or export, from which the imported product has been exempted or has been or will be relieved by means of refund.

5. (a) Except as otherwise provided in this paragraph, where it is necessary for the purposes of paragraph 3 for a Member to convert into its own currency a price expressed in the currency of another country, the conversion rate of exchange to be used shall be based on the par values of the currencies involved, as established pursuant to the Articles of Agreement of the International Monetary Fund or by special exchange agreements entered into pursuant to Article 24 of this Chapter.

(b) Where no such par value has been established, the conversion rate shall reflect effectively the current value of such currency in commercial transactions.

(c) The Organization, in agreement with the International Monetary Fund, shall formulate rules governing the conversion by Members of any foreign currency in respect of which multiple rates of exchange are maintained consistently with the Articles of Agreement of the International Monetary Fund. Any Member may apply such rules in respect of such foreign currencies for the purposes of paragraph 3 of this Article as an alternative to the use of par values. Until such rules are adopted by the Organization, any Member may employ, in respect of any such foreign currency, rules of conversion for the purposes of paragraph 3 of this Article which are designed to reflect effectively the value of such foreign currency in commercial transactions.

(d) Nothing in this Article shall be construed to require any Member to alter the method of converting currencies for customs purposes which is applicable in its territory on the day of this Charter, if such alteration would have the effect of increasing generally the amounts of duty payable.

6. The bases and methods for determining the value of products subject to duties or other charges or restrictions based upon or regulated in any manner by value should be stable and should be given sufficient publicity to enable traders to estimate, with a reasonable degree of certainty, the value for customs purposes.

It will be seen that the basic principles prescribed by the charter are eminently reasonable and desirable, and, in view of the extended discussion of the various issues already given, little will be said at this point. The difficult problem so far as the United States is concerned will be the translation of the broad principles of the charter into the specific form of a new valuation statute and the development of appropriate administrative procedures for its implementation. Some suggestions in this direction are given in the following chapter.[67] The success of this long-overdue program for valuation reform will depend largely upon the determination of those participating to minimize the complexity of the law and to adhere to the basic principle of equating as nearly as possible dutiable value and "actual values." Restated, this proposition calls for a far closer approximation of dutiable value to import transaction prices than is contemplated by the general valuation law of the United States as it is today.

67. The National Council of American Importers has prepared a brochure suggesting a number of desirable changes in the valuation features of customs administrative law. Although these changes were proposed prior to the appearance of the I.T.O. Charter, they have become, as indicated *infra*, pp. 341–44, especially pertinent in view of recent developments (cf. National Council of American Importers, *Customs Administrative Law: Changes in the Special and Administrative Provisions of the Tariff Act of 1930: As Amended* [New York, 1945]; cf. also Harry Radcliffe, Executive Secretary, National Council of American Importers, "Congress Urged To Modify Rules for Valuing Imports," *New York Journal of Commerce and Commercial*, CCXI [February 24, 1947], 18A).

PART IV

Summary and Conclusion

CHAPTER XI

Summary and Conclusion

Historical Recapitulation

1. *Colonial times to 1816.*—A review of the origins of customs valuation in the United States reveals that valuation methods in the initial period of national history were largely a continuation of practices developed in the colonies. Colonial practice based dutiable value normally on "prime cost," or the purchase price of the imported merchandise in the country of exportation. Variations from this basic principle included a constructive landed cost basis, using flat-rate additions in lieu of actual ocean freight and insurance, occasional discriminations in favor of England, and, in the case of New York, arbitrary valuations for "Indian goods" but not for merchandise imported from overseas. The entire period was characterized by low rates of duty, simple administrative procedures, and wide latitude for discretionary action by local customs officers. Among the colonial procedures which were continued and extended in the national customs system were entry under oath, merchant appraisement, and a system of distribution of forfeitures. The national system of the United States adopted the prime or foreign-cost basis of value with differential additions of 10 and 20 per cent to approximate landed cost. This was not a system of "home valuation," as often stated by twentieth-century protectionists but rather a system based on specific purchase price. Invoices were used as evidence of purchase price, with penalties for falsification and provision for merchant appraisement in case of dispute. The "moieties" provisions were by statute made applicable to forfeitures for undervaluation.

2. *Valuation under rising protection, 1816–61.*—This period witnessed the rise of the protectionist movement and the bitter struggles over national commercial policy. Valuation methods played an important part in the implementation of protectionist policy, in the nullification movement, and in the adoption and administration of the Com-

promise Tariff Act of 1833. The use of minimum valuations on cotton goods in the Tariff Act of 1816, and its successors in 1824, 1828, and 1832, gave the American cotton-manufacturing industry virtually complete protection; under the minimum the domestic manufacture flourished and became the nation's leading industry. The simple minimum on cotton goods was followed by the more complicated system of valuation by value brackets on woolens. Both types of minimum tended to conceal, as well as to grant, high protection. The Compromise Act, which averted a threatened civil war, provided for the gradual reduction of all duties to 20 per cent, which would have eliminated the minimum features; this policy was overruled by the Act of 1842, but the Walker Tariff of 1846 abolished the remaining minimum valuations and began an era of declining duties under simple ad valorem rates.

During the period 1816–61 many new administrative features relating to valuation were developed, extended, and standardized. By the appraisement acts of 1818 and 1823 government appraisers were appointed at the principal ports; invoice consulation prior to exportation was required; forms of declarations and oaths were elaborated; and undervaluation penalties were established. Numerous Treasury regulations governing the treatment of charges, commissions, discounts, consigned goods, the administration of forfeitures, and other details were issued throughout the period. In 1851 Congress created the position of general appraiser and provided that four such appraisers be appointed to visit the several ports and to standardize valuation methods. Between 1816 and 1833 there was much antagonism toward foreign importers, especially on the part of domestic producers, because of the foreigners' ability to clear merchandise at low values; this resulted partly from the inadequacy of the law to deal with the problems of valuing nonpurchased goods and partly from the facilities for disposition of merchandise through the auction system and had the effect of concentrating certain lines of imported merchandise into the hands of foreign exporters and manufacturers.

The period of rising protection also marked the appearance of a number of other valuation issues important to customs history. These included the first debates over "home valuation" and its brief trial and abandonment in 1842; the temporary adoption in 1828, and the later permanent adoption by the Act of 1842, of general market price instead of specific purchase price in foreign markets as the basis for dutiable value; the first major custom-house scandals, chiefly at New York, involving political corruption, dubious relationships between the custom house and domestic producers, considerable technical if not actual undervaluation by importers, and a fairly systematic operation of the seizure bureau in conjunction with the "moieties" provision of the law. This was followed by the ad valorem–specific-duty controversy, particularly during the regime of Secretary Walker. During the last fifteen years of this period domestic prosperity and abundant revenue under increased commerce and declining duties were accompanied by the waning of the tariff controversy; at this stage in the nation's history it appeared that low duties, if not free trade, might become the established policy of the United States.

3. *Valuation under high protection.*—The Civil War resulted in a sudden reversal of the policy of low duties and firmly re-established the protective principle which had been bitterly fought by the South for the previous forty years. The war and postwar administrative measures were harsh and punitive. The system of triplicate consular invoices was established coincidentally with the appointment of the first United States foreign-revenue agents and the strengthening of the office of solicitor of the Treasury. Because of poor selections and the methods which they employed, the first Treasury agents acquired a bad reputation in foreign countries and initiated the resentment which was to become the permanent pattern for foreign attitudes toward value investigations abroad. Following the appointment of foreign agents and a corresponding group of special customs investigators in the United States, numerous seizures and forfeitures of imported merchandise for alleged undervaluation were made. From 1867 to 1874 fines, forfeitures, and compromise settlements reached a new high level and the distribution of the proceeds among the principal officers and agents resulted in the personal enrichment of public officials and encouraged initial laxity in the clearance of goods followed by harsh and technical exaction of penalties. The ensuing national scandal, turning upon the Phelps-Dodge case, resulted in a series of congressional investigations and the passage of the Anti-moiety Act of 1874.

The following years witnessed a marked increase in the number and kinds of technical administrative problems and formalities relating to valuation matters. Such problems were most numerous and representative at the port of New York, which cleared over three-fourths of all imports during the latter part of the nineteenth century. The Tariff Act of 1883, by exempting containers and coverings as dutiable charges, created widespread confusion in appraisement and promoted attempts at evasion of duties; the same act established cost of production as an alternate basis of dutiable value. The problem of importers' avoidance of undervaluation penalties by the use of *pro forma* invoices reached substantial proportions; appeals to reappraisement multiplied; the overburdened general appraisers were obliged by necessity to delegate more and more hearings to merchant appraisers; reappraisement proceedings at New York developed into a judicial type of proceeding, opposed by the Secretary of the Treasury but forming the pattern for subsequent legislation. Customs litigation and the activities of customs brokers and lawyers increased rapidly; federal-court calendars, especially in the southern district of New York, became so congested with customs cases that relief to importers for duties excessively exacted did not appear to be possible "within a generation." These conditions led to the passage of the Customs Administrative Act of 1890, the principal feature of which was the creation of the nine-man Board of General Appraisers. At first subject to some supervision by the Secretary of the Treasury because of its presumed administrative functions, the board eventually became an independent judicial body; in its early years it disposed of the accumulated, as well as of the new, customs litigation with such remarkable dispatch that it fulfilled, if not exceeded, the expectations of the framers of the act.

The 1894 and 1897 tariff acts made minor changes in valuation law, the latter introducing the first provision for United States value. In 1898 the Supreme Court handed down the Passavant decision, holding that prices for home consumption rather than prices for export in foreign markets were to be used as the basis for dutiable value. This decision profoundly affected the law of dutiable value, and its repercussions are still felt today.

The Payne Act of 1909 made a number of important changes. In addition to refining the substantive definitions of dutiable value it gave the Board of General Appraisers full judicial powers and created the Court of Customs Appeals. It also established the office of assistant attorney-general for customs and placed under the Department of

Justice the responsibility for the preparation and conduct of the government's interest in court cases, functions formerly divided between the office of solicitor of the Treasury and federal district attorneys. In the interval between 1909 and 1913, under the direction of Collector Loeb and Secretary of the Treasury MacVeagh, there was a resurgence of seizures and forfeitures for undervaluation at the port of New York; fines and settlements amounting to over five million dollars exceeded in dollar terms even those at the climax of the moieties system. The Underwood Tariff of 1913 made a number of administrative changes in valuation procedures, the principal one being the introduction of the "duress entry" privilege, granting importers at least partial relief from hardships under the "entered value minimum" proviso. A number of important changes were made by the Emergency Tariff Act of 1921. This act provided for "export value," to be used in the absence of, or when higher than, foreign value; it established new currency conversion rules, requiring the use of current foreign-exchange rates instead of mint parities in cases of substantial divergence; and it contained the Anti-dumping Law, which required special valuation procedures for its implementation.

The greatest changes in statutory valuation law and in customs administration in many years were effected by the Tariff Act of 1922, the administrative provisions of which were based largely on Tariff Commission recommendations. As a result of the pressure for the general adoption of "American valuation," which reached its climax during the debates on the Fordney Bill, the act incorporated American selling price as the basis for dutiable value for coal-tar products and certain items subject to presidential proclamation under the "flexible" provisions of the tariff. Export value was made a permanent part of valuation law and in subsequent practice became an important basis of valuation. The other bases for dutiable value were carefully redefined and placed in substantially their present form. All dutiable "charges" became part of appraised value, were thus placed under the jurisdiction of the appraiser instead of the collector, and formed a part of value for purposes of classification and the levy of additional duties. The Board of General Appraisers was given general power to make remission of additional duties for undervaluation. A liberalization of "duress entry" and "amended entry" features was made, and "final appraised" rather than "entered" value thereafter determined classification by value.

Relatively few important changes in statutory valuation law have been made since 1922. The Board of General Appraisers became the United States Customs Court in 1926, and in 1929 the appellate court was given jurisdiction over patent matters and became the Court of Customs and Patent Appeals. The Tariff Act of 1930 made a number of refinements and, in response to the continued but somewhat abated pressure for American valuation, directed the Tariff Commission to make studies of valuation methods. These were made but resulted in no additional legislation. Other changes in valuation law, of minor importance, were made by the Customs Administrative Act of 1938.

The most important developments in valuation law in recent years have been accomplished not by statutory changes but by administrative and court interpretation of the statutes. As a result, the structure of valuation law has become highly complicated, giving rise to serious problems of administration, producing anomalies in both substance and procedure, and adding substantially to the burden of administrative protection imposed by the tariff.

Some General Observations

THE PRESENT STATE OF DUTIABLE VALUE
IN THE UNITED STATES

The law of dutiable value in the United States today is exceedingly complex, resulting in a wide measure of uncertainty, delay, and injustice in the levy of ad valorem duties. Administration of the law has become increasingly difficult, with ensuing delays in appraisement of merchandise and liquidation of duties for months and sometimes years after importation. As a result, importers are often obliged to carry a heavy load of contingent liability for increased and additional duties which may fall with crushing effect long after their goods have been sold and distributed in the commerce of the nation.

Accompanying the complication of the law has been an increase in customs litigation, which feeds upon itself and results in further complexity of the law. The costs of such litigation form a part of the tariff burden upon the American consuming public. Even the transaction of routine custom-house business, apart from litigation, has become so highly technical that few importers attempt to handle it themselves, and, since customs brokers must live, the cost of their services is part of the total tariff burden. Many other purely administrative costs of customs valuation add to the general burden of "administrative protection" provided by the tariff.

But the costs of valuation procedures do not stop with purely administrative or "operating" costs and the immeasurable but real costs of uncertainty and delay. Even more important are the substantive effects upon duty levels resulting from increases in dutiable values far beyond the prices actually paid for imported merchandise. Occasionally—as in the case of the minimum-value and American selling-price provisions—the substantive increase in tariff duties by means of special valuation devices has been a deliberate legislative policy adopted by Congress in order to conceal from the public the true costs of the American tariff system. For the most part, however, the increase in dutiable values beyond prices actually paid by importers has been the result of a variety of factors. One such factor of long standing has been the fear on the part of administrators and legislators of widespread undervaluation. This fear, partly justified at the time, was the primary reason for the change from specific purchase price to market price, which relieved customs officers of complete dependence upon evidence of dutiable value furnished by individual importers. So long as dutiable value was based upon specific purchase price, proof of fraudulent undervaluation was exceedingly difficult. It was, in fact, during the period of specific purchase price that additional duties for undervaluation were inaugurated along with other punitive and enforcement measures. Such measures were originally designed for the punishment and prevention of fraud. But these measures persisted long after the adoption of the market-price principle, which gave government officers the power to compel payment of duties on values independent of importers' invoices, thereby providing basic protection to the revenue. The persistence of these measures in varying degree into the twentieth century gives to valuation law today much of its punitive flavor and explains the existence of statutory anomalies and absurdities otherwise difficult to comprehend.

The reasons for the persistence of these features are fairly evident. Legislative delays in the correction of the details of administrative law are notorious. In addition there has been the positive and successful opposition of domestic producers to changes which tend to reduce tariff burdens of any kind. Importers are a small and relatively defenseless minority group, and the nature of their business lends itself to attack with all the force that bigotry and chauvinism can bring to bear. Indeed it is the anomalous nature of the tariff as a whole which explains many of the anomalies of its administrative provisions. It is inconceivable that the Congress of the United States would ever incorporate into the income-tax laws an administrative provision permitting the General Motors Corporation to protest the tax paid by the Ford Motor Company on the ground that it was too low. Yet the tariff act of the United States permits an American businessman to hale another American businessman into court because the tax paid by the latter on merchandise bought and sold in the course of his business is too low to suit his competitor. Clearly it is not a cause for surprise to find less than satisfactory justice in the administrative provisions of a law whose fundamental purpose is oriented in the direction indicated.

Along with the foregoing factors in the shaping of the law have been the inevitably strange results of court-made law built upon an elaborate structure of precedent and technicality. It is sometimes remarked by those who deal with the law that a strange result may not make good sense but often makes "good law." Only upon some such assumption can the layman understand why "price . . . in the usual wholesale quantities" is not the wholesale price for a given quantity but the retail price for that same quantity; why "ordinary course of trade" is not that of 99 per cent of the trade but is governed by the remaining 1 per cent; and why a legally compulsory expenditure between the port of exportation and the place of delivery is not a necessary expense between the port of exportation and the place of delivery.[1]

This mixture of purposes, motives, and circumstances has resulted in laws, administrative regulations, and judicial decisions which have created an ever widening gap between the primary basis of dutiable value and prices actually paid for merchandise imported into the United States. Nevertheless, partly because the letter of the law is impossible of fulfilment and partly because technicality can be matched with technicality, *de facto* dutiable values for a large proportion of imported merchandise do, in reality, approximate prices actu-

1. For relevant cases cf. *supra*, pp. 177–78; p. 295, n. 46; p. 297, n. 51.

ally paid by importers. This has been made possible by the reintroduction into the statute—under its own name—of export value, the basis for dutiable value originally contemplated by the adoption of "actual market price" at the time of the change from specific purchase price. Ironically, the purpose of its reintroduction was not to afford relief to importers and the American public from the existing artificiality of dutiable value but to increase still further the barriers to the internationally profitable flow of commerce. Export value was accordingly made applicable only when *higher* than foreign value. But the same processes of ratiocination and interpretative legerdemain which have operated to complicate "foreign value" beyond recognition have also operated in large measure to complicate it out of existence. As a consequence, export value, by its nature confined to a relatively restricted and homogeneous set of conditions, was left as the applicable basis for an important, if not the dominant, share of importations.

The conclusion to be drawn is that, while there is a substantial degree of injustice, eccentricity, and absurdity in customs valuation in the United States today, there is also a substantial degree of practical justice and sanity. And, to correct any unfortunate impressions that might easily have resulted from the tenor of much that has been said in the course of this study, it should be explicitly stated that customs administrators, appraisers, and judges have contributed their share to the equitable operation of the law. The important task that remains is the extension and generalization of the equitable features of the law to insure their application as uniformly and universally as possible. The greatest single prerequisite to the achievement of this purpose is the categorical elimination of "foreign value" from the tariff law of the United States.

DUTIABLE VALUE AND THE AD VALOREM PRINCIPLE

The history of dutiable value in the United States, the shift from specific purchase price to market price, and the complex of problems eventually associated with the determination of market price for appraisement purposes, all raise some fundamental questions with respect to the nature and effects of the ad valorem principle. It is appropriate at this time, both as a result of a detailed study of dutiable value and as background for specific proposals for valuation reform, to reach some conclusions regarding the principle in question.

A basic assumption underlying the use of ad valorem duties, and generally accepted in the planning and execution of tariff policy, is the proposition that tariff *rates,* not dutiable values, furnish the only legitimate or desirable means of establishing or varying levels of revenue yield and tariff protection. Deliberate legislative departures from this principle for the purpose of increasing and misrepresenting the degree of tariff protection, such as in the case of the use of the American-selling-price basis of value, are recognized as violations of the principle and have succeeded historically in a few cases only because of successful pressure brought to bear by highly organized special-interest groups. Normally the selection of an appropriate standard or definition of dutiable value revolves about two major considerations—administrative workability and the criteria of desirability of the standard itself. The present discussion is primarily concerned with the latter and takes its point of departure from a comparison of the nature and effects of the two general historical types of dutiable value in the United States: specific purchase price, and an ideal type— however defined and applied—known as "market price."

A significant feature of the use of specific purchase price is its reliance upon prices actually paid by importers as the measure of value of the merchandise taxed. It thus results in a uniform, proportional tariff levy upon actual transaction values. It is unconcerned with the fact that differential money amounts per physical unit or "article" of import may be levied as a result of differential quantity buying or other terms of sale. The "market price" principle, on the other hand, represents the compulsion to elicit a single dutiable value for a previously defined physical unit of import. It thus seeks to achieve, at any given time, the results of a specific duty—the levy of a uniform money amount per physical commodity unit. To illustrate the difference in principle, suppose two hypothetical shipments consisting of 10 and 10,000 units of a given article to be imported under a 50 per cent rate at unit prices of $1.00 and $0.40, respectively, representing differential quantity buying. On the basis of specific purchase price each would pay a uniform, proportional rate of 50 per cent upon transaction value. If, however, an arbitrary doctrine of valuation required a single dutiable value per article at the highest price for both importations, the lower-priced article would pay the highly regressive tax of 125 per cent upon actual transaction value.

This last case illustrates, in principle, the type of regressive taxation legally in effect in the levy of "ad valorem" tariff duties in the United States today. It is the end result of a long series of changes beginning with the shift from specific purchase price to market price, progressing through the Passavant decision, the statutory adoption of the Passavant principle, the "major portion of sales" doctrine, the "all purchasers" rule, and culminating in the use of retail prices in foreign markets unrelated to import transactions for the United States.

Among the many causes underlying this development has been a curious conception of justice or equity in taxation—the notion that the levy of a uniform money amount per physical unit of import is either the only or the most equitable type of "uniformity" in commodity taxation. This notion is often expressed in the form of such common-sense propositions as "Why should one man be allowed to pay a lower tariff duty than another merely because he acquired his goods at a lower price?" It is hardly necessary explicitly to cancel out this proposition by giving expression to its converse, nor should it be necessary to debate the relevance of prices to the collection of ad valorem duties. Yet the conception in question is often represented as an essential principle of equitable tariff taxation.

Adequate discussion of the various possible kinds of "uniformity" in the taxation of commodities would lead far afield of the present study. For present purposes it is sufficient to state that there are many possible conceptions of uniformity and that the equitable superiority of one over another requires more than that it belong to the general class. In the levy of ad valorem duties, a prima facie case would appear to exist for the preference of a uniform, proportional levy upon transaction value, rather than a uniform money levy per physical commodity unit. This last species of uniformity, represented par excellence by the specific-duty principle and to a less extent by the "market-price" principle, derives its plausibility as a requirement of the levy of ad valorem duties from the notion that there must exist a "true" value for each unit of imported merchandise and that equity demands that all duties be levied on the basis of such "true" values. For lack of a better assumption, it may be presumed that the notion in question stems from the "normal-price" concept of value theory in economics. Granted that the "normal" or "equilibrium" price concept of economic theory furnishes a useful tool in the description of the operation of the price system and that valid conclusions may be drawn from it with respect to the allocation of resources and the maximization of real income, its specific relevance to equity in import taxation is not at all clear. Certainly it is not to be supposed that importers are seriously concerned with the "inequity" of the levy of ad valorem duties on the basis of prices actually paid.

This has especial force when it is considered that the importation of identical "articles" by different importers under ad valorem rates is the exception rather than the rule. The *raison d'être* of ad valorem duties is the prevalence of dissimilarity and product differentiation, requiring a uniform rule of taxation largely independent of the physical characteristics of the article taxed. The ad valorem principle reflects a more complete adaptation to a money economy than does the specific-duty principle, which results in regressive taxation not only at a given time with respect to differential transaction prices but through time with respect to price fluctuations.

Apart from these considerations the attempt to tie the application of ad valorem duties to the characteristics of the quasi-specific duty or "market-price" principle is bound to defeat the very kind of uniformity which the latter professes, namely, uniformity with respect to hypothetical "true" values. Since different classes of merchandise are imported under widely differing conditions and terms of sale, importations of those classes which are uniformly purchased in the various markets of the country of exportation in large quantities with the benefit of uniformly large quantity discounts will, under the "market-price" principle, pay duty on dutiable values reflecting such large discounts. Other classes of merchandise which are uniformly exported at such large discounts but which are offered and occasionally sold to local dealers at list prices will not receive the benefit of wholesale prices for dutiable value. Thus the attempt to base duties upon a single, hypothetical "true" value actually promotes widespread lack of uniformity in valuation policy for imported merchandise as a whole.

The specific-purchase-price basis of dutiable value, on the other hand, automatically gives effect to all the countless differential terms and conditions of sale for all classes of merchandise. Such terms and conditions explain and "justify" apparent deviations from "true" market price to the extent that they represent genuine economies, as in the case of large-quantity buying, which are really consistent with such "true" market price. Whether or not monopolistic or other elements concerned would lead to an equilibrium price different from "true" competitive market price, it is certain that the necessity of selecting a single dutiable value results in departures from "true" values reflecting bona fide price differentials.

The burden of this discussion is that specific purchase price is the most satisfactory "ideal" form of dutiable value. If it is to be rejected as a practicable basis, this must be done on grounds of administrative unworkability rather than of theoretical undesirability. The only objectionable lack of uniformity in its application is the lack of uniformity resulting from payment of duty by fraudulent importers upon less than the true price actually paid. Whether and to what extent this consideration would be a substantial barrier to its workability under twentieth-century conditions—conditions which permit the successful operation of the income-tax law faced by far greater administrative problems—the writer is not prepared to say. In any case, the satisfactoriness of an alternative basis must be judged largely in terms of its approximation to the actual prices paid by importers for their merchandise.

Proposals for Valuation Reform

This study has indicated, and the proposed charter for an international trade organization recognizes, the need for valuation reform. Although it is not within the scope of this study to present a detailed blueprint for valuation reform in the United States, a basic plan for the implementation of the charter in this country is proposed, with reference to modifications elsewhere proposed and several suggestions for the correction of specific defects of the present law.

Export value as the primary basis of dutiable value.[2]—This plan offers substantial advantages in terms of simplicity, certainty, equity, economy of administration, and a minimum of friction with foreign countries. It proposes the abolition of foreign value and the use of export value, liberally defined, as the primary basis of dutiable value. It would retain, as alternate bases for application to nonpurchased goods, etc., United States value and cost of production, modified to

2. This has also been advocated by the National Council of American Importers in their brochure of suggested changes (cf. *supra*, p. 326, n. 67).

eliminate so far as possible the objections to them as they are currently applied.

The adoption of export value, instead of unqualified purchase price,
would avoid the difficulties experienced by the United States in the
first fifty years of its history—the dependence of customs officers upon
the individual invoices of the merchandise undergoing appraisement.
On the other hand, the plan would avoid the difficulties of the last
fifty years—the use of prices, real or imaginary, which diverge substantially from the prices at which merchandise is actually imported
into the United States. With this as the express policy of valuation
reform, the specific wording of the new definition in the statute—
including the definitions of United States value and cost of production—could be developed by a committee of experts, drawing liberally
from the knowledge of experienced appraisers, customs-court judges,
and importers' representatives. Among the specific objectives of the
new definition would be the elimination of the concept of usual wholesale quantity, allowing the price paid for imported quantities to be
applicable so long as it is freely offered for such quantities; the provision of sufficient flexibility in the definition to insure wide application
of the primary basis of value; and the elimination of the use of offered
prices except in the absence of sales.[3]

It is believed that this proposal fulfils every requirement of the
I.T.O. charter. It would approximate actual import transaction prices
as closely as possible short of adopting specific purchase price itself
as the basis of dutiable value. The elimination of foreign value would
exclude all "home-market" considerations in the country of export,
considerations which often have little or no relevance to market prices
under which merchandise is exported to the United States. This would
automatically exclude from dutiable value the amounts of foreign
taxes, drawbacks, etc.—an exclusion implied by paragraph 4 of
the valuation article of the charter. The close approximation to transaction prices resulting from this proposal would improve the import
statistics of the United States, both for balance-of-payments purposes
and for purposes of comparison with the import statistics of other

3. The elimination of offers except in the absence of sales is the proposal of the
National Council of American Importers (*ibid.*).

nations.[4] Greater equity would be accorded importers, and dutiable values for purposes of both revenue and protection would reflect more nearly the actual underlying economic considerations relevant to such purposes.

Administratively the plan has much to recommend it. Narrowing the field of value investigations to the export markets in the countries concerned would reduce the problem of customs valuation to manageable proportions. A relatively homogeneous set of conditions would replace the multiplicity and complexity which today often make literal application of the law either impossible or absurd. If investigations were confined to actual import transactions, most of the data would be available in the files of importers in this country. Supplementary value investigations abroad would create far less resentment in foreign countries than heretofore for the twofold reason that (1) their scope would be greatly reduced, and (2) their appropriateness and propriety would be greatly enhanced. Few impositions can be more irritating to any businessman than the compulsion to divulge to an agent of a foreign government details of his business which have no apparent or just relevance to the real problem at hand, regardless of their relevance in terms of foreign statutory requirements.

No additional information would be needed by appraisers in the administration of the proposed plan. On the contrary, the information currently most difficult of access to appraisers under the present law, the existence and nature of foreign taxes, price data, terms of sale, and other information pertaining to prices "for home consumption"—information unrelated to export transactions and available only in foreign countries—would no longer be required. Far from upsetting long-established administrative tradition and experience, this proposal would retain the essentials of such experience while making possible greater expedition, certainty, and uniformity in the valuation of imported merchandise.

4. The comparability of foreign-trade statistics of the various nations depends not only upon their relevance to transaction prices but also upon common practice in either including or excluding charges between the port of exportation and the port of delivery. Since the uniform exclusion of such charges is essential for balance-of-payments analysis, it would be desirable that all nations record such charges separately for statistical purposes even when using a "landed-cost" basis for customs valuation.

Other valuation changes.—In its brochure of suggested changes in the customs administrative laws the National Council of American Importers has made a number of other recommendations for the correction of anomalies in valuation procedure. The following are among the more significant of these recommendations.

1. Elimination of the statutory 8 and 8 per cent limitations on deductions for profit and general expenses in the definition of United States value
2. Restoration of the 50 per cent maximum addition for profit in the cost-of-production formula, as carried in the 1909 and 1913 tariff acts
3. Exemption of application of additional (undervaluation penalty) duties in cases where the appraiser's increase over entered value is due to a change in the basis of valuation
4. Elimination of the presumption of fraud and seizure of goods when appraised value exceeds entered value by more than 100 per cent
5. Requirement of appraisement within 120 days after date of entry, with entered value to become final thereafter unless the collector files an appeal within 180 days after entry
6. Elimination of the entered-value minimum provision

As indicated either explicitly or by implication throughout the body of this study, all these proposals are desirable and would appear to constitute minimum requirements in a program of valuation reform. Two other essentials not proposed by the importers' association are the abolition of American selling price and the correction of value-bracket anomalies. American selling price is explicitly incompatible with paragraph 3(a) of the valuation provisions of the charter and in any case is no longer required by its primary beneficiary, the chemical and dye industry. Apart from the fact that its chief competitor has been destroyed and that it has recently gained access to numerous valuable patents and formulas supposedly constituting the principal original foreign advantage, this industry has long left the infant stage and is well able to stand on its own feet. The continued existence of specially exaggerated protection for this industry which has been able for years to export its products at dumping prices is an imposition upon the American consumer which only the most credulous or the most interested would seek to defend.

So far as value brackets are concerned, their complete elimination can be recommended unequivocally. Simple ad valorem rates can grant as much or greater protection without producing the patent absurdities of the specific and compound rates illustrated in the text.

Appraisement procedures are required in any case, and the actual or potential assessment of hundreds or thousands of dollars in increased duties on individual shipments because of a minor fluctuation in a foreign currency or doubts as to the nature of a $7.50 box is an extreme price for the American public to pay for the privilege of being kept in luxurious ignorance of the true levels of tariff rates. If, however, the perpetuation of such ignorance is a "must" item in United States tariff policy, the least that can be done is to adjust rates and to narrow the class limits of value brackets to the point where rough proportionality of taxation obtains for all value classes of a given kind of merchandise. There will always be inevitable injustice in the administration of even the hypothetically most perfect tariff law, but there is no necessity for the perpetuation of manifest and remediable absurdity.

BIBLIOGRAPHY

BIBLIOGRAPHY

BIBLIOGRAPHY

BOOKS

ADAMS, HENRY C. *Taxation in the United States, 1789–1861.* ("Johns-Hopkins University Studies in Historical and Political Science," Nos. 5 and 6.) Baltimore: Johns Hopkins University, 1884.

APPLETON, NATHAN. *Introduction of the Power Loom and Origin of Lowell.* Lowell, Mass., 1858.

BIDWELL, PERCY WELLS. *The Invisible Tariff.* New York: Council on Foreign Relations, 1939.

BOLLES, ALBERT S. *Financial History of the United States, 1789–1860.* New York: Appleton, 1883.

———. *Financial History of the United States, 1861–1885.* 2d ed. New York: Appleton, 1894.

BRICE, JOHN. *A Selection of All the Laws of the United States Relative to Commercial Subjects.* Baltimore: Neale, Willis & Cole, 1814.

BUCK, NORMAN SYDNEY. *The Development of the Organization of Anglo-American Trade, 1800–1850.* New Haven: Yale University Press, 1925.

BUTTERBAUGH, WAYNE EDGAR. *Principles of Importing.* New York: Appleton, 1924.

COKE, ROGER. *A Treatise Wherein It Is Demonstrated, that the Church and State of England, Are in Equal Danger with the Trade of It,* Treatise II: "Reasons of the Increase of the Dutch Trade, etc." London, 1671.

COLTON, CALVIN. *Public Economy for the United States.* 3d ed. New York: A. S. Barnes, 1853.

Custom House Guide. 1946 ed. New York: John F. Budd, 1946.

DEWEY, DAVIS R. *Financial History of the United States.* 12th ed. New York: Longmans, 1934.

EDGAR, WILLIAM. *Vestigalium Systema, or, a New Book of Rates.* 2d ed. London, 1718.

Exporters' Encyclopaedia. 1904———. New York: Exporters' Encyclopaedia Corp., 1904———.

FAIRLIE, JOHN A. *The National Administration of the United States.* New York: Macmillan, 1905.

FUTRELL, WILLIAM H. *The History of American Customs Jurisprudence.* New York, 1941.

GERSTING, J. MARSHALL. *The Flexible Provisions of the United States Tariff.* Ph.D. dissertation, University of Pennsylvania, Philadelphia, 1932.

GOSS, JOHN DEAN. *A History of Tariff Administration in the United States, from Colonial Times to the McKinley Administrative Bill.* ("Columbia University Studies in History, Economics, and Public Law," Vol. I, No. 2.) 2d ed. New York, 1897.

GRAS, N. S. B. *The Early English Customs System.* ("Harvard Economic

Series," Vol. XVIII.) Cambridge, Mass.: Harvard University Press, 1918.

GREGORY, T. E. G. *Tariffs: A Study in Method.* London: Griffin, 1921.

HABERLER, GOTTFRIED. *Der Internationale Handel.* Berlin: Springer, 1933. Available in English under the title, *The Theory of International Trade.* Trans. Alfred Stonier and Frederic Benham. London: W. Hodge & Co., Ltd., 1936.

HARVEY, A. S. *The General Tariff of the United Kingdom.* London: Pitman, 1933.

HEATON, HERBERT. *The Yorkshire Woolen and Worsted Industries.* ("Oxford Historical and Literary Studies," Vol. X.) Oxford: Oxford University Press, 1920.

HIGGINSON, JOHN HEDLEY. *Tariffs at Work.* London: King, 1913.

HILL, WILLIAM. *The First Stages of the Tariff Policy of the United States.* ("Publications of the American Economic Association," Vol. VIII, No. 6.) Baltimore: American Economic Association, 1893.

KOEHLER, GEORGE F. *Importers First Aid.* Washington: Importers First Aid Service, 1919.

KREIDER, CARL. *The Anglo-American Trade Agreement.* Princeton: Princeton University Press, 1943.

LARKIN, JOHN DAY. *The President's Control of the Tariff.* ("Harvard Political Studies.") Cambridge, Mass.: Harvard University Press, 1936.

LEVETT, BENJAMIN ARTHUR. *Through the Customs Maze.* New York: Customs Maze Pub. Co., 1923.

MAYO, ROBERT. *A Synopsis of the Commercial and Revenue System of the United States.* 2 vols. Washington: J. & S. Gideon, 1847.

NEW YORK HISTORICAL SOCIETY. *Collections.* Vol. I. New York, 1841.

NUSSBAUM, ARTHUR. *Money in the Law.* Chicago: Foundation Press, 1939.

OGDEN, E. D. *Tariff or Rates of Duties, etc., in Conformity with the Act of Congress Approved August 30, 1842: Also Containing All the Recent Circulars and Decisions of the Treasury Department Relating to Commerce and the Revenue.* New York: Rich & Loutrel, 1844.

———. *Tariff or Rates of Duties, etc., in Conformity with the Act of Congress Approved July 30, 1846: Also Containing All the Recent Circulars and Decisions of the Treasury Department Relating to Commerce and the Revenue.* New York: Rich & Loutrel, 1846.

PAGE, THOMAS WALKER. *Making the Tariff in the United States.* New York: McGraw, 1924.

PARTON, JAMES. *Life of Andrew Jackson.* 3 vols. New York: Mason Bros., 1860.

PETRUZZELLI, NICHOLAS. *Some Technical Aspects of Foreign Trade Statistics with Special Reference to Valuation.* Washington: Murray & Heister, 1946.

STANWOOD, EDWARD. *American Tariff Controversies in the Nineteenth Century.* 2 vols. Boston: Houghton, 1903.

STERN, CARL W. *Importing, with Special Attention to Customs Requirements.* ("Business Training Corporation, Course in Foreign Trade," Vol. XI.) New York: Business Training Corp., 1916.

STUART, GRAHAM. *American Diplomatic and Consular Practice.* New York: Appleton, 1936.

SUMNER, WILLIAM GRAHAM. *Andrew Jackson.* ("American Statesmen" ser.) Boston: Houghton, 1900.

TAUSSIG, F. W. *State Papers and Speeches on the Tariff.* Cambridge, Mass.: Harvard University, 1893.

———. *Tariff History of the United States.* 7th ed. New York: Putnam, 1923.

VALLOTTON, JAMES. *De la juridiction administrative fédérale des États-Unis et de la Suisse en matière de douanes.* Lausanne: F. Rouge et Cie, 1905.

VANDEGRIFT & Co. *United States Tariff, Act of 1930.* New York: Vandegrift & Co., 1931.

VINER, JACOB. *Dumping: A Problem in International Trade.* Chicago: University of Chicago Press, 1923.

WELLS, DAVID A. *Congress and Phelps, Dodge and Company: An Extraordinary History.* New York, 1875.

WOODWARD, W. E. *A New American History.* New York: Farrar, 1936.

WRIGHT, CHESTER W. *Economic History of the United States.* 1st ed. New York: McGraw, 1941.

ARTICLES

BERGLUND, ABRAHAM. "The Ferroalloy Industries and Tariff Legislation," *Political Science Quarterly,* XXXVI (June, 1921), 245–73.

BROWN, GEORGE STEWART. "Judicial Review in Customs Taxation," *The Forum,* LX (July, 1918), 96–110.

CURTIS, JAMES F. "The Administrative Provisions of the Revenue Act of 1913," *Quarterly Journal of Economics,* XXVIII (November, 1913), 31–45.

GOODNOW, FRANK. "The Collection of Duties," *Political Science Quarterly,* I (March, 1886), 36–44.

HEATON, HERBERT. "Yorkshire Cloth Traders in the United States, 1770–1840," *Publications of the Thoresby Society, Miscellany,* XXXVIII, Part III, 1941 vol. (April, 1944), 225–87.

HOFFMAN, I. NEWTON. "Customs Administration under the 1913 Tariff Act," *Journal of Political Economy,* XXII (November, 1914), 845–71.

KREIDER, CARL. "Valuation for Customs," *Quarterly Journal of Economics,* LVI (November, 1941), 157–59.

MARSHALL, HERBERT. "Recent Developments in Balance of International Payments Statistics," in H. A. INNIS (ed.), *Essays in Transportation in Honour of W. T. Jackman,* pp. 145–57. Toronto: University of Toronto Press, 1941.

MEARS, ELIOT. "The Foreign Trade Statistics of the United States," *Journal of the American Statistical Association,* XXX (September, 1935), 501–16.

MUHLBACH, WALTER. "Tariff Devices To Meet a Problem of Depreciating Currencies," *Journal of Political Economy,* XXXIII (June, 1925), 293–317.

Nussbaum, Arthur. "The Pound-Dollar Ratio before the Supreme Court: *Barr* v. *United States,*" 45 Columbia Law Review 412 (May, 1945).

Radcliffe, Harry S. "Congress Urged To Modify Rules for Valuing Imports," *Journal of Commerce and Commercial,* CCXI (February 24, 1947), 18A.

Rutter, Frank R. "Statistics of Imports and Exports," *Journal of the American Statistical Association,* XV (March, 1916), 16–34.

Taussig, F. W. "The Tariff Act of 1922," *Quarterly Journal of Economics,* XXXVII (November, 1922), 1–28.

Wells, David A. "The Meaning of Revenue Reform," *North American Review,* LXIII (July, 1871), 104–53.

Westerfield, Ray Bert. "Early History of American Auctions: A Chapter in Commercial History," *Transactions of the Connecticut Academy of Arts and Sciences,* XXIII (May, 1920), 159–210.

Wirt, Henry. "The First Legislative Assembly," *American Historical Association, Annual Report for the Year 1893.* Washington, 1894.

PUBLIC DOCUMENTS

UNITED STATES[1]

U.S. Congress. *American State Papers: Class III, Finance.*

——. *Annals of Congress.*

——. *Congressional Debates.*

——. *Congressional Globe.*

——. *Congressional Record.*

U.S. Congress, House. *Letter from the Secretary of the Treasury in Relation to the Collection of Duties on Imports and Tonnage, January 29, 1823.* (House Doc. 50.) 17th Cong., 2d sess., 1823.

——. *Investigation of the New York Custom House: Message of the President in Response to Resolution of the House of Representatives of February 9, 1842.* (House Doc. 77.) 27th Cong., 2d sess., 1842.

——. *Investigation of New York Custom House: Message of the President Transmitting Communication of Benjamin F. Butler, Samuel Lawrence, and William W. Stone in Defense against Mr. Poindexter's Report.* (House Doc. 230.) 27th Cong., 2d sess., 1842.

——. *Duties on Imports . . . Tables Showing the Rates of Duties Imposed by the Tariff Acts of 1816, 1824, 1828, and 1832 . . . to Which Are Appended the Tariff Laws from 1789 to 1833.* (House Doc. 244.) 27th Cong., 2d sess., 1842.

——. *Investigation of New York Custom House: Message of the President Transmitting Reports, etc., of Commissioners.* (House Exec. Doc. 212.) 27th Cong., 2d sess., 1842.

——. *New York Custom House: Report of the Committee on Public Expenditures.* (Report No. 669.) 27th Cong., 2d sess., 1842.

1. Except as otherwise specified, the U.S. government documents listed were printed by the Government Printing Office, Washington, D.C., or by prior government printers.

——. *Validity of Tariff Laws: Report of the Committee on the Judiciary on Collection of Duties under Home Valuation after July 1, 1842.* (Report No. 943.) 27th Cong., 2d sess., 1842.

——. *Navigation, Revenue, and Collection Laws.* (Report No. 145.) 33d Cong., 2d sess., 1855.

——. *Frauds on the Revenue: Report of the Committee on Public Expenditures in Response to House Resolution of April 30, 1866.* (House Report No. 15.) 39th Cong., 2d sess., 1867.

——. *New York Custom House: Report of the Committee on Public Expenditures.* (House Report No. 30.) 39th Cong., 2d sess., 1867.

——. *Suits, etc., for Violation of the Revenue Laws: Letter from the Secretary of the Treasury Relative to the Amount of Money Paid . . . for the Violation of the Revenue Laws at the Boston and New York Custom Houses.* (Exec. Doc. 124.) 43d Cong., 1st sess., 1874.

——. *Moieties and Customs Revenue Laws.* (Exec. Doc. 264.) 43d Cong., 1st sess., 1874.

——. *Undervaluation of Wool and Woolen Yarns: Letter of the Secretary of the Treasury in Response to House Resolution of January 7, 1884.* (Exec. Doc. 101.) 48th Cong., 1st sess., 1884.

U.S. CONGRESS, HOUSE COMMITTEE ON WAYS AND MEANS. *Revision of the Tariff: Hearings before the Committee on Ways and Means.* 51st Cong., 1st sess., 1890.

——. *Tariff Hearings before the Committee on Ways and Means.* (House Doc. 338.) 54th Cong., 2d sess., 1897.

——. *Tariff Hearings before the Committee on Ways and Means.* (House Doc. 1505.) Vol. VII: *Free List and Miscellaneous.* 60th Cong., 2d sess., 1909.

——. *Notes on Tariff Revision.* 1909.

——. *Examination of Custom House Frauds: Message from the President . . . Transmitting a Joint Report of the Secretary of the Treasury and the Attorney General . . . in the Matter of Frauds in the Customs Revenue.* (House Doc. 901.) 61st Cong., 2d Sess., 1910.

——. *Tariff Commission: Hearings.* 1910.

——. *Tariff Schedules: Hearings before the Committee on Ways and Means.* (House Doc. 1447.) Vol. VI: *Free List—Miscellaneous—Administrative.* 62d Cong., 3d sess., 1913.

——. *Report: A Bill To Reduce Tariff Duties, etc.* (House Report No. 5.) 63d Cong., 1st sess., 1913.

——. *Antidumping Legislation: Report.* (House Report No. 479.) 66th Cong., 2d sess., 1919.

——. *Emergency Tariff Bill: Conference Report on H.R. 2435.* 1921.

——. *Hearings on General Tariff Revision before the Committee on Ways and Means,* Part VI: *Administrative and Miscellaneous.* 1921.

——. *Tariff Information, 1921: Comparison of Foreign Selling Prices and Landed Costs with American Selling Prices.* 1921.

——. *Tariff Information, 1921: Customs Administrative Laws: Proposed Revisions Submitted by the U.S. Tariff Commission.* 1921.

——. *Tariff Information, 1921: Explanatory Notes with Information and Authorities Accompanying a Proposed Customs Administrative Act and Suggested Import-Duty Statutes.* 1921.

——. *Customs Administration and Personnel: Hearings before a Subcommittee of the Committee on Ways and Means.* 70th Cong., 1st sess., 1928.

——. *Tariff Readjustment, 1929: Hearings before the Committee on Ways and Means, XVI: Administrative and Miscellaneous Provisions; XVII: Supplemental Statements and Miscellaneous Data.* 70th Cong., 2d sess., 1929.

——. *Adjustment of Duties—People's Counsel—International Economic Conference: Hearings on H.R. 6662.* 1932.

——. *Equalization of Tariff Duties by Compensating for Depreciation of Foreign Currencies: Hearings on House Bills.* 1932.

——. *Equalization of Tariff Duties by Compensating for Depreciation of Foreign Currencies: Hearings before a Subcommittee of the Committee on Ways and Means on H.R. 13999.* 72d Cong., 2d sess., 1933.

——. *Customs House Brokers: Hearings before a Subcommittee of the Committee on Ways and Means on H.R. 8834.* 1935.

——. *Customs Administrative Bill: Hearings before the Committee on Ways and Means on H.R. 6738.* 75th Cong., 1st sess., 1937.

——. *Amendment to Administrative Provisions of 1930: H.R. 8099.* 1937.

——. *To Amend Certain Provisions of the Tariff Act of 1930: Hearings before a Subcommittee of the Committee on Ways and Means on H.R. 7003.* 76th Cong., 3d sess., 1940.

U.S. CONGRESS, SENATE. *Report from the Secretary of the Treasury . . . in Relation to the Cloth Cases Recently Tried in the Eastern District of Pennsylvania, Involving Forfeitures under the Revenue Laws.* (Senate Doc. 83.) 27th Cong., 3d sess., 1843.

——. *New York Custom House Investigation: Report of the Senate Committee of Investigation and Retrenchment.* (Senate Report No. 227.) 3 vols. 42d Cong., 2d sess., 1872.

——. *Report of the Secretary of the Treasury on the Abolition of Moieties.* (Senate Misc. Doc. 36.) 43d Cong., 1st sess., 1874.

U.S. CONGRESS, SENATE COMMISSION OF GOLD AND SILVER INQUIRY. *Foreign Currency and Exchange Investigation.* (Serial 9.) By JOHN PARKE YOUNG. 2 vols. 1925.

U.S. CONGRESS, SENATE COMMITTEE ON FINANCE. *Report on Undervaluation.* (Senate Report No. 1990.) 49th Cong., 2d sess., 1888.

——. *Undervaluations.* (Senate Report No. 295.) 50th Cong., 1st sess., 1888.

——. *Comparison of the Customs Law of 1883 with the New Law of 1890, with Index, to Which is Appended the Administrative Customs Law of 1890: Prepared in Accordance with Senate Resolution of December 5, 1890.* 1890.

——. *Comparison of the Tariffs of 1897, 1894, and 1890, with Index.* (Senate Doc. 192.) 55th Cong., 1st sess. (Senate Doc. 329.) 55th Cong., 2d sess., 1897–98.

———. *Customs Tariffs: Senate and House Reports, 1888, 1890, 1894, 1897.* (Senate Doc. 547.) 60th Cong., 2d sess., 1909.

———. *The Customs Administrative Laws: Hearings before a Subcommittee of the Committee on Finance.* (Senate Doc. 683.) 60th Cong., 2d sess., 1909.

———. *Selling Foreign Manufactures in United States at Prices Lower than the Domestic Prices: Letter from the Secretary of State, Transmitting, with Accompanying Papers . . . Information concerning the Practice.* (Senate Doc. 16.) 61st Cong., 1st sess., 1909.

———. *Comparison of Customs Tariff Laws 1789 to 1909 and Intermediate Legislation, with Import Data.* 1911.

———. *Tariff Handbook: Report on H.R. 3321.* 1913.

———. *Emergency Tariff: Hearings before the Committee on Finance on H.R. 15275.* 66th Cong., 3d sess., 1921.

———. *Emergency Tariff Bill: Report To Accompany H.R. 2435.* 1921.

———. *Tariff Hearings on H.R. 7456,* Part III: *American Valuation;* Parts VI–VII: *American Valuation.* 1921.

———. *Imported Merchandise and Retail Prices: Letter from the Secretary of the Treasury, Transmitting . . . a Report on Foreign and Landed Valuation of Imported Merchandise and the Retail Selling Price in the United States of the Same Merchandise.* 67th Cong., 2d sess., 1922.

———. *Tariff Act of 1929: Hearings before a Subcommittee of the Committee on Finance on H.R. 2667,* XVII: *Special and Administrative Provisions: Valuation.* 71st Cong., 1st sess., 1929.

———. *Confirmation of Members of the U.S. Tariff Commission.* 1930.

———. *Customs Administrative Act: Hearings before a Subcommittee of the Committee on Finance on H.R. 8099.* Rev. ed. 75th Cong., 3d sess., 1938.

U.S. Congress, Senate Select Committee on Investigation of the Tariff Commission. *Hearings on the Administration of the Flexible Tariff.* 2 vols. 1926–28.

U.S. Court of Customs and Patent Appeals. *Court of Customs and Patent Appeals Reports: Customs.* 1911——.

———. *Digest of Reports on Vols. I–XXII of Customs Reports.* 1936.

———. *Rules of the U.S. Court of Customs and Patent Appeals: Customs.* 1931,

U.S. Customs Court. *Reappraisements of Merchandise, 1890——; Reports, 1939——.*

———. *Rules of the United States Customs Court.* 1931.

U.S. Department of Commerce, Bureau of the Census. *Foreign Commerce and Navigation of the United States for the Calendar Year 1944.* 1946.

———. *Regulations for the Collection of Statistics of Foreign Commerce and Navigation of the United States.* Rev. to May, 1946.

———. *Statistical Abstract of the United States, 1878——.*

U.S. Department of Commerce, Bureau of Foreign and Domestic Commerce. *The Balance of International Payments of the United States, 1922——. 1923——.*

———. *Foreign Tariff Notes.* Nos. 1–42. 1910–22.

——. *Handbook of Foreign Currencies.* ("Trade Promotion Series," No. 164.) 1936.

——. "Merchandise Import Statistics in the Balance of International Payments: Report on Official W.P.A. Project No. 365-97-3-20." [New York? 1939?] (Mimeographed.)

——. "Tariff Series." (Nos. 1–42.) 1907–27.

U.S. DEPARTMENT OF JUSTICE. *Official Opinions of the Attorneys-General of the United States, Advising the President and Heads of Departments in Relation to Their Official Duties.* Vols. I—— (August 21, 1791——). 1852–19——.

U.S. DEPARTMENT OF STATE. *Foreign Service Regulations of the United States of America.* ("Loose-Leaf Series.") 1941——.

——. *Havana Charter for an International Trade Organization, March 24, 1948.* (Department of State Pub. 3117, "Commercial Policy Series," No. 113.) 1948.

——. *Papers Relating to the Foreign Relations of the United States, 1862——.*

——. *Press Releases.* Vols. I——. 1929.

U.S. LAWS, STATUTES, ETC. *Comparison of Tariff Acts of 1913, 1922, and 1930, with Index.* 1930.

——. *Statutes at Large.*

——. *Tariff Acts Passed by the Congress of the United States from 1789 to 1895 [etc.].* 1896.

——. *Tariff Acts Passed by the Congress of the United States from 1789 to 1909 [etc.].* 1909.

U.S. SUPREME COURT. *Reports of Decisions.*

U.S. TARIFF COMMISSION. *American Valuation as the Basis for Assessing Duties Ad Valorem.* 1921.

——. *Annual Reports.* 1917——.

——. *Basis of Value for the Assessment of Ad Valorem Duties in Foreign Countries.* 1932.

——. *Canned Clams: Report No. 84.* 2d ser. 1934.

——. *Computed Duties and Equivalent Ad Valorem Rates on Imports into the United States, 1929.* 1931.

——. *Computed Duties and Equivalent Ad Valorem Rates on Imports into the United States, 1929 and 1932.* 1933.

——. *Cotton Rugs: Report No. 95.* 2d ser. 1935.

——. *Customs Administrative Laws: Revision.* 1918.

——. *Depreciated Exchange and International Trade.* 1922.

——. *Depreciated Exchange: Report No. 44.* 2d ser. 1932.

——. *Dictionary of Tariff Information.* 1924.

——. *Domestic Value—Conversion of Rates: Report No. 45.* 2d ser. 1932.

——. *Dumping and Unfair Competition in the United States and Canada's Anti-dumping Law.* 1919.

——. *Effect of Depreciated Currency upon Importations of Wood and Pulpwood: Report No. 43.* 2d ser. 1932.

——. *The Ferroalloy Industries.* Rev. ed. 1921.

——. *The [First] Trade Agreement with Canada: Report No. 111.* 2d ser. 1936.

——. *The Foreign Trade of Latin America: Report No. 146.* 3 vols. 2d ser. 1942.

——. *Handbook of Commercial Treaties.* 1922.

——. *Methods of Valuation: Report No. 70.* 2d ser. 1933.

——. *Optical Fire Control Instruments: Report No. 54.* 2d ser. 1933.

——. *Rag Rugs.* 1928.

——. *Regulation of Imports by Executive Action.* Misc. ser. 1941.

——. *Regulation of Tariffs in Foreign Countries by Administrative Action.* Misc. ser. 1932.

——. *Regulation of Tariffs in Foreign Countries by Administrative Action.* Misc. ser. 1934.

——. *Relation of Duties to Value of Imports.* 1932.

——. *Rubber-soled and Rubber Footwear: Report No. 63.* 2d ser. 1933.

——. *Second Trade Agreement between the United States and Canada.* Vol. I. 1938.

——. *The Tariff: A Bibliography: A Select List of References.* 1934.

——. *The Tariff and Its History.* 1934.

——. *Taximeters.* 1926.

——. *Transportation Costs and the Value of Principal Imports.* 1940.

——. *Wool Knit Gloves and Mittens: Report No. 108.* 2d ser. 1936.

U.S. TARIFF COMMISSION, 1882. *Report.* 2 vols. 1882.

U.S. TREASURY DEPARTMENT. *Annual Reports.* 1790——.

——. *Customs Regulations of the United States, 1943.* 1943.

——. *Customs-Tariff Legislation.* (Special report by EDWARD YOUNG, Ph.D., Chief of the Bureau of Statistics.) 1874.

——. *Digest of Customs and Related Laws and Decisions Thereunder.* 3 vols. and Suppl., *1941.* 1936 and 1941.

——. *Digest of Decisions under the Customs Revenue Laws, 1883 to 1913.* 2 vols. 1918.

——. *General Regulations No. 63.* 1856.

——. *General Regulations No. 67.* 1856.

——. *General Regulations under the Revenue and Collection Laws of the United States.* 1857.

——. *Laws of the United States Relating to the Customs, together with Portions of Certain Commercial Treaties.* 1899.

——. *Report of the Appraisement Commission of the Treasury Department, December 31, 1912.* (Reprinted by the Tariff Service Record, Washington, D.C.)

——. *Revised Customs Regulations, Part IV: Entry and Appraisement of Merchandise.* 1895.

——. *Tariff Act of 1930 on Imports into the United States.* 1930.

——. *Treasury Decisions.* 1868——.

OTHER THAN UNITED STATES

AUSTRALIA. *The Acts of the Parliament of the Commonwealth of Australia, Passed from 1901 to 1935 and in Force on 1st January, 1936: Customs Act.* Canberra: L. F. Johnston, 1936.

CANADA. *The Customs Tariff and Amendments with Index to October 5, 1939, and also with Appendices.* Ottawa: J. O. Patenaude, 1939.

——. *Manitoba's Case: A Submission Presented to the Royal Commission on Dominion-Provincial Relations by the Government of the Province of Manitoba,* Part IV: "The Effects of Federal Tariff Policy on Western Canadian Economy." Winnipeg: James L. Cowie, 1937.

——. *Report of the Royal Commission on Dominion-Provincial Relations, 1940.* 3 vols. and Appen. 3 "The Economic Background of Dominion-Provincial Relations," by W. A. MACKINTOSH. Ottawa: J. O. Patenaude, 1940.

——. *Report of the Royal Commission on the Textile Industry.* Ottawa: J. O. Patenaude, 1938.

——. *The Revised Statutes of Canada, 1927: Customs Act.* Ottawa: F. A. Acland, 1927–28.

GREAT BRITAIN. *Statutes of the United Kingdom.*

GREAT BRITAIN, PARLIAMENT. *Accounts and Papers: Customs and Excise.*
——. *Parliamentary Debates.*

INTERNATIONAL CHAMBER OF COMMERCE. *The Customs Convention and Its Benefits to Trade.* (Brochure No. 33.) Paris, 1923.

——. *Report of Trade Barriers Committee.* (Brochure No. 44.) Paris, 1926.

LEAGUE OF NATIONS. *Proceedings of the Second International Conference with a View to Concerted Economic Action, Geneva, November 17–28, 1930.* 1st ser. Geneva, 1931.

——. *Report and Proceedings of the World Economic Conference, Held at Geneva, May 4–23, 1927.* Vol. II. Geneva, 1927.

LEAGUE OF NATIONS, ECONOMIC AND FINANCIAL SECTION. *International Economic Conference, Geneva, May, 1927,* Documentation, C.E.I. 28: "Methods of Assessment for the Application of Ad Valorem Duties." Geneva, 1927.

MASSACHUSETTS. *The Acts and Resolves, Public and Private, of the Province of the Massachusetts Bay . . . 1692——.* Boston: Wright & Potter, 1869–1922.

——. *The Colonial Laws of Massachusetts.* Boston: Rockwell & Churchill, 1890.

NEW YORK. *The Colonial Laws of New York from the Year 1664 to the Revolution.* Albany, 1894.

——. *Laws of New York, from the Year 1691 to 1751, Inclusive: Published According to an Act of the General Assembly.* New York, 1752.

——. *Laws and Ordinances of New Netherland, 1638–1674.* Albany, 1868.

PAMPHLETS, REPORTS, ETC.

AMERICAN INSTITUTE. *Report of a Special Committee of the American Institute on the Subject on Cash Duties, the Auction System, etc., January 12, 1829*. New York, 1829.

BARBOUR, THOMAS. *Appraisers, Spies, and Informers*. New York: Press of the Chamber of Commerce, 1874.

BRAINERD, CEPHAS. *Book Seizures, Moieties, and Informers—Indefensible*. New York, 1874.

BURKE, HON. EDMUND. *The Protective System Considered in Connection with the Present Tariff*. (A series of twelve essays originally published in the *Washington Union* over the signature of "Bundelcund.") Palmyra, N.Y.: Wayne Sentinel, 1846.

CHAMBER OF COMMERCE OF THE STATE OF NEW YORK. *Report of a Special Committee on Revenue Reform: Undervaluation and Damage Allowances*. New York, 1885.

EATON, SHERBURNE B. *A Discussion of the Constitutionality of the Act of Congress of March 2, 1867, Authorizing the Seizure of Books and Papers for Alleged Frauds upon the Revenue*. New York: Press of the Chamber of Commerce, 1874.

GIBBS, MONTGOMERY. *Letters to the Secretaries of the Treasury in Relation to the Revenue by Montgomery Gibbs, United States Revenue Agent for Europe*. December, 1867.

HOOPER, SAMUEL. *A Defense of the Merchants of Boston against Aspersions of the Hon. John Z. Goodrich, Ex-collector of Customs*. Boston: Little, 1866.

NATIONAL COUNCIL OF AMERICAN IMPORTERS, INC. *Customs Administrative Law: Changes in the Special and Administrative Provisions of the Tariff Act of 1930, as Amended*. New York, 1945.

NATIONAL FOREIGN TRADE CONVENTION. *Official Reports*. New York, 1914——.

OSBORN, WILLIAM H. *The Administration and Undervaluation Frauds on the Customs Revenue: How Manufacturers Are Ruined and Wages Cut Down*. New York, 1887.

PHILADELPHIA CHAMBER OF COMMERCE. *Essay on the Warehousing System and Government Credits of the United States*. Philadelphia, 1828.

Proceedings of a Convention of Delegates Appointed by Persons Interested in the Growth and Manufacture of Wool. (Held at Clinton Hall, N.Y.) New York, 1831.

Report of a Committee of the Citizens of Boston and Vicinity Opposed to a Further Increase of Duties on Importations. Boston, 1827.

Speech of Mr. M'Cord at a Meeting of Inhabitants in the Town Hall of Columbia, S.C., Opposed to the Proposed Woolens Bill. 2 July, 1827. Columbia, S.C., 1827.

WELLS, DAVID A. *Our Revenue System: History of the Proceedings in the Case of Phelps, Dodge and Co. of New York, and Vindication of the Firm*. New York: Martin's Steam Printing House, 1873.

PERIODICALS

Commercial and Financial Chronicle. New York, 1865——.
Economist. London, 1843——.
Federal Reserve Bulletin. Washington, 1915——.
Free Trade Advocate and Journal of Political Economy. Philadelphia, 1839.
Journal of Commerce and Commercial. New York, 1901——.
Merchants' Magazine and Commercial Review. New York, 1840–70.
New York Times. New York, 1851——.
Niles' Weekly Register, Baltimore, 1811–49.

UNPUBLISHED MATERIAL

NATIONAL COUNCIL OF AMERICAN IMPORTERS. Briefs filed with the U.S. Tariff Commission, Washington, D.C.
——. "Statement by Harry S. Radcliffe, Executive Secretary, N.C.A.I., at the Public Hearing, New York, February 28, 1947, on the Proposed Charter for an International Trade Organization." 1947. (Mimeographed.)
U.S. LIBRARY OF CONGRESS, MANUSCRIPT DIVISION. "New Orleans Custom House Collection." (A collection of correspondence, Treasury Circulars, and other documents pertaining to the operation of the New Orleans Custom House during the first few decades after its absorption into the federal customs system of the United States.)

TABLE OF CASES CITED

TABLE OF CASES CITED

UNITED STATES SUPREME COURT

Aldridge v. *Williams,* 3 Howard 9 (1845). Pp. 92–93, 246, 318
Marriott v. *Brune,* 9 Howard 619 (1850). P. 191
U.S. v. *Southmayd,* 9 Howard 637 (1850). P. 191
Greely v. *Thompson et al.,* 10 Howard 225 (1850). P. 97
Stairs v. *Peaslee,* 18 Howard 521 (1855). Pp. 186–87
The Collector v. *Richards,* 90 U.S. 246 (1874). Pp. 260, 262–63
Arthur v. *Goddard,* 96 U.S. 145 (1877). P. 156
Cramer v. *Arthur,* 102 U.S. 612 (1880). P. 264
Hadden et al. v. *Merritt,* 115 U.S. 25 (1885). Pp. 264, 268
Oberteuffer v. *Robertson,* 116 U.S. 499 (1886). Pp. 122–23
Heinemann v. *Arthur's Executors,* 120 U.S. 82 (1887). Pp. 264–65
Seeburger v. *Hardy,* 150 U.S. 420 (1893). P. 70
Muser v. *Magone,* 155 U.S. 240 (1894). P. 159
U.S. v. *Passavant,* 169 U.S. 16 (1898). Pp. 139, 155, 158–62, 339
Hoeninghaus v. *U.S.,* 172 U.S. 622 (1899). P. 136
American Sugar Refining Company v. *U.S.,* 181 U.S. 610 (1901). P. 191
Helwig v. *U.S.,* 188 U.S. 605 (1903). P. 278
U.S. v. *Whitridge,* 197 U.S. 135 (1905). Pp. 266–67
Haviland and Co. v. *U.S.,* 216 U.S. 618 (1910). Pp. 183, 286
Billings v. *U.S.,* 232 U.S. 261 (1914). P. 318
Fish v. *U.S.,* 268 U.S. 607 (1925). P. 279
Barr v. *U.S.,* 324 U.S. 83 (1945). Pp. 269–72

UNITED STATES CIRCUIT AND DISTRICT COURTS

Reiss v. *Magone,* 39 F. 105 (1889). P. 191
U.S. v. *J. Allston Newhall and Co.,* 91 F. 525 (1899). Pp. 260–61, 265–66, 273
U.S. v. *Beebe et al.,* 117 F. 670 (1902). P. 266
U.S. v. *Lawrence et al.,* 137 F. 466 (1905). P. 190
U.S. v. *Haviland and Co.,* 167 F. 414 (1909). P. 183
U.S. v. *Haviland and Co.,* 177 F. 175 (1910). Pp. 183, 286
Kreutz et al. v. *Durning,* 69 F. (2d) 802 (1934). P. 252
Cottman Co. et al. v. *Dailey,* 20 F. Supp. 142 (1937). P. 256
Cottman Co. et al. v. *Dailey,* 94 F. (2d) 85 (1938). P. 256

UNITED STATES COURT OF CUSTOMS AND PATENT APPEALS

Stein v. *U.S.,* 1 C.C.A. 36 (1910). P. 157
Masson v. *U.S.,* 1 C.C.A. 149 (1911). P. 190
U.S. v. *Schwartz and Co.,* 3 C.C.A. 24 (1912). P. 138
U.S. v. *Spingarn Bros.,* 5 C.C.A. 2 (1913). Pp. 181, 192
Thomas and Co. v. *U.S.,* 5 C.C.A. 69 (1914). P. 278

U.S. v. *Alfred Kohlberg, Inc.,* 27 C.C.P.A. 223 (1940). P. 156
U.S. v. *European Trading Co.,* 27 C.C.P.A. 289 (1940). P. 257
Hughes Fawcett, Inc. v. *U.S.,* 27 C.C.P.A. 372 (1940). P. 163
Bolinders Co., Inc. v. *U.S.,* 28 C.C.P.A. 40 (1940). Pp. 280–81
U.S. v. *Mexican Products Co.,* 28 C.C.P.A. 80 (1940). P. 180
F. W. Woolworth Co. v. *U.S.,* 28 C.C.P.A. 239 (1940). P. 271
U.S. v. *Collin and Gissel (Ludwig Baer),* 29 C.C.P.A. 96 (1941). Pp. 198, 200–201
White Lamb Finlay, Inc. v. *U.S.,* 29 C.C.P.A. 199 (1942). Pp. 199–200
American Shipping Co. (General Electric X-Ray Corp.) v. *U.S.,* 29 C.C.P.A. 250 (1942). Pp. 173, 177–78, 336
U.S. v. *John Barr,* 32 C.C.P.A. 16 (1944). P. 269
U.S. v. *Wm. S. Pitcairn Corp.,* 33 C.C.P.A. 183 (1946). Pp 162, 179–80, 295

INDEXES

INDEX OF NAMES

INDEX OF SUBJECTS

371